A Trial of Witches

In 1662, Amy Denny and Rose Cullender were hanged for the "crimes" of witchcraft, including causing the death of a child, overturning carts, bedevilling cattle, and lice infestations. *A Trial of Witches* is a study of this seventeenth-century witch trial, placing it in its social, cultural, and political contexts.

Through an examination of the major participants in the case and their institutional importance in the early modern period (the presiding judge was Sir Matthew Hale, whose work is still cited in English case law, and the verifying doctor was the influential Sir Thomas Browne, author of *Religio Medici*), the authors critique the official process and detail how it led to its erroneous conclusions.

The Lowestoft trial has even broader significance as it was cited as evidence thirty years later at the Salem trials, where many lost their lives. Through detailed discussion of primary sources, the authors explore the important implications of this case for the understanding of hysteria, group mentality and early modern social forces, and the witchcraft phenomenon as a whole.

Gilbert Geis is Emeritus Professor in the Department of Criminology, Law and Society, University of California, Irvine. **Ivan Bunn** is a local historian living in Lowestoft.

A Trial of Witches

A seventeenth-century witchcraft prosecution

Gilbert Geis and Ivan Bunn

London and New York

First published 1997
by Routledge
11 New Fetter Lane, London EC4P 4EE

Simultaneously published in the USA and Canada
by Routledge
29 West 35th Street, New York, NY 10001

© 1997 Gilbert Geis and Ivan Bunn

Typeset in Galliard and Clairvaux by Routledge
Printed and bound in Great Britain by Biddles Ltd,
Guildford and King's Lynn

Cover image: A witch, cat and demon; reproduced with permission of the
British Library; Shelfmark Add.32496

British Library Cataloguing in Publication Data
A catalogue record for this book is available from the British Library

Library of Congress Cataloguing in Publication Data
Geis, Gilbert.
A Trial of Witches: a seventeenth-century witchcraft prosecution/
Gilbert Geis and Ivan Bunn.
p. cm.
Includes bibliographical references and index.
Summary: A case study of the witchcraft trial of two women in 1662
Lowestoft, England, including a description of the accusers and
prosecutors and an analysis of the trial itself, which was cited as a precedent
in the Salem witchcraft trials.
1. Trials (Witchcraft)–England–Lowestoft. 2. Witchcraft–England–History.
[1. Trials (Witchcraft)–England. 2. Witchcraft–England–History.]
I. Bunn, Ivan. II. Title.
KD371.W56G45 1997
345.42'0288–dc21
97–8354 CIP AC

ISBN 0–415–17108–3 (hbk)
ISBN 0–415–17109–1 (pbk)

"God offers to every mind its choice between truth and repose. Take which you please—you can never have both."

Ralph Waldo Emerson, "Intellect"

"For a clever man, nothing is easier than to find arguments that will convince him that he is doing right when he is doing what he wants to do."

Aldous Huxley, *The Devils of Loudon*

To Dolores and in memory of Robley Geis

To Lesley, who has patiently lived with the
Lowestoft "witches" for many years
And also for Dad who never saw the dream
come true

Contents

Illustrations

Preface

The present study of the 1662 trial at Bury St. Edmunds of two women accused as witches offers a comprehensive scrutiny of one of the most important of such cases in England. Besides the focus on witchcraft *per se*, the operation of the assize criminal court at the time is examined through the lens of this particular trial. Those who played major roles in the case and the court's procedures are scrutinized in some depth to show how they figured in the fate of the accused women. As Salo Baron recently noted: "penetrating studies of the personality traits and psychological impulses of . . . leaders have contributed much to the understanding of . . . historical events."[1]

Two particular concerns underlie this element of the study: first, why did an official process, relied upon to discover the truth, reach so erroneous a conclusion? And, second, have the flaws in the belief-system been eliminated and the protections to defendants so broadened and strengthened in the ensuing three centuries that such a miscarriage of justice is now unlikely? "We are," the psychiatrist-historian Robert Jay Lifton reminds us in his study of the Nazi doctors, "capable of learning from carefully examined past evil."[2]

As we wrote this book, we had in mind the point, most recently stated by David Cannadine, that professional history is in danger of collapsing under the weight of its own erudition; "that more and more historians know more and more about less and less."[3] Put more positively, Cannadine observes that "there has in recent years been a growing interest in the revival of narrative history, in the imaginative aspects of historical research and writing."[4] Our aim has been to collect as many significant facts as possible that bear upon the case of the Lowestoft "witches" and to tell an interesting story that has important implications for the understanding of the witchcraft phenomenon. Perhaps the most notable lesson of contemporary relevance is that we should never senselessly succumb in the face of authority. Medical, religious, and legal officials may proclaim that their processes and hearts are pure and their methods impeccable. But they obviously fooled people (and likely themselves) with their high-sounding justifications of witchcraft verdicts in the seventeenth century, and they undoubtedly do so today in other contexts. Bertrand Russell put the matter well: "Most of the greatest evils that man has inflicted upon man have come through people feeling quite certain about something which, in fact, was false."[5]

A great deal has been written on the subject of English witch-hunting in general, including five classic monographs: Wallace Notestein's *A History of English Witchcraft* (1911), Cecil L'Estrange Ewen's *Witch Hunting and Witch Trials* [1929]/(1971), George L. Kittredge's *Witchcraft in Old and New England* (1929), Keith Thomas' *Religion and the Decline of Magic* (1971) and James Sharpe's *Instruments of Darkness: Witchcraft in England 1550–1750* (1996).[6]

There also have been regional studies, the most deservedly renowned being Alan Macfarlane's *Witchcraft in Tudor and Stuart England* (1970).[7] The closest thing to a one-volume study of an English witch-hunt is Richard Deacon's *Matthew Hopkins: Witch-Finder General* (1976), but Deacon deals with a whole series of trials in a relatively jour-nalistic manner. Joyce Gibson, in her *Hanged for Witchcraft: Elizabeth Lowys and Her Successors* (1988),[8] focuses on one trial for a few chapters, but then turns to a general and rather unsatisfactory history of English witchcraft.

There have been some very good short studies of particular trials. The best is Michael MacDonald's review of the Mary Glover case in his introduction to *Witchcraft and Hysteria in Elizabethan England* (1991),[9] from which we draw many insights and ideas in the present study. Edgar Peel and Pat Southern offer a fine study, *The Trials of the Lancashire Witches* (1969), and Annabel Gregory's "Witchcraft, Politics and 'Good Neighborhood' in Early Seventeenth-Century Rye" (1991)[10] is also a first-rate examination of a local witchcraft prosecution. So too is Anne Reiber DeWitt's *Witchcraft and Conflicting Visions of the Ideal Village Community* (1994).

Nothing in the study of English witchcraft compares to the large number of treatises regarding the witch hunt at Salem in 1692 the best known of which is Paul Boyer and Stephen Nissenbaum, *Salem Possessed* (1974), which recently has been challenged in some particu-lars in Bernard Rosenthal's *Salem Story* (1993) and reconsidered in Frances Hill's *A Delusion of Satan: The Full Story of the Salem Witch Trials* (1995). There is also nothing regarding England comparable to studies of specific European witch-hunts, such as Gustav Henningsen's

The Witches' Advocate (1980), which deals with the great Basque trials of 1609 to 1614, or Michael Kunze's *Highroad to the Stake* (1987), which relates the story of the prosecution of the Pappenheimers in early seventeenth-century Bavaria.[11] To this group we can add Carlo Ginzburg's *The Night Battles* (1983)[12] which deals with the prosecution of members of a fertility cult, the Benandanti, in the Friuli region in northeast Italy over the course of some eighty years. These prosecutions involved more than one trial, but they constituted a single witch-hunt in a particular locality.

The authors of the case studies noted above all have had the benefit of a considerable body of primary sources upon which to base their work. Henningsen had a very large cache of inquisitorial records at his disposal, including the papers of a leading inquisitor; Ginzburg also had access to some extraordinarily rich historical records. The materials available for Salem are similarly extensive; the court records alone fill three volumes of *The Salem Witchcraft Papers*.[13]

The result is that scholarship regarding the Salem trials has been something of a cottage industry in which successive scholars seek to put a new twist on what by now is very familiar source material. The social critic Russell Baker, only partially tongue-in-cheek, recently wrote that "[h]istory is constantly being revised these days. It's because there is a glut of historians. Revising history is the only way to keep them busy."[14] Witchcraft history revisionists sometimes fall prey to the tendency to hit upon one or another partial explanation—or correlation—of what occurred and to elevate that singular point to an overarching thesis. In our analyses, we pay heed to Rosenthal's warning that "to create a unified theory to explain the Salem witch trial would be to distort the event, at times to trivialize it.... The methodological challenge is to find reasonable conclusions, generalizations at times, that do more than impose one more myth upon the . . . trials." He adds: "Anyone who offers to adjudicate once and for all the various competing theories about the Salem witch trials should be a soldier not a scholar."[15]

There was no possibility that our intensive examination of one witch trial would permit us to offer a new and novel understanding of the witchcraft phenomenon. Beginners in social science learn early that you cannot generalize with safety and comfort from an N of l. A case study, as a recent essay defined it, represents an "in-depth, multifaceted investigation, using qualitative research methods, of a single social phenomenon. The study is conducted in great detail and often relies on the use of several data sources."[16] We have sought to portray in its narrative richness a notably important and instructive criminal proceeding, a proceeding that William Godwin called "one of the most remarkable trials that occur in the history of criminal jurisprudence."[17] We drew upon information from a variety of sources, both local and national, never before brought together. We have had to deal with the problem that assize court records tell us very little because the depositions were not regarded as official papers and therefore almost never have been preserved with the indictments. For the most part, historians of English witchcraft have had to rely upon the skeletal details of the indictments and, as we did, upon the occasional contemporaneously compiled report of a trial.

It is just such documents—the indictment of Amy Denny and Rose Cullender for witchcraft—and the fifty-nine-page report (included as an Appendix to the present volume), *A Tryal of Witches Held at the Assizes at Bury St. Edmunds* (1682), said to have been written by the judge's marshal, that provided us with the core material for our study. We have fleshed out this information from other sources that tell us about the locale and the trial procedures. We also have examined in considerable detail the lives of the major participants in the case, the very rich and the relatively well-to-do townspeople who brought the charges, the officials who participated in the trial, the expert witness, and the two hapless women who sought to defend themselves against the accusation of witchcraft. Throughout, we have sought to match the details of our case history against the generalizations offered by historians such as Macfarlane and Thomas, who speculated about the general outlines of English witchcraft. Much of what these scholars discovered proves to be true in regard to this particular case, though there are small and larger discrepancies between what happened in Lowestoft and Bury St. Edmunds and their overall blueprint of English witchcraft.

Our examination of the lives and ideas of the individuals who brought about the denunciation and ultimate death of Amy Denny and Rose Cullender indicates, to us, the important role that idiosyncratic circumstances can play in an historical event. Broader political and cultural conditions have to prevail for certain things to happen, but these things—a particular witch trial at a particular place with a certain kind of outcome—do not necessarily follow.

The trial at Bury St. Edmunds did not proceed smoothly from accusation to sentencing; rather there were significant divisions and occasional conflicts between some of the leading participants. It is vital to appreciate that by 1662, English opinion no longer was widely consensual regarding the reality of witchcraft, a matter which allows us to discriminate in this case between the backgrounds of those who clung to the belief now being challenged and those who sought to discredit it. Rosenthal has made the same point forcefully about the Salem Village trials by documenting that many persons refused to buy into the witchcraft prosecutions and saw them for the travesty of justice that they were. Rosenthal notes: "The argument that we must see it from their perspective carries an implicit codicil that, given their perspective, they could not have seen it the way we smarter moderns can," and adds: "However, though patronized by future commentators, they saw it well enough—better, on the whole, than the theorists who have come to explain what happened to them."[18] "It is fair to assess the judges by honorable standards of their own day," Rosenthal insists,[19] and he does so by documenting the skeptical opinion about witchcraft held by prominent people of the time.

This analytical axiom notwithstanding, we have throughout our study sought to be sensitive to the very real concerns of seventeenth-century minds to the perils of witchcraft and to put events into the context of the times. In his recent review of cases which arose in Yorkshire, J.A. Sharpe reminds us that for "[t]hose on the receiving end of witchcraft in the early modern period . . . the witch was frequently a frightening individual who could, on occasion, do harm with terrible speed and terrible effectiveness." "As we have tried to make clear," Sharpe adds, "the experience of thinking oneself to be bewitched, or of thinking that the same fate had befallen one's children or one's cattle, was a deeply disturbing one."[20]

We totally agree with this, but we also would note that, while Sharpe is appropriately sympathetic to the terrors of the supposed victims, he does not attend (in what admittedly is but a brief paper) to the horror of being accused of witchcraft and the ultimate awfulness of being hanged for it. To understand the psychological and ideological climate that prompted the accusations is essential, but to appreciate—albeit by means of a present-day view—what was visited upon the accused is at least equally essential.

There is a further contextual note that needs to be recorded. By profession neither of us is an academic historian. Inevitably, because of our training in sociological criminology and local studies, we do not necessarily look at witchcraft in precisely the same manner as those scholars who traditionally have dominated the study of its occurrence in non-preliterate societies. This book, for instance, presents considerable detail about the manner in which a case of witchcraft was tried, a matter that has not attracted the attention of historians who study witchcraft. Our detailed examination of the views and backgrounds and interactions of the major establishment participants in the witchcraft trial, men such as Sir Matthew Hale, Sir John Keeling, and Sir Thomas Browne, provides much more of this kind of information than traditionally offered by witchcraft historians and offers insight in why *this* trial went as it did. We also present considerable details about the accusers, including their standing, background, and length of residence in the community than is commonly reported. Presumably, this material, combined with further studies of other witchcraft cases, can be crafted into more general statements about the phenomenon.

We also believe that there is something to be gained by looking at the subject in a manner slightly different to that commonly done. We would note, for example, that Kai Erikson's *Wayward Puritans* (1966),[21] a study based on events in Salem Village, may at times be regarded as rather inadequate history by historians, but is considered a classic insight and a theoretical breakthrough by sociologists of deviant behavior who turn to it constantly for interpretations of present-day research about social outcasts. For our part, we have sought historical integrity and have combed the extant historical literature seeking to incorporate its insights where they seem appropriate. At the same time, we have attended to adjacent concerns that generally do not fall within the historical perspective.

Details of our collaboration are worth noting. We met when, out of curiosity, Geis trekked to Lowestoft to follow up on work he had been doing at Cambridge University on the legal background of the crime of rape. He had learned that the pronouncements on rape by Sir Matthew Hale, the preeminent jurist of the seventeenth century, had established the way this offense was regarded for the following three centuries. He also had discovered that Hale had presided over the trial of two women accused of being witches at Lowestoft. A local historian, Hugh Lees, brought the two of us together and, for longer than we sometimes care to admit, we have pursued in tandem our intense preoccupation with seeking to determine what led to and followed the accusation of Denny and Cullender.

A few minutes in the local library during that initial visit established that every discussion of the trial had gotten one of the defendant's name wrong. Not long afterwards we were able to document, by securing a copy of the indictments from the Public Record Office, that a majority of the discussions, probably several hundred, also had misdated the trial. After those heady triumphs there was no turning back, though over many years we often have despaired and fretted about more fundamental issues regarding the case that we sought to learn about and to understand. Almost ritualistically, we occasionally return to St. Margaret's Church in Lowestoft and in silence peer down at the slab marking the grave of Samuel Pacy, the man who pushed the accusations of Denny and Cullender, as if somehow we could gather from our visit an understanding of what he would tell us were we able to discuss this case with him.

If at times it appears that we are harsh upon Pacy and those officials who aided the condemnation of Amy Denny and Rose Cullender we would partially defend our judgments by echoing the observation of John Acton, a leading nineteenth-century historian and essayist. Lord Acton believed that historians should be judges, exercising their right to condemn the sins of the past. In his famous letter to Mandell Creighton, in which he set out the axiom that "[p]ower tends to corrupt, and absolute power corrupts absolutely," Acton insisted in the sentence before that pronouncement that "[h]istoric responsibility has to make up for the want of legal responsibility," that is, that historians have the obligation to hold those who wield power to some moral standard.[22] Creighton, who tended to obsequiousness in his own writings, later would maintain that "[i]t is a real support to them [those with power] that they will be judged by a higher standard than that of their immediate success."[23] Both postulations admit of many qualifications, of course. Certainly the standard by which persons are judged ought to be one that they reasonably should have been able to achieve. Besides, it is arguable how much influence the possible judgment of posterity exercises upon powerful people's actions, though we sometimes are told by the media that it is the verdict of history not the clamor of immediate approval that dictated one or another leadership decision.

We would also point to the words of George Burr, an eminent early witchcraft historian who thought that puritanism played a prominent part in European and American witchcraft prosecutions. Burr's knowledgeable insight has been overridden—indeed, largely repudiated—by later interpretations that highlight neighborhood quarrels, misogyny, political unrest, and numerous other concomitants of witchcraft prosecutions. Our information shows, as we shall subsequently indicate in detail, that at least for the Lowestoft case and its relationship to what went on in Salem Village thirty years later, theology appears to have been a significant contributing factor. Burr also favors making judgments (albeit fairly and properly qualified) rather than exculpating those involved in pressing witchcraft charges by portraying them as no more than creatures of their time. "It is not because we think we are better than our fathers," Burr wrote. "It is because deep within ourselves we still feel the impulses which led to their mistakes. . . . I fear that they who begin by excusing their ancestors may end by excusing themselves" and "repeat their faults."[24] Burr's rhetoric may be a bit overblown, but the point is worth taking to heart, particularly when as sophisticated a historian as Geoffrey Elton maintains that once the evidence is understood in terms of its times—of the attitudes and prejudices of the period—it is professionally desirable to pass judgment about what took place.[25]

Acknowledgements

We owe a debt of gratitude to a large number of persons and institutions that have provided us with information and insights as we have sought to gather and interpret the facts and the dynamics of the 1662 prosecution of Amy Denny and Rose Cullender on charges of bewitching their neighbors. These include David Wright, the Local Studies Librarian in Lowestoft and David Butcher of Corton. David Butcher has been especially helpful in critiquing our work and offering results from his own research on Lowestoft. Others with whom we discussed one or another issue are the late Hugh Lees, Parish Historian of Lowestoft, Jack Rose, Michael Burgess, Richard Haxell, Denis Fletcher, Chris Want, Barbara Turner of CEFAS, and the late Eric Porter, all of Lowestoft. Sir Nicholas Bacon, Baronet of Raveningham, Diana Spelman of Norwich, Susan Moore of London, Eric Stockdale of New Barnet, Dr. G.H. Glanville of Richmond, Helen Phelan of New York, Douglas Salmon of Norwich, Terry Weatherly of Lowestoft, and Ruth Flowerdew of Basingstoke similarly have contributed to our work. Thanks also go to Pete Clements of Lowestoft for his critical appraisal of our manuscript.

Archivists and staff at the following sites were particularly helpful in aiding our research: the Suffolk Record Offices in Lowestoft, Ipswich, and Bury St. Edmunds, Lowestoft Central Library, the Suffolk Genealogy Society, and the Surrey Record Office. In London we received assistance at the Public Record Office, the British Library, Dr. Williams' Library, the Lincoln's Inn Library, the Honourable Society of the Middle Temple, the Honourable Society of the Inner Temple, the Royal Commission on Historical Manuscripts, the Guildhall Library, and the Society of Genealogists.

The University Library at Cambridge was one of our prime initial sources of material. Elisabeth Leedham-Green, the assistant keeper of the University archives, was notably helpful in putting the trial indictments into contemporary language for us. Also at Cambridge

University we received assistance from Donald West, Nigel Walker, Alan Cromartie, Alan Macfarlane, J.H. Baker, D.E.C. Yale, David Thomas, and Richard Wright. N.S. Keeble at Stirling University in Scotland also was of considerable help in answering our queries about Richard Baxter, while Keith Thomas at Oxford provided information about Hale's education there, and J.S. Cockburn of the University of Maryland offered data regarding some of the intricacies of the assignment of judges to the assize circuits. Brian Levack of the University of Texas also provided excellent advice.

The Allegany County Historical Society and the Allegany County Museum, both in upstate New York, provided material regarding Samuel Pacy's descendants, while Susan Szpak of the Salem Public Library provided information regarding Lowestoft immigrants in the seventeenth century. Also in the United States, the librarians at the University of California, Irvine, the William Clark Andrews Library in Los Angeles, the University of Chicago Library, and the Huntington Library in San Marino all answered our questions promptly and fully. Samuel Guze, a professor of psychiatry at Washington University in St. Louis, read the trial report and offered observations on how he viewed the behavior of the accusers.

The manuscript would never have been put into satisfactory shape without the intelligent and skilled work done for us by Carol Wyatt of the University of California, Irvine. Judy Omiya is a superb secretary. Also contributing to the effort on the California front were Dianne Christianson, Cindy Cooper, a skilled editor, Anna Maria Tejeda, Ted Huston, Joseph Wells, Dennis and Lori Suzucki, Paul Jesilow, Steve Reynard, Mary Dodge, and Joseph DiMento. In New York City, Jeff Walsh and Richard Kim at John Jay College of Criminal Justice helped with some of the final library and word processing tasks, while Lesley Bunn and Jim Brown of Lowestoft helped with their proofreading skills and advice.

We want to express our deepest appreciation to all of these people and organizations for their help and to make it known that whatever deficiencies exist in this work are the result of our own shortcomings.

Figure 1 Portrait of Sir John Keeling
Note: The portrait bears signs of water damage suffered when the Guildhall was bombed
in World War II.
Source: Portrait by John Michael Wright; Guildhall Library.

Part 1

The case

1

Witchcrafts here resemble witchcrafts there

On Monday, March 17, 1662, in the English market town of Bury St. Edmunds, an assize site on the Norfolk circuit, two old women were hanged by the neck until dead. Four days earlier, the women had been convicted in a trial by jury for the crime of witchcraft.[1] Because their case was presided over by Sir Matthew Hale, by far the most renowned and respected judge of the time, and featured testimony by the prominent essayist, philosopher, and medical doctor, Sir Thomas Browne, the accused women gained a certain kind of immortality. Their names appear as one of the subject headings in the catalogue of the British Library, though it is ironic that both in the Library listing and in each of the hundreds of references to the case one of the women, Amy Denny, is erroneously called Amy Duny, probably because the composer of the printed summary of her trial erred in transcribing the handwriting of the person who had recorded it.

It is neither right nor decent that two elderly women should have been killed by judicial process for acts they had not done. But injustice is hardly an uncommon matter: it was not so then, and it is not so today. Such matters, it might be argued, should be overlooked—or at least not made much of—lest our knowledge of the sometimes whimsical and brutal nature of official procedures comes to make us uneasy. A nineteenth-century English divine believed so: he insisted that an innocent person about to be hanged ought not to protest, because to do so would undermine citizens' faith in the integrity of their judicial system.[2]

The fatuous attitude of the cleric requires no rebuttal, but it may be only meaningless rhetoric to insist that Amy Denny and Rose Cullender should not have died in vain. We all die in vain, and it will do none of us any real good to have our reputation rehabilitated posthumously. But it seems important to seek lessons from matters that involve gross injustice, lessons that hopefully will deter subsequent injustice. When two women are killed by the state for criminal offenses that they did not, and in fact could not, commit, after a trial involving persons with some of the keenest intellects of the time, something has gone seriously awry. A basic aim of our examination of the witchcraft case of Amy Denny and Rose Cullender is to determine what of present-day value can be learned from this sorry affair.

The trial tarnished evermore, be it only so slightly, the reputations of the two notable personages who played a major part in it—and in this too there are lessons to be learned.

Sir Matthew Hale, the judge, has been regarded, in the more than three centuries that have passed since the witchcraft trial, as a sage, compassionate, and decent human being. The Christian faithful probably best know Hale as the kind jurist who during the summer assize in Bedford in August 1661—seven months before the Bury St. Edmunds trial—paused and listened to the pitiful pleas of John Bunyan's wife for the release of her husband from prison after Hale's colleagues had scornfully brushed her aside. Sympathetically, and predictably, Hale told her that there was nothing that he could do, although he explained the official procedures that she might follow to have her husband's petition reviewed in London.[3] Hale's indulgence of Mrs. Bunyan has drawn high poetic marks:

Law's high chair is filled
By one whose spirit ne'er was known to fail
In gentleness—with goodness all instilled
Mild, merciful, tho' still majestic Hale.[4]

Further fulsome tributes to Hale's wisdom, judicial brilliance, and integrity abound; he regularly is honored as one of the best minds in the history of English jurisprudence, possessor of an incisive analytical ability and an encyclopedic knowledge of the common law. But Hale's record also carries the slight stain of his action against Amy Denny and Rose Cullender; commentators persistently nag at his heels because of his role in the witchcraft case. Thomas Thirlwall, for instance, the nineteenth-century cleric who edited Hale's voluminous religious writings, cannot be altogether forgiving. Thirlwall eulogizes Hale's "learning, wisdom, piety and virtue, which shone in his life with such transcendent luster, and raised him to the highest eminence."[5] But he also feels compelled to call our attention to the fact that it was Hale who "passed the sentence of death upon two crazy old wretches for that supposed crime."[6]

A standard early nineteenth-century biographical dictionary similarly

Figure 2 Portrait of Sir Matthew Hale
Source: Reproduced with permission of the National Portrait Gallery, London.

labels Hale's role in the witchcraft trial as "the most blamable passage of his life."[7] John Lord Campbell, otherwise overflowing in his praise of Hale—he calls him the "most pure, the most pious, the most independent and the most learned of judges"[8]—notes that Hale "was not only under the influence of the most vulgar credulity, but that he violated the plainest rules of justice, and that he really was the murderer of two innocent women."[9] An early nineteenth-century editor, annotating the diary of a contemporary of Hale, observes that Hale's decision at Bury was "unworthy of any judge," and that he "left for execution . . . two unfortunate women, on evidence which now appears to be utterly insufficient."[10] Sometimes, when it has been important in legal disputes to overcome one or another of Hale's powerful juridical pronouncements on the common law, the witchcraft case will be exhumed. Thus, in 1889, Rufus W. Peckham, a New York Supreme Court judge, dissenting in regard to the precedent value of Hale's position on government regulation of businesses affected with a public interest,[11] insisted bitingly that Hale's ideas on this subject were no more substantial than those he had entertained on witchcraft.[12]

The reputation of Sir Thomas Browne bears a similar taint. Browne, appearing in his medical role as expert witness at the 1662 trial, testified that the young girls accusing Denny and Cullender were afflicted with organic problems, but that they undoubtedly also had been bewitched.

Author of the esteemed *Religio Medici*, among other works, Browne has been acclaimed in hundreds of books and articles for the magnificence of his prose, and for his exceptional tolerance of the beliefs and behavior of those who differed from him.[13] But many who write about Browne also feel compelled to attend, if only passingly, to his "unfortunate involvement"[14] in the 1662 witchcraft case. Most often writers dismiss Browne's testimony as little more than a reflection of the ideas of the times: no man, it is maintained, can be held to standards higher than those of the keenest minds around him.[15]

By 1662, however, belief in witches was in retreat in England. As Wallace Notestein observes, the wide range of decisions rendered in English witch trials at the time "betrays the perplexity of judges and juries."[16] Indeed, after 1620 the percentage of acquittals in witchcraft cases in Essex "rose enormously."[17] Surviving Home Circuit records show that between 1647 and 1701, 103 persons were committed for trial for witchcraft, but only 14 were found guilty. Grand juries dismissed 28 cases, and trial juries returned not guilty verdicts in 61 of the 71 cases they heard.[18] In 1664, as one instance among numerous others, Robert Hunt, a magistrate in Somerset, uncovered what he stoutly maintained were two covens of witches, but prosecution was aborted "by the cynical attitude of his fellow justices."[19] In 1736, the witchcraft law under which Denny and Cullender were executed would be repealed. On the continent, doubts about witchcraft also were surfacing. Anne Barstow notes: "[B]y 1662, many French judges and doctors had become skeptical of demonic possession."[20] It needs to be kept firmly in mind that Browne and Hale represented not a mainstream position but rather one rapidly becoming anachronistic.

Some writers take the view that Browne had only an inconsequential impact on the outcome of the trial, a position neither easily rebutted nor defended given our inability to penetrate the minds of the jurors and judge. Certainly, on the face of it, the accusers' evidence alone (at least as it is conveyed in the trial report) would appear sufficient to convict, presuming those hearing it found it believable. But the fact that Browne probably was summoned from his home in Norwich (nearby, but not that close to Bury St. Edmunds in terms of the travails of seventeenth-century travel) might indicate that those pushing the case felt the need for his support.

Interpretations of Browne's performance continue to cut into the integrity of his intellectual and personal credentials. A man's reputation, it becomes obvious, can be permanently sullied by a few words uttered in an event that at the time appears to him to be of little consequence. No reference to the trial has been found in Browne's voluminous correspondence with his son and others:[21] it apparently was not worth a mention.

The case against Amy Denny and Rose Cullender also strongly influenced the most notable of America's witchcraft prosecutions, the Salem trials of 1692. Indeed, the Salem witch-hunts might not have taken place if there had not been a trial at Bury St. Edmunds: the events at Salem notoriously imitated those at Bury. Cotton Mather in his *Wonders of the Invisible World* included a large number of excerpts and interpretations of the Bury trial in order to justify what happened at Salem.[22] "It may cast some light upon the dark things now in America," Mather wrote, "if we just give a glance upon like things lately happened in Europe. We may see the witchcrafts here most exactly resemble the witchcrafts there; and we may learn what sort of devils do trouble the world."[23] John Hale, in his "sad, troubled, and honest"[24] account written shortly after the Salem trials, notes that the judges there made "a conscientious endeavor to do the thing that was right. And to that end they consulted the presidents [precedents] of former times & precepts laid down by learned writers about witchcraft ...[including] Sir Matthew Hales *Tryal of Witches*, printed *Anno* 1682."[25]

Thomas Hutchinson, in his history of the Massachusetts Bay Colony, provides further particulars regarding the connection between the Salem trials and the 1662 English prosecution:

> the great authority was that of Sir Matthew Hale, revered in New England, not only for his knowledge in the law, but for his gravity and piety. The trial of the witches was published in 1684 [actually 1682]. All these books were in New England, and the conformity between the behavior of most of the supposed bewitched at Salem, and the behavior of those in England, is so exact as to leave no room to doubt the stories

had already been read by the New England persons themselves, or had been told to them by others who had read them. Indeed, this conformity instead of giving suspicion, was urged in the confirmation of the truth of both.[26]

At Salem, 141 persons were accused of witchcraft. Of these, there are records of 122 having been imprisoned. Nineteen persons were hanged; one man, Giles Corey, was pressed to death, and two women died while in custody.[27] All, of course, were innocent of the accusations made against them. Those accusations were primarily made by two girls, one nine years old and the other eleven years old. The main accusers of Denny and Cullender, thirty years earlier, were of the same sex and the same ages.

Trials for witchcraft are among the most malevolent occurrences in the annals of the human race, and among the most pathetic. The power of the state is mobilized to stage a trial in which the search for justice often is caricatured. Personal grievances, scapegoating, misogyny, superstition, a quest for notoriety and advancement become transmuted and legitimized in witch-hunts. Accusations can also be leveled to relieve boredom. She did it for "sport, they must have some sport," one of the Salem "girls" would say, trying to explain herself.[28] In witchcraft cases, innocent persons are confronted with a capital charge which it is impossible to rebut in any literal way. How can those accused as witches satisfactorily demonstrate that they had not conspired with the devil to bring about the death of an infant in the neighborhood? How can they prove it was not their image that their accusers claimed to have seen cavorting just beneath the ceiling of the meeting house or in the corner of the bedchamber? It is only when the charges themselves are not regarded as creditable, not when they are rebutted, that an accused might be set free. A person was always in danger of being taken for a witch, since, as Montesquieu noted, "the most unexceptional conduct, the purest morals, and the constant practice of every duty in life are not a sufficient security against the suspicion of those crimes."[29] Montesquieu obviously was thinking of persons of standing in the community.[30] How much more vulnerable were persons of little power and poor reputation?

Highly intelligent and able officials accepted as accurate what now appear to have been patently fabricated and unbelievable tales. Why were they so gullible in these instances, when in other matters they could be so shrewd? Answers to such questions can forewarn us about circumstances that pose danger to rational thought and procedure. The prosecution of witches offers a cautionary tale of wrong-minded self-righteousness, of bull-headedness about a position in the face of obvious insufficiencies in the evidence presumed to support it. If the witches had the power they were alleged to possess, why did they not employ it to extricate themselves from their judicial predicament? Why did they not strike down their accusers in the same manner that they allegedly had smitten others? Why, with all those diabolical resources at their disposal, were they usually so poor, their lives so wretched and miserable? Only rarely were such obvious matters taken up. About 1140, according to William of Malmesbury, a witch had escaped by flying through a window after her arrest,[31] but similar kinds of tales are notably absent in the later annals of witchcraft. In the early sixteenth century, Paolo Grillando, a papal judge, insisted that the devil did not free witches from prison because such an act would be apt to seduce judges and officials to adopt the practice of sorcery; therefore, God, who had the final word on what the devil would be permitted to do, had interdicted such rescues.[32] In all but a few such exceptional instances, the self-evident absence of the supposed powers granted by the devil to the witches was a matter ignored, as it would be during the trial at Bury St. Edmunds.

The parish of Lowestoft, where the witch case began, lies 112 miles northeast of London. In the seventeenth century about 660 of its 1,486 acres were used for arable purposes and most of the rest for grazing. Lake Lothing, called the Fresh Water in the seventeenth century, stretched westward from the sea shore, and formed a natural southern boundary of the parish. A small town, little more than a compact village, was located at the extreme northeast corner of the parish, perched at the top of a cliff overlooking the North Sea which then, as now, formed the parish's eastern boundary.[33]

Lowestoft is part of East Anglia, a region that includes the counties of Norfolk and Suffolk as well as segments of Essex and Cambridgeshire. As late as 1948, East Anglia was said to be "rather remote and backward." "Since it is sort of a hump on the east coast," John Appleby wrote, "one does not pass through it on his way to somewhere else."[34] The out-of-the-way location of the area undoubtedly is the major reason so little attention was paid to the witchcraft case: had it taken place in London or its environs we would have much more official and second-hand information about it.

Lowestoft is a particularly isolated site in an isolated region. The town lies at the easternmost point of England, and is swept in winter by fierce polar winds that come uninterrupted off the North Sea. Edmund Gillingwater, the historian of Lowestoft, writing in 1790, found the town eminently appealing, a view not widely shared now—and perhaps not then either. Gillingwater supported his advocacy in the following terms:

> Lowestoft . . . stands upon a lofty eminence, and commands an extensive prospect of the German ocean [the earlier name of the North Sea], and when beheld from the sea, has the noblest and most beautiful appearance of any town upon the coast between Newcastle and London; it chiefly consists of an extensive arrangement of houses, whose line of direction is nearly north and south, and, consequently faces the sea. It stands upon a dry soil, upon the summit of a cliff, and enjoys a most salubrious air, keen, but bracing; and not being exposed to any of those unwholesome damps and vapors which generally arise from low grounds and marshes, it is rendered not only a very pleasant, but a very healthy situation.[35]

Using the town's parish registers, historian and demographer David Butcher recently calculated a population of 1,500 persons for the town in the mid-seventeenth century. During his research, Butcher unearthed a notebook that listed almost every building in Lowestoft from the early 1600s until the 1720s, usually with the name of its owner. The book had been compiled from the Manor Court records in the cramped handwritten Latin of John Tanner, the town vicar from 1708 to 1759, and had lain unattended in a cast iron safe in the vestry of the parish church. Discovery of the inventory enabled Butcher and Bunn to map Lowestoft as it was in the seventeenth century[36] and to locate with some precision where the participants in the witchcraft trial lived in relation to each other.

The main road of Lowestoft was known in the seventeenth century, as it is now, as High Street. It rises in a gentle slope from south to north for a distance of three-quarters of a mile. The more prosperous merchants, tradesmen, and successful mariners dwelt along the High Street, many of their houses built upon foundations dating back to the fourteenth century and a few to an even earlier period. It is on this street that most of the accusers of Amy Denny and Rose Cullender lived. The more ordinary folk tended to live in the narrow streets and lanes to the west of the High Street.

Ownership of a dwelling house on the east side of High Street usually included possession of the cliff upon which the house was constructed. These homes offered a striking panoramic view of the

Denes, the beach, and the sea beyond. The steepest parts of the cliff were often terraced and made into what a guide book later would describe as attractive hanging gardens. At the bottom of the cliff stood the fish-houses and curing sheds where the fishing trade was pursued. The arrangement kept offensive smells from rising too obtrusively up into the area where everyday life went on. At the foot of the cliff there was a wide trackway parallel to the sea called "Whapland" or "Whaplode" Way. It was, and still is, connected to the High Street by a number of steep, narrow lanes, unique to the Lowestoft district, known then as today as "scores," probably from the Old Norse *skor*, meaning a notch or cleft.

In the seventeenth century the parish church, dedicated to St. Margaret of Antioch, lay in the fields about one mile west of the populated core of Lowestoft. The siting of St. Margaret's far from town probably was occasioned by its original proximity to an ancient settlement, called Akethorpe, which by medieval times was incorporated into the parish of Lowestoft. The church stands on the brow of rising ground, close to the highest point in the parish to the north of the main road into Lowestoft from Beccles. The present nave, aisle, and chancel of the church date from the 1480s; the flintstone outer walls also are part of the original construction. It has been said of St. Margaret's that "many great parish churches have more varied details; few, if any, has so gracious a detail."[37]

Conspicuous black marble slabs can be seen prominently embedded in the floor of the chancel of St. Margaret's, directly in front of the altar. These commemorate Samuel Pacy and members of his family, persons especially important in the prosecution of Amy Denny and Rose Cullender. Pacy, a prominent Lowestoft merchant and the owner of several herring boats, was the father of two young girls who accused Denny and Cullender of bewitching them and, as we shall see, himself played a leading role in the case, at one point helping the court extricate itself from an embarrassing situation that followed an attempt to demonstrate that his daughters were liars.

Lowestoft's name is derived from a Scandinavian settlement called "Hlover's Toft"—the homestead of a settler named Hlover. This toft probably lay on, or close to, the location of an earlier Saxon settlement. The 1086 Domesday book refers to the settlement as Lothu Wistoft.[38] In the seventeenth century, the town and parish of Lowestoft were controlled primarily by two manorial courts of ancient origin. The Court Baron, which met monthly, dealt primarily with property transactions and with what today would be called civil suits. The Court Leet, which met annually on the first Friday of Lent, primarily selected petty officials, such as overseers, surveyors, constables, and alefounders—the last responsible for testing the strength of the ale produced by the town's brewers. The Leet court also heard cases involving trivial misdemeanors. Both local courts were presided over by a steward, representing the Lord of the Manor, and each consisted of a jury, or "homage," constituted by the chief tenants of the manor. Most felonies were tried at the Quarter Sessions which were held four times a year at Beccles, ten miles by road in a west-south-west direction, though particularly serious crimes, such as witchcraft, were reserved for the assize court that met twice a year at Bury St. Edmunds.

Lowestoft's economy was based mainly on agriculture and fishing, though like most seventeenth-century market towns, it offered a wide range of services, with millers, blacksmiths, coopers, wheelwrights, bakers, maltsters, and brewers; in all, seventy different occupations have been recorded among the town's working population.[39] In the seventeenth century, the North Sea waters of Lowestoft and Great Yarmouth were regarded as the greatest herring fishery in the world.[40]

Lowestoft has a modest roster of native-son luminaries and historical associations. It was the birthplace of Thomas Nashe (1567–1601), a satirist who spent most of his short life in London, and who was portrayed by William Shakespeare as Master Moth, the knavish page boy, "that handful of wit," in *Love's Labour's Lost*.[41] Colonel Oliver Cromwell had come to Lowestoft in March of 1643 to apprehend a group of "strangers" about to escape by way of the North Sea to Holland, about 120 miles due east. Cromwell believed that they were plotting a Royalist uprising.[42]

Benjamin Britten, the composer, pianist and conductor, was born in Lowestoft on November 22, 1913, the day of St. Cecilia, the patron saint of music.[43] The Britten house at 21 Kirkly Cliff Road, built in the second half of the nineteenth century, lay a mile and a quarter due south of where the Pacys had lived, and also faced the North Sea. When he was but seventeen, Britten touched briefly on the subject of witchcraft, setting to music the poet Walter de la Mare's "I Saw Three Witches," the first verse of which reads:

I saw three witches
That bowed down like barley
And took to their brooms 'neath a louring [scowling] sky,
And, mounting a storm-cloud,
Aloft on its margin,
Stood back in the silver as up they did fly.[44]

Twenty-four years later, Britten composed his *Hymn to St. Peter* to help mark the quincentenary of St. Peter Mancroft Church in Norwich, where Sir Thomas Browne lies buried.[45]

Vera Brittain, arriving at Lowestoft during the First World War to meet her fiancé's parents, writes of the "grim strangeness of the shrouded east coast."[46] To her, Lowestoft presented an alien face:

> In the vanishing light the sea was visible only as a vast gray shadow, scarcely distinguishable from smaller shadows of floating cloud in a gently wind-blown sky. Far out to sea, the tiny twinkling eyes of buoys and vessels starred the vague dimness. As we drove through the streets, the faint outlines of the buildings and the muffled stillness broken only by the smooth wash of waves on the shore, gave the curious impression of a town wrapped in fog.[47]

A prominent explanation of witch trials is that people invent scapegoats, such as witches, during times of turmoil and danger to ease the anguish of an uncertain existence. When the witch trial was held in 1662, the interregnum had ended only two years earlier with Charles II's assumption of the throne, and religious nonconformists, Samuel Pacy prominent among them, now stood in strong fear of persecution.

For Pacy, one of Lowestoft's leading fish merchants, there also was at the time of the witchcraft upheaval an even more immediate and threatening problem that may well have contributed significantly to the panic that underlay the accusations against Denny and Cullender. A centuries-old dispute between Lowestoft and Great Yarmouth, its prosperous northern neighbor, had again heated up. The argument was over fishing rights. It reached a climax in 1660 when Great Yarmouth blockaded the North Sea waters off Lowestoft so that no fish could be landed. Unable to pierce the blockade, and threatened by economic disaster, the Lowestoft people took the matter to court.

The anxiety associated with the Lowestoft cause can be seen from a petition that inhabitants of the town sent to the House of Lords in 1660:

> having been grievous sufferers for our constant fidelity to his sacred majesty: [Lowestoft, unlike Yarmouth, had supported the King during the Civil War]: several times plundered, grievously burthened with taxes above the neighbouring towns, soldiers living at free quarters, great losses by sea, depopulated of our principal inhabitants by their being

engaged in his Majesties service . . . besides . . . many who have lost their lives in contending with these oppressors, and also a most lamentable fire in this town which consumed 140 houses, together with tackling and goods to the amount of ten thousand pounds and upwards, for which we never had any favour [redress]: And now having made large provisions for the fishery of all sorts, [such as] receiving, salting and drying such herrings as they should bring in, being able to hang [smoke] about 700 lasts,[48] which time out of mind have been the sole subsistence of this town, are now bespoiled at once and like to perish if speedy remedy be not obtained, being no ways able to wage war with them [Great Yarmouth], for reasons above.[49]

The "most lamentable fire" of 1645 in fact had destroyed only 39 houses, twenty of them fish-houses (none belonging to the Pacys),[50] though it had caused damages that at today's prices would perhaps equal one million pounds or even more. Despite its exaggerations, the petition conveys the sense of desperation in Lowestoft because of its dispute with Great Yarmouth.

At the heart of the conflict lay the question of which waters of the North Sea fell under Yarmouth's jurisdiction. The Bailiffs of Yarmouth had the legal right to insist that, up to a certain distance from their town, all fish must be landed and sold at their town quay. In this way, they could collect custom fees on fish hauls taken or brought into them.

The Town of Great Yarmouth had developed in the seventh or eighth century on a large sandbank straddling the confluence and estuary of three important rivers that provided the main inland access from the North Sea, and during the Middle Ages and for some time afterward it had been the world's leading market for herring.

Since Protestantism, the product of England's Reformation, did not require the eating of fish instead of flesh, the market for herring had been seriously reduced by the seventeenth century, thereby aggravating the trade rivalry between Lowestoft and Great Yarmouth. In addition, the Dutch had begun to dominate the fishing trade. A 1614 pamphlet offering advice on how to improve the English fishing and maritime fleets referred to the fishing towns in Norfolk and Suffolk as "decayed."[51] Yarmouth had experienced other problems as well, as the mouth of its harbor silted up, making navigation to the town increasingly difficult, and detouring many boats to Lowestoft. No less than seven alternative channels that were cut also quickly became unnavigable, until a new entrance, dredged in 1567, proved usable—and is still in use today.

The dispute had come to a head in 1660 as Yarmouth fishing interests increasingly infringed on what Lowestoft people believed should be open waters, and virtually blockaded approaches to Lowestoft. At issue was a law enacted in 1357[52] and its arguable repeal by an Act that came twenty-two years later, during the second year of Richard II's reign. This second enactment was a general law which granted "free trade for all persons to buy and sell at any place within the realm, notwithstanding any statute, grant or usage to the contrary."[53] The original decree had given Great Yarmouth a monopoly over fishing rights for a distance of seven leucae from a given point within the town. The dispute involved three questions: first, precisely what distance equalled a leuca? The measure had originated in antiquity and probably was derived from a leuga, the Roman league of 2,500 yards or 1500 paces,[54] but its meaning had become befogged over time. Second was the question of the point from which the seven leucae were to be measured: the statute had stipulated Kirkley Road, but by this time it was arguable precisely where Kirkley Road lay. Finally, there was also the issue of whether the 1379 law automatically had repealed the earlier legislation.

At stake was the ability of Lowestoft's fish merchants to buy herring caught not only by its own fishermen but from others as well. As there was no harbor at Lowestoft, herring boats would anchor in the roads, the name given to stretches of sea contiguous to the coast. Local merchants then would sail out to the boats to negotiate purchase of the haul. Some herring were sold locally, some were shipped inland either fresh or pickled, while most of the haul was smoked and cured in the town for sale throughout England and on the continent. Many of the fishermen preferred to market their wares in Lowestoft because they could avoid Great Yarmouth's harbor dues and its fixed prices. There was the added advantage of a speedier turn-around as the boats did not have to wait for the tides as they did at Yarmouth.

But Yarmouth's leaders, insisting that they had jurisdiction over these adjacent waters, often intercepted boats bound for Lowestoft. A ship they dispatched into the Lowestoft roads in the fall of 1659 to prevent the unloading of fish was driven off only after the local fishermen threatened to set fire to it. The following year, during the traditional Free Fair for herring trade, Lowestoft was successfully blockaded by a fully equipped warship from Yarmouth—described in Lowestoft annals as "a vessel . . . with a flag on the main top mast head, having 25 men on board, armed with swords, half-pikes, musketts, and a great store of stones."[55] So successful was this blockade that Lowestoft merchants declared that they had been deprived of at least 1,000 lasts of herring.

The principal manager of the Lowestoft suit against Great Yarmouth was James Wilde. He was primarily assisted by Thomas Mighells and by Samuel Pacy. Wilde and Pacy were cousins who lived next door to each other in the High Street.

As they fought their case in London for commercial survival, the Lowestoft petitioners would find themselves in contact with some of the country's most powerful legal presences, including Sir Matthew Hale or, at least, members of his entourage. It was these associations that may well have been instrumental in provoking very soon thereafter the prosecution of Amy Denny and Rose Cullender for witchcraft.

The legal system commonly swings into action as soon as a criminal offense becomes known and its perpetrator apprehended. The case against Amy Denny and Rose Cullender, however, largely represented stale allegations. The lone charge involving a death by witchcraft concerned events that had taken place in 1659, three years before the trial of the Lowestoft women. Illnesses suffered by Elizabeth and Deborah Pacy, two young girls, said to have been brought about by Amy Denny's witchcraft, were the only alleged serious recent crimes. And only four months before her assize trial, Amy Denny had been placed in the Lowestoft stocks for witchcraft, a punishment once, but no longer, decreed for the first such offense, and one most typically used for drunkards, scolds, and other minor community irritants.

Why, suddenly, were the old allegations revived and redefined as a capital crime?

We strongly suspect that there was some form of collaboration between Samuel Pacy, the father of the ill girls—or someone acting on his behalf—and Matthew Hale—or someone close to him—that led to the new witchcraft charges. We do not know the precise nature of what passed between Pacy and Hale or their representatives prior to the trial, but we know that there had been several opportunities for meetings.

Hale apparently knew that he would be judging a witchcraft case when he rode out to the Suffolk assizes on the Norfolk circuit that spring in 1662. Although the practice was not sanctioned by statute, records of examinations and depositions collected by justices of the peace sometimes were sent to the assigned assize judges before they left London.[56] Evidence that Hale knew what he would meet with in Bury St. Edmunds is offered in the Preface to *A Collection of Modern Relations of Matters of Fact Concerning Witches & Witchcraft Upon the*

Persons of People, published in 1693. The Preface, written by Edward Stephens,[57] the husband of Hale's elder daughter, Mary, notes that Hale understood "by his kalendar before-hand what a cause he was to try."[58] Stephens also tells us that the trial lasted "from seven or eight in the morning to seven or eight at night," that Hale had summoned to his assistance "diverse physicians and other learned men," and that the trial report, prepared by Hale's marshal, "which I suppose is very true," nonetheless was, "to the best of my memory, not so complete as to some observable circumstances, as what he [Hale] related to me at his return from that circuit."[59]

This was not Hale's first witchcraft case. He had been one of two judges on the Home Circuit who sentenced Judith Sawkins of Aylesford to be hanged at the end of March, 1658. Sawkins, a widow, had been indicted two years earlier for bewitching Frances Long who died after a languishing illness. The jury acquitted her. Later the same year she again was indicted, both for bewitching the daughter of Elizabeth Meadows and for burning a barn and corn by means of witchcraft. This time, with Hale presiding, she was convicted.[60]

The stress by Stephens on Hale's foreknowledge seems a bit unusual, but not much more than that. Hale often rode the Norfolk circuit—a prized assignment because the area was so accessible from London; and he sat at Bedford, a Norfolk circuit site, at least fifteen times between 1660 and 1674.[61]

To remove suspicion of partiality, judges by law were prohibited to hold their sessions in counties where they had been born or where they lived.[62] As a very senior judge by the spring of 1662, Hale had a high priority in choosing the circuit he would ride. First choice went to the Chief Justice of the King's Bench, Sir Robert Foster; second to the Chief Justice of the Common Pleas, Sir Orlando Bridgeman; Hale as Lord Chief Baron of the Exchequer had the third selection. The judges would pick their circuits toward the end of the Hilary term, that is, some time between January 11 and the last day of the month.[63] The meeting in London between Hale and Pacy—or persons speaking for them—would have come about during the final stages of the fishing rights dispute between Lowestoft and Great Yarmouth, very close to the time when Hale would choose his circuit for the spring.

We can recreate the work of the Lowestoft advocates from the detailed account of expenditures kept by James Wilde, who headed the town's petitioners. In December 1660, Pacy and Thomas Mighells were each given an advance of one pound for expenses as they set out on what would be almost a four-month trip to the south coast of England to solicit support from fishermen in Folkestone, Hastings,

Ramsgate, Dover, and Rye, for the fight against Great Yarmouth. They came home by way of London, joining Wilde there in support of his petition to the Attorney General. Five months later, Pacy and Mighells received an additional £10, presumably to cover costs incurred on their trip.[64]

By mid-1661, the battle between Lowestoft and Great Yarmouth had heated up. The case was sent on June 20 from the Privy Council, which included the King and his brother, the Duke of York, to the House of Lords for a hearing. It seems certain that Samuel Pacy attended both this hearing and the second shortly thereafter, since the reimbursements he received for expenses in London are dated June 25 and June 27.

Following a brief hearing on June 20, and a longer one on June 22, the Lords decided to defer judgment until they had obtained the opinion of a panel of ten judges concerning the intricate points of law under dispute. But the designated judges were preoccupied with the weightier matter of preparing for the trials of twenty-nine regicides and they were attempting to sort out the legality of laws passed during the Commonwealth. Consequently, they deferred the fishing rights case. Then, on December 4, 1661, after a brief preliminary meeting, they directed that on January 24 representatives from Lowestoft and Great Yarmouth should appear to argue their position. Matthew Hale had been appointed Lord Chief Baron of the Exchequer on November 7, 1661, and therefore was a member of the judicial panel adjudicating the Lowestoft dispute.

Interestingly, Hale is the only judge mentioned in Wilde's accounts, with the first of two references indicating the following expenses during a journey to London:

> December 4th, 1661—To money paid Lord Chief Baron Hale's man and Mr. Robert Lumley for their trouble for waiting upon the Judges and getting their hands[65] [i.e., obtaining their signatures] . . . £1.0.0.

The other reference to Hale in Wilde's accounts, concerning another trip to London, reads:

> February 1st, 1662—To a barrel of choice red herrings, given as a present, viz. to captain Allen 100, to Lord Hollis 200, to lord chief baron Hales 200, to Mr. Hall Solicitor 100, to myself 100, and the remainder to several others . . . £1.3.0.

To Mr. Moore (Mr. Attorney's brother), a basket of herrings . . . £0.2.9.[66]

Putting aside the disingenuous—and marvelously honest—detail of Wilde's present to himself for his efforts, the rendering up of gratuities to judicial officers and their staff was a commonplace occurrence, not to be seen as a form of bribery (although, of course, it could be that), but as a recognition of services, albeit services done as part of a person's required duty. "Hollis" was Denzil Holles, a Privy Councillor, and Parliamentary representative from Dorchester, described by the Lowestoft group as "one of our most worthy gentlemen (conscious of the justice of our cause)."[67] Except for Hale, the recipients of the herring were openly partisan supporters of Lowestoft's cause, which had found favor with the judges the previous week: the presents likely were a token of gratitude. Later, following further resolution of the case, "Lord Hales Gentleman" would be given another 100 red herring (in March 1663)[68] and a share of a further 600 fish (in October 1664).[69]

On February 26, 1662—just two weeks before the witch trial would begin—the House of Lords adopted the judges' findings in favor of Lowestoft, indicating that a leuca was to be regarded as a standard mile and that the distance of Great Yarmouth's monopoly extended only from a site called Crane Key, where the annual Free Fair, the grandest of the medieval age's fish markets, had been held, rather than from farther south. This placed Lowestoft one and a half miles outside the range of Yarmouth's territorial rights.[70] The verdict was made even more satisfactory for Lowestoft by King Charles' proclamation earlier the same month enjoining the observance of Lent, a custom which had been in abeyance since 1640, and reinstating Wednesdays, Fridays, and Saturdays as fish days, when the eating of meat was forbidden. The King's act specifically sought to preserve "the young brood" of fish and thereby to avoid "the hazard of dearth" as well as to redound to the "profitt and encouragement of many poor families who live by fishing."[71]

Though Wilde's accounts demonstrate that Pacy had been in London, documents in the House of Lords Record Office show only James Munds and Samuel Wilde as Lowestoft's witnesses before the judges.[72] Nor is there a claim by Pacy for a December 1661 trip. We are persuaded that either Pacy or someone close to him discussed the Lowestoft witchcraft disturbances with Hale or with persons who were working for him. We presume that the people from Lowestoft were offered or sought procedural help, and were informed about the status of witchcraft under existing criminal law, and advised what particular steps needed to be taken to initiate a prosecution. This is the part that Hale had played with John Bunyan's wife. Similarly, in another case presided over by Hale, that of "the perjur'd fanatick," involving a spurious robbery charge against an Aylesbury minister, the minister tells of "the incouragement I had from the Lord Chief Baron to prosecute several of the conspirators." "He himself," he says of Hale, "was pleas'd to direct the process for special bail" and "to order the undersheriff to demand 500 pounds security of each."[73]

What is especially notable is that within two weeks of the first gift of herring to those in Sir Matthew Hale's employ, back in Lowestoft Amy Denny and Rose Cullender were arrested for witchcraft and held for trial before Hale at the forthcoming assize session. Samuel Pacy's daughters had been suffering for at least four months, and Amy Denny had been sent to the stocks because of their sickness. But only directly after the meetings in London was felony action taken against the suspected witches. One person who might have forged the link between Hale and Pacy was William Moore, a lawyer working on behalf of Lowestoft, who was related to the Attorney General, Sir Geoffrey Palmer,[74] and was one of the recipients of a gift of herring. Palmer was married to Margaret Moore, an aunt of Sir Matthew Hale's wife, and it was at the Palmers' house that Hale had met his wife.[75] It is also possible that Hale's marshal, the man who wrote the report of the trial, played the intermediary role in getting the trial of Amy Denny and Rose Cullender for witchcraft on its way. If so, Lowestoft's leaders had not only triumphed in their age-old battle with Great Yarmouth, they serendipitously had found a likely solution to another local problem that had been frightening and vexing them.

2

The toad in the blanket

The legal path that led Amy Denny and Rose Cullender to the Bury St. Edmunds courtroom on March 10, 1662 began with the lodging of a formal complaint before Sir Edmund Bacon of the parish of Redgrave, one of the county's justices of the peace. The trial report points out that "about the beginning of February last past, the said Rose Cullender and Amy Duny were charged by Mr. Samuel Pacy for bewitching his daughters. And a warrant being granted at the request of the said Mr. Pacy, by Sir Edmond Bacon . . . to bring them before him."

It is unclear why Sir Edmund Bacon was selected to process the witchcraft charges. Redgrave, Bacon's home, is a considerable distance from Lowestoft. Also there were more than sixty justices of the peace in Suffolk, some of them living within ten miles of Lowestoft. At least six justices were actively engaged in assisting the town in its legal struggle with Yarmouth. While some of these men were in London for the fishing rights hearing, others were much more accessible than Bacon.

Perhaps Bacon had been in Lowestoft when the charge was ready to be made, and he had heard the accusations there rather than, as was common, having them placed before him in his own residence. More likely, we suspect that Bacon was deliberately chosen because it was known that he would be receptive to the allegations against Denny and Cullender. His was a delicate task: had Bacon turned his back on the charges presented to him by Samuel Pacy, the entire episode likely would have come to an abrupt end.

Perhaps Bacon's ties to Thomas Browne and Sir John Pettus were what brought him into the case. Pettus was a staunch Royalist and one of Lowestoft's leading supporters in its law suit against Great Yarmouth, in which he worked closely with Wilde and Pacy. Wilde's accounts show that in February 1662 he had presented Pettus' "gentleman" with a gold ring inscribed "Lowestoft's Deliverance—this

26th February 1661/62."[1] There is little doubt that Pettus was a frequent visitor to Lowestoft during the 1660 to 1662 period, and he must have been well aware of the talk of witchcraft there.

Pettus' linkage to Browne has been established by Frank Huntley, who determined that Browne's *Letter to a Friend, Upon the Occasion of the Death of His Intimate Friend* (published by Browne's son in 1690) was written to Pettus by Sir Thomas to acquaint him of the death of Robert Loveday, a mutual friend. At that time, Pettus was living away from his Chediston home in Suffolk because of the Civil War.[2]

The Bacon–Browne linkage is verified in the Epistle Dedicatory segment of Browne's *Garden of Cyrus*. The work is dedicated to "my worthy and honoured friend Nicholas Bacon of Gillingham, Esquire." This is Sir Edmund Bacon's uncle, the brother of his father, Robert. In the final paragraph of the dedication, Browne refers to Nicholas as "being a flourishing branch of that noble family . . . [o]f the most worthy Sir Edmund Bacon, prime Baronet, my true and noble friend . . . "[3] Since *Garden of Cyrus* was published three years after Edmund had been created fourth Baronet of Redgrave, Browne clearly is referring to the man who served as justice of the peace for the arrest of Amy Denny and Rose Cullender.

Justices of the peace, such as Bacon, were chosen from among the most prominent men in the community, were unpaid, usually amateur, and only lightly subject to discipline.[4] The office had been initiated at least by the fourteenth century, with some historians placing its origin as early as the late twelfth century.[5] The work of a justice of the peace, at least as the eminent minister Richard Baxter, a close friend of Matthew Hale, saw it, was "[t]o encourage the good, and be a terror to and avenger to the evil." "And therefore," Baxter advised, "be not the same to persons who are not the same, be a lamb to lambs, and a lyon to the wolves."[6] In Norfolk, a typical working justice of the peace (many of the appointments were purely honorary) would be concerned with about 50,000 persons scattered over a circular area with a perimeter usually not more than twenty-five miles from his home.[7]

Sir Edmund Bacon had been baptized on November 10, 1628, which would have made him thirty-three years old when he was confronted with the accusation of witchcraft against Amy Denny and Rose Cullender.[8] He had become the fourth Premier Baronet of Redgrave in 1655, and was the great-great grandson of Sir Nicholas Bacon (1509–1579). Sir Nicholas had been the Lord Keeper of the Great Seal for Queen Elizabeth I, and the father of Sir Francis Bacon, the renowned essayist, philosopher, and Lord Chancellor. Sir Edmund's great-grandfather, also Sir Nicholas Bacon (1540–1624),

Figure 3 The Raveningham Portrait of Sir Edmund Bacon, which has not been
published to date
Source: The origianl hangs in Raveningham Hall, Norfolk; reproduced by kind permission of Sir
Nicholas Bacon (photo: Dr. P. O. Johnson).

was the first person to be created a baronet when the title was established by King James I in 1601.

Sir Edmund would have six sons and ten daughters, all of whom
save four of the daughters died before his own life ended in 1685.

Today, his portrait, encased in an ornate gold frame and hung near the top landing of the main staircase, is the largest in a gallery of Bacon ancestors at Raveningham Hall in Norfolk. He wears dress armor in the portrait, with a plumed helmet lying on the table in front of him. He is portly, and seems to be making an effort to look stern and important, though to recent visitors, being shown the painting by Sir Nicholas Bacon, the fourteenth Baronet of Redgrave (and fifteenth Baronet of Mildenhall), Sir Edmund's expression seems kindly.

After he had listened to the charges, Bacon issued a warrant on the first or second day of February 1662 for the arrest and examination of Amy Denny and Rose Cullender. They would have been taken into custody by a constable and questioned by Sir Edmund, but by law they were not put on their oath, primarily because doing so was considered worthless.[9] Sir Edmund was required to put the results of his inquiry into writing within two days;[10] the document he had to prepare was less a deposition than a memorandum recounting the evidence.[11] Such documents served primarily to refresh the memories of the justices during their oral testimony at the trial.[12] They were not made part of the assize record, and for the Denny–Cullender witchcraft case, as for almost all other criminal trials of the period, they have not survived.[13]

Witchcraft had been declared a crime far back in English history. In the time of Alfred (844–899) it was decreed that "women who are wont to practice enchantments, and magicians and witches, do not allow them to live."[14] The later line of English statutes outlawing witchcraft had begun with a 1542 enactment under Henry VIII.[15] This law was repealed in 1547,[16] and for the next 16 years England was without a statutory prohibition of witchcraft, though other juridical avenues, particularly the laws against heresy, were employed to try persons believed to be engaged in diabolic schemes.

In 1563, the Parliament of Elizabeth I again outlawed witchcraft. The new measure included the death penalty for murder by sorcery. For witchcraft that was not deadly there could be a year's imprisonment and placement in the pillory during a fair, where the convicted person would be exhibited for six hours and had to "openly confess his or her error and offense." The statute outlawed divination, including predicting the sovereign's death and seeking to locate hidden treasures or stolen property, as well as the use of love philters and the attempt to murder by diabolic means.[17]

The 1604 statute, the law under which Amy Denny and Rose Cullender were tried, retained much of the phraseology of the Elizabethan measure, but was harsher: it has been estimated that more than 40 per cent of those executed under the 1604 statute would have avoided death under the earlier law.[18] The new statute decreed hanging for maleficent witchcraft done with harmful intent, even though the bewitched person had not died. It also added the taking of dead bodies from graves to the list of witchcraft acts meriting death, and imposed capital punishment for some offenses when committed for a second time, such as provoking a person to "unlawful love."[19] In practice, according to Robert Filmer, writing in 1653, judges were inclined to interpret the statute benevolently, and "condemn none for witches unless they be charged with murdering some person."[20] The one-year penalty remained for the lesser offenses, such as divination. The new statute also attempted to spell out the nature of a pact with the devil, making it a capital offense "to exercise any invocation or conjuration of any evil and wicked spirit, or [to] consult, covenant with, entertain, employ, feed, or reward any evil and wicked spirit to or for any intent or purpose."[21]

It was Sir Edmund Bacon's responsibility to square the statutory definitions with the accusations against Amy Denny and Rose Cullender. Once he had issued the warrant and conducted the examination, his only options were to place the accused in custody or release them on bail: he did not have the right to discharge them.[22] Witnesses examined by Sir Edmund could be bound by recognizance to appear at the following assize to present their evidence. The two women accused of witchcraft probably were kept under house arrest in Lowestoft until the time they were transported to Bury St. Edmunds by one or several of the town constables. Four men, unpaid, served in that capacity in Lowestoft each year, one of whose descendants, as we relate below, later would spin a tale of his ancestor's bewitchment during the trip to the Bury St. Edmunds jail.

Sir Edmund's written report would be handed over to the commission of jail delivery. Then indictments would be drawn up by the court clerk and submitted to the grand jury, whose members—somewhere between a dozen and two dozen "middling" men—had been selected two weeks earlier by the sheriff from among freeholders in the community.[23] The sheriff himself ranked above the justices of the peace, and often was drawn from their ranks. He was appointed from a list of three put together at a special session of high government officials and the Council of the Exchequer. The King then "pricked" out one name from the roster. That person secured a letter patent and was sworn in as sheriff for a one-year term.[24]

The accused and the witnesses—the Pacys and the others—probably traveled together to Bury St. Edmunds as one party at the beginning of March. At least eighteen people made the trip to Bury St. Edmunds,

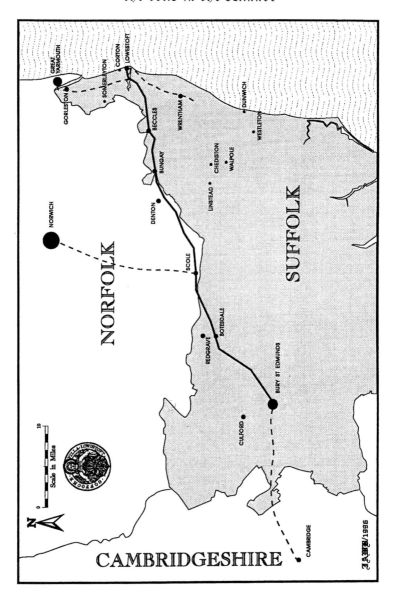

Figure 4 Map of East Anglia, showing the relative positions of Lowestoft, Bury
St. Edmunds, Norwich, and Cambridge (and other locations of
relevance), together with the route taken by the trial party
Source: Drawn by Ivan Bunn.

and they must have required a cart to transport the sick among them. They probably stopped one or two nights along the way—in those days the word "journey" adhered to its etymological root[25]—perhaps one night in or near Bungay, where Samuel Pacy's wife's family lived. The fifty-mile journey from Lowestoft to Bury was notably arduous, with highways nothing more than wide bumpy tracks that were likely to be wet and water-logged in February and March: "the wayes and common roades in this countrye [county] are very fowle and uncomfortable in the winter tyme to travyle on," a chronicler had written in 1605.[26] January had been an exceptionally warm month in the area; Samuel Pepys indicates in his diary that in the middle of the month a general fast was held to urge divine assistance in producing colder weather.[27] But if the February and March weather ran true to form it would have been cold, wet, and windy.

Beginning at Lowestoft, the road to Bury St. Edmunds followed the comparatively high ground south of the river Waveney for about the first ten miles and then passed through the old market town of Beccles. From Beccles the road wound westward to Bungay, after which the route became more irksome, descending into low-lying marshlands, and involving the fording of small tributaries of the Waveney. It skirted the parish of Denton, where Samuel Pacy and his wife were landholders, and passed through Wortwell and Redenhall. Houses hugged the road, with wide-open lands behind them. After Needham and Billingford, the travelers would have reached Scole, a bustling site that stood on the crossroad of this highway and the old north–south Roman road that led to Norwich and Ipswich, along which Thomas Browne would come on his way to the trial.

From Scole, the road crossed the river and then swung westward, skirting Stuston and its expansive heaths and commons, passed over another ford, and rose steadily, until it came close to the village of Wortham. West of Wortham it ran within half a mile of Sir Edmund Bacon's estate at Redgrave Hall, where Browne well might have rested on his way to the assize. From Redgrave, the road traversed Botesdale, Rickinghall Superior and Rickinghall Inferior. Town folklore later would have it that Edward Yowell's father, a town constable who reportedly was in charge of Amy Denny and Rose Cullender on the trip, was told by one of the women that it would have been better had he stayed at home. On the return trip, the story goes, he fell from his horse near Botesdale and broke a leg.[28] At Wattisfield, there was a length of highway, the Wattisfield Causeway, whose upkeep was paid for by a Bacon legacy set up in 1628. Then came Hepworth Common and Stanton and after that another dozen miles along the bleakest part of the trek, with high exposed ground, and only two inhabited towns—Ixworth and Great Barton—and the rest unfenced open heath and common.

At last, there was Bury St. Edmunds. The party would have entered by way of the narrow Eastgate Street, crossed a bridge, and passed through the ancient portals. A few more yards brought them into the open vista of Angel Hill, over which stood the great gateway to the famed abbey, then in ruins. A short distance more took the officials and their prisoners to the Great Market where the women would have been handed over to the jailer.

The jail in which Amy Denny and Rose Cullender were incarcerated no longer exists. It stood at the west side of the Great Market. If it was like others of its kind at the time, it would have been appallingly squalid. In 1655, a number of Quakers had been put into the Bury jail, and on their release a year later they claimed that they were surrounded by drunkenness and were constantly beaten and abused by the jailer and that his assistant had "cast a stone violently, and hit one of us in the back with it" as well as "buffetted some of us severall times together with his fists violently on our faces." Other prisoners, saying that they had been encouraged to do so by the jailer, were reported to have seized the Quakers' food. Straw was provided for sleeping, but the prisoners were expected to pay for their keep.[29]

Assize sessions, held twice a year, in the spring and during the summer, were a time of ceremony for Bury St. Edmunds and the other court sites. The out-of-town arrivals—the judges and a train of law officials, barristers, and servants—were met near the boundary of the county by a cavalcade that included the leading local notables: the High Sheriff, decked out in fine apparel, his tenants and retainers, the latter often in new livery for the occasion, carrying javelins and halberds, and with two trumpeters at their head. The officials usually were followed by a large assembly of gentlemen, who escorted the representatives of the King.

When the assize officials and the local delegation met, trumpets sounded, all dismounted from their horses or coaches, and a welcoming speech was made by the High Sheriff.[30] Roger North, writing toward the end of the century, would report how fatiguing it was to ride circuit on a trotting mare, and how his horse came to recognize the "first clangours" of the trumpets and "would always brisk up as a good news" of their arrival.[31] After the greeting ceremonies, the judges went to their lodgings where they received the leading members of the gentry, who were expected to report on the state of the county. Then the assize officials, with the judges dressed in their scarlet robes, were taken to church where the local minister read prayers and the sheriff's chaplain delivered a sermon.[32]

In 1662, when the assize proceedings against Amy Denny and Rose Cullender took place, Bury St. Edmunds was a town of about 6,000 persons, four times larger than Lowestoft, and about half the size of Norwich, then England's second largest city.[33] It had taken its name from Edmund (841–869), king of the East Angles. Captured by the invading Danes, Edmund allegedly had been brutally murdered when he refused to renounce his Christian faith. His body was interred in a rough grave, and when the corpse was exhumed a number of years later, it was said to be "perfect and uncorrupted." Edmund was canonized, and his body reburied in a newly constructed abbey, where it was to be guarded by a college of priests. The three major focal points of Christendom in the Middle Ages are said to have been St. Peter's in Rome, Cologne Cathedral, and the Bury Abbey Church.[34]

At the middle of the seventeenth century, Bury was a thriving town. It was so situated that travelers from London to more distant points had to pass through it. It also was a virtually unavoidable crossroad for those going to and from Norwich, Cambridge, and Ipswich.[35] Daniel Defoe, in his *Tour Through the Eastern Counties*, would praise Bury for "its pleasant situation and wholesome air" and call it "the Montpelier of Suffolk, and perhaps of England."[36] The town was not an industrial center of any importance, but it served as the commercial and social hub for the prospering agricultural region of west Suffolk.[37] Its wealth was built on the wool trade, and its annual fair was the most flourishing in the kingdom.

The King's itinerant justices had been sitting at Bury St. Edmunds from at least as early as 1187. In 1662, the assizes met at the Shirehall, located near the center of the town. The L-shaped building had two main courtrooms that overlooked the churchyard of St. Mary's to the north. Crown court cases were heard in one room, while the other served as a *nisi prius* court, where civil cases were adjudicated. There also were two small rooms, about 15 by 20 feet, which were used by the grand jury and for witnesses and officials, and a small enclosed yard containing a privy.

The crown courtroom was a lofty chamber measuring 35 by 48 feet, two stories high with stout posts supporting the exposed roof timbers. The judges, the justices of the peace (who were required to attend the assizes but did not always do so), and other dignitaries sat on a raised dais along the eastern wall. Behind and above them was a large window that provided the courtroom with its main source of light. The west wall had a door leading into the *nisi prius* courtroom, which

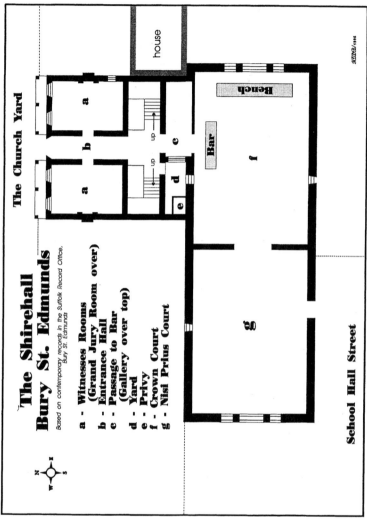

Figure 5 Plan of the Shirehall, Bury St. Edmunds
Source: Drawn by Ivan Bunn; based on contemporary plans and documents in the Suffolk
Record Office, Bury St. Edmunds.

was similar to the crown court chamber. The north wall had a small
window overlooking the yard, and directly opposite there was another
window which provided a view of the garden of an adjoining house.

Spectators from the general public were permitted to attend the
assizes. At Bury, they apparently occupied a gallery over the witness
room that adjoined the courtroom. The gallery was reached by a
corridor staircase; a similar staircase at the opposite end of the corridor

provided access to a grand jury room. This chamber was 38 feet by 20 feet, had four windows overlooking the churchyard, and probably a large open fireplace at each end.[38] The court building was in a poor state at the time of the witchcraft trial, for in the year following an order was made to raise £200 for the "alteration and repairing of the Shire House." It was noted that the north wall of the *nisi prius* courtroom, behind where the judge sat, was ruinous and likely to fall, and that the windows and great post in the middle of the court needed replacing.[39] Ten years later, the Corporation finally ordered work on the court, under the threat that "if not built as it is promised and the judges expect, the assizes, as it is conceived, will be removed from the town."[40]

This was the setting in which the trial of Amy Denny and Rose Cullender took place. Most often, women accused of witchcraft (and overwhelmingly those so accused were women) were old, poor, and without the support of males, particularly husbands. Rose Cullender fit some of these conditions, but not all of them. She probably was not born in Lowestoft, since the parish register contains no record of her baptism. As Rose Hicks, "single," she was married at Lowestoft on April 18, 1625 to William Cullender, a "singleman."[41] He too probably was from another place since the Lowestoft parish registers do not list his baptism. It is interesting to note that there was a family named Hicks living at Denton in the early seventeenth century. It is from this parish, or its vicinity, that Samuel Pacy's wife originated.

On June 24, two months after her wedding, Rose Cullender bore her first child, Elizabeth. At this time, about 12 per cent of the brides married in Lowestoft went to the altar pregnant, but no particular stigma seems to have been attached to their condition.[42] During the next twelve years, Rose Cullender had eight more children. Of the nine, five had died before reaching the age of ten, including twins, Peter and Mary, born in 1632. Four of the deaths of Rose's children occurred during the 1635 plague when the town's burial register contains 170 entries compared to only thirty for the year before.[43] The Cullenders, following common practice, had given three of their nine children the name of Mary, reusing it as it became available with the death of an earlier Mary.

The single messauge that the Cullenders had rented, probably soon after their marriage in 1625, was part of a large building called "The Hall House." In the yard of the house was a barn that formerly had served as a blacksmith's shop. During the Cullenders' occupancy of The Hall House, the barn was leased to a local brewer, Francis Ewen, who had three teenage daughters, the second of whom was Ann, aged fifteen in 1630. Thirty-two years later, as Ann Landefield, she would be an important witness against Rose Cullender at the witchcraft trial. The Cullender family probably was reasonably well off, at least before William died. In 1638, he held a mortgage on the house of Richard Church, and two years later he purchased the house from Church and used it as his family home. William Cullender died within a year after the house purchase, probably in the fall of 1641, though the Lowestoft parish register contains no reference to his death or his burial. This suggests that he might have been buried in the parish in which he was born or, perhaps, that he was a sailor or fisherman and was drowned at sea. The following entry is found under the date of November 3, 1641, in the record of the Manor Court, which dealt with land transactions:

> William Cullender . . . customary tenant of this Manor, died since the last court, and . . . at the time of his death held divers lands and tenements copyhold of this Manor. . . . [44]

It was necessary for the legal heir to present himself to the Manor Court to claim his inheritance and to be officially admitted to it. Rose Cullender, as a wife, did not have the right to inherit. Seven months later, in June 1642, the court record notes that, for the moment, this moiety (a piece of property physically divided into halves) of one curtilage (an area of land occupied by a dwelling and its yard and outbuildings) had been seised (taken) by the lord of the manor, as was his right. We do not have further details on the court's actions, but commonly the seizure was no more than a formality, and the land would be placed in trust, often with an uncle, until the heir, in this case fourteen-year-old Thomas Cullender, reached his majority. Rose Cullender likely lived at least passably well during the period between her husband's death—twenty-one years earlier—and her trial for witchcraft. At no time did she claim parish relief; in fact, she herself contributed to the poor rate.

A scant seven months after his mother's execution, Thomas Cullender would transfer the family house to his sister, Susan. We learn from the Manor Court records that Thomas was married and had children of his own, though neither the marriage nor the baptism of the children is recorded at Lowestoft, indicating that he lived elsewhere. Like so many elderly women accused of witchcraft, Rose Cullender apparently did not have any adult male near at hand to protect her against the charge.

If Rose Cullender had been twenty-four or twenty-five years old when she married, the average age for women to do so in the seventeenth century,[45] she would have been sixty at the time of the trial. Despite the high mortality rate, if a person lived past the age of twenty-five and married, there was one chance in four to survive to seventy.[46] Old age during this period, according to Steven R. Smith, was neither revered nor despised, though Smith fails to distinguish between men and women or to take into account social status, particularly the status of elderly women without family and means.[47] Caricatures of the elderly as a group were common then as now: Henry Cuffe, for instance, accused old people of being excessively talkative, and said that this was because their mouth and tongue were among the "least decayed" parts of their body.[48]

Less information is available regarding Amy Denny than Rose Cullender. The name Denny is common in Lowestoft and the surrounding area, though the vagaries of seventeenth-century spelling, coupled with the local dialect, can make it difficult for the uninitiated to understand it properly. Lowestoft parish registers of the day variously list the name as "Danye," "Dany," "Danny," "Danie," "Daney," and "Dennie," as well as the more usual "Denny." The name originally indicated a person who worked in the woodland or in the swine pasture.[49]

There exists a slender clue that might identify the origins of Amy Denny. The marriage register for Beccles, ten miles from Lowestoft, records that on October 28, 1634, John Denny of that town married Emma Heckelton at the parish church.[50] "Amy" commonly was used affectionately for Emma (being a corruption of "Emmy," a pet form of Emma).[51]

Given the vagaries of seventeenth-century spelling, this Emma Heckelton could have been related to Margaret Eccleston who eleven years later, during the 1645 witch-hunt in Suffolk, "confessed" to being a witch and employing an imp for diabolical purposes. Margaret Eccleston lived in the parish of Linstead, nine miles south-south-west of Beccles. She was found guilty, though her fate was not recorded.[52] As we shall see, one of the most damaging allegations raised against Amy Denny was that she was related to a known witch.

There also is a possibility that Amy Denny's husband was descended from an earlier John Denny who, together with two other men, was burned to death at Beccles on May 21, 1556 for heresy. The executions were part of a purge by Queen Mary as she sought to reestablish Catholicism in England. John Denny refused to recognize the supremacy of the Catholic Church or to participate in the Catholic rites that Mary was reintroducing into the Church of England service.

Denny and the two men executed with him became known as the Beccles Martyrs, and the place where they are believed to have died is marked today by The Martyrs' Memorial Chapel.[53]

The Beccles parish register records three children born to John and Emma Denny: John in 1636, Richard in 1639, and Thomas in 1642: there are no further entries after 1642, while the first mention of John and Amy Denny in the Lowestoft parish register occurs on May 11, 1651, in regard to the baptism of a son, Samuel.[54] This child could have been another offspring of the Beccles–Lowestoft Dennys, its birth record pinning down their move to the latter town.

There also exist a series of references to a John Denny in the records of the Lowestoft Manor Court, the Court Baron, which heard what basically were civil suits, cases typically involving trespass, debt, or damage, where the amount involved did not exceed forty shillings. Unfortunately, only the names of the plaintiff and the defendant survive from hearings of about fifteen cases at each monthly session.

There are many references to John Denny in these records. His name first appears in November 1644, affording some credence to the idea that the family had relocated to Lowestoft from Beccles soon after the birth of their third child in 1642. Many of the cases against him dragged on for more than a year: three of the suits, one filed in September 1646 and two more in January 1647, were by John Soan, who a decade and a half later would level witchcraft accusations against Amy Denny at her trial. Robert Sherrington, also an accuser in the witch trial, pressed a suit against Denny in January 1653. Another plaintiff, in September 1650, was Nicholas Pacy, either the father or the brother of Samuel Pacy.

Between November 1644 and December 1653 John Denny's name appears in the manor court records sixty-nine times, in all but three of them as a defendant.[55] These appearances are far in excess of those of any other townsman during this time. Unfortunately, records for the following ten years are missing. When we pick them up from 1665 onwards, we find that they no longer record civil cases, which were apparently transferred to the Court of Gunton Score, which heard only civil cases and was responsible for a geographical area much wider than Lowestoft. Its records commence in 1667 and contain no mention of John Denny.[56]

Two men in Lowestoft carried the name John Denny, so there is an even chance that the John Denny who appeared so regularly before the manor court was the husband of Amy, though perhaps both John Dennys were consistent malefactors. If the manor court Denny was

Amy's spouse (or, perhaps, a close relative), we can reasonably expect that we can identify at least one source of the vindictiveness that characterized the witch trial. We may presume that John Denny—or the pair of John Dennys—were very unpopular, men either constantly in debt or reluctant bill payers, and/or men who committed actions of trespass and caused other civil injuries to neighbors.

The Lowestoft parish register notes the burial of a John Denny at Lowestoft in January 1657:[57] this may have been Amy's husband; at the time of the trial she was a widow. In 1662, she lived at the south end of Lowestoft close to the seashore in a house on a plot of land south of a lane called "Henfield Score." The house was demolished in the eighteenth century, when a nearby gun battery was extended.

The assize records show that there were nine criminal trials before that of Amy Denny and Rose Cullender during the session at Bury St. Edmunds. One involved two indictments while the other eight consisted of a single criminal charge. The indictments, now abraded and often illegible, provide partial information on seven of the eight trials. There was one murder: Robert Rushford, the indictment alleged, at the instigation of his wife, Catherine, also charged with murder, had "with a sword in his right hand mortally wounded one William Nutt." The theft of an animal and sodomy were charged against John Cromptom of Helmingham. The kind of animal stolen can no longer be deciphered, but it was grey and said to be worth forty shillings. The sodomy charge was listed as "that diabolical felonie against nature, that sodomitical, detestible and abominable crime called buggerie." There follows in the indictment the puzzling observation: "But on questioning revealed no names." Three other cases also involved theft of animals. George Wincoate of Wickhambroke was charged with stealing a cow worth £3.2s.0d. as well as three heifers; Richard Mile of Yoxford, a laborer, was said to have stolen a gander worth one shilling and six pence as well as a goose; while Thomas Cutting of Mickfield had taken from Arthur Dod a red and a black-brindled heifer each worth forty shillings and a brindled heifer valued at £5.

A badly worn indictment, in which the accused's name cannot be read, appears to have involved a burglary and to have listed the goods that were taken and their value. Legible only is "a wooden platter worth two pence." Finally, in what probably also were burglaries, Thomas Barton of Barham, a laborer, was accused of stealing from Edward Andrewes of the same town, on July 10, a coat worth eight shillings, and slightly more than a month later stealing eight shillings and a penny from a person identified only as Barwell.[58]

The summary statement standing at the head of the report of the trial for witchcraft of Amy Denny and Rose Cullender, a statement prepared by the printer or by Sir Matthew Hale's marshal and published in 1682—twenty years after the trial—tersely sums up all that needed to be known from an official viewpoint about the events that occupied the court at Bury from morning until evening during those three days in mid-March in 1662:

> *At the Assizes and General Gaol delivery, held at* Bury St. Edmonds *for the County of* Suffolk, *the Tenth day of* March, *in the Sixteenth Year of the Reign of our Sovereign Lord King* Charles II:* *before* Matthew Hale, *Knight, Lord Chief Baron of His Majesties Court of* Exchequer: Rose Cullender *and* Amy Duny, *Widows, both of* Leystoff *in the County aforesaid, were severally indicted for Bewitching* Elizabeth *and* Ann Durent, Jane Bocking, Susan Chandler, William Durent, Elizabeth *and* Deborah Pacey: *And the said* Cullender *and* Duny, *being arraigned upon the said Indictments, pleaded* Not Guilty: *And afterwards, upon a long Evidence, were found* Guilty, *and thereupon had Judgment to dye for the same.*[59]

"The Evidence whereupon these Persons were convicted of Witchcraft," the headnote goes on to observe, "stands upon divers particular circumstances."[60]

The indictment had been endorsed as a "true bill" by the grand jury which then, as today, had the right to question complainants in secret as it sought to determine if there were grounds for further proceedings and if the indictments were technically sound.[61] The grand jury had to have at least twelve members to return an indictment, and typically was made up of an odd number to prevent a tie vote. Defendants were not told precisely what was alleged against them, on the assumption that the truth would best be revealed if prisoners were first confronted with

---

* This dating, like the 1664 date given on the cover of the trial report, is incorrect, and one of the errors probably prompted the other. The reign of Charles II is counted as beginning from January 29, 1649, when his father was executed by beheading, as if the Commonwealth period never had existed. The year of Charles II's return from exile and restoration, 1660, is reckoned as the twelfth year of his reign. The 1662 trial therefore took place in what would be called the fourteenth year of his reign. (On regnal dates for Charles II, see Christopher R. Cheney, *Handbook of Dates for Students of English History*, London: Offices of the Royal Historical Society, 1945, p. 26.)

the evidence in the courtroom so that the jury could judge their immediate, unprepared response to it.[62]

The trial of Amy Denny and Rose Cullender, as did other criminal
trials, presumably began with the clerk of arraignment publicly
requesting the crier to "make proclamation." The crier would
announce that those having business with the court should "draw near
and give your attendance." The accused then would be called to the
bar by the clerk by name and commanded to hold up her hand. This,
"though it may seem a trifling circumstance," Sir Matthew Hale noted
in his treatise on pleas of the crown, "yet is of importance, for by
holding up his hand . . . he owns himself to be of that name."[63] The
indictment would then be read, and the accused asked to plead
"Guilty" or "Not Guilty." If they said "Not Guilty," as Amy Denny
and Rose Cullender both did, they were asked "How wilt thou be
tried?" with the expected response being "By God and the country,"
country meaning by a petit jury which would be made up of freeholders with enough income to be "a sufficient support of life, and a
delivery of the possessor from temptation to perjury."[64] The reply of
the accused would prompt the clerk to say: "God send thee a good
deliverance." After this, the crier would request those who could
inform the court about the charge to "come forth and they shall be
heard, for now the prisoner stands upon his deliverance."[65]

The report of the 1662 trial at Bury St. Edmunds apparently
adheres to the sequence in which information came to the court's
attention. Immediately after the headnote, for instance, we learn that
three of the girls named in the indictment—Ann Durrant, Susan
Chandler, and Elizabeth Pacy—had come to the assize proceedings in
a "reasonable good condition."[66] But on the morning that they
entered the courtroom to provide instructions to the clerk to draw up
the bills of indictment, they had fallen into "strange and violent fits,
screeking out in a most sad manner, so that they could not in any wise
give instructions to the court who were the cause of their distemper."
After a while—the passing of "some certain space"—the girls recovered
from their fits, "yet they were every one of them struck dumb, so that
none of them could speak neither at that time, nor during the assizes
until the conviction of the supposed witches."

This brief paragraph about the inability of three major witnesses to
come face-to-face with the authorities and in their presence to accuse
Amy Denny and Rose Cullender of the capital crime of witchcraft
raises a crucial issue that we will address at some length in our later
discussion of the case. The girls' strategy was eminently sensible. By
remaining mute, they were able to avoid direct responsibility for

sending the two women to their death. But important questions remain. Was their dumbness a last-minute attempt to escape what could be devastating personal consequences, and an awful sense of guilt? Did they deliberately feign the fits and simulate muteness or was this an involuntary response to fear and awe brought on by the judicial surroundings and the possibility that they might be caught in a web of insupportable lies? It seems unlikely that each of the three girls independently designed an escapist ruse: did one inaugurate the behavior and the other two copy her actions?

The report provides no sense of its writer's view regarding the possibility of deception. He seems to accept what he saw at face value, with the underlying implication that the disorders had been visited upon the girls by maleficent acts by the accused. But why does he end the discussion of the girls' indisposition with a phrase calling Amy Denny and Rose Cullender "supposed" witches? Had the court proceedings not totally persuaded him of their guilt? Or was he merely at this point suggesting his impartiality, since the accused at this stage were still unconvicted?

The indictment was written on parchment in Latin (though it would be read to the prisoners in English), a usage grandly defended by Sir Matthew Hale in his treatise on the pleas of the crown because Latin "it being a fixed, regular language, it is not capable of so many changes and alterations, as happen in vulgar languages." Hale noted that if there existed a proper Latin word for an offense or other matter contained in the indictment the indictment would be quashed if it were written "with general words, and in Anglice."[67] In the case against the Lowestoft women, Elisabeth Leedham-Green, who translated the indictments for us, notes that the court clerk did fine while writing the repetitive, formal parts of the charges, but when he had to branch out into translating the actual occurrences into Latin, his Latin deteriorates markedly and at one point collapses altogether. The accused were not allowed a copy of the indictment, based on the argument that, if they were supplied with one, they would be able to take advantage of technical errors and either waste the court's time or secure an unreasonable acquittal.[68]

There were fourteen counts in the indictments against Amy Denny and Rose Cullender. Typical of each is that concerning Ann Baldinge, who is identified correctly in the indictment but miscalled Ann Baldwin in the trial report. The allegation is stated in the formal language repeated in each of the other charges, which vary only in the details of the alleged criminal act. It reads in translation as follows:

The King's sworn officers maintain upon their oaths that Rose Cullender late of Lowestoft in the aforesaid county, widow, on the lst day of February in the 14th year [1662] of the reign of our lord Charles the second King of England, Scotland, France and Ireland, Defender of the Faith etc. being a common witch and "enchantress" and not having God before her eyes but moved and seduced by the instigation of the Devil did at the aforesaid Lowestoft in the aforesaid county violently, unlawfully, diabolically and feloniously use, practice and employ certain evil and diabolical "fascinations"—in English "witchcrafts"—and "incantations"—in English "enchantments"—on one Ann Baldinge, spinster then and there living in the peace of God and the said lord King and by the aforesaid evil and diabolical witchcraft and enchantments then and there did feloniously bewitch and enchant her, by which evil and diabolical witchcraft and enchantments aforesaid the aforesaid Ann Baldinge from the aforesaid lst day of February of the above-mentioned year to the day of the holding of the inquisition at Lowestoft aforesaid in the aforesaid county has languished and languishes still and is greatly wasted in her/his body and is consumed to the injury of the same Ann Baldinge and in breach of the peace of the said lord King now crowned and of his privileges and also in breach of the form of the state given forth and provided for such cases.[69]

Next to this indictment count, as well as all the others but one, is written *po se cul*, a contraction from the Latin. *Po se* stands for *ponit se super patriam de bono et malo*, meaning that the defendant pleads not guilty. *Cul* is short for *culpabilis*, standing for guilty. Thereafter, the clerk had written *ca nu*, the abbreviation for *catalla nulla*, indicating that the women had no chattels for forfeiture. Then comes the judgment: *sus per coll*, short for *suspendendae per collum*—to be hanged by the neck.[70]

The most serious accusation, causing a death by bewitchment, was the first matter addressed at the trial. Dorothy Durrant, probably in her late twenties or early thirties, was the opening witness. Both she and her husband, William, apparently had been born elsewhere than in Lowestoft, for the parish register holds no notice of their baptisms. William Durrant is first mentioned in Lowestoft records in October 1653, when his wife, Marie, was buried there.[71] The next mention is his marriage to Dorothy Fox, a "single woman," on July 25 of the following year.[72]

The parish register identifies William Durrant as a "dauber," that is, a person who constructed walls using "daub," a mixture of clay, dung, and horsehair that was spread over the wattles of a timber-framed building to weatherproof it. William's occupation suggests that in all probability he came to Lowestoft to work on rebuilding houses destroyed in the severe fire of 1645. As a tradesman, Durrant had a standing slightly above that of persons in the ordinary laboring class. But it is noteworthy that the charge against Amy Denny involved child-minding, which indicates that the Durrants were not sufficiently well off to afford a maid, although servants were common in the households of the town's more successful citizens.[73]

William and Dorothy Durrant produced six children; in 1662, there also was at least one daughter still with the couple from William's earlier marriage, the child who with her stepmother would play a significant part in the trial of Amy Denny and Rose Cullender.

There is no evidence of the Durrants' place of residence in the Lowestoft Manor Court books, which suggests either that they owned and lived in one of the freehold properties in the town or that they were tenants in a copyhold house. The second explanation seems the better, because the Lowestoft Poor Rate Books for the seventeenth century contain no record of William Durrant paying the tax assessment levied against property owners.

Dorothy Durrant (her name is spelled Durent in the trial record, but Durrant in the indictment) told the court that on March 10, 1657—precisely five years before the date on which she was now testifying—she had to leave her house for an errand and needed someone to care for her infant son, William, who was still nursing. William was baptized at Lowestoft on May 26, 1655,[74] so he would have been about 20 months old (he would have been weaned at 13.75 months if he had met the average for the time).[75] Dorothy Durrant asked Amy Denny, her neighbor, to look after the child in her absence, and promised to give her a penny for the service. But she did not want Amy to suckle her child, and laid "a great charge upon her not to do it."

At this point, Matthew Hale interrupted to ask why that instruction had to be given, since Amy Denny was an old woman and not capable of giving suck. Dorothy Durrant replied that she "very well knew that she did not give suck," but that Amy Denny had the reputation of being a witch, and that the instruction not to suckle the child was in part based on that reputation. She also pointed out that it was customary with old women that if they were caring for a nursing child and nothing seemed to satisfy it "they did use to please the child to give it the breast, and it did please the child, but it sucked nothing but wind, which did the child hurt."[76]

Despite the warning, Amy Denny apparently suckled William, and when Dorothy Durrant returned, according to her testimony, Amy told her that she had done so. The mother was "very angry," and had it out with Amy Denny. For her part, "Amy was much discontented, and used many high expressions and threatening speeches toward her; telling her, That she had as good have done otherwise than to have found fault with her, and so departed out of her house."

That night, the infant "fell into strange fits of swounding" and was so wretchedly ill that his mother was "much affrighted therewith." The sickness continued for several weeks, eventually leading the mother to consult a "Doctor Jacob," who lived in Great Yarmouth, and who had the reputation of being able to help bewitched children.

Dr. Jacob's advice proved to be rooted in something other than the science of medicine, however primitive medicine's understanding of health and sickness at the time. Dorothy Durrant was told to hang the child's blanket in the chimney corner through the day, and then at night, when the child was put to bed, to place it inside the same blanket. If she found anything in the blanket at this time, she was not to be afraid, but to throw whatever it was into the fire.

When the blanket was taken down "there fell out of the same a great toad, which ran up and down the hearth." Having only a "young youth" with her in the house, Dorothy Durrant asked him to catch the toad and put it into the fire. He did so, holding it with tongs. Almost immediately, "it made a great and horrible noise, and after a space there was a flashing in the fire like gun-powder, making a noise like the discharge of a pistol, and thereupon the toad was no more seen nor heard."

The judge interrupted here to ask if Dorothy Durrant had seen the substance of the toad consumed in the fire. She told him that after the flashing and the noise "there was no more seen than if there had been none there."

The next day, a niece and neighbor of Amy Denny told Dorothy Durrant, according to her testimony, that her aunt was "in a most lamentable condition having her face all scorched with fire, and that she was sitting alone in her house, in her smock without any fire." Dorothy Durrant went to Amy Denny's house to corroborate this, and told the court that she found the matter to be as it had been related to her. Amy Denny's face, legs, and thighs were seen to be very much scorched and burned with fire, "at which this deponent seemed much to wonder." Amy Denny, asked what had happened, replied that Dorothy Durrant was the cause of it, and that, because of what she had done, "she should live to see some of her children dead, and she upon crutches."

Following the burning of the toad, William Durrant recovered, and was alive at the time of the assize, though, the indictment notes, "he languishes still"; he would die in Lowestoft thirteen months to the day after Amy Denny was found guilty of having bewitched him.

Then, on the sixth of March in 1659—just about three years before the trial—Dorothy Durrant's stepdaughter, Elizabeth, then about ten years old, suffered the same symptoms as William had shown. In her fits, Elizabeth complained that Amy Denny had appeared to her, presumably in spectral form, and afflicted her as she had her younger brother. When Dorothy Durrant returned from the apothecary, where she had gone to get some medicine for Elizabeth, she found Amy Denny in her house, and asked her what she was doing there. Amy Denny said that she had come to see the sick child and to give it some water. Dorothy Durrant responded angrily, and "thrust her forth of her doors." Outside, Amy Denny reportedly said, "You need not be so angry, for your child will not live long." That was on a Saturday; the child died the following Monday. The indictment, but not the trial report, indicates that the cause of the death was quartan ague, a form of malaria, one of the ailments, along with apoplexy, epilepsy, stone, gout, and strangury (a condition characterized by slow and painful emission of urine) on Robert Burton's 1621 list of diseases that doctors "cannot cure at all."[77] Since there is no record of Elizabeth's burial in Lowestoft, she presumably was interred in the parish where she had been baptized.

Dorothy Durrant informed the court that she believed that Elizabeth's death was caused by Amy Denny, who, she said, had long been reputed to be a witch, "and a person of very evil behavior, whose kindred and relations have been many of them accused of witchcraft, and some of them have been condemned."

Curiously, Dorothy Durrant did not mention another son, John, who was eleven months younger than William, and had died in January 1658, in the period when Amy Denny allegedly was bewitching William and the time when she was supposed to be fashioning Elizabeth's death. Perhaps there had been no contact between John Durrant and Amy Denny, a matter that seems doubtful. More likely, John had died from something that had routinely come to be interpreted solely in medical terms. Nonetheless, there was not then (and it should be appreciated that there is not today) any reasonable, scientific way of understanding why any particular child, and not someone else, caught a fatal disease. Witchcraft could always be imputed, though with less persuasiveness in some instances than others.

Dorothy Durrant, ending her testimony, told the court that shortly after the death of her daughter she had developed a lameness in both her legs from the knees downward and that she had to use crutches to walk. The judge asked whether "that at the time of the lameness, if it were with her according to the custom of women?"; that is, whether she was menstruating. She answered that it was so, and that "she never had any stoppages of those things, but when she was with child."

This was the extent of Dorothy Durrant's evidence. Defendants were not allowed to have lawyers, so there was no cross-examination. Immediately after reporting Dorothy Durrant's testimony, the marshal felt compelled to point out the astonishing outcome of her lameness:

> There was one thing very remarkable, that after she had gone upon crutches for upwards of three years, and went upon them at the time of the assizes in the court when she gave her evidence, and upon the juries bringing in their verdict, by which the said Amy Duny was found guilty, to the great admiration of all persons, the said Dorothy Durent was restored to the use of her limbs, and went home without making use of her crutches.

At the root of this matter, as indicated by the judge's query to Dorothy Durrant, was the issue of menstruation. Menstruation then was referred to in gynecological texts as "the terms," "the courses," or "the flowers," the last term because "they go before conceptions, as flowers do before fruit."[78] It was believed in seventeenth-century England that, absent pregnancy, unexpelled menstrual blood could produce physical disorders.[79] Apparently, the judge was seeking to determine if there might be a physiological explanation for Dorothy Durrant's lameness. Since she still was nursing William, she might have been experiencing post-partum amenorrhea,[80] a condition that a judge conversant with the ideas of the time might suspect to be related to a hysterical state that would render her testimony less reliable.[81] A French medical text, translated into English in 1655, explained that "when seed and menstrual blood are retained in women besides [beyond] the intent of nature, they putrefie and are corrupted, and attain a malignant and venomous quality."[82] Accumulated menstrual blood was believed to become a decaying sink of ill humors which attracted more ills and, because the blood might beat back from her womb to her brain, could produce melancholy in the unfortunate sufferer.[83]

It has been argued that the theological and social definitions of menstruation—including Leviticus (xv:20) which defined menstruating women as unclean and polluting—were promulgated by men to justify keeping women inferior,[84] but there is no trace of such usage in the brief interchange in the witchcraft trial: what is notable is the open discussion of a subject that at the time, much more than now, was regarded as highly private.

Dorothy Durrant's lameness, and its cessation at the end of the trial, offers the first and perhaps the clearest indication of hysteria among those testifying against Amy Denny and Rose Cullender. The diagnosis of hysteria most assuredly suffers from a long history of controversy, and is marked by convoluted, flailing attempts to achieve medical consensus regarding symptoms;[85] as Eliot Slater, a British psychiatrist, has noted: "the concept of hysteria fragments as we touch it"; it is, he observes, "not only a delusion but also a snare."[86] Hysteria, as another of many writers similarly indicates, has been "one of the most ill-defined concepts in psychiatry";[87] it "has taken on some of the attributes of both a fossil and a chameleon."[88]

But there is considerable agreement that if anything can be said to be hysterical in origin some forms of conversion symptoms, like lameness, fit that requirement. In their pathbreaking work on hysteria, Josef Breur and Sigmund Freud noted: "We choose to designate the term 'conversion' as the transformation of psychic excitement into chronic physical symptoms, which characterize hysteria."[89] Conversion reactions, said to constitute an unconscious simulation of illness, are believed to distract a person who is convinced of their somatic origin from conflicts, stresses or inadequacies that would otherwise be emotionally distressing.[90]

By these medical criteria, Dorothy Durrant's lameness clearly was an hysterical symptom. And her cure fits precisely with the observation of Sir Benjamin Brodie that it "still more frequently happens that recovery from hysterical symptoms immediately follows from a forcible impression of any kind made upon the nervous system."[91] Brodie believed that four-fifths of supposed joint diseases are hysterical in origin.[92]

There lies within the testimony by Dorothy Durrant an element that half a century later was highlighted in a telling critique of the proceedings at Bury St. Edmunds. In 1692, Francis Hutchinson was named the vicar of St. James's Church at Bury St. Edmunds and, in

1718, while still resident there, he published *An Historical Essay Concerning Witchcraft*, a contribution which has been judged by the historian Wallace Notestein, a preeminent pioneer in the study of English witchcraft, to have "levelled a final and deadly blow at the dying superstition."[93]

Fulminating against "one ill translated text of scripture"—the tale of the Witch of Endor—which allows a "crack'd-brain girl" to accuse people of witchcraft,[94] Hutchinson provides a conspectus of English witchcraft cases, critically reviewing in chronological order each instance about which he had information.

It is disappointing, though, that neither in the first or later (1720) edition of his work does Hutchinson offer a single detail that is not found in the published report of the 1662 trial at Bury, though he readily could have gathered first- and second-hand information from persons alive at the time of the trial or their surviving kin. Adding fuel to frustration is the fact that Hutchinson sets forth new information about a much earlier case, "having spoken with persons of credit, who attended the trial." That case involved John Lowes, the Vicar of Brandeston, Suffolk, who persistently had been hounded by his neighbors and parishioners.[95] Lowes was more than seventy years old when he was kept awake several nights in a row, made to run backward and forward about a room, rested briefly, and then run again, till "he was weary of his life and scarce sensible of what he said or did."[96] Lowes, with another man and sixteen women, was hanged in Bury St. Edmunds on August 27, 1645.

In his sixteen-page chapter on the Bury St. Edmunds' trial, presented in the form of a dialogue between a believer (an English juryman) and a skeptic (a clergyman) about the reality of witchcraft, Hutchinson first deals with the issue that had puzzled many others, how "that great and good man" Lord Chief Baron Hale could have erred. Hutchinson suggests kindly that it was not "strange for a great man to be in one error," given the "common frailty of our human nature."[97]

Dorothy Durrant, Hutchinson emphasizes, voluntarily confessed things that were more serious crimes than anything that was proved against Amy Denny and Rose Cullender. "Now I own I do not believe this witness," Hutchinson writes of Dorothy Durrant. "[S]he must be a silly loose woman or she would not have gone to the witch-doctor." Nor is her testimony "rational." Hutchinson notes that Dorothy Durrant said that she believed Amy Denny a witch, yet she had left her child to be tended by her. She made out that giving the child an empty breast is both a usual way to quiet a child and yet also an act of witchcraft. She said that the prisoner was very much scorched and burned with fire, yet no scars or signs of burning were shown, though such scars, where real, do not readily disappear. Therefore, says Hutchinson, "I believe she was a lying old woman."[98] But, even if the accusations were true, what follows?

> Why the only sure conclusion is, that she charged herself with real sorcery in all its several steps and gradations. She first departed from God by forsaking his way of prayer and natural means, and leaving the event to his providence. She employed the devil by the use of a charm, which she knew could have no effect without the devil's help. After she found a toad in the child's blanket, which could not get into it in the chimney but by the same power. As witches use[d] to root the representation of the party to be afflicted, so she burnt the toad, and if there be any truth in her words, afflicted this Rose Cullender [actually Amy Denny] the prisoner by that act of hers. And what judgment can be made of this matter? Why first, take it in the hardest sense against the prisoner, and imagine, that by some prior acts of sorcery, she had made herself subject to this power of the devil, yet both [Amy Denny and Dorothy Durrant] are guilty within the statute, and are but two witches trying to persecute one another.[99]

But this way of looking at things, Hutchinson points out, is the least fair to the accused; the true story makes a better case for them. At the time Dr. Jacob prescribed his remedy neither Denny nor Cullender had been formally accused and they therefore remained under the protection of the law; thus, they were the innocent victims of an act of witchcraft. The believer in Hutchinson's dialogue demurs at this argument, suggesting that what Dorothy Durrant had done was common practice, and that the blanket was hung not as an act of witchcraft but to uncover a suspected witch. To this the cleric responds:

> But how, and by whom, and by what did she try to make the discovery? She tried to discover by a charm and sorcery; for the blanket in the chimney was not a common act, but designed for a spell or call to a spirit; And therefore she tried to discover the witch by employing the Devil to inflict another, and by that to let her know, whether that other was a witch. And is not this a hopeful evidence and fit to be laid before a Christian court of justice? Had this wife witness

another charm to cure the Devil of his double dealings, and hold him so fast by the ears, that he should have only power to burn Rose Cullender [actually Amy Denny], but not to deceive her self by any juggling delusion? This doth not appear very evident. But as it is plain that she used a charm and sorcery, and tried to employ a spirit; it is as plain, that at least she should have been set in the pillory as part of the punishment that the Act of Parliament appoints for those evil practices.[100]

Had such a punishment of Dorothy Durrant come about, Hutchinson suggests, those who testified after her at the trial might well have been more careful.[101]

Hutchinson's interpretation did not go unchallenged. Richard Boulton, who earlier had put together a two-volume collection of "authentic" tales of witchcraft,[102] sprang to the attack. Boulton grants that the Durrants were guilty of consulting a witch doctor, but he insists that "what Cullender [Denny] did was a long continued practice, excited by the malice of the Devil; but what Durrant did was but an experiment, a single action, with no ill design, nor with a design to continue it, and to be a professor of that ill practice." Besides, the actions of the accused witches had fallen upon innocent persons, while Durrant's recourse to Dr. Jacob had only served to do justice to "an old sinner that deserved punishment."[103]

At first we came up empty-handed in our quest for further information about Dr. Jacob: like thousands of other Englishmen of his time, he apparently lived and died unremarked in any formal manner by those who convert transient mortality into permanent records. Then surprisingly—and inadvertently—our search appeared to have been successful when a handwritten description of the witch trial was donated by an elderly man to the town museum run by the Lowestoft & District Local History Society. We had earlier heard, in one of our own visits to a local bookseller, that the man had attempted to sell the material to him. At the museum, the desk attendant was expected routinely to ask all persons making a gift to leave their name and address, but on the day that the notebook was handed over there was a volunteer unfamiliar with that requirement, and the donor's identity was not obtained. Nor did strenuous efforts around town to discover the owner and how he had come by it prove successful.

Bearing the title *Trial of the Lowestoft Witches*, and with the date 1794 inscribed besides the footnotes, the material is written on hand-made paper with lines made by wire. The paper bears the watermark G.R. and shows a crown, so that it probably came from some official source. Essentially, it is a verbatim copy of the 1682 trial report plus the discussion of the event by Francis Hutchinson as well as Edmund Gillingwater's review of the court proceedings in his history of Lowestoft. There is some attention to more current spellings (Edmunds for Edmonds; Leostoft for Leystoff; and die for dye), and a goodly number of transcription errors. Only one substantive omission occurs: the question to and the response by Dorothy Durrant about menstruation had been excised.

The material in the notebook is in the handwriting of Isaac Gillingwater, and the occasional annotations are signed by him. Isaac was the brother of Edmund Gillingwater, Lowestoft's early historian, and we believe that he put together the notebook with an eye toward publication, since there are catch words at the bottom of each page, a practice designed to aid illiterate printers. Isaac was the elder of the brothers by four years, and was described by an acquaintance as a man "singular in his habits but very intelligent"—presumably meaning that his eccentricity was balanced by his brightness.[104] Isaac worked in his house on the High Street in Lowestoft as a barber and hairdresser, a particularly good situation to acquire details about local history.[105]

Isaac Gillingwater's notebook entry has this to say of Dr. Jacob:

> It is supposed that Jacob Travers is the person here alluded to, he was a tailor and then lived at Yarmouth but afterwards boarded with a widow Ayers in the south west corner house in the old Market Place at Lowestoft. He was tall, had very grey hair and much addicted to drunkeness. But had the reputation of being able to counteract the machinations of witches and on that account resorted to by the superstitious.
>
> Travers once being at a public house called "The Cock" (but now the "Jolly Sailor") sent Matthew Butcher, afterwards Master of Mr. Robert Barker's fishing boat, at time a boy, to his lodgings for a paper under strict command not to open it. Upon delivering it to Travers, Butcher received from him a severe blow as a punishment for disobeying his orders. Butcher, who at first denied the charge, after this rebuke, confessed his having looked in to the paper and that it was filled with unintellible characters.
>
> These anecdotes among sundry others I had from Alice Gowing, widow, now eighty years old who well remembers Travers and was acquainted with Butcher.[106]

The footnote proceeds to another anecdote, this one supplied by John

Sead Gowing, Alice's son and a twine-spinner, a man who spun hemp into the thin cord used to make fish nets. The footnote tells of efforts to beach a fishing boat that were frustrated by broken ropes and shattered tackle, mishaps attributed to witchcraft. Travers, who was in a nearby cooper's shop, was asked to dissolve the spell: he "cut two notches in a twig and delivered it to the messenger, desiring him to carry this talisman down to the boat." The messenger did so, and after the talisman arrived the fisherman "to the amazement of all present ha[u]led [the boat] up with the greatest of ease."[107]

As a portrayal of the work of a white witch—or, more accurately, a white wizard—this brief vignette of Jacob Travers is exemplary, but it is not likely that it is historically accurate. Jacob Travers does not appear in the Lowestoft parish registers, but Alice Gowing died in Lowestoft in 1803 at the age of ninety-three, which would put her date of birth at about 1710. Perhaps she did remember Travers from when she was a very small girl. Matthew Butcher, we know, was baptized in Lowestoft in 1703 and died there in 1774. If we assume that between the ages of eight and fourteen Butcher was a boy who could be sent on errands and smacked on the ear, then we can place both the episode involving him and Alice Gowing's memory of Travers somewhere around 1715. But it was during 1659 that Dorothy Durrant had visited Dr. Jacob in Great Yarmouth for advice. If Dr. Jacob were no more than 25 years old at the time (it seems likely he would have been considerably older), then he would be about 80 in 1715. It is all possible, but not very likely. Jacob Travers seems to have been a person suspected of having supernatural powers, and was probably the subject of tales told to Alice Gowing rather than matters remembered by her. The story supplied by John Sead Gowing, Alice's son, certainly is not a first-hand report, since Gowing was not born until 1754, and by that time Travers undoubtedly was long dead. The identity of "Dr. Jacob" remains a mystery to us. Perhaps, we sometimes think, the name was a clever alias, since the word "jacob" is an old East Anglian dialect term for a large toad.[108]

It also seems unlikely that the toad, immured in the Durrant fireplace, exploded with a "great and horrible noise": more reasonable would be a popping noise or sharp crack. There are two species of toad in East Anglia, the common toad (*Bufo bufo bufo*) and the smaller natterjack toad (*Bufo calamita*). The first comes out of hibernation about mid-March, the second at the end of February. Both species inflate themselves to twice their normal size when frightened, and the natterjack, the more likely of the two to have been in the blanket, can offer a particularly formidable appearance.[109] The late Ted Ellis, East Anglia's foremost naturalist, pointed out to us that there is a great deal of water in a toad's body "and this would account for the explosion when the poor creature was thrust into the flames." Ellis added that a toad's bones are very fragile and would quickly be reduced to ashes.[110]

It was ominous that it was a toad that tumbled from the blanket, since toads figure prominently in the annals of witchcraft.[111] They were part of the potion brewed by the witches in *Macbeth* ("Toad, that under cold stone/Days and nights has thirty-one").[112] Toads were particularly adapted for the mythology of witchcraft because witch creatures were expected to be tailless.[113] Toads also were believed by many to be able to spit poison.[114]

Toads had figured prominently in earlier witch cases both on the continent and in England. In 1599, at Bauzel, a village in northern France, Reyne Percheval, accused of witchcraft, told her judges after being tortured that she had dressed her team of toads in red, green, and yellow cloth, and had mixed their venom with water to make a concoction that could rot apples and pears.[115] In England, the details of a notorious case tried at the Chelmsford Assizes in 1579 are worth noting because they so resemble what would take place at Lowestoft more than half a century later:

> The sonne of . . . Ellen Smith, of the age of thirteene yeres, or thereaboutes, came to the house of one Jhon Estwood of Malden, for to begge an almose, who chid the boy awaie from his doore, whereuppon he wente home and tolde his mother, and within a while after the said Estwood was taken with very greate paine in his bodie, and the same night followying, as he satte by the fire with one of his neighbours, to their thinkying they did see a ratte runne by the chimeny, and presently it did fall dowune again in the likeness of a tode, and takying it up with the gonges, thei thruset it into the fire, and so helde it in forcesibly, it made the fire burne as blewe as azure . . . and at the burnying thereof the saide Ellen Smith was in greate paine . . .[116]

Toads also figured in the case of Oliffe Barthram, who had been executed at Bury St. Edmunds in 1599 for "divellish and wicked witcheries practiced upon Ioane Iorden." Barthram was said to have sent her victim three toads "to trouble her in bed."[117] A similar instance took place in King's Lynn in 1606, when a servant took a suspect toad and put it into the fire. The toad "made a groaning noise for a quarter of an hour before it was consumed." Marie Smith, who reportedly had sent the toad, during this time "did endure (as was reported), torturing paines, testifying the felt griefe by the outcryes then made."[118]

Much less explicable in commonsense terms is the testimony that Amy Denny showed signs of being burned on her face, thighs, and legs when she was visited by her niece the following day. It might be noted that the niece is reported to have said only that Amy Denny "seemed" to have been burned. There is no indication that Amy Denny denied this charge; but neither is there any report of an attempt to verify it directly from the niece or to corroborate it through the word of others or by physical examination.

The idea of the transfer of wounds to a human, who had taken the shape of an animal, also had a long history in European folklore. The most famous tale is that told by the Roman Petronius who, during the first century, wrote of a hired man running a spear through the neck of a wolf, and the protagonist in the tale coming home to find his acquaintance bleeding profusely from the neck. "Then I knew he was a werewolf."[119] Gervase of Tilbury, writing in the thirteenth century, insisted: "In England we often see men changed into wolves at the changes of the moon. If one of a wolf's limbs was cut off, the bewitched human being might be freed from enchantment, and the wound would be reproduced in the corresponding part of the human body as proof that the witch had shape-shifted."[120] In England in 1640, John Palmer would confess that after "falling out with a young man, he transformed himself into a toad, and [put himself] in the way where the young man came." The young man kicked the toad, and Palmer himself soon after began complaining of a sore shin. In revenge, for many years thereafter he bewitched the young man to his "great woe and torment."[121] A few years later, John Stearne, Matthew Hopkins' assistant, told of an old woman who displayed a wound she had received while in the likeness of a dog.[122]

The main thrust of Dorothy Durrant's testimony against Amy Denny, then, was that Denny had used her diabolic powers to kill Elizabeth Durrant. Amy Denny had been offended on two occasions and each time she had responded by angry outbursts and threats of evil (actions that formally were labeled *damnium minatum*). Each time something bad had resulted (the *malum secutum*). Presumably too, Amy Denny's statement that Elizabeth Durrant was doomed represented not a tactless diagnosis, but rather a foretelling of her plan to murder the girl. Only the wisdom of Dr. Jacob had managed to save William's life, though it had not averted the curse of lameness placed on Dorothy Durrant.

At this early point in the trial, on the basis of the testimony of but one witness, the evidence against Amy Denny (that against Rose Cullender had yet to be presented) already satisfied four of the seven "presumptions of guilt" set out by William Perkins, an eminent seventeenth-century Calvinist divine, any one of which "at least probably and conjecturally note one to be a witch."[123] The first and fourth of the items are much the same; so too are the second and third, which could make an accused seem doubly culpable for a single condition. The four items noted by Perkins that applied to Amy Denny were:

1 Notorious defamation by people among whom the suspect resided which "yieldeth a strong suspicion."
2 If after cursing, there followed death, or at least some mischief, since witches are wont to practice their mischievous acts by cursing and "banning."
3 If after enmity, quarreling, or threatening, a present mischief doth follow.
4 If the party suspected be the son or daughter, the manservant or maidservant, near neighbor or old companion of a known and convicted witch, since dying witches pass the secrets of their trade on to some of the "forenamed heirs."[124]

A reputation for witchcraft persistently was regarded as particularly powerful evidence of likely guilt. English folk culture recognized this; rural people were wont to say: "He that hath an ill name is half hanged."[125] Amy Denny, the testimony by Dorothy Durrant indicates, was related to adjudicated witches, among them probably some of the victims of the mania that swept through East Anglia in 1644–45, precipitated by Matthew Hopkins who for a fee agreed to uncover witches.

At this stage of the trial, a large portion of the evidence hinges on Amy Denny's reputation for witchcraft, her scalding tongue, and her proximity to the Durrant children before they suffered illness and, in the case of Elizabeth, death. There undoubtedly were numerous other persons who had been near the child prior to her sickness, and Elizabeth's crying out against Amy Denny can be tied to her family earlier having associated Denny with their son's indisposition.

The episode of the transmogrified toad and Amy Denny's alleged scorching may have carried weight with the jurors, at least in attaching an eerie feeling to matters concerning the accused woman. But those who wanted Amy Denny and Rose Cullender hanged had to add more fuel to the flickering flame they had created in order to overwhelm the court with so much evidence that the flimsiness of any single part would be lost in the massive totality of it all.

It is notable that the precise manner in which Amy Denny had been able to produce the evil attributed to her is nowhere specified, only inferred. Though the indictment in its required formality indicated that the acts charged were done in consort with the devil, the testimony of Dorothy Durrant and other witnesses pays no heed to any presumed compact between Amy Denny and diabolical legions. As Roger Thompson has noted of English witch trials: "Where theological ideas of devil worship did appear, they were most probably the intellectual gloss of lawyers and clerics on rustic accusations."[126] In England, unlike on the continent, witchcraft cases did not involve such wondrous and blasphemous events as sabbats reached by flight, in which the devil's fundament was licked and kissed by his devoted adherents, baptism was renounced, the mass parodied, babies cooked and eaten as part of sumptuous banquets, and all this followed by windershins dances and "wild orgies of lust."[127] The main reason for the relative tameness of witchhunting in England, Brian Levack suggests, is that the concept itself came to Britain belatedly and incompletely and that the great medieval heresies never crossed the Channel.[128]

The failure to attend to the devil's complicity in diabolic acts by the accused also spared courts what could have been a perplexing legal dilemma: how can you convict an accessory to a crime without convicting the principal?

Neither did English witch trials involve the official use of torture, though on rare occasions torture was invoked in treason and other cases by the Privy Council or the sovereign, who insisted that its employment fell within the royal prerogative.[129] Matthew Hopkins had "walked" persons suspected of witchcraft, depriving them of sleep and compelling them to pace back and forth for seemingly endless periods. But these were exceptional occurrences. On the continent, unbearable pain inflicted under the supervision of agents of the Inquisition was the routine lot of most of those who denied witchcraft accusations. Such torture almost invariably succeeded in securing confessions to any charges that the accused could invent in order to obtain surcease from the awful pain. It also elicited the names of other persons said to be involved in diabolic practices, thus feeding a continuous supply of victims to the courts, a "domino process." The process, H.C. Erik Midelfort has demonstrated, stopped only when a community came to appreciate the ghastliness of what it had done. This often happened when witchcraft accusations began to be levelled against some of the community's holiest and most exemplary citizens.[130]

The elegant analysis by John Langbein of the jurisprudential basis of torture traces its initial employment to the decree against the continued use of trials by ordeal at the Fourth Lateran Council in 1215. Such trials had been deemed infallible, since God's judgment was seen to keep the innocent, in one such kind of trial, from being burned while walking barefoot over hot coals. There now was a need for new standards of certain proof—proof "so high that no one would be concerned that God was no longer being asked to resolve the doubts."[131]

In continental witchcraft cases such proof could come only from the victim. In England, on the other hand, a jury system rather than the Roman canon law of proof had replaced ordeals. The jury, England's substitute for God, could convict on circumstantial evidence: it did not require absolute certainty. "[B]ecause criminals could now be punished on evidence short of full proof, confession was no longer essential."[132] The English legal scholars, Frederick Pollock and Frederic Maitland have observed, were not possessed of "any unusual degree of humanity or enlightenment." Rather, they benefited from legal institutions so crude that torture was not necessary.[133] Torture would come to an end on the continent only when judges were deemed able to evaluate the evidence presented to them and to reach an independent decision. Convicted continental witches were burned to death at the stake, a fate confined in England to heretics and those found guilty of high treason (murdering or plotting to murder the sovereign) and petty treason (murder of a husband by his wife or the murder of a master or mistress by a servant).

Thus, the manner in which witchcraft was dealt with in England differed in significant ways from the approach on the continent; the "fantastic complications of continental demonology and inquisitorial practice" were never adopted in England.[134] It might even be said that in contradistinction to the demonology of Germany and France, "English witchcraft was a flat, dull, vulgar, unimaginative affair."[135] In this regard the approach to witchcraft in England often is referred to as "unique,"[136] a term that has been forcefully rejected by Christina Larner.[137] Larner grants that English procedures, unlike those of much of Europe, "were simple, related to local experience and not very closely integrated with official Christianity,"[138] but she insists that English trials were not "unique" but only somewhat "different." Amy Denny and Rose Cullender presumably would agree with this position. Though they were spared physical torture, there can be no doubting the mental torture they must have suffered as the court processes surely dragged them to their ultimate fate. Whatever distinctions existed between the trials of witches in England and those on the continent in the end would be matters of no particular importance to them.

3

The swouning sisters

Eleven-year-old Elizabeth Pacy and her nine-year-old sister, Deborah, were the key witnesses in the case against Amy Denny and Rose Cullender. Matters concerning them—their fits, contortions, agonies, and antics—occupy more than a third of the trial report—twenty of the fifty-nine pages. This is more than twice the amount of space accorded to any other witnesses. The tale of Samuel Pacy's daughters, as it unfolded, seemed to doom Amy Denny and Rose Cullender, but, as we will see subsequently, a sense of skepticism arose among some persons at the trial. That element of doubt would fuel a dramatic showdown that largely determined the fate of the accused women.

Neither of the Pacy sisters entered a word into the court proceedings. Deborah was too ill to attend the assize and Elizabeth remained mute throughout the trial, unable even to take part in the drawing up of the indictments. Nonetheless, consciously or unconsciously, she performed in ways that must have been horribly absorbing, and probably terrifying to many of those who watched her. The trial report offers a graphic description of Elizabeth's behavior in the courtroom at Bury St. Edmunds:

> as to the elder, she was brought into the court at the time of the instructions given to draw up the indictments, and afterwards at the time of tryal of the said prisoners, but could not speak one word all the time, and for the most part she remained as one wholly senseless[,] as one in a deep sleep, and could move no part of her body, and all the motion of life that appeared in her was, that as she lay upon cushions in the court upon her back, her stomack and belly by the drawing of her breath, would arise to a great height: and after the said Elizabeth had lain a long time on the table in the court, she came a little to her self and sate up, but could neither see nor

speak, but was sensible of what was said to her, and after a while she laid her head on the bar of the court with a cushion under it, and her hand and her apron upon that, and there she lay a good space of time.[1]

However persuasive Elizabeth's awful state might have been of witchcraft at work, Amy Denny and Rose Cullender had to be tied directly to her condition. After all, anybody—or nobody—could have been responsible for what had happened and obviously still was happening to Elizabeth Pacy. The judge sought to fill this evidentiary gap by staging a courtroom drama, a not uncommon procedure in witchcraft trials of the time.[2] He arranged a confrontation between Elizabeth Pacy and one of the accused women:

> by the direction of the judg, Amy Duny was privately brought to Elizabeth Pacy, and she touched her hand; whereupon the child without so much as seeing her, for her eyes were closed all the while, suddenly leaped up, and catched Amy Duny by the hand, and afterwards by the face; and with her nails scratched her till blood came, and would by no means leave her till she was taken from her, and afterwards the child would still be pressing towards her, and making signs of anger conceived against her.

To draw a witch's blood in order to annul the power of her spell—called "scoring about the breath"—was an idea of ancient origin, routinely remarked upon in writings on witchcraft,[3] though it had its disbelievers, primarily because for purists it represented yet another form of illicit countermagic—"a foule sinne among Christians to thinke one witch-craft can drive out another."[4] William Perkins had rejected scratching and similar tactics, such as setting fire to the thatch of an alleged witch's house, describing them as "after a sort practices of witchcraft, having in them no power or vertue to detect a sorcerer, either by God's ordinance in the creation, or by an special appointment since."[5] In 1616, we are told, Edward Newton of King's Lynn found that "his nailes turned like feathers, having no strength" when he resorted to countermagic and tried to scratch Marie Smith, whom he insisted had bewitched him.[6] Such considerations notwithstanding, the drama of a wildly suffering eleven-year-old girl pressing forward angrily to get at her tormentor in order to find relief must have been a sight that deeply etched itself into the minds of those watching it.

Deborah, the other accuser, it may be remembered, had not made the journey to Bury St. Edmunds. She was "in such extream manner," the report observes, "that her parents wholly despaired of her life, and therefore could not bring her to the assizes."

That neither Elizabeth nor Deborah would personally testify made moot the question of whether they were legally competent to offer evidence acceptable in court. Common law disqualified witnesses for reasons such as infancy, mental derangement, and marital relationship. Fourteen, being the age of discretion, was the legal cutoff point at which children routinely were permitted to testify; but age was not an absolute disqualification. Sir Matthew Hale in his *Pleas of the Crown* had pointed out that persons of "tender years" might be examined without taking an oath, a procedure presumably used to convey to the jury the lesser evidentiary value their words carried.[7] A judge's decision rested on whether the youngster appeared to be intelligent. The kind of case being tried also figured into the conclusion, Hale observed, writing: "[T]he nature of the fact may allow an examination of one under that age [14], as in a case of witchcraft an infant of nine years old has been allowed a witness against his own mother."[8]

The age requirement often was waived in witchcraft cases because of the difficulty of otherwise sustaining the accusations. In Sweden, although testimony of minors under the age of fifteen was not acceptable, judges got around the restriction by adding the ages of several minors together to make one witness.[9] In England, as Wallace Notestein notes, the testimony of children from six to nine was "eagerly received,"[10] and Thomas Potts reports in detail on the case which Hale had in mind, that of the Pendle Forest witches at the Lancaster Assizes in 1612, where nine-year-old Jannet Device testified about events that had taken place three years earlier.[11] The mother, son, and Alison Device, Jannet's eleven-year-old sister, all were convicted and hanged.[12]

Because of inability of his daughters to tell their own stories, Samuel Pacy was called as the witness after Dorothy Durrant. He is described as a "merchant," and praised as "a man who carried himself with much soberness during the tryal" and one "from whom no words either of passion or malice" were heard, "though his children were greatly afflicted." Pacy is the only witness who is called "Mr.": the other men and women who testified are referred to either by their full name—such as Dorothy Durrant—or only by their first name such as " . . . and after the return of said Dorothy, the said Amy did acquaint her . . . "

The Pacy family had been residents of Lowestoft for almost a century by the time of the witch trial. The Pacy line probably originated in the French town of that name, a site where in 1691 the last execution for sorcery ordered by the Parlement of Paris took place.[13] Samuel's immediate English ancestors probably came from the rural parishes near the Suffolk town of Wrentham, eight miles south of Lowestoft. His grandfather, Mark, a sailor, is the first of the family to appear in Lowestoft records; he, his wife, and their three children were living there at least by 1571. The wife died shortly after that, and within six months Mark Pacy married Elizabeth Whight, the daughter of a Lowestoft merchant.[14] Soon after, he became a fish merchant and in 1586 he purchased two pieces of "waste land" at the foot of the cliffs below the High Street. A little later he acquired a salt house to dry herring.[15] When Mark Pacy died in 1596, probably suddenly (his will was nuncupative), he left all his property to his widow.[16] In the two dozen years before her own death, Elizabeth Pacy added considerably to the family fortune. Her will mentions a maid, a very large house and grounds on the east side of High Street, a small cottage in the south of the town, a number of fish houses, and two fishing boats, "The Johne" and "The Marke," together with their nets and tackle.[17]

Nicholas, the eldest son of Mark and Elizabeth Pacy, was born in Lowestoft in July 1581, and took over the family business from his parents. He married Margaret Eache, the daughter of a Lowestoft cordwainer, in 1609.[18] In his will, Nicholas would refer to himself as a "mariner," and the history of Lowestoft mentions him as "Capt. Pacey."[19] He probably had sailed with the merchant fleet until he settled down to manage the family interests.

Nicholas and Margaret had four daughters and four sons. Samuel was the youngest of the eight and clearly the favorite. He was born in 1624 in Lowestoft and baptized there on January 8,[20] making him thirty-eight years old at the time of the witch trial. He had married Elizabeth Bardwell, the daughter of William Bardwell, probably in 1647. Her father owned copyhold property in the parishes of Topcroft and Denton in Norfolk that he later bequeathed to her.[21] It is possible that Elizabeth grew up in the Topcroft and Denton area, but there is no record of her in the local parish registers. When he married, Samuel received most of his parents' property;[22] they obviously had elected to place their hopes on their youngest child. In his will, Samuel's father would name his wife as the sole executrix, but would add that "my sonne Samuell shall bee assisting unto my executrix in and about the execution of this my said last will and testament."[23] This was despite the fact that several older brothers and sisters were still alive.

In time, Samuel became one of the wealthiest and most influential men in Lowestoft. He styles himself as a "merchant" in his own will, but he was one with a wide range of business interests. He owned two fishing boats and by the 1670s was curing more herring than any other person in the town; in the fall of 1663 alone he handled 72 lasts of fish, the equivalent of 720 barrels or more than three-quarters of a million fish.[24]

Pacy also owned a merchant vessel, the "Red Lyon," held quarter shares in two other ships, the "Black Lyon" and the "Baltic Merchant," and smaller shares in the merchantmen, the "Riga Merchant" and the "Neptune." Colliers such as the "Black Lyon" were infamous for smuggling, often carrying goods that would demand high customs fees into England from Holland and Flanders under their coal cargo.[25] There is no evidence that Pacy dabbled in smuggling, but early in 1663 an informer accused James Wilde and Pacy of dealing in cordage stolen from the Navy dockyard at Chatham.[26] The charge grew out of an investigation by William Blackbourne, an admiralty field agent, who was told that the rope had been taken by ship to Lowestoft, where it had been purchased by James Wilde and Pacy. The accused men dispatched a letter to the Admiralty denying having "any pt nor parcell of said ropes."[27] Blackbourne's later report to navy officials in April 1663 noted that Wilde willingly had given him leave to search his storehouse and that he had not found the cordage there. Wilde was reported to have said that he had planned to purchase the rope but could not agree with the vendor on a price. There the matter appears to have ended, though Blackbourne apparently subsequently recovered some of the cordage.[28]

Samuel Pacy's other business interests included property speculation; he also apparently loaned money at interest.[29] His principal residence, part of which still stands, contained eight hearths, making it one of the largest houses in Lowestoft,[30] and he owned additional land, cottages, storehouses, and fish-houses that he had inherited from his parents. In 1672, he would purchase a large barn and a piece of land, and the following year add a small freehold meadow called "Pond Pightle," situated at the edge of the town. In 1674, the Pacys acquired a second house at the north end of High Street[31] and five years later a stable and a piece of land, "which piece is used to throw excrement or in English muck."[32] He also owned a six-acre enclosure known as "Pacy's Great Meadow."[33] In addition, there was the fifty-five acres of land in Denton in Norfolk that the Pacys had inherited from Elizabeth's father.[34]

By the time he died in 1680, Pacy would be in a position to leave £2,387 in cash bequests alone. As he provided no instructions in his will for the disposing of any property or estate to pay these bequests, it is reasonable to assume that he had the money on hand.[35] His wife's will, probated two years later, shows goods and chattels worth £2,849.4s.9d. (2,849 pounds, 4 shillings, and 9 pence).

Working from the Lowestoft probate records, David Butcher has calculated that Samuel Pacy was the richest merchant in Lowestoft. The only person in the town with more money than Pacy during this period was Riches Utber, a retired admiral.[36]

Pacy served Lowestoft in a number of official capacities. In 1647, he was appointed a trustee of the Lowestoft Townlands, together with twenty-three other men who were to be, according to the original feoffment, " . . . four and twenty of the best and most sufficient inhabitants of the town." He was still a trustee when he died thirty-three years later.[37] He was many times a juryman, or "Chief Pledge" at the Manor Court, twice served as Churchwarden,[38] and in 1663 was an Overseer of the Poor.[39]

Several documents, mostly wills, that Pacy drew up for his neighbors in his very small, neat, and fussy handwriting survive, as do a number of petitions from the town to the government that he signed. Pacy clearly was a religious man, and his leanings were toward the nonconformist sect that had coalesced into the Congregational movement. In 1665, three years following the witch trial, Pacy and several others had to appear before the justice of the peace at the Quarter Sessions, charged with holding illegal conventicles in his Lowestoft home.[40] The Conventicle Act of 1664 had decreed that any person aged sixteen or over who attended an unorthodox religious gathering of more than five persons was to be fined up to £5 for the first offense and £10 for the second. A third offense incurred payment of £100 and transportation overseas for seven years. Those unable to pay the fine faced imprisonment.[41] Pacy was bound over to appear at the summer assize at Bury St. Edmunds, but the assize records contain no reference to the case having been heard.

Samuel Pacy told the court in the witchcraft trial at Bury St. Edmunds that his youngest daughter, Deborah, by his own admission a sickly child, had, on the previous October 10, suddenly been taken with a lameness in her legs, so that she could not stand, and she had no strength to support herself. She continued this way until a week later. The "day being fair and sunshiny, the child desired to be carried on the east part of the house, to be set upon the bank which looketh upon the sea." While Deborah was sitting there, Amy Denny came to the house to buy some herring. This is what was said to have happened:

being denied she went away discontented, and presently returned again, and was denied, and likewise the third time and was denied as at first; and at last going away, she went away grumbling; but what she said was not perfectly understood.

What is very different between this brief episode and the corpus of witchcraft cases in Essex reviewed by Alan Macfarlane[42] is that Amy Denny sought to purchase the herring, that she was not begging. This departure from the pattern overwhelmingly reported in other English witchcraft episodes, if indeed it was so, places this trial in a starker light. For the convenience of local residents, Lowestoft merchants involved in large-scale fishing expeditions traditionally sold small amounts of their catch from their home.[43] Amy Denny's persistence in seeking to purchase herring suggests that she thought that she had a right to do so. Pacy's denial may have been related to his belief that Amy Denny was a witch; if so, he should have appreciated that it was reckless of him to risk her anger. Perhaps, though, since the incident occurred when the blockade against Lowestoft by Great Yarmouth severely restricted the herring haul, Pacy may have been conserving what herring he had gotten ashore for a more profitable outlet, leading him to abandon the fish-merchant's traditional role of providing cheap and much needed nourishment to the town's poorer people.

Selectively scrupulous in not claiming more for his case than he could square with his conscience, Pacy had informed the court that what Amy Denny had grumbled about in her discontent upon being refused the herring "was not perfectly understood." The implication, nonetheless, was that the grumbling was understood well enough to appreciate its drift. There certainly for Pacy was no questioning the consequences of Amy Denny's irritation, for "at the very same instant of time the said child was taken with most violent fits, feeling most extream pain in her stomach, like the pricking of pins, and shreeking out in a most dreadful manner like unto a whelp, and not like unto a sensible creature."

Deborah continued in this state for thirteen days. During that time, the family sought the help of "Dr. Feavor, a Doctor of Physick," regarding the child's distemper. The doctor witnessed Deborah's fits, but, the trial report observes, he "could not conjecture (as he then told this deponent, and afterwards affirmed in open court, at this tryal) what might be the cause of the childs affliction," leaving the impression, of course, that it might have a diabolical root.

As far as we have been able to discover, no person named "Dr. Feavor" existed in the Lowestoft area. The name is probably a corruption of the old French surname LeFebre. Almost a century before the trial, a Fever is found twice in the Lowestoft parish registers. In September 1567, James Fever's marriage to Margaret Browne is recorded, and then the baptism of a daughter, Elizabeth, the following April.[44] After that, the name disappears from local records. That a descendant of James Fever was a doctor and resident in Lowestoft, but went unrecorded, is very unlikely.

There were two doctors known to be living in the area in 1662. James Reeve, described on his tombstone as "A physician of this town and most skilful in his profession," resided in the adjoining parish of Carlton Colville, and had strong family ties with Lowestoft.[45] The second man was Robert Peake (often spelled Pake), who is recorded in the parish registers in the 1640s as a "chirurgian" (surgeon) and in his burial entry in 1680 as a "doctor."[46] Although Peake had an estate in the nearby parish of Worlingham he apparently lived in Lowestoft. He was a contemporary of Samuel Pacy, and his son Joseph, the youngest of six children, would marry Deborah Pacy. Logic would dictate that Peake would be the doctor consulted by Pacy. But it may be that Sir Matthew Hale's marshal, who did not attend diligently to names and dates in reporting the trial, succumbed to a moment of whimsy, and invented for the Pacy doctor a name that would serve well in a Restoration comedy.

There is another possibility, perhaps far fetched, but not altogether unlikely. We documented in the previous chapter the close relationship between Sir John Pettus and Sir Thomas Browne, and Pettus' close affiliation with Lowestoft's leaders. Could Browne possibly have been the physician who diagnosed the Pacy daughters as bewitched? It is noted in the trial report that Dr. Feavor testified in court, but no details are provided regarding what very likely was highly significant diagnostic evidence. All other witnesses about whom we are aware from the indictment get at least a summary and more often an extended statement of their contribution to the proceedings.

Browne himself, later in the trial, would provide a brief medical assessment of those claiming to be bewitched. The trial reporter, as we will see on occasion, was not above playing loose with information in order to make a point he wanted to convey to his readers. He might have found it easier to camouflage Browne as the "Dr. Feavor" who saw the stricken girls rather than to detract from Browne's more formidable position as an impartial expert witness who brought medical wisdom to bear on the phenomenon of witchcraft.

That the Pacys had consulted a doctor testifies to their relatively high social standing; only at the highest levels of society, and then often only for serious ailment, were physicians called in.[47] Medical men were scarce and for the average person too expensive. At the time, England had about one physician for every 8,000 persons,[48] and there were many complaints about the cost of medical services. One disenchanted contemporary wit, for instance, noted that "meer dull physicians" always pronounced "a disease incurable but by an abundant phlebotomy of the purse."[49]

Reinforced by the judgment of "Dr. Feavor," Pacy told the court that he was convinced that the condition of his daughter could be blamed on Amy Denny. He testified that she was "a woman of an ill fame, & commonly reported to be a witch & sorcerer," and that Deborah would cry out that Amy Denny was the cause of her malady, and that she did "affright her with apparitions of her person (as the child in the intervals of her fits related)."

Pacy's first step to deal with this situation had been taken on the previous October 28, very shortly after he had consulted Dr. Feavor. He had Amy Denny put in the stocks, presumably on the basis of the now-defunct Elizabethan statute that decreed such punishment for a first offense of non-lethal witchcraft. A sentence to the stocks normally would have had to be imposed by the court leet. Such courts had been established, Sir Edward Coke notes, "for the ease of the people, so that they should have justice done unto them at their own doors without any charge or loss of time."[50] The court leet had the authority to sentence persons to the stocks, to whip offenders, to put them on a cuckstool, and to amerce adjudged violators, that is to impose a fine not fixed by statute.[51]

In 1661, the Lowestoft court leet met on March 9. But Amy Denny was not put into the stocks until October. Since the stocks came under the jurisdiction of the Manor of Lowestoft, presumably some official blessing had been granted for this act. In 1661, Lady Mary Heveningham, Lady of the Manor, did not reside locally, and it is unlikely that she ever presided personally over the leet court; her local steward-of-courts probably handled its business.[52] Presumably Samuel Pacy persuaded the steward to place Amy Denny in the stocks. The Manor Court Book for 1661 is no longer extant, so it is not possible to determine if the penalty was an official act. The records of the local quarter sessions court, which was held before a panel of justices of the peace at the nearby town of Beccles, show that Denny was never brought before it. Pacy's action in having Denny put in the stocks was technically illegal, for there was no such statutory provision.

The stocks consisted of two heavy timbers, the upper one of which could be raised. Two half circle notches were cut in each of the timbers, which formed round holes when they met. The legs of offenders were held tightly in place in notches either by chaining the timbers or by placing weights or "legstones" on them.[53] Sometimes there also were holes for the hands and even the neck,[54] though offenders usually sat on a low bench with only their legs confined.[55] The agony of the experience could be heightened by forcing the ankles far apart or raising the stocks so that the trapped person's feet were far above his or her head.[56] A leading Puritan divine, Richard Baxter, lamented that a stint in the stocks often became for offenders a moment of glory rather than of shame, because "their companions get about them and feast them openly, and feed them there with wine and ale, so that they are never so jovial as in the stocks and justice made an open scorn."[57]

Amy Denny's experience, however, was to be different from the high hilarity deplored by Baxter. While in the stocks, located on Goose Green on the western edge of Lowestoft, she was confronted by two women—Jane Buxton and Alice Kittredge. Jane Buxton was the twenty-seven-year-old daughter of a Lowestoft merchant, Thomas Fullwood. Like his father before him, Thomas was a scrivener, someone who could read and write, and could draw up simple legal documents, and a person of some importance in any seventeenth-century community. Jane Buxton, then twenty-two, had been married in 1656 to John Buxton at nearby Somerleyton.[58] Her second child was born not long before her encounter with Denny.

The second woman is incorrectly called Alice Letteridge in the trial report, though the manuscript version of the trial spells her surname correctly. Little is now known of her; she probably was in her mid-thirties, but as her marriage does not appear in the Lowestoft parish records, we have been unable to ascertain either her date of birth or her maiden name. She married Thomas Kittredge, a local seaman, around 1650—and bore him four children before his death in 1668. In 1662, Thomas, the youngest, was just over one year old. Jane Buxton and Alice Kittredge, both with young babies, were probably friends out for a stroll and might deliberately have made their way to the stocks to have a good look at the pinioned miscreant.

The two women demanded of Amy Denny (they would testify in court) that she tell them why Deborah Pacy was so sick, and they said that she herself was believed to be the cause of Deborah's trouble. To these comments, Amy Denny is said to have retorted: "Mr. Pacy keeps

a great stir about his child, but let him stay until he hath done as much
by his children, as I have done by mine."

When asked exactly what she meant by these words, what it was
that she had done with her own children, Amy Denny replied: "That
she had been fain to open her child's mouth with a tap [a hollow
tube, usually made of wood, used for drawing liquids] to give it victuals."

Within two days after Amy Denny had said these words from the
stocks—on the last day of October—the bewitchment spread in the
Pacy household. According to the trial report, this is what happened:

> the eldest daughter Elizabeth fell into extream fits, insomuch,
> that they could not open her mouth to give her breath, to
> preserve her life without the help of a tap which they were
> enforced to use; and the younger child was in the like manner
> afflicted, so that they used the same also for her relief.

Francis Hutchinson would shrewdly point out in 1718 that by
employing a tap rather than another appropriate instrument the Pacys
had produced a self-fulfilling prophecy:

> who put those taps into their mouths? Did any invisible
> agents in a supernaturel way? Did Amy Duny's imp stick them
> in, when nobody else touched them? No, the people them-
> selves put them in. . . . Why did they do it by "taps," rather
> than by anything else? Why not a quill or a pipe or anything
> else that would have given breath in a fit? . . . Had the Devil
> laid all things out of the way save taps? If not, what made
> them voluntarily choose to lay the children in such a ridicu-
> lous posture, with taps sticking out of their mouths. . . . It
> seems very plain to me, that as before they had perverted the
> poor woman's words, they did this to make an appearance of
> fulfilling them.[59]

Samuel Pacy also told the court that, in addition to their problem
with breathing, both his children, thus "grieviously afflicted," would
complain that Amy Denny and a woman they did not know, but whose
person and clothes they described, were afflicting them, and that they
saw the apparitions of these women before them, "to their great terror
and affrightment." Sometimes the children would cry out, saying,
"There stands Amy Denny, and there Rose Cullender," who, the trial

report notes, was "the other person troubling them." This is the first evidence offered against Cullender.

The evidence that apparitions plagued Pacy's daughters and that these apparitions were in the form of Amy Denny and Rose Cullender represented the most arguable kind of prosecution offering. Such "spectral evidence" was impossible to rebut, except by categorically declaring that the person testifying was lying or deluded. An explanation that the accused had been elsewhere during the moment of affrightment offered no hope since it was presumed that the devil readily was able to accomplish such duplicity. More satisfactory might be a defense that relied upon the theological premise that the devil often assumed the form of innocent persons in order to mock them and to inject confusion and consternation into the ranks of the godly.[60] George Gifford, writing in 1587, had offered a form of this kind of explanation: The devil, he argued, knows when people are going to die or fall ill from natural causes, and for his own glory he stirs up some quarrel so that the sufferer may think he has been bewitched.[61]

To mount such defenses, however, took a good deal more knowledge and self-assurance than either Amy Denny or Rose Cullender was likely to have possessed. At Salem, where spectral evidence constituted the core of the proceedings, various accused persons tried ineffectually to deal with it. "Does she hurt you?" one of the young Salem accusers was asked about the alleged witch. "Yes, she came in her shift and choked me," was the girl's reply. Then the alleged witch was asked: "What do you say, Goody Proctor, to these things?"—and Goody Proctor could but respond lamely: "I take God in heaven to be my witness, that I know nothing of it, no more than the child unborn."[62] Susanna Martin, more strong-willed, did better, but to no greater avail: "How comes your appearance just now to hurt these?" she was asked, and replied: "How do I know?" When it was then demanded that she tell the truth, she answered, "He that appeared in Samuel's shape can appear in any one's shape."[63] Her response was regarded merely as impertinent.

The reported apparitions, with their imagery of supernatural marvels, must have been awesome evidence against the accused. That such information was accepted at the Bury St. Edmunds trial accorded with precedent: Michael Dalton's authoritative *The Country Justice*, published first in 1616 and reprinted numerous times thereafter, decreed that "the afflicted parties thinking they see the person who torments them . . . may be given in evidence."[64]

In his testimony, Pacy piled on additional accusations, relating things that had happened to his daughters because of what he believed was their bewitchment by Amy Denny and Rose Cullender:

> Their fits were various, sometimes they would be lame in one side of their bodies, sometimes on the other: sometimes a soreness over their whole bodies, so as they could endure none to touch them: at other times they would be restored to the perfect use of their limbs, and deprived of their hearing; at other times of their sight, at other times of their speech; sometimes by the space of one day, sometimes for two; and once they were wholly deprived of their speech for eight days together, and then restored to their speech again. At other times they would fall in swounings, and upon the recovery to their speech they would cough extreamly, and bring up much flegme, and with the same crooked pins, and one time a two-penny nail with a very broad head, which pins (amounting to forty or more) together with the two-penny nail were produced in court.

Samuel Pacy testified that he was present when the nail and most of the pins were vomited. He said that commonly his daughters would vomit up a pin at the end of every fit, and sometimes they would have four or five fits in a day.

Both Elizabeth and Deborah, Pacy reported, continued in this condition for two months. Strongly suspecting witchcraft, Pacy had them read chapters of the New Testament. They would do well until they came to the name of the Lord, or Jesus, or Christ; and then, before they could pronounce these words, they would fall into fits. But when they came to the name of Satan, or that of the devil, they would "clap their fingers upon the book, crying out, This bites, but makes me speak right well."

The girls could be brought out of their fits by others reciting the name of the Lord, or Jesus, or Christ. Pacy asked his daughters why they could not themselves speak Jesus' name, and they told him that Amy Denny had said that they must not say it. They also reported that Amy Denny and Rose Cullender appeared before them, shaking their fists, and threatening that if they related what they saw or heard, they would be tormented ten times more than ever they had been before. While in their fits, Pacy testified, the girls would indicate sometimes one place in the room where the alleged witches were, sometimes another, and then they would run "with great violence" to the spot where they fancied them to stand and strike at them as if they were present. The witches, the girls reported, sometimes appeared before them spinning, sometimes reeling or in other postures, and they derided and threatened them.

Baffled—"finding no hopes of amendment"—Samuel Pacy chose a strategy that two centuries later would form the background for a major essay by one of England's foremost writers and critics. Pacy's tactic was to dispatch his ailing children to his sister, Margaret Arnold, who lived in Yarmouth, to determine "whether the change of air might do them any good." Pacy sent his daughters away just four days before the House of Lords was to hear the fishing rights case involving Lowestoft and Great Yarmouth.

Margaret Arnold was the sixth of the eight children of Nicholas and Margaret Pacy, and, at 42, was almost four years older than her brother Samuel. She had married Matthew Arnold on May 23, 1640 at Somerleyton, a small village six miles northwest of Lowestoft, by special license, required because neither was a resident of the parish in which they were wed.[65] Lowestoft records indicate the birth of a daughter to the couple in 1641, and we have found notations in the register of the nonconformist Congregational (or, as it usually was called, the Independent) church in Great Yarmouth of a child born to the couple in May 1653 and another in January 1656.[66]

Margaret Pacy Arnold's brother-in-law, William, was the great-great-great-grandfather of Dr. Thomas Arnold, clergyman, historian, and the famed headmaster of Rugby. Dr. Arnold's even more illustrious son, Matthew, would spend a "lifetime of inspired drudgery"[67] as an inspector of public schools, and nonetheless find time to produce a large body of poetry, literary criticism, and religious essays, in the process becoming, as one of many critics similarly notes, "indubitably the central man of letters of his age."[68]

Matthew Arnold would use the Bury St. Edmunds witchcraft trial (though never indicating the involvement of his ancestors in the case) in an essay, "A Psychological Parallel" (1876),[69] that was part of his campaign to render Christianity palatable to Englishmen by retaining its ethical core but stripping away its excesses.[70] Arnold portrays as synonymous the belief of St. Paul in the physical resurrection of Jesus and that of Sir Matthew Hale in witchcraft. With witchcraft, as with the resurrection story, Arnold observes that evidence which no longer would be accepted by a reasonable person was, in the seventeenth century, "quite compatible with trustfulness of disposition, vigor of intelligence, and penetrating judgment on other matters."

As the trial that would be interpreted by her renowned descendant continued, Margaret Arnold testified that the Pacy children had come to her house on the 30th of November, and that her brother, after telling her what they had said and done, declared that they were bewitched. Margaret Arnold told the court that she "gave no credit to that which was related to her, conceiving possibly that the children might use some deceit in putting pins in their mouths themselves." She sewed the children's clothes, removing all pins. But, "notwithstanding all this care and circumspection of hers," the children vomited up at least thirty pins in her presence, and had "most fierce and violent fitts." They cried out against Amy Denny and Rose Cullender, affirming that they saw them, and repeated that they had been threatened with torment ten times greater than what they were suffering if they complained (a threat that they obviously did not take much to heart). Sometimes, Margaret Arnold told the court, "the children would see things run up and down the house in the appearance of mice; and one of them suddainly snapt one with the tongs, and threw it into the fire, and it screeched out like a rat."

On another occasion, Deborah, being relieved of her fits for the moment, ventured outside the house to get some fresh air, "and presently a little thing like a bee flew upon her face, and would have gone into her mouth, whereupon the child ran in all haste to the door to get into the house again, screeking out in a most terrible manner." Margaret Arnold sought to help, but before she could get to Deborah the child had fainted, "and at last with much pain straining herself, she vomited up a two-penny nail with a broad head." After this, Deborah "came to her understanding," and when she was asked about the nail, she told her aunt that "the bee brought this nail and forced it into her mouth." Elizabeth, the older child, not to be outdone, said that flies had come to her bearing crooked nails in their mouths; afterwards, she fell into a violent fit and raised several pins. At another time, Elizabeth claimed to have captured a mouse (she had been under a table at the time, so Margaret Arnold was unable to see what was happening). She acted as if she held the mouse in her apron, and ran to the fire and threw the creature into it, whereupon Margaret Arnold witnessed something that appeared like the flashing of gunpowder, though she had seen nothing in the child's hand.

At another time, though said to be speechless, "but otherwise of perfect understanding," Elizabeth had run about holding her apron and crying, "Hush, hush" (apparently she was able to say this much), as if there were a small animal in the house, though again Margaret Arnold could perceive nothing. Elizabeth scooped something into her apron, then made a gesture as if she had thrown it into the fire.

Margaret Arnold asked Elizabeth what was going on. Elizabeth's answer was that "she saw a duck."

Margaret Arnold, testifying with the help of notes that she had taken, told the court that Deborah Pacy, recovering momentarily from her fits, had declared that she had seen the apparition of Amy Denny, who tempted her to drown herself, to cut her throat, or otherwise to destroy herself. The girls also cried out to the figures they claimed to see: "Why do not you come yourselves, but send your imps to torment us?"

Her nieces' actions overcame Margaret Arnold's initial skepticism. The trial report summarizes her testimony: "for the reasons aforesaid, she doth verily believe in her conscience, that the children were bewitched, and by the said Amy Duny, and Rose Cullender; though at first she could hardly be induced to believe it."

Edmund Durrant, who would testify about the condition of his daughter, Ann, followed Margaret Arnold as a witness. Despite extensive research, he remains an obscure character for us. Although some distant kinship cannot be ruled out, he does not seem to have been a relation of Dorothy Durrant, who had testified earlier. Then forty-eight years old, Edmund Durrant was the eldest son of Peter Durrant, a husbandman and ale house keeper, by his second wife, Margaret (née Parker). His younger brother Peter had occupied the house next door to the Pacys from 1654 onward.

Apart from his baptism, there is no other record of Edmund Durrant to be found in Lowestoft. We learn from the trial report that he was married, but his wife's name is not known, nor is the date of their marriage. There is no record of the baptism of a child of his in Lowestoft, and the Manor Court records do not show him to have been a house owner, unless he had one of the few freehold properties, the details of which are not recorded in the court books. Neither was he a rate payer. Despite this absence of local supporting evidence, Edmund Durrant is said in the indictment and the trial report to be a resident of Lowestoft. It is possible that he lived in the adjoining parish of Oulton for the records show that an Ann Durrant (his daughter?) married Peter Paine there in August 1676. However, another Ann Durrant married Riches Canham, a seaman, at Lowestoft on Christmas Day in 1672; this could equally well have been Edmund's daughter.

Samuel Pacy's two daughters frequently are referred to in the trial report as "children"; Ann Durrant, however, is called a "maid," a contraction of maiden, a young, unmarried woman and, presumptively, a virgin. The term usually was applied only to a young woman who had reached puberty but had not yet married. Peter Laslett indicates that at the end of the sixteenth century the average age at menarche was not much lower than sixteen;[71] therefore it is fairly safe to assume that Ann Durrant was at least sixteen in 1662 and probably not older than 21. This could explain why her baptism is not recorded in Lowestoft; her birth would have occurred during the Civil War when parish registers were neglected.

Edmund Durrant bore witness to the tribulations of his daughter because she, though present, was unable to "speak to declare her knowledge, but fell into most violent fits when she was brought before Rose Cullender." Durrant's story was in most details a replica of Samuel Pacy's. He told the court that toward the end of the previous November Rose Cullender had come to his house to buy herrings from his wife. When she was refused, she "returned [presumably to her own dwelling] in a discontented manner." Then, on the first of December, Ann Durrant was "sorely afflicted in her stomach, and felt great pain, like the pricking of pins." She fell into faints and, when recovered, said that she had seen the apparition of Rose Cullender, who had threatened to torment her. She remained in this condition to the very moment and, like the Pacy girls, had been throwing up pins, which were displayed in court.

Next came Ann Baldwin, whose allegations appear in the portion of the indictment presented in the previous chapter. She is an enigmatic figure in terms of local records. She was the daughter of John and Barbara Baldinge (here again the casualness of seventeenth-century spelling: the surname is variously spelled Balden, Bolden, Balding, Baldinge, and Baldwin), and was baptized at Lowestoft on December 1, 1644; therefore she was seventeen years old at the time of the witchcraft trial. Ann's father, John, had died at Lowestoft in 1654.[72]

Apparently seeking to avoid the monotony of repetition, the report uses only eighteen words to handle Ann Baldwin's part of the case, merely indicating that it concerned "the same thing" as "touching the bewitchment of the said Ann Durent." Ann Baldwin (though the spelling makes positive identity a bit uncertain) would find her way into the Lowestoft parish records three years after the trial when the burial register indicates for July 22: "Ann Bolden shot to dead by Tho. Base."[73]

Two more episodes, both again involving the bewitching of young females, finish this segment of the trial report. Jane Bocking, midway between her fourteenth and fifteenth birthdays, was also too weak to undertake the trip to the assize, and was represented by her mother, Diana. Diana Bocking would live until 1680 and be described at that time in the parish register as "an antient woman."[74] At the time of the trial, she was probably in her late 50s.

Diana's husband, Henry, was born in Lowestoft in 1616. He was likely dead by 1653 because in that year Diana purchased in her own right a house overlooking the sea at the north end of town. In 1656, a "widow Bocking," probably Diana, received four pence from the poor rate. The following year she sold off all the land belonging to her house and eighteen months later she sold the house. By the mid-1660s, Diana was living in a small rented tenement in the northern section of the town. It is apparent that in the year preceding the trial, Diana Bocking's fortunes were very much in decline.

Diana Bocking told the court that her daughter, like Ann Durrant, had been afflicted with "swooning fitts" and with great stomach pains, again described as like the pricking of pins. She recovered but again became ill in February when the accusations against Denny and Cullender were common knowledge. Her physical symptoms—combined with apparitions—were said to be the evil doings of the accused. Her illness had continued to the present. Jane ate little or no food, and vomited crooked pins daily; indeed, the previous Sunday she had raised seven such pins. In her fits, "she would spread forth her arms with her hands open, and use postures as if she catched at something, and would instantly close her hands again." If the hands were forced open, several pins, "diversly crooked," would be found inside, but it could not be understood how they "were conveyed thither." Jane Bocking in her fits also talked as if she was discoursing with some person in the room, though she would not respond nor appear to notice anybody then present. She would throw up her arms and say: "I will not have it, I will not have it." In the end, she would capitulate, saying: "Then I will have it." Again, she made a fist and when it was forced open, a lath-nail was discovered inside. Jane Bocking also was said to complain in her fits that Rose Cullender and Amy Denny stood at the foot and head of her bed and in other places.

Though the fits ceased, her mother testified that Jane Bocking was stricken dumb, and could not speak a word for several days. When speech returned, she requested her mother to get her some meat, and when asked the reason for her muteness said that Amy Denny would not suffer her to speak. The court was presented with the nails and pins that Jane Bocking had vomited.

Mary Chandler, speaking for her eighteen-year-old stepdaughter, Susan, was the final witness in this portion of the trial. Mary Chandler, née Draper, probably was born outside of Lowestoft. In 1633, she had married Thomas Coe, member of a well-to-do Lowestoft family, and probably was about fifty when she testified at Bury St. Edmunds.[75] She bore five children between 1635 and 1645; in 1646, Thomas Coe died, aged 44. In his will, which he signed with his mark, he described himself as a "yeoman," and left all his houses and lands to his wife.[76] Two years later, Mary Coe married Robert Chandler, an innkeeper (or innholder, as it was then called) at "The Crown," Lowestoft's principal inn, and became stepmother to his children, Susan amongst them.[77] Robert Chandler would die thirteen years after the Bury St. Edmunds trial, and leave his property to Mary, with the provision that on her death it go to his son, John, who, in turn, was charged to give one third to Susan when he received it.[78] By then Susan was the wife of Samuel Pearson, a widower she had married in 1668.[79] Pearson previously had been married to a Margaret Pacy from a branch of the Pacy family other than Samuel's.[80] Mary Chandler may well have been a member of the Yarmouth Congregational Church to which Margaret Arnold belonged: a person of that name was propounded on September 14, 1652, and formally admitted two weeks later.[81]

Mary Chandler told the court that in February (February 2, according to the indictment), when Amy Denny and Rose Cullender had been brought before Sir Edmund Bacon on the warrant requested by Samuel Pacy and had "confessed nothing," Sir Edmund had appointed her and five other women to examine the bodies of the accused. The women went to Rose Cullender's house, where "they did acquaint her with what they were come about, and asked whether she was contented that they should search her?" Rose Cullender "did not oppose it." The failure, if it was so, to search Amy Denny as well as Rose Cullender, might well suggest Sir Edmund Bacon's lesser comfort with the evidence demonstrating the alleged witchcraft of Cullender. Bacon could have concluded that there was sufficient "real-life" testimony to convict Denny, but could have been uneasy about the fact that, except for the report of Edmund Durrant, the evidence against Cullender involved only "spectral" sightings and acts. Perhaps Bacon believed he needed to locate more physical evidence in order to get a true bill finding by the grand jury regarding Cullender. They began at her head, then they "stript her naked" and continued the search:

> in the lower part of her belly they found a thing like a teat of an inch long, they questioned her about it, and she said, *That she had got a strain by carrying of water which caused that excrescence.* But upon narrower search, they found in her privy parts three more excrescences or teats, but smaller than the

former: This deponent farther saith, that in the long teat at the end thereof there was a little hole, and it appeared unto them as if it had been lately sucked, and upon the straining of it there issued out white milkie matter.

After reporting this finding to the court, Mary Chandler testified that her stepdaughter, eighteen years old and working in Lowestoft as a servant, had gotten up to wash early the next morning (apparently the day following the examination of Rose Cullender's body) and at that time Rose Cullender appeared to her and took her by the hand, which frightened her greatly. She immediately went to her stepmother and told her what had happened. She then fell "extream sick, much grieved at her stomach." That night, after being in bed with another young woman (unmarried people customarily shared their bed), she shrieked, fell into fits, and cried out that Rose Cullender wanted "to come to her bed to her." She continued this way, beating herself and wearing herself out, so that Mary Chandler required help to attend her. Susan also declared that at one time there was a great dog accompanying Rose Cullender. Susan vomited crooked pins and sometimes was stricken with blindness, and became mute. This last was her state when the trial began. She had fallen into a fit when she was brought into court, but half an hour after she had been carried out she came to and recovered her speech. Immediately returned to the court and asked whether she was in a condition to take an oath and give evidence, Susan Chandler said that she could:

> But when she was sworn, and asked what she could say against either of the prisoners? before she could make any answer, she fell into her fits, screeking out in a miserable manner, crying *Burn her, burn her*, which were all the words she could speak.

The words "Burn her" offer a curious twist, since, while burning was the penalty for witchcraft on the continent, hanging was the mandated penalty in England.

Robert Chandler, Susan's father, repeated the evidence that his wife had given except, the report notes, he did not testify in regard to the searching of Rose Cullender's body.

The "excrescences" or supernumerary teats discovered on the body of Rose Cullender (there is no mention of a similar search of Amy Denny) traditionally had been regarded in England as marks of enlistment in the service of the devil. In continental witchcraft lore, the devil was believed to stamp upon members of his corps an insignia of some sort so that his followers could be distinguished from the orthodox. This belief, however, did not emerge with any clarity until the early sixteenth century, and then was largely confined to the writings of Protestant demonologists.[82] By 1548, witchcraft suspects in France and Switzerland systematically were searched for a mark of the devil,[83] and the French demonologist Henri Boguet would write in 1582 that "all witches have a mark, some on the shoulder, some on the eyelid, some on the tongue or lip, and others on the shameful parts."[84] Francis Hutchinson, however, pointed out that if examined closely enough most people would show "scurvy spots, or mortified or withered part, or hollow spaces between muscles."[85] Another critical voice was that of the English iconoclast, Thomas Ady, who asked the "witchmongers": "Where is it written [in the Bible] that the devill setteth privy marks upon witches, whereby they should be known or searched out?"[86]

In England, the doctrine of witch marks had shaded into the belief that the devil's human minions had extra nipples at which they fed their familiars, the animals that carried out their nefarious deeds. It was a "peculiarly English notion" that a witch was likely to possess such a familiar imp, which would usually take the shape of a cat or dog, but possibly a toad, a rat, or even a wasp or butterfly.[87] George Gifford, asking his parishioners how witches did their work, was told: "O syr, they do it not by themselves. They have their spirites which they keep at home in a corner: . . . these they send when they be displeased, and will them for to plague a man in his body, or in his cattle."[88]

The special English fondness for household pets, especially among the elderly, perhaps underlay this part of the country's lore regarding witchcraft. Ronald Seth suspected that "the ancient crones who represented the majority of the con-fraternity [of women accused as witches] sought comfort from the presence of small animals in the loneliness of their cottages."[89] As early as 1510, John Steward of Knaresborough in Yorkshire had been accused of keeping familiars like "humble bees,"[90] and a woman in Haverhill in Essex "confessed" in 1645 that a fly seen in her chamber was one of her imps, designated for diabolic doings.[91]

Richard Bernard, in his handbook for grand jurors, provided a comprehensive guide to the bodily mark that would signify allegiance to the devil and would also serve as a feeding station for familiars:

> Search diligently therefore for it in every place, and lest one
> be deceived by a naturall mark, note this from that. This is
> *insensible* and being pricked will *not bleede*. When the mark

therefore is found, try it, but so as the witch perceive it not, seeming as not to have found it, and then let one pricke in some other places, and another in the meane space there: it sometimes is like a little *teat*, sometimes but a *bluish spot*, sometimes *red spots* like a *fleabiting*, sometimes *the fleshe is sunke* in and hollow, as a famous witch confessed, who also said that witches cover them, and some have confessed, who also said that they have been taken away; but, saith that witch, they grow againe, and come to their old forme. And therefore, though this mark be not found at first, yet it may at length, once searching, therefore must not serve: for some out of fear, some others for favor, make a negligent search. It is fit therefore searchers should be sworn to search, and search very diligently, in such a case of life and death, and for the detection of so great a height of impiety.[92]

Searchers rarely encountered much difficulty in locating a postule, wart, wen, or other bodily growth on those they examined. For one thing, extra nipples—polythelia is the medical term—are common in both men and women, often appearing on the so-called Milk Line which runs under the armpits and across the chest.[93] An insensitivity to pricks is a usual characteristic of such a growth, though sometimes insensitivity is the result of an anesthesia induced by fear. At other times, searchers, such as the notorious Matthew Hopkins, possibly used pricking instruments with a retractable point to pretend that they had discovered an insensitive spot.

By this point in the trial the strategy of the accusers, conscious or illness-driven, appeared to be working admirably. Witnesses had told the court essentially the same story, that Amy Denny and Rose Cullender malevolently had caused awful personal harm to a number of girls and young women. The testimony indicated that twenty-month-old William Durrant, the only male victim, had been saved by the timely intervention of Dr. Jacob, but that his sister Elizabeth had been killed by the sorcery of Amy Denny. Thereafter Elizabeth and Deborah Pacy (through Samuel Pacy and Margaret Arnold), Ann Durrant (through her father, Edmund), Ann Baldwin (speaking for herself), Jane Bocking (through her mother, Diana), and Susan Chandler (through her stepmother and father, Mary and Robert) had testified to the terrible things that had happened to them because of the machinations of the accused. In addition, Alice Kittredge and Jane Buxton reported that Amy Denny had predicted (and therefore presumably caused) Elizabeth Pacy to have her mouth opened with a tap in order to feed her. Besides, incriminating teats had been located on the body of Rose Cullender. The case against the accused seemed to be overwhelming. Many English women had been hanged on testimony no stronger and often much weaker than this. But the case was not destined to proceed smoothly. There was discontent among prominent persons at the trial.

4

Lice of extraordinary bigness

"This was the sum and substance of the evidence which was given against the prisoners concerning the bewitching of the children before mentioned," the trial summary observes immediately after reporting that Robert Chandler had confirmed his wife's testimony.[1] Then, abruptly, a very different note intrudes:

> At the hearing this evidence there were divers known persons, as Mr. Serjeant Keeling, Mr. Serjeant Earl, and Mr. Serjeant Barnard present. Mr. Serjeant Keeling seemed much unsatisfied with it, and thought it not sufficient to convict the prisoners: for admitting that the children were in truth bewitched, yet said he, it can never be applied to the prisoners, upon the imagination only of the parties afflicted; for if that might be allowed no person whatsoever can be in safety, for perhaps they might fancy another person, who might altogether be innocent in such matters.

This paragraph is the first jarring note in the smooth progress of the trial. It is unclear precisely how Keeling's objection was raised. Was it expressed in the open court after Robert Chandler had presented his evidence and before the following witness was to appear? Or if the trial occupied several days, as Edward Stephens, Hale's son-in-law, wrote, was Keeling's position expressed informally after the trial had recessed and the officials were airing their views?

More important than the manner in which Keeling's concern became part of the record is the questionable accuracy of the trial report on this matter. A close reading of the paragraph quoted above indicates the awkwardness with which the point is made. First, there is the roster of the three "divers known persons" who were present in the courtroom; then the reader is told that one of them had voiced reservations about the persuasiveness of the evidence. Why bother to list all three serjeants when but one is of concern? The answer can be found in the significant difference between the printed version of the trial and a handwritten manuscript version that is among Richard Baxter's papers in Dr. Williams' Library in London and obviously predates it. The manuscript reads:

> At the hearing there were divers known persons, as Mr. Serjeant Keeling, Mr. Serjeant *Parker*, and Mr. Serjeant Bernard present. *They* seemed much unsatisfied with it, and thought it not sufficient to convict the prisoners . . . [italics added].

The substitution in the printed version of Mr. Serjeant Earle for Mr. Serjeant Parker and the relocation of the objection to the evidence from the trio of serjeants to Keeling alone represent the only important differences between the handwritten and printed versions of the trial, except for another alteration later in the report in which, again, Keeling is said in the printed version to be a lone holdout, while the manuscript indicates that others shared his view.

Both Serjeants Parker (handwritten manuscript) and Earle (printed version) may well have been present at the Bury St. Edmunds proceedings. Perhaps Parker had not been one of those objecting, while Earle, who was something of a curmudgeon, had expressed reservations and the names subsequently had been changed when the manuscript was prepared for printing to accord with what actually happened. Or perhaps a mistake in identity had been corrected. But why change the text in order to place the onus of objection solely on Keeling? It is possible, of course, that this too corrected an error in the manuscript. But it is at least as likely that by the time the trial report was being made ready for the printer—twenty years following the trial itself— Keeling had so poor a reputation, particularly in relation to Hale, with whom he often had bullheadedly disagreed, that to list him as the person who thought the evidence inadequate was seen as tantamount to proving its strength. The change may also represent an attempt by survivors sympathetic to Hale to further darken Keeling's already much tainted reputation, since the two men were competitors for recognition and had taken antagonistic positions on several prominent political, moral, and legal issues.

The writer of the most comprehensive review of Keeling's career has found his stand at the Bury St. Edmunds witchcraft trial noteworthy because "it was the only recorded occasion on which Kelyng [the more common spelling of the name at the time] tried to behave fairly!"[2] That judgment may be somewhat overstated, but it is eminently understandable, given Keeling's lifetime record of unsavory opinions and actions in a series of highly publicized cases. Yet it is Keeling's eminently sensible objection that introduces the first breath of fresh air into the trial. His statement that "the children were in truth bewitched" may well have been no more than a concession that had to be made, given the temper of the times, however little he might have believed it: or, as he says, he may have believed in witchcraft but distrusted this particular attempt to demonstrate it. Certainly, the point that the girls could just as well have chosen to "fancy another person" for their charges implies a willful and malicious persecution of the accused women.

Keeling and the men named with him were persons of some distinction and power. The title "serjeant"—standing for serjeant-at-law—is now obsolete; the last induction to the rank was made in 1874. It had been in existence since at least 1382 and was achieved by royal appointment, placing the holder just below judges in importance. Serjeants wore elegant scarlet and violet cloth costumes, with a white coif—a close fitting, skull-shaped linen cap—constituting their special badge of office. As Chaucer noted of the serjeant-at-law in *Canterbury Tales*: "For his science, and for his high renoun,/Of fees and robes he had many on."[3] On admission to the order, each designee "gave gold," that is, he distributed about 400 rings with his special motto (the motto was called a "posy") to predesignated recipients and others.[4] It was in character for Keeling that in 1669, after he had been made a judge, he would complain that the rings he was given were underweight.[5]

Though we are not certain, it is possible that Keeling—as serjeants sometimes were—had been appointed as coadjudicator with Hale to conduct the assize proceedings at Bury in the spring of 1662—that, in Trollope's pleasant phrase, he was a "bench fellow."[6] J.S. Cockburn, the leading authority on seventeenth-century assizes, notes that Hale was the only judge commissioned in the normal manner to ride the Norfolk circuit that spring but he believes that, as such matters often were arranged, Keeling later was appointed to fill the vacancy for the second position. Typically, the junior of the two judges at the assize, which would have been Keeling, handled the civil side, but when either judge was not occupied he would share in the work of his colleague, especially in cases of unusual importance or complexity.[7]

It is also possible, of course, that the grouping in the trial report of Keeling with his fellow serjeants—Erasmus Earle (and/or John Parker) and Robert Bernard—might indicate only the presence of these eminent personages, none in judicial capacity, since they all typically handled cases at Norfolk assize sessions.

At the age of seventy-one, Earle was the best known of the group, and was particularly likely to have been at the assize: Francis Blomefield notes that "such was his reputation in business, being esteemed one of the most able lawyers of his time, that in the Norfolk circuit he almost monopolized it."[8] Earle lived at Heydon in Norfolk, and among his clients were members of the Bacon family, relatives of the justice who had committed Amy Denny and Rose Cullender for trial. A graduate of Peterhouse at Cambridge University, he had been created a serjeant in 1657 by Oliver Cromwell, and reappointed by Richard Cromwell in 1658.[9] He was nominated for reinstallation in 1660, but it seems that no formal investment procedure ensued.[10]

Sir Robert Bernard (sometimes spelled Barnard or Baynard) first had been raised to the rank of serjeant-at-law in 1648, and then, because their interregnum advancement was deemed invalid, he and twelve other serjeants (including Matthew Hale) were reappointed to the order in June 1660, following Charles II's return to England. Bernard was a justice of the peace for Ely, and would be created a baronet later in 1662.

There are two men who might have been the John Parker, the serjeant listed only in the manuscript version of the trial; the *Dictionary of National Biography*, for its part, confuses one with the other.[11] A John Parker was created serjeant in 1648 and, along with Hale and Bernard, was reinstalled in 1660. His patron on becoming serjeant was Thomas Edgar, the grandfather of Robert Gibbon, Hale's factotum.[12] He is believed to have died in 1668, and seems the more likely of the pair to have been at the trial. The second John Parker was created serjeant in 1655, and also reinstalled in 1660.[13]

John Keeling, the last of the group, a man about whom we will have much more to say later, was cantankerous, discourteous, hot-headed, and intensely doctrinaire. Unlike Hale, he had neither patience for infinite reflection on the complexity of things, nor inclination to indulge in expressions of amazement and awe about the ways in which the creator's hand was at work. Keeling, above all, was not receptive to nor confused by a wide range of diverse viewpoints; neither did he find some portion decent and admirable in each of them or—as regards Hale, Thomas Browne, and Richard Baxter—in almost all of them. Keeling was certain that he was correct, and he was not to be bothered with fine distinctions.

The trial report abruptly leaves the comment about the reservations of Keeling (and, presumably, those of his two colleagues as well), to proceed to the evidence of Dr. Browne of Norwich, "a person of great knowledge." We do not learn how Sir (as he would become in 1671) Thomas Browne, author of the well-known autobiographical reflection, *Religio Medici*, came to be in the court. Some commentators regard his presence—about 60 miles from where he lived—as fortuitous; others presume that he had been summoned, perhaps by Matthew Hale. Both men had overlapped at Oxford, with a student body of about 2,000, when they were in residence.[14] Browne, a Winchester graduate, was at Pembroke College from 1623 to 1629 and Hale at Magdalene Hall from 1626 to 1628, but we have found no personal connection between them, then or later.[15]

It is uncertain whether Browne's expert witness testimony was originally part of the trial plan, or whether he was thrust into the proceedings to offer his medical opinion as a means to cope with the reservations of Keeling and the other two serjeants. This last interpretation is suggested by the phrase directly before the summary of Browne's testimony, a phrase that the text editor had overlooked when he sought to make the printed text conform with the redaction that had reduced the objectors to Keeling alone. Note the words we have italicized in the following sentence. Browne, it reads, "after this evidence given, and *upon view of the three persons in court*, was desired to give his opinion, what he did conceive of them." It is possible, of course, that the italicized words mean that the medical testimony was requested by the "three persons in court" (obviously the named serjeants), but it seems more likely that the phrase speaks directly to the trio's reservations about the testimony.

This is what Browne told the court:

> He was clearly of the opinion, that the persons were bewitched; and said, That in Denmark there had been lately a great discovery of witches, who used the very same way of afflicting persons, by conveying pins into them, and crooked as these pins were, with needles and nails. And his opinion was, That the Devil in such cases did work upon the bodies of men and women, upon a natural foundation, [that is] to stir up, and excite such humors super-abounding in their bodies to a great excess, whereby he did in an extraordinary manner afflict them with such distempers as their bodies were most subject to, as particularly appeared in these children; for he conceived, that these swounding fits were natural, and nothing else but that they call the Mother, but only height-

ened to a great excess by the subtilty of the devil, cooperating with the malice of these which we term witches, at whose instance he doth these villanies.*

Browne was a man ensnared between two epochal historical periods, that of the emergent scientific spirit and that of traditional and unquestioning religious faith. He prided himself as a medical man on the depth of his commitment to science, while a line in *Religio Medici* captures his religious orthodoxy well: "[W]here the Scripture is silent, the Church is my text, where that speaks, 'tis but my comment."[16]

There was a very important precedent for Browne's appearance as an expert witness at Bury St. Edmunds. In 1602—sixty years earlier—at a witchcraft trial in London, Edward Jorden, a doctor educated at Cambridge and Padua, had sought to persuade the court that Mary Glover, the fourteen-year-old daughter of a prominent Puritan merchant family who had accused Elizabeth Jackson, a charwoman, of witchcraft, was suffering from hysteria. The young girl had reported that Jackson shouted terrible curses at her. Following a further confrontation with Jackson, Mary Glover was struck dumb and blind, did not appear to eat for eighteen days, and suffered from a series of fits. The fits worsened, and they now combined with an elaborately choreographed pattern of hand motions. When Elizabeth Jackson was in the vicinity, the words "hang her" came out of Mary Glover's mouth in a peculiar nasal tone. The touch of Elizabeth Jackson also produced fits in the young girl. When another woman was dressed in Jackson's clothes, however, and touched Mary Glover, the girl gave no response.

Testifying at the trial, Jorden said that he believed the girl's symptoms were produced by hysteria. He also said that he did not think that she was a fraud, but that she suffered from a real ailment. Sir Edmund Anderson, the chief justice of the Court of Common Pleas, who was presiding, dismissed Jorden's views angrily: "Then in my conscience," he said, "it is not naturall; for if you tell me neither a naturall cause of it, nor a naturall remedy, I will tell you that it is not naturall." Anderson asked the jurors if they ever had heard of hysterical fits that occurre d regularly, in different forms, on alternating days and intensified when one particular person was present. The judge then

---

* A curious sidelight on this testimony is that in 1578, forty-four years earlier, another Dr. Browne, also a Norwich physician, had been accused of "spreading a misliking of laws by saying there are no witches" (*A Calendar of State Papers, Domestic Series, Addenda 1566–79*, p. 693).

again indicated the small worth he placed in Jorden's testimony: "Divines [and] phisitions," Anderson told the jury, "I know they are learned and wise, but to say this is naturall, and tell me neither the cause, nor the cure of it, I care not for your judgment." "After . . . pawsing a while," Anderson also told the jury, according to one report, that

> the land is full of witches; they abound in all places: I have hanged five or sixe and twenty of them; ther is no man here, can speake more of them than my selfe; few of them would confesse it, som of them did; against whom the proofes were nothing so manifest, as against those that denyed it. They have on their boodies divers strange marks, at which (as som of them have confessed) the devil sucks their bloud; for they have forsake god, renounced their baptisme, and vowed their service to the divill . . . [17]

Elizabeth Jackson was quickly found guilty, but under the much more benign 1563 witchcraft statute her sentence was but a year in prison, though she was required to stand in the pillory on several occasions during that period.

The statement by Browne in his trial testimony that a witchcraft episode similar to that facing the Bury court had occurred in Denmark is characteristic. It exhibits a display of worldliness but contributes virtually nothing to the situation that Browne had been called upon to interpret. Certainly, witchcraft in Denmark and England had strong historic interconnections. During his flamboyant voyage in 1589 to Denmark to spend the winter there and to personally claim his bride, the Princess Anne, James VI of Scotland (later James I of England) claimed to have brushed closely against witchcraft. He believed that malevolent forces in league with his rebel cousin, the Earl of Bothwell, had used demonic acid to raise the storms that initially forced the couple to return to Denmark after they had set sail for his home following his six-month stay:[18] cynics maintain that the idea that he was of such importance as to attract the attention of the devil was not the least basis for James' position. Later, the King would argue that one of the old Scottish women accused of this malevolence had told him things that were said between him and his bride that could not have been known to anyone but a person with diabolic powers.[19]

Scholars, including Francis Hutchinson writing in 1718, and Dorothy Tyler in 1930, have presumed that Browne was referring to the burning of eleven women in Køge in Zealand in his Bury St. Edmunds testimony, but that trial had taken place fifty years earlier, in 1612 and 1613.[20] Browne had a more contemporary source for information about what was going on in Denmark. He had maintained a correspondence in Latin, beginning in 1650, with the Icelandic priest Theodor Jonnsen, who was acquainted with Copenhagen's leading scholars. Jonnsen sailed each year from Iceland to Yarmouth, and routinely visited Browne. We also know that Browne communicated to the Royal Society the fact that, though the previous winter of 1662 was persistently cold in England, it was the mildest that had been seen in Iceland for many years.[21]

The leading contemporary Danish historian of witchcraft today, Jens Christian Johansen, reports that no case that he encountered in his study of seventeenth-century Danish witchcraft could have formed the basis for Browne's testimony.[22] Knud Bogh, writing two decades earlier, when discussing Browne's *Vulgar Errors*, which was translated into Danish but never published, suggested in passing that at Bury St. Edmunds Browne probably was referring to a case that had taken place in Bergen, in Norway, which then was under Danish rule.[23]

Details of the Norwegian case appear in a 1663 Latin treatise by Thomas Bartholin,[24] a professor at the University of Copenhagen, who was a physician, naturalist, and philologist. Bartholin was a man with whose works Browne was familiar and with whom he may have corresponded: they shared the same partiality for singular topics and novel disquisition.[25] The witch case involved a fourteen-year-old boy who was said to be expelling fishbones from wounds and abscesses on his body. Later, the boy was reported to vomit nails, needles, crooked pins, small pieces of iron and pewter, and a half-inch-long piece of wood. We are told only the first name of the woman accused of bewitching the boy—Synneve. She admitted her guilt, then hanged herself in her prison cell during the night before she was to be executed. The authorities burned her body underneath the town gallows.[26]

Thomas Browne's testimony notwithstanding, all apparently still was not lost for Amy Denny and Rose Cullender, though the chronology of the trial procedure, as detailed in the report, is puzzling at this point. Right after detailing the testimony of Sir Thomas Browne, the report returns to the earlier matter of the objection raised against the reliability of the young girls' evidence. It may be that the sections before and after Browne's testimony originally were together and that the summary of Browne's court appearance was awkwardly inserted between them.

The report now provides additional information about the objections that had been raised by Keeling and, very likely, by the other serjeants. "Besides the particulars above mention'd touching the said persons bewitched," it notes, "there were many other things objected against them for a further proof and manifestation that the said children were bewitched."

The only specific objection mentioned concerns an attempt to verify that the girls were not stage-acting their outbursts. An experiment had been conducted during the trial that had Rose Cullender touch one of her young accusers. The result had been dramatic:

> [I]t was observed that when they were in the midst of their fitts, to all mens apprehension wholly deprived of all sense and understanding, closing their fists in such manner, as that the strongest man in the court could not force them open; yet by the least touch of one of these supposed witches, Rose Cullender by name, they would suddenly shriek out opening their hands, which accident would not happen by the touch of any other person.

To make certain that the girls were not faking, they also had been "blinded with their own aprons," and the touching by Rose Cullender, we are told, "took the same effect as before."

But this attempt to demonstrate the awful consequences of the touch of one of the accused women on the girls did not satisfy everyone. There was "an ingenious person" who objected that "there might be a great fallacy in this experiment," and that "there ought not be any stress put upon this to convict the parties for the children might counterfeit their distemper." "Perceiving what was done to them," it was said, "they might in such manner suddenly alter the motion and gesture of their bodies, on purpose to induce the persons to believe that they were not natural, but wrought strangely by the touch of the prisoners."

The objection, like the earlier one, is again worded differently in the manuscript than in the printed trial report. The report tells us that it was "an ingenious person" who objected: the manuscript says that there were "ingenious persons" who objected. We presume that the objectors noted in the manuscript are the three serjeants.

Another experiment, seeking to deal with the "scruple" raised by the ingenious person(s), saw Hale appoint Sir Edmund Bacon, Serjeant Keeling, and Lord Charles Cornwallis to oversee a further test. Cornwallis was the second Baron Cornwallis of Eye in Suffolk. A few weeks short of his thirtieth birthday, he had just succeeded his father, Frederick, a supporter of Lowestoft in its law suit with Great Yarmouth, who had died two months earlier. Cornwallis belonged to an ancient and influential county family, was a member of Parliament, and a county magistrate: it was in this last capacity that he would have been at the assize. Through his grandmother, Lady Jane Cornwallis, he was related to Sir Edmund Bacon, since Lady Jane had taken for her second husband Sir Nathaniel Bacon, the seventh son of Sir Nicholas Bacon, the premier baronet of England.

The three men, together with "some other gentlemen," were instructed to attend one of the girls in the farther part of the hall and there to send for one of the accused witches to determine what would happen. This time the experimenters resorted to a ruse. Amy Denny was brought from the bar to the young girl. Then they put an apron over the girl's eyes, and while she was blindfolded they had her hand touched by "one other person." This "produced the same effect as the touch of the witch did in the court." The gentlemen appointed to conduct the experiment, we are told, "returned, openly protesting, that they did believe the whole transaction of this business was a meer imposture." Keeling, we learn for the first time from the trial report, had found support for his resistance to what was taking place.

For the moment, the lives of Amy Denny and Rose Cullender seemed on the verge of being spared. The trial report succinctly indicates how the result of the experiment was received: "This," it tells us, "put the court and all persons into a stand."

Three hundred and thirty years later, it is difficult for us to comprehend why the mistaken response by the blindfolded girl to the touch of a woman not accounted to be a witch did not put an end to the trial of Amy Denny and Rose Cullender. W.H. Davenport Adams has called it "remarkable" that Sir Matthew Hale remained unconvinced of the innocence of the accused women.[27] The failure of the experiment to derail the prosecution may testify to an intense determination to gain a guilty verdict. Or perhaps disinterest ruled; perhaps nobody cared enough to take the outcome of the experiment to its logical conclusion.

For the Lowestoft women accused of witchcraft, rescue came tantalizingly within reach, but then, salvation was snatched from them. Amy Denny and Rose Cullender lost their opportunity for rescue when Samuel Pacy convinced the court that what had happened during the experiment was not what it appeared to be. The trial report tells how Pacy, the "man who carried himself with much soberness during the tryal," and "from whom proceeded no words either of passion or malice," resolved the dilemma created by his daughter's unsatisfactory response:

> But at length Mr. Pacy did declare, That possibly the maid might be deceived by a suspicion that the witch touched her when she did not. For he had observed divers times that although they could not speak, but were deprived of the use of their tongues and limbs, that their understandings were perfect, for that they have related divers things which have been when they were in their fits, after they recovered out of them.

It is difficult to determine from this non-sequitur precisely what it was that Samuel Pacy was suggesting to the court. He appears to be arguing that his daughter had been maneuvered into her error by the machinations of the devil. The second sentence in Pacy's statement indicates that he told the court that the diabolic ruse could be verified when Elizabeth recovered sufficiently from her fit to relate to others what had gone on, though this idea hardly appears to resolve the issue satisfactorily.

Cotton Mather, in summarizing the Bury trial in his *Wonders of the Invisible World*, draws back slightly from accepting Pacy's interpretation. Mather was a deep believer in the reality of witchcraft and it was with considerable relish that he pounced upon tales of bewitching to frighten the wayward back into the fold. But Mather was notably hesitant about crediting spectral evidence that presumed to show disembodied spirits performing diabolical acts. He reasoned that, given the devil's power and malevolence, it would be in his interest to torment the good by misleading afflicted persons into the belief that individuals otherwise beyond reproach had caused their agony. Nobody would be safe if the courts paid heed to such evidence. At the Salem Village witch trials Mather ultimately was led to endorse—or, at least, to accede to—spectral evidence, as the witnesses testified to seeing the forms of their tormentors haranguing them from the rafters of the hearing room. For Mather to have fought the Salem trials would have undermined a situation that fitted too neatly with his role as the grand savior of New Englanders suffering from divine displeasure and in danger of damnation.

Mather indicates both his concern about spectral evidence and his difficulty with Pacy's explanation to the Bury St. Edmunds' court:

The experiment about the usefulness, yea, or lawfulness, whereof good men have sometimes disputed, was divers times made, that thou the afflicted were utterly deprived of all sence in their fits, yet upon the touch of the accused, they would so screech out, and fly up, as not upon any other persons. And yet it was also found that once upon the touch of an innocent person, the like effect followed which put the whole court unto a stand: altho' a small reason was at length attempted to be given for it.[28]

The trial report offers no additional enlightenment concerning the nature of Pacy's "small reason," though it lets us know that what he said "was found to be true afterwards, when his daughter was fully recovered (as she afterwards was)":

For she was asked [when she had recovered] whether she did hear and understand any thing that was done and acted in the court, during the time that she lay as one deprived of her understanding? and she did say, she did: and by the opinions of some, this experiment, (which others would have a fallacy) was rather a confirmation that the parties really were bewitched, than otherwise.

This information is followed by an attempt to demonstrate that what the young girls did could not have been triggered by other than witchcraft. The trial reporter argues that the idea that they might have committed fraud is highly implausible, and that to believe otherwise would be to believe in things so contradictory to common sense as to be absurd:

It is not possible that any should counterfeit such distempers, being accompanied with such various circumstances, much less children; and for so long time, and yet undiscovered by their parents and relations: For no man can suppose that they should all conspire together, (being out of several families, and as they affirm, no way related one to the other, and scarce of familiar acquaintance) to do an act of this nature whereby no benefit or advantage could redound to any of the parties, but a guilty conscience for perjuring themselves in taking the lives of two poor simple women away, and there appears no malice in the case. For the prisoners did scarce so much as object it.

Thus, the youth of the accusers, the nature and duration of their symptoms, the unlikelihood that they would be able to continuously deceive their parents and their relatives, the absence of particularly close relationships among them, and the fact that there did not appear to be anything that the young girls might gain from what they had done are set forth to convince anybody who would give the matter adequate thought that the charges of witchcraft are legitimate. This appeal to common sense shifts the burden of proof from those prosecuting the case to those seeking to undermine it.

The assumption that the feeble defense offered by Amy Denny and Rose Cullender testified to their guilt is a theme that would be repeated later in the trial report. Its force is considerably undercut by the fact that neither woman conceded any of the charges. Nor does this line of reasoning explain adequately the inability of Elizabeth Pacy to respond "properly" to the touching. But the reporter again feels compelled to revert to Elizabeth's awareness of what was happening—though blindfolded?—as the key to interpreting the episode:

> it is very evident that the parties were bewitched, and that when they apprehended or understand by any means, that the persons who have done them this wrong are near, or touch them; then their spirits being more than ordinarily moved with rage and anger at them being present, they do use more violent gestures of their bodies, and extend forth their hands to lay hold upon them; which at other times not having the same occasion, the instance there falls not out the same.

Perhaps this double-talk was comprehensible to a seventeenth-century mind steeped in the lore of witchcraft. It appears to be very important to the trial reporter to emphasize that Elizabeth Pacy, though comatose, was conscious of what was going on, and therefore that her response was not automatic, for if it had been her body should have known it was being touched by a person not a witch. There also is the hint of an idea that the true witches may have been nearby and that this might have caused the incorrect reaction. On the face of it, the fact that Elizabeth Pacy is deemed to have been aware of what was going on during the experiment would seem to undermine rather than to support her credibility.

Taken as a whole, the reporter's interpretation reads as if he had a preordained conclusion and that he had to find some explanation, more or less plausible, that might appear to support that judgment. The wrap-up sentence epitomizes the inadequacy of the effort: "while at other times not having the same occasion, the instance there falls out the same"—that is, sometimes things don't work out the way they are expected; sometimes the touch of a witch produces fits; and sometimes it does not.

Having dealt with objections that might be made about the result of the experiment, the trial report turns to testimony about other acts of witchcraft said to have been practiced by Amy Denny and Rose Cullender. Except that the matter was one of life and death, the remaining witnesses are at least as amusing as they are informative. Their purpose either was to rehabilitate a case that had been brought into question or perhaps, by introducing further accusations, to blunt or remove from immediate recollection the unsatisfactory outcome of the experiment, presuming that the jury had been made aware of it. Matthew Hale, writing about both religion and jurisprudence, had himself set forth the advantage of piling on evidence in order to carry a point:

> [I]f to any one quantum of fact there be many probable evidences, which taken singly have not perchance any full evidence, yet when many of those evidences concur and concenter in the evidence of the same thing, their very multiplicity and consent makes the evidence the stronger as the concurrent testimonies of many witnesses make an evidence more concludent.[29]

This statement is accurate enough as a guideline to good scientific practice, but it needs to be applied cautiously: after all, a dozen misinformed persons are neither better nor worse than one misguided witness. And Hale fails to appreciate that it is often better to obtain an estimate from one skilled person than to rely on the guesses of a multitude of amateurs. At Bury St. Edmunds, myth and misinterpretation merely piled one upon the other to make it acceptable to take away the lives of Amy Denny and Rose Cullender.

John Soan (also spelled at times Soane, Soon, or Sone, but never Soam, which is the way the trial report identifies him) was the first of the new round of witnesses. His name does not appear on the indictment, so technically Denny and Cullender were not being tried for bewitching him. The trial report labels him a yeoman and he is said to be "a sufficient person."

Soan was not born in Lowestoft, but town records verify the relatively high social standing that he enjoyed there by 1662. His birthplace may have been Beccles or Somerleyton where the surname

Soan is very familiar. In August 1633, he had married Jeane Robinson, who apparently was much older than he was.[30] She was the widow of William Robinson, a "husbonman." Robinson was a Lowestoft resident, but his wife was not, for there is no local record of their marriage, which took place prior to 1614. The couple had seven children; Jeane Robinson was pregnant with the eighth in 1630 when her husband died.[31] It is possible that when she married Soan, Widow Robinson brought with her a decent inheritance, and she certainly provided him with an instant and sizeable family, though three of the children died during the plague of 1635.[32] No children from the Soans' marriage are listed in local records.

The ship money returns for 1639–40 show that Soan possessed about 126 acres, a substantial holding;[33] unlike Pacy, he derived his livelihood from farming rather than fishing and merchant adventuring. During the 1650s Soan was one of the largest single contributors to the town poor rate, which was calculated on the basis of land holding.[34] He served in 1649 with Samuel Pacy as a trustee of the Lowestoft Townlands, and, together with Pacy, he was a churchwarden at St. Margaret's in 1649 and 1650.[35] His name appears many times in the Manor court proceedings, invariably as a plaintiff in a civil dispute. In the fall and winter of 1646 he filed a suit against John Denny though, as in all these cases, no details are provided in the records of what the dispute involved.[36] Soan had enough money to lend some of it. In January 1660, Henry Ward mortgaged his inn, "The White Horse," to him and two years later Soan, who presumably had foreclosed, sold the inn.

When Soan's wife died in 1656, the church entry reported: "November 30: Mrs. Soane, ye wife of Mr. John Soane, buried ye last of November."[37] Use of the terms "Mrs." and "Mr." was uncommon in the Lowestoft Parish Registers in the seventeenth century and indicates that the couple was considered to be a cut above the common folk. Soan probably inherited a public house called "The Sun" by way of his wife's first marriage: it stood in Blue Anchor Lane next to the house occupied by the Cullender family during the 1630s and 1640s.

At Bury St. Edmunds, Soan told the court a tale about wayward carts, whose disturbing behavior he was certain could be traced to the acts of Rose Cullender. The story begins thus:

> That not long since, in harvest time he had three carts which brought home his harvest, and as they were going into the field to load, one of the carts wrenched the window of Rose Cullender's house, whereupon she came out in a great rage and threatened this deponent for doing that wrong.

The carts then proceeded into the fields, where all three were loaded. Two got back home with no trouble and made a pair of additional round trips without difficulty. But the cart that had touched against Rose Cullender's window encountered problems:

> After it was loaded, it was overturned twice or thrice that day; and after that they had loaded it again the second or third time, as they brought it through the gate which leadeth out of the field into the town, the cart stuck so fast in the gateshead, that they could not possibly get it through, but were inforced to cut down the post of the gate to make the cart pass through, although they could not perceive that the cart did of either side touch the gate-posts.

This puzzling repudiation of physical law would lead Francis Hutchinson half a century later to wonder why "if it [the cart] did not touch the posts what made them cut the posts down?"[38] But, undaunted by any mundane consideration such as this, Soan told the court that after they had managed to work the cart through the gateway, there was trouble getting it into his yard at home: "but for all that they could do, they could not get the cart near unto the place where they should unload the corn, but were fain to unload it at a great distance from the place." There also was a problem with the unloading itself, "it being so hard a labor that they were tired that first came; and when others came to assist them, their noses burst forth a bleeding." This led to a postponement of the task to the following morning, "and then they unloaded it without any difficulty at all."

Narrow roadways often made the passage of carts difficult. Isaac Gillingwater identifies the field in which the cart overturned as the North Field, lying northwest of the town center.[39] John Soan's farmhouse was situated on land which today has been incorporated into the Town Hall. The route toward the field would certainly have taken his cart past Cullender's house on the narrow Swan Lane.

The story of the stubborn cart, however, like so many aspects of the Bury St. Edmunds trial, was derivative, part of the baggage of witchcraft belief. At a St. Osyth trial in 1582—eighty years earlier— John Sayer had told the court that "his cart stood, and that he could not make it forward nor backward by the space of one hour or more." Sayer blamed the intransigence of the cart on the diabolic magic of Alice Manfield before whose door it had become stalled. The record appears to indicate that Manfield, despite this testimony, was acquitted.[40] Fourteen years after the Bury trial, a similar complaint about a bewitched cart was lodged against Chatrina Blackenstein in a trial near Naumberg in Saxony. A finding that the cart was overloaded contributed to the defendant's acquittal.[41]

Robert Sherrington was the next witness after John Soan. He too is misnamed in the trial transcript, being called "Robert Sherringham" rather than by any of the considerable variants of his name that appear in Lowestoft records. Sherrington was not Lowestoft born, but descended from generations of yeoman farmers living in the parish of Westleton in Suffolk, in a line going back to William Sherington (also known as Cudon) in 1510.[42]

Robert Sherrington probably had settled in Lowestoft soon after marrying Elizabeth Chamberlin of Beccles on April 23, 1640.[43] Four children born to the couple and given typical names—Elizabeth, Robert, Susan, and William—are recorded in the parish register.[44] Both of the parents would die within a day of each other in November 1667, presumably of the plague.[45]

Sherrington is an elusive character to pin down in existing records. His house probably was situated on the east side of High Street, opposite the Crown Inn and the entrance to Bell Lane. During the 1640s and 1650s he filled a number of official posts. He was in turn aletaster, constable, swine reeve, and an overseer of the poor. In August 1653, he became yet another on the long list of plaintiffs who brought a civil action against John Denny at the Court Baron of Lowestoft.[46]

The testimony of Sherrington, like that of John Soan, was directed against Rose Cullender. He maintained that two years earlier, while he was passing along the street with his cart and horses, the cart touched against the Cullender house and broke down some part of it, making her "very much displeased, threatening him, that his horses should suffer for it." And it happened that those horses, four in number, died within a short time. The horses are specifically identified in the indictment (which spells Sherrington's name correctly) as a bald-colored gelding worth £5; a bay gelding worth forty shillings; a sorrel mare valued at £5, and another mare said to be worth £4.

Since that time, Sherrington testified, he also had suffered great losses by the sudden dying of his cattle. Also "so soon as his sows pigged, the pigs would leap and caper, and immediately fall down and die." Sherrington himself had been taken with a lameness in his limbs so that for some days he could neither walk nor stand. As if this were not enough, he also was vexed with a great number of "lice of extraordinary bigness," and although he many times "shifted himself" (changed his clothes)[47] he could not achieve any release; he would soon again swarm with lice, "so that in the conclusion he was forc'd to burn all his clothes, being two suits of apparel, and then was clean from them."

The mournful recital of Robert Sherrington was followed by the testimony of Richard Spendlar (incorrectly called Spencer in the trial report, though correctly identified in the manuscript at Dr. Williams' Library). Spendlar, not of Lowestoft birth, seems to have settled with his wife, Charity, in Lowestoft in the early 1630s, and the couple apparently leased a house at the south end of the town, not far from the residence of John and Amy Denny. The baptisms of two children are noted in the parish registers for 1631 and 1647.[48] Spendlar was a parish constable in 1644 and an overseer of the poor in 1665.[49]

At the trial, Spendlar directed attention from the misdeeds of Rose Cullender toward those of Amy Denny. The previous September 1, or thereabouts, according to the witness, he had in his own house heard Amy Denny say that "the devil would not let her rest until she were revenged on one Cornelius Sandeswell's wife." Here again the trial document misreports a name: Sandeswell should be Landefielde. We have found no seventeenth-century record of a Sandeswell surname anywhere in Suffolk; the witness was talking about Cornelius Landefielde, a mariner, and his wife, Ann, whose rather unusual last name not only confused the trial reporter, but also befuddled many generations of Lowestoft parish clerks who had it spelled at least once in fifteen different ways. Cornelius spells his name Landefielde in his will; thus, we will stay with that version. The name is of French origin, and it can be found in Lowestoft as far back as the early sixteenth century.

The close connection between persons involved as witnesses against Amy Denny and Rose Cullender can be seen from a brief inventory of the Landefielde heritage. Cornelius and Ann Landefielde had been married at Lowestoft on the second day of January in 1640.[50] Born in February 1616[51] (which would make her forty-six years old at the time of the trial), Ann was the second of four daughters of Francis Ewen and his wife, Mary. Mary Ewen died in 1620,[52] and soon after that Francis Ewen married Ann Arnold, the widow of Matthew Arnold, a sailor, who had died in 1619, leaving her with three sons and two daughters.[53] Francis Ewen, Ann's father, seems to have been a person who delighted in court cases and who was also a strong minded man not frightened to take the law into his own hands if he thought fit. During the period 1634 to 1639, his name appears eight times in the records of the Court of Common Pleas. The first case involved a suit he brought for the recovery of £13.10s. owed him by Thomas Pacy (a Lowestoft innkeeper and Samuel Pacy's uncle) for the sale and delivery of twenty-seven barrels of "ale made with hops." This case dragged on until the following year when Ewen was awarded forty shillings damages. Other cases involved Ewen suing various local people for outstanding debts. The majority of these cases were found in Ewen's favor and he was awarded damages.

It is obvious though that Ewen himself was not exactly a blameless character. In 1635 he was taken to the Court of Common Pleas by Thomas Utber, who said that Ewen, "with force of arms," stole sixty barrels from him at Beccles. Ewen pleaded not guilty to the charge and no judgment is recorded. At the Court Leet of Lowestoft, held in 1636, Ewen was indicted for brewing beer on a Sunday. Francis Ewen died in 1640; perhaps his hard-headedness lived on in his daughter.[54]

Ann Arnold, Ewen's second wife, was the daughter of William Drake, a Lowestoft blacksmith, and Joan Drake (née Wilson). Her cousin, Richard Drake, was married to another Ann Landefielde, an aunt of Cornelius. Besides this, Elizabeth, a sister of Matthew Arnold senior, had married Henry Ward of Lowestoft in 1608: they were the grandparents of another Henry Ward who, in the 1670s, married Elizabeth Pacy, the eleven-year-old whose condition, testified to by her father and aunt, helped condemn Amy Denny and Rose Cullender. In addition, Francis Ewen owned a brewery in Lowestoft that stood close to the house of John Soan, and in the 1630s he had rented a barn located in the yard of the "Hall House," then occupied by Rose Cullender and her family.

Cornelius Landefielde had been born in Lowestoft in March 1611,[55] one of the five children of the 1604 marriage of John Landefielde and his second wife, Mary Peterson of Great Yarmouth. Cornelius lived with his wife at the southern end of town in a house at the foot of the cliff, close to the seashore. After the death of her step-mother in 1644, Ann had come into a legacy from her father, derived from the sale of the brewery he owned;[56] in 1651 the Landefieldes purchased a plot of land at the top of the cliff and immediately to the west of their house.[57] Cornelius later erected a house on this plot, which he would describe in his will as "ye house or tenement standing above ye clift which I lately built." His will also informs us that both of his houses were divided into two tenements. Amy Denny was the tenant in the northern part of the house at the top of the cliff, while the Landefieldes lived in the eastern part of the lower house.[58]

It was the landlord–tenant relationship between the Landefieldes and Amy Denny which gave rise to one of the witchcraft charges of the Landefieldes against Amy Denny, charges which, like those of John Soan, were not included in the indictments.

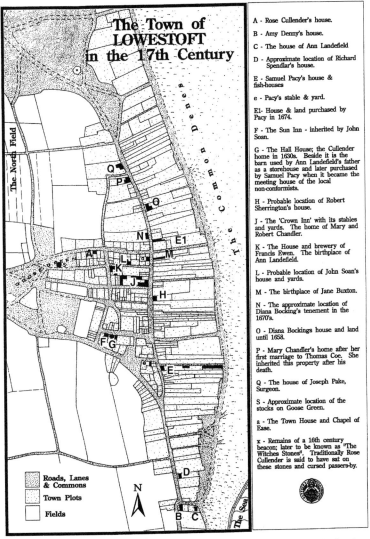

The Town of
LOWESTOFT
in the 17th Century

A - Rose Cullender's house.

B - Amy Denny's house.

C - The house of Ann Landefield

D - Approximate location of Richard Spendlar's house.

E - Samuel Pacy's house & fish-houses

e - Pacy's stable & yard.

E1- House & land purchased by Pacy in 1674.

F - The Sun Inn - inherited by John Soan.

G - The Hall House; the Cullender home in 1630s. Beside it is the barn used by Ann Landefield's father as a storehouse and later purchased by Samuel Pacy when it became the meeting house of the local non-conformists.

H - Probable location of Robert Sherrington's house.

J - The 'Crown Inn' with its stables and yards. The home of Mary and Robert Chandler.

K - The House and brewery of Francis Ewen. The birthplace of Ann Landefield.

L - Probable location of John Soan's house and yards.

M - The birthplace of Jane Buxton.

N - The approximate location of Diana Bocking's tenement in the 1670's.

O - Diana Bockings house and land until 1658.

P - Mary Chandler's home after her first marriage to Thomas Coe. She inherited this property after his death.

Q - The house of Joseph Pake, Surgeon.

S - Approximate location of the stocks on Goose Green.

a - The Town House and Chapel of Ease.

x - Remains of a 16th century beacon; later to be known as "The Witches Stones". Traditionally Rose Cullender is said to have sat on these stones and cursed passers-by.

Roads, Lanes & Commons

Town Plots

Fields

N

Figure 6 Map of the town of Lowestoft in the seventeenth century, indicating the residences of the trial participants, the place where the stocks were, and similar trial-related locations

Source: Drawn by Ivan Bunn in collaboration with David Butcher using 17th-century Manor Court records of Lowestoft.

Ann Landefielde told the court that seven or eight years earlier she had purchased some geese, and afterwards had met Amy Denny who reportedly told her that "if she did not fetch her geese home they would all be destroyed." And, indeed, this came to pass a few days later. Then, after Amy Denny had "become tenant to this deponents husband for a house," Cornelius (according to the trial report) is said to have told her "that if she looked not well to such a chimney in her house, that the same would fall." The report obviously errs here, because the context makes it clear that the complaint about the defective chimney was delivered by Amy Denny to her landlords. Ann Landefielde said that she replied that the chimney was a new one (as was the house), and paid no further attention to the matter ("not minding much her [Amy Denny's] words"). But a short time later the chimney fell down, "according as the said Amy had said."

We learn no more of this incident from the trial report. An episode which most reasonably could be expected to show the inadequacy of the workmanship and the danger of the chimney toppling and perhaps injuring Amy Denny instead stands as testimony to her uncanny and diabolical prescience.

The final evidence set out in the trial report deals with Ann Landefielde and one of her brothers. He was a fisherman who worked the northern seas, and, at her request, he had sent her a firkin (about a quarter barrel) of fish. When told that the fish had arrived at Lowestoft Road, Ann Landefielde asked a boatman to bring the firkin ashore with the other goods he had to transport. She then asked Amy Denny to go with her to meet the boatman and help carry the fish home. Amy's answer, reported by Ann Landefielde, was that "She would go when she had it"; that is, when Ann had gotten her hands on the fish, a reasonable enough reply. This is the remainder of the story:

> And thereupon this deponent went to the shoar without her, and demanded of the boatman the firkin, they told her, that they could not keep it in the boat from falling into the sea, and they thought it was gone to the divel, for they never saw the like before. And being demanded by this deponent, whether any other goods in the boat were likewise lost as well as hers? They answered, Not any.

Fishermen are noted for their superstitious nature, a matter said to be related to their exposure to the dangerous vicissitudes of the sea. Some seamen of the time believed that violent storms at sea could be caused by witches ashore stirring boiling water in which eggshells floated;[59] thus in East Anglia empty eggshells often were carefully crushed before being thrown away.[60] We suspect, however, that Ann Landefielde's firkin of fish met a much more mundane fate, stolen by a boatman who took advantage of the gullibility of its intended recipient. The fish story finished the trial testimony. Amy Denny and Rose Cullender then were asked if they had anything to say for themselves. They replied, we are told, undoubtedly in the reporter's and not their own words: "Nothing material to any thing that was proved against them."

It was now left to Sir Matthew Hale to direct the jury. Hale brought to this task formidable erudition in the history and the nature of English law, and a deep and unquestioning religious faith. These traits combined with a high degree of tolerance for religious dissent and a personality that traditionally has been regarded as extraordinarily decent, but which, as we shall see, has been painted in less flattering colors by several observers, most notably Roger North, who knew Hale personally.

How a judge chose to sum up the trial evidence typically played a large part in determining the fate of the defendants.[61] James Fitzjames Stephen, reviewing the *State Trials* volumes for this period (which include a reprint of the witchcraft proceedings at Bury St. Edmunds), wondered why any judge should have thought it necessary to be openly cruel or unjust to prisoners. The judge's position, Stephen observed, "enabled him, as a rule, to secure whatever verdict he liked, without taking a single irregular step, or speaking a single harsh word."[62] Sir Matthew Hale, in extolling the virtues of trial by jury, "certainly the best manner of trial in the world,"[63] had emphasized the prominent role played by judges. They are, he pointed out, always present when evidence is offered. They also are able to direct the jury in matters of law, and in matters of fact "to give them a great light and assistance by . . . weighing of the evidence before them, and observing where the question and knot of business lies, and by shewing them his opinion . . . which is a great advantage and light to laymen."[64] Such judicial power was supposed to be employed to achieve fairness and justice. Isaac Barrow, a seventeenth-century theologian and scientist, indicates what ideally was expected from a judge:

> A judge should never pronounce final sentences, but upon good grounds, after certain proof, and upon full conviction. Not any slight conjecture, or thin surmise; any idel report, or weak pretense is sufficient to ground a condemnation upon; the case should be irrefragably clear before we determine on the worse side. . . . Every accusation should be deemed null, until both as to matter of fact, and in point of right, it be firmly

proved true; it sufficeth not to presume it may be so; to say, It seemeth thus, doth not sound like the voice of a judge. . . . [65]

There is some controversy regarding whether judges in Hale's time usually went into great detail in their jury summations. J.M. Beattie maintains that judges rarely found it necessary to sum up for the jury, partly because most trials were so brief, but also because their view of the matter had been made eminently clear during the course of the trial.[66] On the other hand, Sir John Hawles noted in *The Englishman's Right*, published in 1680, that judges "do often recapitulate and sum up the heads of evidence,"[67] and Gilbert Burnet reported that it was Hale's practice to do so: "He was not satisfied barely to give his judgment in causes, but did especially in all intricate ones, give such reasons that prevailed with him."[68] Hale himself noted that "[w]hen the case was good, and fully so appeared to me, I thought was that season, that the use of that ability [eloquence] was my duty . . . and I spared not the best of my ability," indicating that he did so because of a divine obligation:

> I was warm and earnest; the setting forth of thy glory; the asserting of thy truth; the detection and conviction of errors; the clearing of the innocent; the aggravating of sins, oppressions, and deceits; and though I was careful I did not exceed the bounds of truth, or due moderation; yet I ever thought that these were the seasons for which that talent was given me, and accordingly, I employed it.[69]

We also know at least one criminal case in which Hale took conspicuous pains to go over the testimony in minute detail and to make absolutely certain that the jury understood his view. Tried in Aylesbury in 1668, the case involved a charge of theft against Robert Hawkins for stealing two rings, an apron, and one pound nineteen shillings from the Reverend Henry Larimore, an Anabaptist minister. During the trial, Hale called Larimore "a very villan, nay I think thou art a devil,"[70] and at its end he laid out the essence of the evidence, and then emphasized the strength of the defense's position. The summary of what Hale told the jury shows how he maneuvered it into seconding his version of what had taken place:

> Thus I have repeated the evidence to prove him guilty, and have not, I think, omitted any thing in it that is material; which if you do believe, he must needs be guilty: And also the

prisoner's defense, which, I think, is sufficient. It is a plain case, and I suppose you need not go from the bar; but that I leave to you.[71]

The jury did not stir from the bar, and quickly returned the called-for verdict of Not Guilty. One lawyer, reviewing the case years later, concluded that it demonstrated that Hale was "better provided with solemnity, respectability, and learning than mother-wit,"[72] a judgment concordant with that of a commentator on Hale's treatise on the prerogatives of the King, who decided that "the wealth of learning displayed by Hale . . . cannot conceal the fact that argument, good or bad, was not his strongest point."[73]

At Bury St. Edmunds Hale chose to be cryptic and, on the surface, noncommittal, specifically telling the jury "[t]hat he would not repeat the evidence unto them, least by doing so he should wrong the evidence on the one side or on the other." Then he informed those who would decide Amy Denny and Rose Cullender's fate that "they had two things to enquire after." The first was "whether or not these children were bewitched?" And second: "Whether the prisoners at the bar were guilty of it?" This partitioning of the issues may have been Hale's response to Keeling's objection that, though he granted the bewitchment, there had been no satisfactory proof that the accused women were the cause of it.

Hale followed his opening pronouncement with these words:

> That there were such creatures as witches he made no doubt at all; for first, the scriptures had affirmed so much. Secondly, the wisdom of all nations had provided laws against such persons, which is an argument of their confidence of such a crime. And such hath been the judgment of this kingdom, as appears by that act of Parliament which hath provided punishment proportionable to the quality of the offense.

These thoughts left unheeded the warning of John Selden, a man who had a great influence on Hale's thinking. "*Scrutamni scriptura* [search ye the scripture]; these two words have undone the world," Selden had written.[74]

After having established that witches exist by relying on the bible and the law, Hale moved on to what he expected from the jury:

> And desired them, strictly to observe their evidence; and desired the great God of Heaven to direct their hearts in this

weighty thing they had in hand: For to condemn the innocent, and to let the guilty go free, were both an abomination
to the Lord.[75]

Perhaps Hale was echoing the sentiment of King James I, who in
Daemonologie (1597) had written: "Judges ought indeede beware
whom they condemne: for it is as great a crime ... to condemne the
innocent, as to let the guiltie escape free."[76] Hale himself in another
context had observed: "Let me remember, when I find myself inclined
to pity a criminal, that there is likewise pity due to the country."[77]
There is a striking contrast between these comments and the observation of Increase Mather: "It is better that ten suspected witches should
escape," Mather maintained, "than that one innocent person should be
condemned. . . . I had rather judge a witch to be an honest woman,
than judge an honest woman to be a witch."[78]

To some, Hale's instructions seem even-handed and neutral. One
scholar has written: "[G]iven his sincere belief in witchcraft, Hale acted
in a completely impartial manner favoring neither prosecution nor
defense."[79] But most persons read the charge as clearly tilted against
the defendants. "After a charge of this description," notes one critic,
"the jury naturally brought in a verdict of 'Guilty'."[80] Barbara Shapiro
traces Hale's bland charge to the jury to his ambivalence about
witchcraft because of its conflict with the emerging scientific spirit.
"Hale's refusal to sum up the evidence and his statements about
witchcraft," she writes, "were considered extraordinary at the time. . . .
It seems fair to conclude that Hale's zeal against atheism overcame his
commitment to the new [scientific] methodology, with his refusal to
sum up indicating his awareness of the cognitive dissonance which he
had created for himself."[81] Perhaps Keith Thomas' general observation
is the most pertinent: "Men seldom seek a high degree of proof for
what they already believe to be true."[82]

To us, Hale's attempt at neutrality is at best unfortunate, particularly since the accused women had no counsel or any legal advice,
except what the judge might deign to offer. Nor were they allowed to
see the depositions. Also, they had been confined since they were
accused and therefore were unable to obtain witnesses on their behalf.
Generally too, as C. L'Estrange Ewen adds, "ill-treatment . . . reduced
the prisoners to a state of collapse and worse."[83]

Hale, of course, was under some public pressure to satisfy the better
citizens of Lowestoft about the quality of justice delivered in a king's
court. Writing of a time not much later, Roger North tells us how his
brother Francis was "infinitely scrutinous" in capital cases, but "never

more puzzled than when a popular cry was at the heels of a business; for then he had his jury to deal with, and, if he did not tread upon eggs, they would conclude sinistrously, and be apt to find against his opinion." Francis particularly "dreaded" trying a defendant accused of witchcraft:

> It is seldom that a poor old wretch is brought to trial upon that account, but there is, at the heels of her, a popular rage that does little less than demand her to be put to death: And, if a judge is so clear and open as to declare against the impious vulgar opinion, that the devil himself has power to torment and kill innocent children . . . [the triers] cry this judge hath no religion, for he doth not believe witches; and so, to shew they have some, hang the poor wretches.[84]

To avoid a "tendency to mistake," North declares, a clever and discrete judge had to manifest "a very prudent and modest carriage" with which "to convince, rather by detecting the fraud, than by denying authoritatively such power given to old women."[85] This is, of course, part of the strategy that was pursued, though unsuccessfully, by Serjeant Keeling.

The witchcraft trial was near its end. The reporter verifies that he had not unduly truncated the judge's remarks to the jury by noting that after Hale's "short direction" its members departed from the bar. In seventeenth-century criminal trials, jurors typically heard a series of cases and then rendered their verdicts on each of the group. They discussed their views in "some convenient place,"[86] usually a corner of the courtroom or perhaps in a nearby house or church.[87] There was some pressure to reach a decision rapidly, for the rule was that jurors were to be kept without meat, drink, fire, candle, or lodging until they had agreed.[88]

The witch trial at Bury St. Edmunds apparently had occupied enough time so that judgment upon the defendants was the only matter concerning the jury, and its members were back within the space of half an hour. Presuming that the standard procedures for a capital case were followed, the clerk would have called each juror by name, asked that person whether he had reached a verdict, and who would speak for the group. One of the prisoners then would be called to the front of the court, and asked to hold up her hand. The clerk would say: "Look upon the prisoner you that be sworn; what say you is she guilty to the felony whereof she stands indicted, or not guilty?" The process then was repeated for the second prisoner.[89]

At Bury, the jury spokesman declared that Amy Denny and Rose Cullender both were "guilty upon the several indictments, which were thirteen in number, whereupon they stood indicted." The trial reporter does not indicate that there were in fact fourteen indictments and that the count involving Robert Sherrington's overturned cart and four dead horses resulted, as noted on the indictment, in a "Not Guilty" verdict. The omission of this acquittal in the report may have been inadvertent or it may have been a deliberate deceit, an attempt to make things appear even more unequivocal than they had been. This meaningless acquittal on the single charge may reflect some juror bias against Sherrington, whose evidence was hardly more far-fetched than that of several other accusers. Or does it demonstrate an attempt by the panel to solemnly weigh the evidence supporting each charge?

After the verdict had been announced, the jury foreman was asked what lands, tenements, goods, or chattels the prisoners possessed at the time the crime had been committed. The common answer, and that given at Bury St. Edmunds, was that the jurors knew of no such possessions. The spokesman also presumably gave the same answer to the required question about whether the prisoners had tried to abscond before their trial.[90]

A single sentence paragraph concludes the discussion of the jury's verdict. "This was," it is noted, "upon Thursday in the afternoon, March 13, 1662."

Thereafter, the report ties up a few loose ends. We learn that three children (apparently Elizabeth Pacy, Ann Durrant, and Susan Chandler) and their parents came to Lord Chief Baron Hale's lodging the morning after the jury's verdict. Two of the girls now "spake perfectly," and "were as in good health as ever they were." Susan Chandler, a few years older than the other two, was the exception. Susan was said to appear "very thin and wan . . . by reason of her very much affliction." Her failure to be restored to full health would add another ember to the coals of Francis Hutchinson's burning scorn for the proceedings. "[I]f it be really true," Hutchinson noted, "that the judgment of law and authority hath this supernatural effect in this case . . . what was the reason the effect was partial, and only cured some of the afflicted, and not others?"[91] For Richard Boulton, the answer to Hutchinson was obvious if tautological: "the effect . . . was partial, and only cured some of the afflicted, and not others."[92]

The children were questioned by Hale about their well-being. Samuel Pacy again acted as a proxy, indicating that within less than half an hour after the women were convicted, "they were all of them restored, and slept well that night, feeling no pain." Susan Chandler, again the exception, Pacy noted, had felt a pain like a pricking of pins in her stomach.

The children were then taken to the court, but Ann Durrant remained so fearful that she would not confront Amy Denny and Rose Cullender. The other two girls affirmed under oath ("in the face of the country"), and before the convicted women, those matters that earlier had been testified to by their friends and relations, "the prisoners not much contradicting them."

This procedure apparently served the function of what might be regarded as a sentencing hearing. "In conclusion," the trial report notes, "the judge and all the court were fully satisfied with the verdict, and thereupon gave judgment against the witches that they should be hanged." Hale presumably preceded his sentence by reciting the formula, called the *allocutus*, that reminded the accused of the charges against them, repeated the judgment of the jury, and asked the prisoners: "Now what can you say for yourselves why according to law you should not have judgment to suffer death?"[93]

This ceremonial procedure provided an opportunity to plead pregnancy or other mitigating circumstances. All we learn about the response of the women at Bury St. Edmunds is communicated in a terse sentence: "They were much urged to confess, but would not."

That same morning, Hale and his marshal left Bury St. Edmunds for Cambridge. In his *Pleas of the Crown*, Hale had noted that "[s]ometimes the judge reprieves before judgment [is carried out], as where he is not satisfied with the verdict, or the evidence is uncertain."[94] At Bury, we are told, "no reprieve was granted," undoubtedly because Hale had not suggested one.

"But they confessed nothing," are the final words of the trial document.

While there is no way to be certain about it, we take these concluding words—which repeat an earlier, similar statement—to carry with them a note of perplexity, perhaps even of concern in the mind of the trial reporter.

"Justice" was dealt out swiftly in seventeenth-century England. On Monday, March 17, three days after they had been sentenced, Amy Denny and Rose Cullender were hanged by the neck until dead. The deed presumably was carried out at the Thinghow, originally a tumulus or burial mound situated on the heathland outside the North Gate of Bury St. Edmunds. The site had been the ancient assembly point for the Thing, a word meaning "court of justice," first used when Suffolk lay under Danish law.[95] This was the traditional place of execution, and later would be known as "Betty Borrough's Hill" in memory of the last person to be hanged there.

The King's commission would have been read out to the prisoners when they reached the gallows. Sometimes this would be accompanied by a proclamation that those present should move back if they had not been appointed to play a role in the hanging. Only a chaplain, the sheriff, and the executioner, perhaps with an assistant, were allowed to remain close to the prisoners.[96] A drink of spirits always was offered to condemned persons: in 1653, Ann Bodenham, executed at Salisbury for witchcraft, understandably kept asking for more and would have died drunk if she had been permitted.[97]

Following death, the bodies of Amy Denny and Rose Cullender presumably would have been burned and their ashes scattered.[98] On the other hand, another possibility exists. By the nineteenth century a community known as the Beach Village had grown in Lowestoft between the foot of the cliffs and the North Sea. During work to improve the roads there, a human skeleton, pinioned in its grave by a stake, is said to have been unearthed. An elderly lady raised in that neighborhood who had heard the tale in her youth told us that the skeleton was found at the foot of the cliff just outside the boundary of Samuel Pacy's house. The woman's mother, who told her the story, said that the remains were reputed to be those of a witch.

Part II

What might it mean?

5

Wrinkled face, furrowed brow, and gobber tooth

What can be said to explain the accusations and the trial for witchcraft of Amy Denny and Rose Cullender? Attempts to interpret witchcraft, like attempts to explain most complex historical phenomena, face formidable hurdles. The more general the roster of causes put forward, the less likely they are to have specific predictive value. It seems to be true, for instance, that outbursts of witchcraft prosecutions were associated with unsettled political and social conditions, but there has been an almost endless array of such conditions in places where no attention was paid to the possibility of witchcraft. Other explanations also falter when looked at in a cross-cultural context. Misogyny clearly seems to play a role in much of the world's witchcraft, but why is it that in some places, such as Iceland and Finland, men rather than women overwhelmingly bore the brunt of witchcraft charges?[1] While broad-based studies of witchcraft can cite political, social, and psychological irregularities that seem to be associated with the presence of prosecutions, case studies, such as ours, can merely affirm that in one particular instance the forces said to be at work generally did or did not prevail. At the same time, a case study can offer rich detail by being able to focus on aspects of the situation that tend to be overwhelmed or camouflaged in inquiries which summarize a great number of episodes over a longer period of time.

The fear and persecution of witches, as Alan Kors has noted, involved practices linked with the most complex areas of human behavior, matters such as social conformity and deviation, magic, helplessness and mastery, responses to aging, and the etiology of mental states. Witchcraft accusations also were tied to jurisprudence, theology, medicine, and the popular mentality. "To provide sound data on which to test theories that might deal with issues of such scope," Kors observes, "is no small accomplishment."[2]

Brian Levack has similarly pointed out that it would be difficult to think of any other historical problem over which there has been more disagreement and confusion than witchcraft. During the present century alone, he observes, the persecution of witches has been attributed in whole or in part to the Reformation, the counter-Reformation, the Inquisition, the religious zeal of the clergy, the rise of the modern state, the development of capitalism, the widespread use of narcotics, changes in medical thought, social and cultural conflict, an attempt to wipe out paganism, the need of the ruling classes to distract the masses, and hatred of women. In his own analysis of witchcraft, Levack chose not to endorse any all-encompassing explanation, but rather to adopt a "multi-causal approach which sees the emergence of new ideas about witches and a series of fundamental changes in the criminal law as the necessary preconditions of the witch-hunt, and both religious change and social tension as its more immediate causes."[3]

In such terms, neither misogyny, unrest, nor any of the other explanations can, by themselves, provide a total understanding of what happened and why it happened, but each can offer insight into the kinds of matters that fed—or did not feed—into the persecution of witches. The unraveling of causation in regard to human events most often locates certain established circumstances and then focuses upon noteworthy matters that appear to trigger these preexisting circumstances. Witchcraft charges, for instance, however auspicious other causal components might have been, never would have been laid had there not been a social and judicial climate that, for a variety of reasons, would not ridicule such charges. In the end, as Christina Larner says approvingly of Macfarlane's work on witchcraft, there is a tendency to lay out a grabbag of partial causes, chance combinations of circumstances, and the apparently perverse. The picture that then emerges, she observes, "is as untidy and as rich as life itself."[4]

Such eclecticism does not rule out a search for correlates associated with witchcraft accusations. In this regard, it is worth exploring how what took place at Bury St. Edmunds in the trial of Amy Denny and Rose Cullender in 1662 fits with ideas such as Puritan–Anglican conflict, hysteria, misogyny, and the tension caused by the demands of charity and those of self-interest that traditionally have been advanced to shed light on the phenomenon of witchcraft. It also seems valuable to try to seek understanding in terms of the positions and personalities of the protagonists who played so prominent a part in the case—Sir Matthew Hale, Serjeant John Keeling, and Sir Thomas Browne. It is arguable whether the case would have gone forward had another set of authorities been involved or, if the case was tried, whether it would have ended as it did.

In these following chapters, we will examine major ingredients that fed into the trial of Amy Denny and Rose Cullender to establish a background that permits a more comprehensive understanding of the case of the Lowestoft "witches."

The suggestion that there is "a rough temporal coincidence between energetic phases of witch prosecution and natural or man-made disasters"[5] is commonplace in the literature on the subject. Julio Caro Baroja notes: "It is certainly true that the practice of witchcraft increases . . . when a general state of anxiety exists or catastrophes occur; at moments, in fact, when collective misery is a stronger force than individual passions."[6] In 1662, when Amy Denny and Rose Cullender were accused, England was only barely emerging from the strain of the interregnum and was deeply embroiled in highly unsettling religious friction, a matter particularly unnerving for a family of dissenters such as the Pacys. More directly, Lowestoft and Yarmouth were involved in litigation over fishing rights that immediately threatened the primary means by which Lowestoft's people lived. Samuel Pacy was one of the main players in this conflict, and his absence from home, while he sought support for his town's cause, very likely was unsettling for his family.

That people need to lay the blame on someone in order to reduce their own anxieties lies at the heart of scapegoating, a process that is critical to an understanding of the Lowestoft witch case. Amy Denny and Rose Cullender proved to be irresistible targets when life-threatening, prolonged, and incomprehensible illness struck at a time when the town was under the stress of its conflict with Great Yarmouth over fishing rights. The prerequisite was the social belief, widely held at the time, that "[a]ll afflictions were necessarily providential, and demonic afflictions merely a special case."[7] Matthew Hale gave strong voice to this idea in his religious writing: "Afflictions," he proclaimed, "are most certainly fruits and effects of sin: and worldly crosses and calamities do as naturally flow from precedent sins, as the crop doth from the seed that is sown."[8] The appropriate response to affliction was a patient "searching of our waies . . . to the acknowledgement of our sinnes."[9] An easier path is to locate others upon whom to displace personal guilt. Anthropologist Lucy Mair puts a high priority on this particular condition: "This book," she writes in her overview of witchcraft, "starts with the premise that in a world where there are few assured techniques for dealing with everyday crises, notably sickness, a belief in witches, or the equivalent of one, is not only not foolish, it is indispensable."[10] Particularly compelling are Alan Macfarlane's interpretative remarks:

Witchcraft accusations were a method of splitting apart, of distancing people. On the personal level they justified disruptive feelings of anger and hostility which ran contrary to the traditional pressures towards harmony and charity instilled by Christianity. Furthermore, witchcraft beliefs did not force people to examine their own conduct to see in what way they had deviated from traditional ideals of behavior. If suffering had been accepted as the consequence of personal sin, then people would have had to admit that they had failed in charity, that the old woman was justified in laying a curse. The whole organic, distributive rather than acquisitive, communal rather than individual, "thou art thy brother's keeper," traditional Christian ethic would have had to be adhered to. As it was, the enormity of the witch's reciprocal retaliation, and her association with foul behavior and hidden power, so overshadowed the situation that the victim's original offense was forgotten. In a subtle way the whole traditional morality could be altered without appearing to change. Charity and love were fine, but could not, of course, be expected to include those beast-like witches—just as today we are to love all brethren, except for those foul and scarcely human protagonists of "enemy" states we fear.[11]

Experimental research on scapegoating indicates that it is particularly likely to occur when people behave contrary to sex-role expectations. Lynn Kahn found that criticism of women was greatly intensified when they expressed anger or distress, and that when the pressure was extreme the groups of people she studied seemed to behave as if their survival depended upon finding suitable scapegoats.[12]

The Puritan doctrine that the death of a wife or child often was the result of the father's transgressions increased the urgency for nonconformists to find someone else upon whom to place blame. Ann Kibbey notes: "The Puritan adult male, if he married, acquired a power commensurate with the witch's," a situation which in the face of everrecurring family tragedies could produce grief and guilt—and hostility as well.[13] And witches, unlike infidels and Jews, could be located in any town, and be held responsible for what had gone wrong. In fact, in places and times when there were many Jews available for scapegoating, there were correspondingly fewer witch-hunts.[14]

Scapegoating vulnerable persons also deflected tensions from coming to rest on social and political institutions, particularly those which made the poor so demanding and burdensome and the rich so resentful of them. Because of the witchcraft outlet, it has been said, "dysfunctional institutions were allowed to struggle on instead of being rapidly transformed."[15]

Mair points out that cross-culturally witchcraft most commonly is associated with quarreling, "not with naked midnight revels or keeping pet snakes." "It is malice and hatred," she observes, "and not sinister mystical powers, that disrupt the small community and that the villagers want to drive out, not foreseeing that they must endlessly return."[16] John Denny obviously had been a troublesome creature, unwilling to abide by the rules, as the innumerable court actions against him demonstrate. Amy Denny, likely the widow of this disturbing creature, also was notably cantankerous. So too was Rose Cullender, always on the alert to forcefully upbraid those whose vehicles brushed against her house as they made their way through town.[17] For Keith Thomas the important point is the paradox that, as in Lowestoft, it tended to be the accused woman who was morally in the right and the alleged victim who was in the wrong.[18]

Anthropologists point out that witchcraft accusations virtually never occur among nomadic and transient groups, but that they require a sedentary existence in which people cannot readily avoid one another. Tensions build up; witchcraft charges allow them to be resolved. Hunting groups, on the other hand, among whom there is little witchcraft, "have a great deal of latitude to vote with their feet, to walk out of an unpleasant situation."[19] Witchcraft accusations also are particularly likely to arise in small communities, especially those dependent on the land or the sea, where people must rely on each other. These contrast with urban sites, in which the autonomous nature of the nuclear family style and the separation of home and workplace defuse the build-up of antagonisms.[20] Nor are witchcraft accusations commonly directed against strangers, but rather fall upon neighbors and persons in some regular communication. Philip Mayer, commenting on witchcraft both in preliterate and western societies, puts the matter well:

> [W]itches and their accusers are individuals who ought to like each other but in fact do not. The two elements in the situation—the demand for a positive sentiment and the inability to provide it—are equally essential for the picture. . . . By the standards of society one ought to get on well with one's kinsman or neighbor or one's co-wife or maternal uncle. If in fact one cannot . . . the situation may become tense. When such a tension becomes insupportable, the only ways to

resolve it are reconciliation on the one hand or rupture on the other.[21]

To accuse someone of witchcraft—when that possibility has social sanction—also offers a legitimate outlet for aggression that cannot otherwise be satisfactorily expressed. "If one could convince oneself and others that these people were in fact witches, one was perfectly justified in kicking out the pauper, slamming the door on the neighbor and forcing mother-in-law to live in an outhouse on the scraps one put out for her," Gustav Henningsen notes. "When one had once established the fact that someone was no ordinary human being, but a witch, there were no limits to how far one could go in setting aside moral and social norms."[22] Amy Denny and Rose Cullender were close neighbors to their accusers and often involved intimately in their lives, but they were quarrelsome, demanding, and largely unprotected old women which made them ideal targets upon whom to deflect anxiety and anger when a child died, other children became fearsomely ill, and matters in the community seemed to have gotten sickeningly out of control.

The trial of the Lowestoft witches allows a close scrutiny of the relationships among the persons who were involved. David Butcher's demographic survey of the town in the seventeenth century found that there were about twenty "long-stay" families. These were extended family groups that had lived in Lowestoft for many generations. These long-stay families in the main belonged to the wealthier merchant class rather than to the lower classes. Then there were the "settlers," persons from elsewhere who, usually after their marriage, made the town their home. The males in these families often were yeomen or artisans. Finally, there were "transients," families that moved into town, stayed for a short period, and then moved on. Butcher calculated that during the seventeenth century, about 26 per cent of the population was transient in any given three-year period. Extend the period to twelve years and the migratory figure rises to 33 per cent.[23]

Only a very small proportion of the persons taking part in the witchcraft trial were from "long-stay families." The Landefieldes fully qualified; so did the Pacys, the only other long-stay family, except that Elizabeth Pacy had come to Lowestoft after her marriage.

The bulk of the accusations against Amy Denny and Rose Cullender, who themselves were "settlers," came from others in the same group: 65 per cent of the adults, either directly or indirectly involved in the trial, were "settlers," persons less secure in their identification with the community and perhaps less secure personally.

Samuel Pacy, of course, was the catalyst, the man who made it happen by lending his standing and his connections to the prosecution. Consistently, the accusers had themselves rejected those they would accuse: Samuel Pacy refused to sell herring to Amy Denny in the time-honored fashion immediately before his daughter became ill. Similarly, Edmund Durrant's wife had turned Rose Cullender aside in her request for herring right before her daughter Ann was stricken. Mary Chandler's daughter was bewitched shortly after the mother had engaged in the ignominious search of Cullender for witch marks; and John Soan's cart was "bewitched" after he had damaged the window of Cullender's house. So too had Robert Sherrington damaged Cullender property. Finally, Cornelius Landefielde complained against Denny after he failed to heed her request to fix the chimney in the dwelling she rented from him. In seventeeth-century English society, there was a form of *noblesse oblige* relied upon by people in the lower order of things. Those with status and rank were expected to fulfill obligations to those beneath them. The system also extended sideways, with expectations of neighborliness and mutual aid. The "victims" of witchcraft had failed to carry out their designated roles. They deflected their guilt on the women they had wronged; their impudent acts fade into insignificance in the face of the charges they level.

Historians of witchcraft, particularly in recent years, have been attending to the striking disparity in the number of accusations leveled against women compared to men. The lopsided ratio is most generally blamed on a deep misogynistic streak in societies of the time that combined with the particularly vulnerable situation of older women, especially widows such as Amy Denny and Rose Cullender.

King James I in *Daemonologie* indicated that women were twenty times more likely than men to be witches, and he thought he knew the reason why. Women were lured into witchcraft, James supposed, by three passions: curiosity, thirst for revenge for some wrongs deeply apprehended, or greedy appetite caused through great poverty. It is said that when James sought from his advisers ideas regarding why older rather than younger women engaged in witchcraft, Sir James Harrington replied with the "scurvey jest" that "the devil walketh in dry places."[24]

Of the some 100,000 persons said to have been executed for witchcraft in Europe between 1400 and 1700, at least 80 per cent were women.[25] In England, sixteen years before the Bury trial, John Gaule noted the strong tendency of "antient" crones to be charged with witchcraft:

Every old woman with a wrinkled face, a furrowed brow, a hairy lip, a gobber tooth, a squint eye, a squeaking voice, or scolding tongue, having a ragged coat on her back, a skullcap on her head, a spindle in her hand, and a dog or cat by her side, is not only suspected but pronounced for a witch.[26]

C. L'Estrange Ewen found women to outnumber men by 102 to seven among those executed on the Home Circuit for witchcraft.[27] Alan Macfarlane, in his study of Essex witchcraft prosecutions, discovered that 266 of the 291 persons accused were women. In regard to the twenty-five men, eleven were married to an accused woman or were named in a joint indictment with a woman. Macfarlane, however, specifically repudiates the idea of hostility between the sexes as basic to witch prosecutions, though he grants a "mounting hatred" toward women that was rooted in their social position. Macfarlane's explanation takes the following form:

If . . . witchcraft reflected tensions between an idea of neighborliness and the necessities of economic and social change, women were commonly thought of as witches because they were more resistant to such change. It was their social position and power which led to mounting hatred against them. As wives and mothers and gossips, [a contraction of God-sib, often referring to a god-parent][28] they tended to be more intimately connected with various village groups; they were the coordinating element in village society. People would feel most uneasy about them when society was segmenting. It was they who borrowed and lent most, and it was their curse which was most feared.[29]

This explanation concentrates on items which seem secondary to us. It was not the social role played by women that appears most significant, but rather the nature of the dominant male views and behaviors in regard to women that made them vulnerable to witchcraft charges and that led to the allocation of social roles and their valuation.[30] The derogation of women was reflexive, bound up in omnipresent religious beliefs. Note, among innumerable contemporary observations on the standing of women, those of William Gouge, writing about domestic life:

In handling the duties of the first forenamed couple [Adam and Eve], the Apostle beginneth with wives, and layeth down their particular duties in the first place. The reason of this order I take to be the *inferiority* of the wife to the husband. I do the rather take it to be so, because I observe it to be his usual method and order, first to declare the duties of inferiors, then of superiors.[31]

The hostility toward women associated with witchcraft prosecutions was most notoriously illustrated in the pages of *Malleus Maleficarum* (1487), a book that with truth has been called "morally obtuse and pornographically obsessive"[32] and "a most hideous document."[33] Compiled by two German Dominican Inquisitors, James Sprenger and Heinrich Kramer, *Malleus Maleficarum* noted with egregious etymological error that the word "feminine" derives from the roots *fe*, meaning "faith" and *minus*, meaning "less." The Dominicans also told why witches were to be found among women rather than among men:

> They are more credulous . . . more impressionable . . . they have slippery tongues . . . she is more carnal than a man . . . they are more prone to abjure the faith . . . women also have weak memories . . . and it is a normal vice in her not to be disciplined. . . . As she is a liar by nature, so in her speech she stings while she delights us. . . . There was a defect in the formation of the first woman, since she was formed from a bent rib . . . which is bent in the contrary direction to a man. And since through this defect she is an imperfect animal, she always deceives.[34]

The book is saturated with fears of omnivorous women, who are said to be bursting with carnality and unrelenting in their efforts to satisfy their lust. Its authors support their hatred of women with the authority of classical writers—thus Seneca's "wisdom": "A woman either loves or hates; there is no third grade. . . . When a woman thinks alone she thinks of evil." They also rely heavily upon the Bible, quoting Ecclesiasticus, for instance: "All wickedness is but little to the wickedness of women."

That men were not involved in any significant numbers in witchcraft was credited in *Malleus Maleficarum* to God's blueprint. "[B]lessed be the Highest Who so far preserved the male sex from so great crime," its authors wrote, "for since He was willing to be born and to suffer for us, therefore He has granted man this privilege." While the direct impact of *Malleus Maleficarum* on English witchcraft often is considerably overstated, the screed put forward doctrines that found their way, either subtly or directly, into later interpretations of the roots of witch behavior. Note, for instance, the explanation offered in 1627 by Richard Bernard for the predominance of women within the ranks of witches:

1 Satan is setting on these rather than on men, since his unhappy onset and prevailing with *Eve*.

2 Their more credulous nature, and apt to be misled and deceived.

3 For they are commonly impatient, and more superstitious, and being displeased, more malicious, and so more apt to bitter cursing, and farre more revengeful, according to their power, than men, and so her[e]in more fit instruments of the divell.

4 They are more tongue ripe, and lesse able to hide what they know from others, and therefore in this respect, are more ready to be teachers of witchcraft to others, and to leave it to children, servants, or to some others, than men.

5 And, lastly, because where they thinke they can command, they are more proud in their rule, and more busie in setting on worke whom they may command, than men. And therefore the divell laboureth most to make them witches; because they upon every light displeasure, will set him on work, which is that which he desireth. . . . [35]

The intersexual hostility associated with witchcraft charges might, as some psychoanalysts see the matter, have been rooted in competition and fear between men and women. Karen Horney, for instance, notes: "Everywhere the man strives to rid himself of his dread of women by objectifying it." " 'It is not,' he says, 'that I dread her; it is that she herself is malignant, capable of any crime, a beast of prey, a vampire, a witch, insatiable in her desires. She is the very personification of what is sinister.' "[36]

There is in this statement the suggestion that women are particularly likely to be victimized when female sexuality is most unbridled. Keith Thomas suggests that "the mythology of witchcraft was at its height when women were generally believed to be more voracious than men,"[37] an idea which then declined (as did witchcraft cases), to be replaced by the view that women were sexually passive and disinterested.

The close relationship between witchcraft and poisoning, another crime that was regarded (probably correctly in this instance) as falling largely within the female domain, is instructive. The biblical designation for a poisoner is the same term as that employed for a witch.[38]

Reginald Scot, the sixteenth-century rationalist who inaugurated the English crusade against witchcraft prosecutions, suspected that one basis for accusations of witchcraft lay in a fear of feminine recourse to poisons for revenge on persons oppressing them. "It appeareth," Scot noted, "that women have been the first inventers and greater practitioners of poisoning, and more naturalie given unto than men."[39] Macfarlane points out that "witchcraft, like murder by poison, was considered a crime apart."[40] The leading manual of the time for justices of the peace noted that for both (and only) cases of witchcraft and poisoning "half proofes are to be allowed."[41]

Male hostility might also eventually lead to witchcraft charges, other things being favorable, when women were seen to be standing in the way of male achievement or when they became redundant to overarching male goals. Alice Clark has suggested that economic rearrangements in the seventeenth century, particularly the emergence of work outside the home, freed men in England from the dependence on their wives that characterized domestic industry. "Henceforth," she notes, "the ideal of the subjection of women to their husbands could be pursued, unhampered by fears of the . . . lessening of the wife's economic efficiency."[42] Looking at the same situation from another angle—in terms of future rather than past trends—Christina Larner has argued that witchcraft accusations were a "rearguard action against the emergence of women as independent adults."[43] She notes that in 1662 Margaret Lister of Fife was described in her indictment as "a witch, a charmer, and a libber," and that "libber" had the same meaning then as today, "a liberated woman who insists on making an issue of it."[44]

Sir Thomas Browne, as we shall see, held a number of notably idiosyncratic and unflattering views of women. There is also evidence that Sir Matthew Hale might have been somewhat below the norm for the times in terms of his views of women.

Hale was twice married. His first wife—the mother of their ten children—plagued Hale by what he deemed to be her extravagance; it also was gossiped that she cheated on him.[45] In a treatise containing admonitions to his children, Hale warned that "an idle or expensive wife is most times an ill bargain, though she bring a great portion."[46] This attitude appears to be projected into Hale's judicial ruling in *Lord Leigh's Case* that the common law prerogative of a husband to impose *salva moderate castigatione* upon his wife was not meant to imply that he could beat her, but only that he might admonish her and confine her to the house if her extramural activities threatened his finances.[47] An unpleasant caricature of young gentlewomen by Hale further documents a certain distaste for at least some of that gender:

They make it their business to paint or patch their faces, to curl their locks, and to find out the newest and costliest fashions. . . . The morning is spent between the comb, the glass, and the box of patches; though they know not how to make provision for themselves, they must have choice diet provided for them. . . . [They] sit in a rubbed [cleaned] parlor till dinner. . . . After they go either to a ball or to cards. . . . They spend their parent's or their husband's money or estate on costly clothes, new fashions, and changeable entertainments. . . . Their house is their prison and they are never at rest in it, unless they have gallants and splendid company to entertain.[48]

In 1687, nine years after his first wife's death, Hale married a woman who Roger North says was a servant, though the Hale family maintained that while she lived with the Hales she did not work for them.[49] Richard Baxter indicated that "many censur'd him for choosing his last wife below his quality," and adds that the virtues of the match were that Hale's new wife was a person of "his own judgment and temper" "and for to please him . . . would not draw upon him the trouble of much acquaintance and relations."[50] Francis North had the Chief Justice saying that this marriage suited him as well as any other might, since with women "there is no wisdom below the girdle."[51] Such a remark does not sound like vintage Hale. Hale was fulsome in his praise of his second spouse, noting of this "deare wife" that he held for her "great and deserved love" and that she had been a most dutiful, faithful, and loving mate and a tender and loving mother to his children and grandchildren.[52]

Hale's obvious respect for his second wife, who in traditional fashion he appointed one of the executors of his estate,[53] and the compassion he showed John Bunyan's wife, have to be laid to his credit. But esteem for individual women need not be exculpatory of a course of action that can sensibly be interpreted as rooted in an indifference to, if not a disdain for, the humanity of women as a group. Such attitudes, as we shall see, characterized Hale's judicial position on rape and witchcraft.

On his death, Hale bequeathed to Lincoln's Inn, where he had been trained, what he called his "Black Book of the New Law," 502 folio pages written in law French and containing his summary of legal doctrines. Hale instructed that the volumes be bound in leather, chained, and neither disposed of nor lent out, except that any of his posterity were to be allowed to borrow one book at a time if they desired to make transcriptions, provided they gave adequate caution to restore it by a prefixed date. These books were, Hale proclaimed, "a treasure that are not fit for every man's view; nor is every man capable of making use of them."[54]

The manuscripts, written in Hale's hand, are arranged in alphabetical order, with the headings running from abuttals to withernam (the reprisal of other goods in lieu of those first named for recovery). The w's include warrant, watch and ward, as well as withernam—but there is no heading for witchcraft.

Rape—though it is one of the listings in the Black Book—is followed only by four inches of white space. However, in his monumental *Historia Placitorum Coronae* (usually shortened to *Pleas of the Crown*), Hale dealt with rape at some length and with enormous effect, and specifically linked it with witchcraft:

> but of all the difficulties of evidence, there are two sorts of crimes that give the greatest difficulty, namely rapes and witchcraft, wherein many times persons are really guilty, yet such an evidence, as is satisfactory to prove it, can hardly be found; and on the other side persons really innocent may be entangled under such presumptions, that carry great probabilities of guilt.[55]

In the same volume Hale set out what would become his famous stricture regarding rape, a view that would pervade Anglo-American jurisprudence for more than two hundred and fifty years. "It must be remembered," Hale wrote of rape, "that it is an accusation easily to be made and hard to be proved, and harder to be defended by the party accused, tho never so innocent."[56] He supplemented this observation by recital of a story from a Sussex court where he had presided in a case involving a rape accusation by a fourteen-year-old girl against a fifty-three-year-old man. The man cleared himself by demonstrating that he suffered from an ailment that made it "impossible he should have to do with any woman in that kind, much less commit a rape, for all his bowels seemed to be fallen down into those parts, that they could scarce discern his privities, the rupture being full as big as the crown of a hat."[57]

In virtually all regards, Hale's warning about rape is singularly inaccurate. Rape is not, and never has been, an easy charge to make and a difficult one to rebut. It certainly was not so in or before Hale's time. J.M. Kaye notes that, though the Statute of Westminster in 1285 decreed death for rape,[58] he could find no trace of an execution during the period between 1285 and 1330.[59] An earlier penalty of blinding and castration, solemnly noted by Bracton,[60] was so far from representative of actual practice, Kaye observes, that a thirteenth-century judge entertained friends with jokes about it,[61] a vignette with a contemporary ring. Joel Samaha's report about the Elizabethan period also has direct parallels today:

> Most women did not relish walking down their village streets if they had been sexually abused, especially in a society prone to assume that her invitation and not her partner's licentiousness prompted the assault in the first place, an assumption jurors usually acted on, judging by the number of accused rapists who were acquitted.[62]

In the United States, appellate court judges deciding rape cases paid continuous tribute to Hale's "impressive observations"[63] on the subject. Hale's stricture about being particularly wary of rape charges became, in the words of Judge David Bazelon, "one of the most oft-quoted passages in our jurisprudence."[64] In California, where judges were required until 1975 to charge juries deciding rape cases in terms adopted virtually verbatim from Hale's warning,[65] an 1856 appellate court opinion reflected the credence placed on that view almost two centuries after its first enunciation:

> There is no class of prosecutions attended with so much danger, or which afford so ample an opportunity for the free play of malice and private vengeance. In such cases the accused is almost defenseless, and courts, in view of the facility with which charges of this character may be invented and maintained, have been strict in laying down the rule which should govern their finding.[66]

It took the militant efforts of the 1970s feminist movement to erase Hale's dictates from the statute books and from the standardized instructions that judges recited to juries in rape trials.[67]

The irony is that Hale's dicta about rape being an easy charge to level and a notoriously difficult one to rebut, associated with his warning to be wary of "malicious and false witnesses,"[68] however wrong-minded in regard to rape, is eminently accurate concerning witchcraft, though neither in his writings nor in his behavior at Bury St. Edmunds did Hale display any comprehension of this fact. The tie between witchcraft and Hale's off-target caveats about rape is perhaps best illustrated in Keith Thomas' treatise on magic in which Thomas echoes, seemingly unaware of its origin in Hale's writings about rape, the following minatory observation: "The accusation [of witchcraft] was easy to make and hard to disprove." Witchcraft charges therefore, Thomas notes, "were particularly likely to be animated by malice or imposture."[69]

Writing in 1599, Samuel Harsnett, who was to become the Archbishop of York, suggested that youngsters accused others of witchcraft because "they have their brains baited and their fancies distempered with the imaginations and apprehensions of witches, conjurers, and fairies, and all that lymphatic chimera,"[70] while centuries later Jeffrey Russell would offer the idea that young persons were inclined to lodge charges of witchcraft because they were less sensitive than adults to the pain that such accusations would inflict on others.[71] Freudians, for their part, focus on pre-pubescent crises and the ability of accusations of witchcraft to permit young girls to vent murderous hostility against oppressive female elders, who in the normal course of events are for them powerful and unassailable.

Besides the Pacy sisters, nine- and eleven-year-old girls appear as accusers in several other cases in the annals of witchcraft. In 1597, at Pamplona in Spain, a pair of nine- and eleven-year-old girls told officials that they would provide details on witchcraft if their own involvement was overlooked. They said that witches could be recognized by examining their left eyes. The authorities took into custody all persons in the vicinity suspected to be witches, covered them completely with blankets and cloth, lined them up in the sun, and then uncovered only their left eyes. The girls had been separated, but the records insist that they were in total agreement on which of the suspects were guilty. As a result, more than 150 persons were imprisoned.[72] At the Salem trials, the initial accusations were laid by nine-year-old Betty Parris, the daughter of the town minister, Samuel Parris, and her eleven-year-old cousin Abigail Williams.[73]

That young girls, such as the Pacy sisters, figure prominently in accusations of witchcraft both in Europe and on the American continent (though, oddly, neither as accusers nor as principals in Russia)[74] has been used to challenge the theme of misogyny in witchcraft cases.[75] Francis Hill also suggests that in all western cultures, girls and women torment each other with words, looks, and silence, while boys and men tend to fight physically. "Women's habitually more covert tactics in any struggle for power make them more suspect when the methods of attack are invisible."[76] While there may be some underlying truth in Hill's ideas, Clive Holmes' observation seems more persuasive. "Women were simply better placed than men to describe the incidents and activities that conformed to the . . . perception of the nature of witchcraft as a criminal offense."[77]

But while intra-gender hostility likely contributed to what went on,[78] the true power in the trials invariably lay with men: the justices of the peace, the judges, the grand and petit jurors were all men. And at Bury St. Edmunds, it was Samuel Pacy, not his wife, who played the most prominent role in the prosecution of Amy Denny and Rose Cullender. Had the men of the community dismissed their wives' and daughters' reports as routine female mischief-making, the witch trials would not have occurred.

At Bury St. Edmunds it appears to be the quarrelsome character of the two women that aroused enmity. Most noticeably, the accused women were far more sharp-tongued than was considered proper and comfortable. Amy Denny was a woman ready with a venomous retort to slights. She threatened Dorothy Durrant when Durrant scolded her for putting her baby to the breast. This form of "nurturing" hostility between women has recently been interpreted as part of a "complex struggle within a patriarchal society" in which "both women stood in an uneasy relation to definitions of female identity which privileged nurturing behavior and well-governed speech."[79]

Denny also threatened the Pacys when they would not sell her herring; and she spoke scornfully, and perhaps threateningly, of the fate of the Pacy daughter when she was challenged while in the stocks. Relatively marginal women could, by such behavior, put the community on warning that they were not to be trifled with. There was something to be said for being regarded as a person who possessed diabolical skills; neighbors would be well advised to treat you with circumspection, lest they incur your wrath.[80] Writing about witchcraft among the Nyakyusa of Tanganyika, anthropologist Monica Wilson notes that witches are believed to attack people who are stingy with food, and "a direct connection is made between feeding potential witches a beef and protecting oneself against attack." After all, she writes, "[w]ell-fed pythons are quiet."[81] But this is a dangerous game and, if Amy Denny and Rose Cullender might understandably have played it, it could have been a main route that led them to the courtroom at Bury St. Edmunds.

The involvement of Denny and Cullender as a pair of witches raises interesting questions. No evidence is offered that the women collaborated in diabolic endeavors nor that they might have been affiliated in any way beyond an acquaintanceship probably inevitable in so small a town. Cullender is the more unlikely witch suspect since she belonged to a social stratum clearly a level or so above that of Denny. The Pacy girls apparently did not know Cullender, though they embraced her in their accusation, saying that two women had plagued them, but they knew the name of only one of them. The other, Cullender, they identified by her clothing. It seems reasonable that a sighting of Cullender on the street or elsewhere by the Pacys had included some information conveyed in the presence of the girls about her unsavory reputation that legitimized their outcry against her.

We do not know for certain, but the trial report suggests that Amy Denny was the prime target of the witchcraft accusations and that, while they were at it, the townsfolk pushed Cullender into the brew. For one thing, as we saw, she was cantankerous and in no position to offer much resistance to the allegations. Also, presumably, it made a stronger case—it was more fearsome and a bit more believable—to have two of the devil's disciples in the town's midst rather than just a lone crotchety old woman. The accusation of just one alleged witch runs the risk of appearing idiosyncratic and vengeful: with two, there are overtones of a significant diabolic presence.

What was in the minds of the young girls such as the Pacy sisters and the other accusers as they fell into fits, threw tantrums at the mention of Christ's name, clenched their fists so that the strongest man in the court could not open them, captured and burned enchanted insects, and scratched wildly at their alleged tormentors? Were they improvising, drawing upon the common knowledge about witchcraft, or were they disturbed to the point that they were acting out of impulses over which they had no conscious control?

There are three major explanations of the behavior of the accusers. First, of course, things could have been as they said they were; their behavior could have been the result of witchcraft. Though there are other reasonable explanations for the condition of the girls, these do not preclude the operation of supernatural forces. The situation is rather like that of the person who insists that waves that remain beyond our capability of discovery are emanating from electric sockets. We believe that the person making the claim is deluded, but we have no absolute assurance that we are correct. "[It] is a sound principle, and a widely accepted one," D.P. Walker has noted, "that historians should not ask their readers to accept supernatural phenomena." But regarding that point of view, he adds: "I cannot demonstrate its validity."[82] For us, more to the point is the fact that, whatever had happened to their accusers, Amy Denny and Rose Cullender did not voluntarily cause those things to happen. Both in this case, and over wide areas of geographic space and centuries of time, the lack of support for the ability of humans to do things that Amy Denny and Rose Cullender purportedly had done should reasonably exonerate them from suspicion of guilt.

There remain the possibilities that the accusers consciously improvised their story or that they suffered from a condition that gave rise to their behavior. In the latter realm, hysteria is almost invariably the diagnosis offered to explain why the young girls behaved as they did.

The presumption is that a diagnosis of hysteria relieves the accusers of personal responsibility or culpability for their contribution to the conviction of Amy Denny and Rose Cullender. But a great deal of difficulty inheres in seeking to separate malingering and fraud from hysteria. Part of the problem lies in the fact that psychiatrists, who today maintain professional control over diagnoses of hysteria, understandably balk at rendering retroactive judgments on the mental condition of persons based only on fragmentary and selected evidence. "We have too little information, especially about the past history and subsequent clinical course of these girls," Samuel Guze, one of the preeminent medical figures in the study of hysteria, indicated to us after reading the Bury St. Edmunds trial record.[83]

For another matter, there is the very complicated question of the limits, if any, of determinism: do any of us ever have an option to do as we please, and is hysteria merely another contributing factor that predetermines how we behave? How are we to decide and to differentiate the ingredients—incorporated from her social world—that led a very young girl to try to convince others that a bee had placed a large nail into her mouth? There are in this world, to use Gabriel Garcia Marquez' telling phrase, "learned lunacies,"[84] and the precise mechanisms that lead to the learning of such lunacies are not easily disassembled.

Other matters, however, could have been tested to try to see if the girls were faking. The vomiting of pins and nails, for instance—medically known as allotriophagy[85]—was susceptible to oversight; a number of witchcraft cases had arisen before the Bury trial in which episodes of vomiting were exposed by skeptics. In 1574, Agnes Briggs and Rachel Pinder, eleven and twelve years old, had been discovered inserting pins into their mouths, and then claiming, when they vomited them out, that they had been bewitched. They had to stand before the preacher at St. Paul's in London and acknowledge their deceit.[86]

Thirty years later, in 1604, Anne Gunter had sneezed, vomited and voided pins, sometimes several hundred at a time, and pins were said to have been exuded from her breasts and fingers. She was dispatched to the home of Henry Cotton, the Bishop of Salisbury, the father of nineteen children,[87] who marked certain pins in his house, and later identified them as the ones that Anne vomited. Charged with fraud, she confessed, and said that she had been put up to the charade by her father. Father and daughter both were charged with conspiracy, but there is no record of the outcome of that accusation.[88] Anne Gunter's duplicity had been suspected by Edward Jorden, the contemporary medical authority on hysteria, who reported his findings to James I in what apparently was the beginning of the King's skepticism, following his strong endorsement of witch-hunting in *Daemonologie*, which he had published in 1597.[89]

Forty years after the Bury case, in 1702, it would be observed in court that the pins produced by Robert Hathaway, a blacksmith's apprentice, were dry. Hathaway's hands were tied behind his back, and he was urged to vomit into a jar held before his mouth. No pins were forthcoming.[90] Then a search revealed packets of pins and nails in his pockets.[91] Hathaway was fined and sentenced to a year's imprisonment and three appearances in the pillory.[92]

Many writers on witchcraft of the time offered a variety of ingenious explanations for the phenomenon. Johan Weyer, a physician, had observed that there were no traces of hard or angular substances in the stomach of persons claiming to be bewitched before they vomited pins and other objects, and no trace of food on the things vomited, though the individuals had only recently eaten. Weyer, therefore, thought that the devil, with a quickness so astonishing that his hand deceived the human eye, placed the objects vomited in the mouth of the bewitched person, who never actually swallowed them.[93] Peter Binsfield, writing in 1591, believed that the devil put people to sleep, inserted objects through a hole that he made in their body, and then closed the hole.[94] For his part, Ignatius Lup Da Bergamo, an Italian who wrote in 1648, was persuaded that the devil introduced things into a body in a state of powder and then recomposed them as they were discharged.[95]

Many persons were so marvelously impressed by the vomiting of objects that so often was part of witchcraft accusations that they used the behavior as the basis for their conviction that witchcraft was a real thing. Joseph Glanvill, a leading figure in the work of the newly created Royal Society and a man deeply committed to the emergent scientific spirit,[96] berated those who doubted the authenticity of the vomiting episodes:

to think that pins and nails, for instance, can by the power of imagination be convey'd within the skin; or that imagination should deceive so many as have been witnesses in objects of sense, in all the circumstances of discovery; this, I say, is to be infinitely more credulous than the assertors of sorcery and demonick contacts.[97]

Glanvill's insistence on strict logic and scientific criteria to assess the truth of witchcraft charges deserves special emphasis because it contains so contemporary a ring, and because it indicates how craftily emotional commitment can masquerade as rational thought. Glanvill offers the following arguments as to why reasonable people ought to believe in witches:

> For these things were not done long ago, or at far distance, in an ignorant age, or among a barbarous people, they were not seen by two or three of the melancholic and superstitious, and reported by those who made them serve the advantage and interest of a party. They were not the passions of a day or night, nor the vanishing glances of an apparition; but these transactions were near and late, publick, frequent, and of divers years continuance, witnessed by multitudes of competent and unbyassed attestors, and acting in a searching and incredulous age: Arguments one would think to convince any modest and capable reason.[98]

At least one reader of the times, however, of considerably greater than modest and capable reason, remained unpersuaded. Samuel Pepys noted about Glanvill's work in his diary: "well writ, in good stile, but methinks not very convincing."[99]

Today, the swallowing of an astounding array of articles is occasionally reported, usually in cases diagnosed as severe medical illness. In 1960, for instance, a pathological swallower was said to have ingested 258 items, including a three pound piece of metal, twenty-six keys, three sets of rosary beads, sixteen religious medals, thirty-nine nailfiles, and eighty-eight assorted coins.[100] Writing about a present-day prison for women, Jessie O'Dwyer and Pat Carlen point out that inmates sometimes swallow safety pins and pieces of glass. "I've even known women to swallow batteries and bedsprings. . . . It happens so often that you could call it an epidemic."[101]

John Putnam Demos, in a careful review of the Salem trials marked by the application of insights from psychiatry, observes in a footnote that he had decided to avoid altogether dealing with the concept of hysteria: "the term . . . has been so widely and loosely applied that its meaning is now quite elastic—not to say, confused," Demos writes.[102] Demos' position is understandable. One writer has maintained that among the classifications of current psychiatry, "hysteria holds pride of place for ambiguity,"[103] and in his comprehensive review of the literature on hysteria Mark Micale notes that the phenomenon is characterized by "a speculative etiology, an obscure pathogenesis, and a flexible and far-flung symptomatology," all of which have made it "ideally suited to reflect a range of subjective nonscientific factors through the ages."[104] Micale avoids addressing the question of whether in fact hysteria is a "real" disease.[105]

Venturing into the intellectual quagmire that marks the vast and complicated medical literature on hysteria often seems like a journey to a land of babel. How does one deal, for instance, with the idea that the conscious simulation of hysteria, rather than an indication of malingering, is a strong indication of hysteria?[106] To discover a genuine dividing line between fraud and illness probably is an insurmountable task; nonetheless, it seems appropriate to examine information that bears upon the role that hysteria might have played in the witchcraft accusations against Amy Denny and Rose Cullender.

In ancient times, Greek doctors regarded hysteria only as a medical condition not as a personality disorder; the latter sense of the term did not arise until the late eighteenth century.[107] The disorder (if there is one) was confined to females. Hysteria was said by the Greeks to produce a sensation caused by the discontented womb wandering upward in the sufferer's body. Malodorous substances were inhaled and sweet substances placed by the vagina to induce the womb to return to its usual niche. Better yet, intercourse and conception were believed to represent effective tactics for coaxing the womb into a more amiable mood and having it move back to its proper place.[108] The womb, Plato observed, is an animal which longed to generate children,[109] while Hippocrates declared: "My prescription is that when virgins experience this trouble, they should cohabit with a man as quickly as possible. If they become pregnant, they will be cured."[110] As late as 1885, hysteria was treated in Paris by removal of the ovary, and in London and Vienna by surgical removal of the clitoris.[111]

Sigmund Freud and Jean Martin Charcot were the major proponents of the idea that hysteria was a personality disorder susceptible to medical therapy. In their first contribution, Josef Breur and Freud in 1893 reported that hysterical symptoms were the product of a traumatic accident or a frightening psychological event such as a hallucination or a distressing feeling of shame. These experiences were repressed in the unconscious but might be expressed by hysterical behavior. Breur and Freud, for instance, regarded hysterical vomiting as a possible expression of moral disgust.[112] Charcot's insistence that children suffering from hysteria ought above all else be separated from the "pernicious" influence of their parents has obvious relevance to the Bury trial.[113]

By 1908, however, a German alienist was insisting that within a few years the concept of hysteria would belong to history, since there was no such disease and there never had been.[114] But a more recent writer accurately notes that the term continues to outlive its obituaries.[115] Perhaps one reason is nostalgia. The term hysteria, the Frenchman Pierre Janet has written, seemingly more in terms of sentiment than science, "possesses so great and so beautiful a history that it would be painful to give it up."[116]

Hysteria today most usually is defined by those who still employ it diagnostically as a disorder with a medical basis, and not a conscious dramatic performance, yet it is said to be marked by "successful manipulation" and it has been noted that hysterical seizures do not occur when the patient "is alone or out of reach of an audience."[117] Hysterical fainting is distinguished from other syncopes by the fact that the person slumps rather than falls to the ground in order to avoid injury.[118]

A survey has demonstrated a pervading lack of agreement among experienced clinicians about specific criteria which can identify the presence of hysteria, though histrionic behavior was the most often mentioned symptom.[119] Hysterics are said to give the impression that they are "always on stage" and have difficulty "distinguishing fantasy from reality."[120] The condition is believed to result from an emotional conflict and to offer some subtle gain to the sufferer.[121] At the same time, feminists, with reason, have echoed the observation of Paul Chodoff and Henry Lyons that hysteria is "a picture of women in the words of men, and . . . what the description sounds like is a caricature of femininity."[122] Another writer believes that the idea of hysteria was used to stigmatize women as weak or wicked and simultaneously to protect them from blame by explaining such undesirable traits as the product of illness beyond their control.[123]

Robert E. Kendell offers an explanation of why hysteria appears to be particularly prominent in the young:

> [T]he adoption of a role in which one is dependent and cared
> for comes most readily to those who have only recently been

required to forego the privileges of childhood and are least experienced at coping with the demands of the adult world. . . . Manipulative behavior is essentially a strategy for achieving power in the context of a role which does not normally provide it. . . . [124]

Kendell further suggests that successful manipulation "requires a degree of willing acquiescence on the part of the person manipulated" and that therefore it is no accident that so many hysterics are strikingly good-looking.[125]

The question regarding whether the girls who accused older women of witchcraft were vicious brats or victims of hysteria has been discussed at length in regard to the Salem trials. The inconclusiveness of that thoroughly aired debate suggests that there is no resolving the question, presuming, of course, that it is worth resolving. Just a snippet of the argument merits consideration. Charles Upham, a later mayor of Salem, thought that the girls there engaged in "splendid acting," marked by "manifestations of contrivance, or deliberate cunning and cool malice." "It is dreadful to reflect on the enormity of their wickedness," Upham adds.[126] Others have joined the denunciatory chorus. Rossell Robbins points out, again referring to Salem, that "never . . . even during the hangings, was the slightest compunction shown. . . . They knew exactly what they were doing,"[127] while Marion Starkey thought that the accusing girls at Salem were "having a wonderful time" because their "infantile cravings for attention" were being satisfied.[128]

Among English writers, Francis Hutchinson thought that witchcraft accusers typically displayed "counterfeit" symptoms,[129] a position echoed by Sir Walter Scott, who believed that it was "terrible to see how often the little impostors, from spite or in mere gaiety of spirit . . . made shipwreck of men's lives."[130] C. L'Estrange Ewen blamed "spite on some hated elder" as well as a desire for "self-glory" for the accusations.[131]

Cotton Mather, however, attacked those who suggested that the behavior of the girls at Salem was play-acting. Mather deemed such an idea "most unchristian and uncivil, yea a most unreasonable thing to imagine that the fitts of the young women were mere impostures." "Scarce any," Mather added, "but people of a particular dirtiness will harbor such uncharitable thoughts."[132] Other writers have relied upon hysteria to explain what prompted the accusations. The behavior of the Salem girls, Chadwick Hansen insisted, was not fraudulent but pathological,[133] a view echoed by Ernest Caulfield, who found the same

children "not cold-blooded malignant brats," but rather "sick children
. . . living in fear for their very lives and the welfare of their immortal
souls."[134]

Our view of what has been written about hysteria by physicians
and historians of medicine—considered in regard to the proceedings
at Bury St. Edmunds—is that the term "hysterical," as C.D.
Marsden, a neurologist, has noted, "is often applied as a diagnosis to
something that the physician does not understand." "It is used," he
adds, "as a cloak for ignorance."[135] The diagnosis can also be a
weapon. "The definition and diagnosis of hysteria had a function
similar to that found in the prosecution of witchcraft," David Allison
and Mark Roberts maintain. "It sought to eradicate outbursts of
nonconformity and emotionally threatening conduct of women."[136]
Eliot Slater, a British doctor, who has been among the severest critics
of the concept, seems to us to be correct when he writes: "Unless a
doctor is convinced that the syndrome exists he will never see it, just
as ghosts are only seen by those who believe in them."[137] In this
regard it is worth remembering that one of the best-known observations uttered about witch-hunts was that of a Spanish inquisitor
whose good sense dramatically reduced the prosecutions in his
country. "I have observed," Alonso de Salazar Frias said almost half a
century before the Bury trial, "that there were neither witches nor
bewitched in a village until they were talked about and written
about."[138]

A hybrid explanation, which we favor, is that at Bury St. Edmunds
the accuser's actions were marked by elements of what currently is
called hysteria, however loosely defined, as well as by play-acting. We
agree with Thomas Szasz that the language of the phenomena defined
as hysteria is a form of rhetoric and a method of persuasion and coer-
cion that cannot convey information accurately, but can induce
feelings and promote action in others.[139] What likely lay behind the
role of the young girls involved in the Lowestoft witch case, as we see
it, is that, driven by fear as well as by other motives, they fell back
upon a repertoire of responses that they had absorbed as possible
behaviors for someone in their situation. These actions were reinforced by those around them, who themselves, for their own reasons,
now helped shape what was taking place. Thereafter, the girls did the
kinds of things necessary to sustain what continuously developed into
a satisfying scenario—though they also now found themselves so
deeply involved that they could not effectively stop what they had
started.

Francis Hutchinson, writing about the Bury trial, saw essentially the process we have suggested as characteristic of many witchcraft proceedings:

> Though a distemper at first be surprising, and puts the afflicted person beyond the thoughts to trickery, yet a little time makes them familiar with their calamity, and when they find themselves come safely out of the strange fits, and begin to have the use of their thoughts while they are in them, they manage their calamity to their own interest.[140]

The recent testimony of an eighteen-year-old female comprehensive school student in London who set off an epidemic of "falling" among eight other girls in her classroom accords with what we believe to be the pattern that unfolded in the Lowestoft witch case centuries earlier: we have italicized the sentences that seem important in interpreting the phenomenon.

> At the end of Christmas term I fainted. At the time I was sitting my mock "O" level examinations, was very depressed, and slept little. I fainted several times that term over a period of a month.
>
> I enjoyed the attention the malady afforded me and the general concern of everyone around me. At the beginning of the next term I fell again, but this time it was not genuine. Again I received much attention and fell several more times. *I was extremely ashamed of my deceitfulness and it became out of my control and I found it impossible to stop.* I used it as an escape from the problems I could not face at home and at school, and became completely wrapped up in it. It was the only thing from which I gained pleasure. . . .
>
> At first, I would not admit to myself that it was not genuine. I was convinced that, because I really had fainted several times, that I was still doing so. *When I did face up to the fact that it was false, I couldn't stop.*[141]

Certainly, the manner in which all the accusers evaded courtroom testimony at Bury St. Edmunds supports the idea that, consciously or unconsciously, they were structuring matters in a way best designed to protect themselves from exposure: after all, while accusations of witchcraft could not be disproved by those accused, neither could they be self-evidently demonstrated by those making the allegations. It was wise, therefore, to place oneself as far as possible from the direct scrutiny of those who might press for firmer proof of the allegations or might challenge inconsistencies in the tale being told. At the Bury St. Edmunds trial, the young accusers had become enmeshed in a deadly game from which they were unable to extricate themselves readily; therefore, employing some intricate combination of conscious and unconscious tactics they had recourse to the only self-saving behaviors they believed were available to them.

6

A man of bilious
complexion and a pedant
with power

How did Sir John Keeling, the disbeliever, and Sir Thomas Browne, the scholarly doctor, come to the parts they played in the Bury St. Edmunds trial? Browne, the intellect and the proclaimed skeptic, might have been presumed to stand back and question the accuracy of the allegations and the integrity of the proceedings, especially the experiment to prove the women guilty. Keeling, fearful, bombastic, and intolerant of opposition, might reasonably have `been expected to have taken an aggressive position in condemning the accused women. Both, however, defied such expectations. What might explain the counter-intuitive outcome?

Though subordinate to Hale at the time of the Bury St. Edmunds trial, Keeling would move past him in the judicial ranks when he became Chief Justice of the King's Bench three years later, in 1665. He held that position until his death in May 1671, when Hale was named to replace him. Subsequent judgment on that succession is epitomized in the colorful language of Lord Campbell, himself a chief justice and lord chancellor almost two centuries later, in his *Lives of the Chief Justices*:

> We pass from one of the most worthless of Chief Justices to one of the most pure, the most pious, the most independent, and the most learned—from Keylinge to Sir Matthew Hale.[1]

So uncompromising is Campbell that he insists that Keeling's death occurred "to the great relief of all who had any regard for the due administration of justice," and then viciously adds: "No interest can be felt respecting his place of interment, his marriages, or his descendants."[2]

Sir John Keeling had been born in Hertford in July 1607, which made him two years older than Hale, and four months short of fifty-

135

five at the time of the Bury St. Edmunds trial.[3] He was educated at Trinity College, Cambridge, and followed his father, also a lawyer (as his own son would be), to the Inner Temple. By the time he was thirty, Keeling had accumulated enough wealth to be assessed "for the buylding & erecting of two pesthouses & for the daylie relief of those persons that have or shall be visited with the foulness of the plague."[4]

Early in the civil war Keeling was incarcerated in Windsor Castle because of his support for the King's cause. The imprisonment probably did not last until the restoration of Charles II, though Lord Clarendon, Charles' chancellor, told the King that Keeling was "a person of eminent learning [and] eminent suffering, [who] never wore his gown [practiced law] after the rebellion, but was always in gaol."[5]

Keeling was among the first batch of serjeants-at-law appointed by the King on his return from exile in 1660, receiving the rank on July 4. He was knighted in late March 1661, and appointed a justice of the King's Bench on June 18, 1663. Two years later he presided at the Old Bailey during the trial of a group of Quakers, and his bullying so incensed them that they published a pamphlet, setting forth its theme in the title, *The Innocency and Conscientiousness of the Quakers Asserted and Cleared from the Evil Surmises, False Aspersions, and Unrighteous Suggestions of Judge Keeling.* Among other things, Keeling had charged the jury that the Quakers were not worthy of pity, "for they are a stubborn sect, and the King hath been very merciful with them." "It is hoped," he added, "that the purity of the Church of England would ere this have convinced them, but they will not be reclaimed." The failure of the Quakers to swear oaths, Keeling told the jury, was subversive, since "without swearing we can have no justice done, no law executed; you may be robbed, your houses broke open, your goods taken away, and be injured in your persons, and no justice or recompense can be had, because the facts cannot be proved." Soon, said Keeling, the Quakers might be up in arms, a result of plots hatched when they held their secret meetings.[6]

Keeling was known for dispatching judicial business at a furious rate: it is said that he raced through sixty-five cases in three days at one assize, and that at the spring and summer assizes in 1670 he wound up the Crown business in less than a day.[7] Hale, for his part, was known for the diligence and painstaking manner with which he did his job. "He had one peculiarity," the Earl of Birkenhead observes of Hale, "in that he encouraged counsel to correct his inaccuracies when summing up."[8] Hale was concerned to convey a sense of fairness: a transcript of a trial he conducted has him proclaiming: "If you have any more witnesses call them, and they shall be heard, and do not say when I am gone that your witnesses could not be heard."[9]

In *A Report of Divers Cases in Pleas of the Crown*, a collection of some of Keeling's decisions, which appeared posthumously in 1708, there is an episode that indicates particularly well the uncompromising frame of mind that Keeling could bring to bear on his judicial work. The situation involved the practice of sparing most felons from death if they were able to read, or, more often, to pretend to read the first verse of the fifty-first psalm, dubbed the "neck verse." If they were deemed to be literate, this supported the fiction that they were clerics, possessing a legal right to be spared the gallows. Judges routinely allowed illiterates to claim "benefit of clergy." But Keeling would have none of it:

At the . . . assizes at Winchester, the clerk appointed by the bishop to give clergy to the prisoners, being to give it to an old thief; I directed him to deal clearly with me, and not to say *legit* in case he could not read; and therefore he delivered the Book to him, and I perceived the prisoner never looked upon the Book at all, and yet the bishop's clerk, upon the demand of *legit* or *non legit*, answered *legit*; and thereupon I wished him to consider, and told him I doubted [not] he was mistaken, and bid the Clerk of the Assizes . . . not to record it, and I told the parson he was not the judge whether he read or no, but a ministerial officer to make a true report to the court. And so I caused the prisoner to be brought near, and delivered him the Book, and then the prisoner confessed he could not read; whereupon I told the parson he had reproached his function; and unpreached more that day than he could preach up again in many days; and because it was his personal offense and misdemeanor, I fined him 5 marks. . . . [10]

It is on this same issue—benefit of clergy—that Alan Cromartie faults Matthew Hale, calling him "politically obtuse" for standing up for the practice. "[A] sincerely committed reformer," Cromartie maintains, "would hardly have defended this abuse, still less have remarked to shore up this position, that 'tis in the parent's power to breed his child to read!"[11]

Keeling was in poor health during the final three years of his life: "sick the whole term," a law reporter noted in regard to the Michaelmas assize of 1670. On May 9, 1671, at the age of 63, he died, or, as a contemporary put it, he had an old statute executed upon him, "a writ of *statum est omnibus semel mori*" (it has been ordained for all men to die once). The cause of death was given as "lethargy," a form of apoplexy, which prompted the same writer to observe that it "was most to be admired that a man of so bilious a complexion should have so phlegmatic a conveyance to the other world."[12]

Besides the Bury trial, there are several major instances in which Keeling came into contention with Hale, and a number of others in which they acted in a very different manner in regard to a similar set of circumstances. A sample of these episodes helps tie down the character-istic manner in which the men dealt with legal problems and the habits of mind they brought with them to the Bury witchcraft trial.

Whatever reputed claim Keeling may have on immortality must lie in the role he played in the trial that led to John Bunyan's imprison-ment. In 1660, Bunyan, a few months short of thirty-two years of age, was indicted under the Elizabethan law against conventicles, which, among other matters, decreed that any person absenting himself from his parish church for a month could be committed to prison until he conformed. When first charging him, the authorities sought to reason with Bunyan: "How can you understand the scriptures when you know not the original Greek?" he was asked. Bunyan was told that he made "poor simple ignorant people . . . neglect their calling," a remark which prompted him to insist that it was these very folk who had need of his ministry. Asked to desist from preaching, on the promise that he would be released, Bunyan refused, and was placed in jail for about seven weeks prior to his trial.

Keeling, sitting with four other judges during Epiphany in 1661, presided at that quarter sessions trial at the old chantry chapel of Herne, which served for the shire hall in Bunyan's Bedford.[13] The trial is reported in *A Relation of My Imprisonment*, the printed version of a manuscript discovered only in 1756, when Bunyan's great grand-daughter offered it for sale.[14] The report is believed to be virtually a verbatim transcript of the proceedings, probably written in prison immediately after the trial, perhaps in the form of a pastoral letter to console and fortify Bunyan's Bedford congregation.[15]

Keeling (Bunyan spells the name Keelin in his report) first wanted to know why Bunyan had not gone to the parish church. "Because," Bunyan said, "I did not find it commanded the word of God." Keeling countered by saying that God had commanded his followers to pray. "[B]ut not by the Common Prayer-book," Bunyan answered. Keeling, obviously caught up in the interchange, asked: "How then?" and was told: "[W]ith the spirit. As the Apostle saith, 'I will pray with the spirit and with understanding.'" That could be done, Keeling offered, with the common prayer book. But Bunyan insisted that the common prayer book was the work of mere mortals, that it did not derive from "the motions of the Holy Ghost, within our hearts."

Keeling, still curious, persisted by asking what Bunyan had against the common prayer book, though now he warned him, in what appears to be a not unfriendly manner, to watch his words: "Let me give you one caution; take heed of speaking irreverently of the common prayer book: For if you do so, it will bring great damage upon yourself." Another of the judges, however, insisted that Bunyan be silenced: "He will do harm; let him speak no further." But Keeling ruled otherwise: "No, no, never fear him, we are better established than so; he can do no harm, we know the common prayer book hath been ever since the Apostle time, and is lawful to be used in church."

This historical reference by Keeling has been a standing jest among Bunyan biographers ever since: it is ridiculed as "astonishingly illiterate"[16] and a "ludicrous overstatement,"[17] and also labelled "a fact apparently not known to any church historian prior to Kelynge,"[18] though one commentator, James Froude, suggests kindly that we should not take Bunyan's report literally, and that perhaps Keeling had said—or meant—that parts of the prayer book, such as the Apostles' Creed, had been in such continuous use, which would have been "strictly true."[19]

Bunyan demanded to be told the precise citation in the scriptures that commanded use of the common prayer book: if shown such a passage he would use the book. At this point, several of the justices turned on Bunyan, one accusing him of worshipping Beelzebub, and another insisting that he was deluded and possessed by the devil. Bunyan, ignoring the vituperation, began to pray, but Keeling interrupted, demanding that Bunyan stop his "canting," and his "pedlers French,"* which drew from the accused the observation: "The Lord open his eyes!"

Then Keeling and Bunyan began to argue about the scriptural basis of Bunyan's right to preach. Bunyan cited chapter and verse for his view, while Keeling lectured on the biblical theme, "*As every man hath received the gift*," interpreting this to mean that Bunyan ought to stick

---

* Pedlar's French: "the language used by vagabonds and thieves among themselves; . . . hence unintelligible jargon" (OED, 2nd edition, 1989, Vol. XI, p. 427). Paul Slack notes that references to such canting slang outside of literary contexts are extremely rare (Slack, *Poverty and Policy in Tudor and Stuart England*, London: Longman, 1988, p. 96).

to his trade of tinkering, and let the divines do the preaching. But Bunyan went further into the verse, saying that it called upon all who felt compelled to preach to do so. Only to their families, retorted Keeling. If what a man said was worthwhile for his family, Bunyan replied, surely he ought to be able to carry the message further.

In the end, Keeling lost patience, saying, according to Bunyan, that "he was not so well versed in Scripture as to dispute, or words to that purpose." He now wanted Bunyan to plead to the indictment. Bunyan granted that he had conducted meetings, both to pray and to encourage members to support one another, and that "we had the sweet comforting presence of the Lord among us for our encouragement, blessed be his name therefore." Finally, he noted: "I confessed myself guilty no otherwise."

Keeling pronounced the verdict:

> [H]ear your judgment. You must be had back again to prison, and there lie for three months following; at three months' end, if you do not submit to go to church to hear divine service, and leave your preaching, you must be banished the realm: And if, after such a day as shall be appointed to you to be gone, you shall be found in this realm, or be found to come over again without special license from the King, you must stretch by the neck for it, I tell you plainly.

Laxity, indulgence, or some other circumstance kept the authorities from implementing the dictate of the statute and transporting Bunyan to America three months later.[20] Instead, Bunyan would use his prison time to write *Pilgrim's Progress*, and in it he would draw upon his trial experience to portray Lord Hategood, the judge at Vanity Fair who sentences Faithful to death for having, among other things, "made commotions and divisions in the town, and won a party to their own most dangerous opinions, in contempt of the law of their Prince."[21]

Though Keeling is usually said to be caricatured in the portrait of Lord Hategood, some glossators of *The Pilgrim's Progress* have suggested that the fury and vitriol of the judge more accurately reflected the legendary courtroom mockery and venom of Judge George Jeffreys, who was at work at the time Bunyan was writing, though the "Bloody Assize" at which Jeffreys unleashed a barrage of drunken vituperation against those on trial did not take place until nearly a decade after publication of *The Pilgrim's Progress*.

Matthew Hale, as we noted earlier, entered the picture (as reported by Bunyan) when he responded indulgently to Bunyan's second wife,

Elizabeth, still a teenager, when she approached him in Bedford during the midsummer assize in 1661. Elizabeth, seeking a means to have Bunyan released, had made a difficult trip to London, where she was told to seek aid from the assize judges. She was first fobbed off by Hale. The next day she threw a petition into the coach of one of Hale's colleagues, who snapped at her that her husband would not be set free until he promised not to preach. Once again, she tried to approach Hale, but was intercepted by another judge.[22]

Finally, Elizabeth made her way into the Swan Chamber, a room in the inn where the justices were in session, and confronted Hale, explaining pitifully that she was the stepmother of four children, one of them blind, and that, with Bunyan imprisoned, she was dependent on charity. Hale's advice that she sue for a pardon or a writ of error apparently went unheeded: Elizabeth wanted action, not information about the procedures that she might pursue, and she was bold enough to accuse the judges of discrimination: "Because he is a tinker, and a poor man, therefore is he despised, and cannot have justice."[23] The kind demeanor that Hale showed drew praise from Bunyan, who reports that Hale offered his advice "very mildly," saying that he was "sorry, woman, that I can do thee no good," while his fellow justices intruded harsh and critical observations on Bunyan's case.[24]

On the record, and it is Bunyan's record, Keeling's performance, though hardly admirable, seems less vicious than the reputation he gained from it. Apart from telling Bunyan to cease the canting, and calling the Puritan parlance which Bunyan employed "pedlers French," Keeling showed himself almost genial.[25] Certainly, his attitude fell far short of the bitter contempt that could mark attitudes toward nonconformity. One writer, for instance, has noted that at the time nonconformists were accounted "the pudenda of the nation" and looked upon "not as sons but bastards, and taken no more account of than a man makes of vermin."[26]

Keeling would behave much more nastily and peremptorily in other judicial situations: as Monica Furlong points out in regard to Bunyan's trial, there was at least an element of aggravation that might mitigate his intolerance:

> It must also be said that the Puritans could be insufferably priggish when brought to justice. Regarding themselves as martyrs for their faith after the manner of the Apostles and their followers, they tended towards a self-righteous manner and bearing that were intensely irritating, and which helped to guarantee their martyrdom.[27]

Keeling's behavior toward Bunyan is also granted some exculpation by Christopher Hill, the preeminent English historian, who has noted that "the fact that we know the end of the story enables us to speak of [Keeling's] overreacting." Hill points out that the jittery rulers of Bedfordshire had some basis for their uneasiness about the likelihood of a political uprising against the King.[28]

There are, therefore, saving elements in Keeling's behavior toward Bunyan. At the regicide trials, however, where he had an opportunity to gain revenge for what had happened to him during the interregnum, Keeling was unreservedly mean and ill-natured. Eleven men were condemned to die (and ten were executed) for treason in these 1660 trials for their part in the execution of Charles I. Keeling's role, a temporary appointment, was that of King's serjeant, an especially high office. Keeling acted as supporting prosecuting counsel against the regicides. He was a state counsel in the trial of Colonel Francis Hacker, who had signed the warrant for the King's execution and commanded the guard during Charles' trial and at his beheading,[29] and that of William Heveningham, who had been one of the men appointed to try the King, but had attended only three hearings, and then had refused to sign Charles' death warrant.[30] Condemned to be executed, Heveningham was spared by the King and died while he was confined at Windsor Castle.

Sir Henry Vane was not a regicide but had been excluded from the Act of Indemnity by a Parliament in which he had fierce enemies:[31] it was said of him that he wished to rule the world but otherwise without ambition.[32] As had Bunyan, Vane wrote his own account of the proceedings against him. He portrays Keeling as a rabid, jeering antagonist, a fanatic whose conduct was unfeelingly harsh and insulting.

Vane complained bitterly that Keeling "had often showed a very snappish property towards the prisoner" and he maintained that on the day of the arraignment Keeling had told a judicial colleague that "though we know not what to say to him, we know what to do to him."[33] Vane was executed for treason on June 14, 1662, three days short of three months following the hanging of Amy Denny and Rose Cullender. His status as a martyr was enhanced by a biography published soon after his death that included a sonnet of tribute by John Milton.[34]

In the case of the bawdy house riots—tried in 1668 as *Rex v. Messenger*—we again see a more restrained and benign attitude expressed by Matthew Hale juxtaposed with Keeling's uncompromising toughness toward a group that, however remotely, might represent a threat to the King's peace. Hale was more relaxed about such behaviors, perhaps because he had done well for himself during the civil war, moving up through the judicial ranks. Keeling had spent much time in prison and had been faced with the loss of his property by what he regarded as usurpers; he would not tolerate a specter of rebellion.

The word "riot" had first made its appearance in an English statute in 1361. That act gave authority to keepers of the peace to pursue, arrest, chastise, and imprison "offenders, rioters, and other barators [brawlers]."[35] Those responsible for the law probably had in mind the unruly behavior of soldiers returning from the French war, men who resorted to the pillaging and robbing they had practiced overseas.[36] But treason, as Pollock and Maitland note in their history of English criminal law, always had been "a crime which has a vague circumference, and more than one center."[37]

The *Messenger* case concerned the indictment for high treason of leaders of a riot that involved thousands of people over a five-day period. Members of the mob ripped down bawdy houses at several sites, but most notably in Moorfields, near London, "a most noisome and offensive place . . . burrowed and crossed with deep stinking ditches . . . and common sewers."[38]

The *State Trials* report portrays the episode as little more than a high-spirited, if reckless, enterprise. Rioters carried clubs and some held a green apron attached to a pole as their rallying flag. Peter Messenger, one of the leaders, waved a drawn sword, crying, "Down with the bawdy houses." Some bawdy houses were destroyed, and a constable who sought to interfere with the crowd was beaten.[39]

The standard interpretation of the event has been that it "was well known to the court that the affair was merely an apprentices' riot,"[40] a bursting forth of pent-up energy that took place each year before Easter. But a recent, more careful examination of the circumstances indicates that, though he assuredly overreacted, Keeling had some basis for believing that the riot represented a threat to the King. Tim Harris, analyzing manuscript material, points out that brothel riots often were used to make political statements, and he insists that the demonstration was essentially a protest against the irreligion of a licentious royal court, aggravated by the failure of the plans for religious liberty, a failure reflected in the 1662 Act of Uniformity (largely drawn up by Keeling), which, among other matters, declared that the Book of Common Prayer had to be used in all public worship. The Act of Uniformity had drowned hopes for religious tolerance anchored in the liberal Comprehension Bill, which had been drafted by Hale the previous January, but had been sidetracked in the House of Commons. It had led to the removal of hundreds of clergymen from their posts, including one-third of London's ministers. Harris indicates that the slogans of the rioters were distinctly political and that the government was convinced that the affair had been instigated by former soldiers in Cromwell's army.[41]

Keeling obviously agreed that the riots had a deeper root than bawdy house bashing. "These people do pretend that their design was against bawdy-houses," he told the jury,[42] but theirs was "a strange kind of reformation." "If a rabble come and say . . . this [man] keeps a bawdy house, and would pull it down: this is a mad reformation."[43] In his own report of the case Keeling used the phrase: "for then no man were safe,"[44] words very similar to those he would utter at Bury St. Edmunds, when he declared that to give credence to the witchcraft charges of the young girls could indiscriminately expose everyone to such unsupported allegations.

Keeling found the riot a "desperate consequence," and declared that "we must make this for a public example."[45] He explicitly explained the basis for his concern:

> We are but newly delivered from rebellion, and we know that that rebellion first began under the pretense of religion and law . . . therefore we have great reason to be very wary that we fall not into the same error.[46]

The four King's Bench judges and seven judges of the common law courts met in Keeling's chambers to discuss whether the acts at Moorfields and other sites represented high treason or were only a felony. Hale held out against the other ten, all of whom agreed with Keeling that the malefactors were guilty of treason. Later, despite his reservations ("it seemed but an unruly company of apprentices . . . usually repressed by officers"[47]), Hale would refer to the verdict in the *Messenger* case without censure and with a certain respect for what had been declared to be the law. Messenger and three others were executed in the barbarous tradition of drawing, hanging, and quartering. Though Keeling pressed for conviction, Alfred Havighurst gives him credit for taking care to distinguish between the ringleaders and others, and to acquit or to direct lesser sentences for the remaining twenty-five persons indicted.[48]

Keeling's final appearance on the center stage of judicial controversy involved his bullying and fining grand and petit jurors. This was not an uncommon practice among assize judges, though Hale, when Chief

Baron of the Exchequer, stayed such fines whenever they had been escheated.[49]

In 1554, the entire common-law bench had ruled that assize judges could not fine or imprison jurors. But some judges ignored the ruling, and others at times bound jurors over to the Star Chamber, which punished a total of forty juries during the second half of the sixteenth century.[50] The charge typically was that they willfully had found a verdict contrary to the evidence, which usually meant that the judge believed the jurors had been bribed, or that they had acted for personal gain or out of favoritism. In most instances, the jurors defended themselves by insisting that they had not behaved corruptly but that they possessed evidence of their own which overrode what they had heard in court.[51] This defense coincided with Hale's opinion that juries could not be convicted of malfeasance "because [it is] impossible that all the circumstances of the case, that might move the jury to acquit a prisoner, would be brought in evidence."[52] Hale's view clearly is much more in keeping with today's standards of justice than that of Keeling.

Keeling's harassment of jurors was so brazen that it prodded Parliament to take up the matter in its 1667 session.[53] As he often was, Keeling had been downright reckless in his choice of those he antagonized. Earlier that year, he had berated Sir Hugh Wyndham, a member of Parliament, after the grand jury of which Wyndham was the foreman declared that a death it examined had resulted from misadventure. Keeling insisted that as a point of law the grand jury had to find a true bill or return an ignoramus (we do not know) verdict. The grand jurors refused to do either, and Keeling thereupon fined each member £20, though he later remitted the levy.[54] Keeling also told Wyndham that "he was now his servant, and that he would make him stoop."[55]

Another case of jury fining by Keeling involved a weaver who had been delegated by the shop master to oversee his workers and to correct them if they neglected their tasks. One of the workers, a young boy, had failed to wind some yarn spindles; the supervisor beat him about the head with a broomstaff and the boy shortly died from his injuries. The jury found that the killing, lacking malice aforethought, was manslaughter. Keeling told the jurors that he would fine each of them £2 if they did not return a verdict of murder. They acquiesced and the supervisor was hanged.[56] At times, Keeling showed a powerful streak of sentiment for the underdog when the underdog had been the passive victim of harm. When those without power acted forcefully, however, as Bunyan and the Moorfields rioters, Keeling lost sympathy for them.

For his highhanded tactics with jurors, Keeling was summoned before a committee of the House of Commons, which reported at the end of 1667 "that he hath used an arbitrary and illegal power" which "tend to the introducing of an arbitrary government," and that he "hath undervalued, vilified, and contemned Magna Carta."[57] This last of the charges arose from a report that Keeling had dismissively waved aside England's sacred legal document with the observation, "Magna Carta, Magna Farta."[58] But the story may be apocryphal since the comment was by then mildewed, having earlier been credited to Cromwell,[59] though Keeling certainly equivocated mightily in his defense against this charge, saying only that "he did not remember, nor believe that he said those words, yet he was not absolutely certain that he did not speak them, but it might be possible, Magna Carta being often and ignorantly pressed upon him."[60]

When the House was on the verge of adopting a resolution against Keeling, he asked to be allowed to address it. Samuel Pepys records in his diary seeing Keeling enter the Commons "to have his business heard . . . a great crowd of people to stare upon him."[61] Six months earlier Pepys had been at a dinner party that included Keeling, where, Pepys reported, Keeling had boasted of a case that he was trying that he "do intend, for these rogues that burned this house, to be hung in some conspicuous place in the town, for an example."[62] Keeling insisted that his fining of the jury for its verdict in the case of the beating of the young weaver was deserved. The assault had been brutal, with the boy being hit "until the blood gushed out of his nose, mouth and ears." He maintained that he had turned down a request for a reprieve for the killer because "I am very strict and severe against highway robbers and in case of blood."[63] On the other hand, Keeling elected not to respond to the accusation that he had insulted Sir Hugh Wyndham with some "unhandsome passionate speeches"; at the Commons hearing, John Milward, who was present, noted that "Sir Hugh very nobly said that since the Chief Justice did forget it, he would also do it and forgave it," a result which, Milward observes, "was very much for the Chief Justice's advantage."[64]

Keeling made a self-righteous and humble statement to the House, declaring:

> Mr. Speaker, I have infirmities sufficient not only to desire grains but greater weights of charity of this honorable House. I acknowledge I have the failings of a man, but I cannot accuse myself of injustice, bribery, or perverting or acting against the known laws, nor do I believe it can by any man be justly laid to my charge, and therefore I humbly crave and

hope to obtain the favor and charity of this honorable House upon which I cast myself.[65]

The House thereafter declared that fining and imprisoning jurors for their verdicts was illegal, and asked that a bill to that end be introduced. The measure, however, was not enacted into law, and it would be another three years before the practice of fining juries was ended by the decision in the *Bushell* case.[66] That case, in which William Penn was a co-defendant, involved a jury verdict that peaceful preaching was not tantamount to the criminal offense of holding an unlawful assembly or disturbing the peace. The judge, believing otherwise, had fined the jurors.[67]

After a four-hour debate, the House of Commons resolved the charge against Keeling with a decision that no further action should be taken. Lord Chief Baron Atkyns, who was present at the hearing, thought that Keeling carried out his part "with [such] great humility and reverence, that those of his own profession and others were so far his advocates that the House desisted from any further prosecution."[68] John Milward observed that Keeling spoke to the House with "very great reverence and respect."[69] These tributes suggest that the unconnoted subsequent portrait of Keeling by persons such as Lord Campbell who called him "worthless," and said that he was viewed with "utter contempt," is overwrought.[70] Counterweights include the praise of several of Keeling's contemporaries: "He died much lamented for his great integrity and worth," one said,[71] while Sir Thomas Raymond, a man not given to easy praise, declared on Keeling's death that he had been "a learned, faithful, and resolute judge."[72] Had they been able (though by then they were more than five years in their graves), Amy Denny and Rose Cullender might have contributed further kind words for the man who momentarily offered them a ray of hope.

Keeling's conduct during the trial of Bunyan highlights the bombast he displayed, though often combining it with an urge to engage in debate to prove his point rather than to mutely invoke his power. He could be particularly skeptical about criminal offenses charged to people acting alone: his fury was reserved for those who came together in groups that appeared to represent the organized threat that had led to his own imprisonment and occupational exile during the interregnum. This mindset seemingly led Keeling to speak his piece at the Bury St. Edmunds witchcraft trial.

What can we suggest in regard to Browne that would help us better understand his testimony at Bury St. Edmunds? Jonathan Post, the author of a study of Browne's life and work, indicates that the matter he finds most interesting is Browne's utter "consistency." We take this to refer to Browne's single-minded ability to pursue a line of thought to a preordained conclusion, be it correct or erroneous.

Browne was fifty-six years old at the time of the trial at Bury St. Edmunds, about twenty months older than Keeling and slightly more than four years older than Hale. He had been born in London on October 19, 1605, and would die in Norwich on the same day in 1682. Browne received his undergraduate degree from Oxford, and underwent most of his medical training abroad—at Leyden, Montpellier, and Padua, the last the most liberal center of scientific influence in Europe.[73] He was admitted to practice in England by the common mechanism of "incorporation," a formal process of recognition of a foreign medical education.[74] John Whitefoot, a friend and neighbor, tells us that Browne's hair and complexion were answerable to his name. He was of moderate stature, and dressed plainly, but never was without a cloak and boots, even in mild weather, because he believed it healthful always to keep oneself warm. Moderate in all things, Browne was said never to be transported either with mirth or sadness. He seldom jested, but often blushed.[75]

Reconciling the demands of a thriving medical practice with a productive literary career made for a hectic personal schedule; a reader of Browne sometimes has the impression of "a man writing with one hand and compounding an electuary with the other."[76] His work has aroused great enthusiasm through the centuries: Samuel Pepys recorded in his diary the remark of a Sir William Petty ("one of the most rational men that ever I heard speak with a tongue") that *Religio Medici* was one of the three books that had been "most esteemed and generally cried up for wit in the world."[77] Samuel Taylor Coleridge rated Sir Thomas "among my first favorites," noting that he was "exuberant in conceptions and conceits, contemplative, imaginative, often truly great and magnificent in his style and diction,"[78] while Charles Lamb named Browne as one of two worthies he should feel the greatest pleasure to encounter on the floor of his apartment in their nightgown and slippers, ready to exchange friendly greetings.[79]

Religious doctrine and scientific knowledge—and the interpenetration of the two—were the major themes that preoccupied Browne's written work; as one critic has noted, Browne "uses his amassed details of scientific knowledge most effectively in support of nonscientific propositions."[80] Browne's literary style was arcane: hypnotic, with haunting rhythms, and very richly-textured prose.[81] His vocabulary was highly idiosyncratic, at times almost a private language, replete with neologistic constructs built upon Greek, Roman, and Hebrew bases.* In *Urne-Burial* Browne employs such words as lapidifical, ampliate, tripundary, desume, congelation, supernation, farranginous, tripudary, and stillicidious: a few of those words he coined, such as electricity, hallucination, suicide, umbrella, and antediluvian, gained currency. Samuel Johnson would observe that the words used by Browne "were originally appropriated to one art, and drawn by violence into the service of another."[82] Edmund Gosse was appalled by the way Browne used language: "There was something abnormal in Browne's intellect," he wrote, "and it is shown in the rather mad way in which he tossed words about."[83] James Joyce in *Ulysses* parodied Browne's phrase "forget not how assuefaction unto any things minorates the passion from it" into "assuefaction minorates atrocities."[84] Browne's style, like his ideas, could be dazzling, disconcerting and, as happened at Bury St. Edmunds, darkly dangerous.

Sixteen years before the trial at which he was to play so prominent a role, Browne had taken upon himself the task of setting humankind straight about faulty knowledge, inadequate logic, and other concomitants of ignorance. His 1646 treatise, *Pseudodoxia Epidemica*, or *Vulgar Errors*, as it often is called, is a mélange of accurate information, shrewd reasoning, and appalling naïveté. The book, seeking to rid others of their belief in "fabulosities," is particularly disconcerting in the discrepancy shown between the high-minded doctrines that Browne proclaims for the exercise of judgment and the testimony he advanced at Bury St. Edmunds.

In *Vulgar Errors*, Browne advocates that readers exorcise "credulity . . . whereby men often swallow falsities for truth." He seeks to set aright those who unthinkingly rely upon authority, that "mortallest enemy unto knowledge," since it involves a "resignation of our judgments." Similarly, he berates those who let the "dictates of antiquity" preclude skepticism and clearheaded reexamination of hoary doctrine. Browne further warns against "men . . . erecting conclusions in no way inferable from their premises" and those who "swallow falsities for truth, dubiosities for certainties, feasibilities for possibilities, and things impossible as possibilities themselves."[85] An additional source of error upon which he lays great stress is the machinations of that great enemy

---

* We have avoided describing Browne's style as "quaint," forewarned as we were by the underlining of the term in a journal in the University of Texas library, and the marginal observation by an exasperated critic: "Jesus H. Christ! Can't anybody write of Browne without this word!"

of truth, Satan. The devil is so shrewd, Browne insists, that "to lead us farther into darknesse, and quite to lose us in this maze of error, he would make men believe there is no such thing as himself . . . insinuating into mens mindes there is no divell atall" and using "many wayes to conceale or indubitate his existency."[86] These words, as we saw, provided the rationale that permitted Samuel Pacy's explanation of his daughter's response to the touch of the non-witch to prevail at Bury St. Edmunds. They also allow their author to create an unassailable polemical position: what you believe, he can say to those who oppose him, is merely the product of what the devil has tricked you into believing.

Browne's paean for clear thinking and the traps that should be avoided are advanced in a book that ridicules the idea that an ostrich can digest iron and that the world was created in the month of March but, at the same time, one that agrees that elephants might be able to write sentences, and that music will cure the consequences of the bite of the tarantula. Defying his own warning about undue reliance on authority, Browne defends this last myth by pointing out that "the learned [Arthanasius] Kircherus has positively averred it, and had set down the songs and tunes solemnly used for it."[87] Kircherus, it can be noted, would be accused in later times of "gullibility, error, ignorance, and filched ideas" and characterized as "an egotistical fabricator and mountebank":[88] in one tale, he told of a Sicilian diver who spent so much time under water that a web grew between his fingers like that on the foot of a goose, and his lungs became so distended that they held enough air to last an entire day.[89] William Dunn captures this pattern of thinking very well: Browne, he observes, "breaks off a stick here and there instead of testing the whole faggot; he carries his candle into a corner and thereby darkens the room."[90]

How can we reconcile Browne's astute dicta about clear thinking with what he said at the trial of the alleged witches? Two fundamental interpretations can be offered: the first involves intellectual timidity, the need to hold onto sufficient orthodoxy to support a calm faith; and the second, an unwillingness to press against the tide in matters that count. No subject addressed by Browne could remotely be regarded as controversial; as Jonathan Post observes: "Whether John the Baptist lived on locusts and honey while in the wilderness is not likely to cause a ripple of commotion at any moment in the history of scriptural hermeneutics."[91]

Browne's approach may be viewed as a form of cowardice or, perhaps, laziness. Jean-Jacques Denomian put the matter well: "[T]his bold, stubborn, high-spirited personality is prone to bow at obstacles and shirk the encounter . . . perhaps out of the inactivity of his disposition."[92] Stanley Fish has emphasized the same point: Browne's vaunted tolerance, he believes, is really indifference: "He doesn't want to be bothered and he doesn't want to bother us."[93] Browne believed that core concepts of doctrinal religion stand or fall as a whole. Should one stanchion of the intricate theological edifice be shown to be faulty, the whole structure would collapse—at least for Browne. The existence of witchcraft was a linchpin of Christian orthodoxy; to entertain the notion of its foolishness was to run the risk of plunging into a pitiless world of uncertainty. Egon Merton agrees: "The supernatural structure of [Browne's] faith," he writes, "was firm but delicate; the removal of one tier like that of devils or witches would cause a stupendous fissure, undermining the position of the human soul, of angels, and of God, destroying the order of the universe."[94]

Second Browne, like Hale, was a shrewd survivor. Survival depended not only on carefully avoiding the transient view, but particularly on predicting how matters were going to go in years ahead. It was one thing to ridicule, as Browne did, the idea that women can conceive in a bath by absorbing the semen of men bathing nearby— "'tis a new and unseconded way in history to fornicate at a distance," he wrote[95]—but quite another to challenge so entrenched a religious doctrine as that of witchcraft. During the civil war, for instance, Browne noted that discretion was the best path: to become a martyr needlessly was to commit suicide.[96] Browne remained secure within the breakwaters, doing battle with the little superstitions, while endorsing some monumental ones. He was, in Joan Webber's words, "[c]autious, self-conscious, often claiming melancholy, scarcely able to make a positive statement about anything."[97] For a man to challenge the belief in witchcraft could lead to suspicion of a person's real motive. Who but a devil's disciple would dare doubt divine doctrine?

These are, of course, inferred motives offered to explain an irrational idea held in a mind singularly dedicated to the eradication of irrationality. A belief in witches recurs in Browne's writings, a matter about which those who called him to testify at Bury undoubtedly were well aware. He had, for instance, that Satan "runs in corners . . . acting his deceits in witches, magicians, diviners, and . . . inferior seducers." In *Religio Medici*, written when Browne was but thirty years old, he offered his most elaborated observation about witches:

For mine owne part, I have ever beleeved, and do now know, that there are witches: they that doubt of these, do not onely deny them, but spirits; and are obliquely and upon consequence of a sort, not of infidels, but atheists.[98]

Note the obvious limits which Browne sets. He will not entertain the notion that both witchcraft and religious orthodoxy are false. Challenge of fundamental doctrine is beyond the pale. Browne's writing on witchcraft drew from Sir Kenelm Digby, in his critique of *Religio Medici*, the more sensible observation: "Neither do I deny there are witches," Digby wrote. "I only reserve my assent till I meet with stronger motives to carry it."[99]

In regard to Browne and the possibility that the taint of misogyny underlay his testimony at Bury St. Edmunds, it can be noted that he apparently had little regard for women: "The world was made for man, but only the twelfth part of man for women. Man is the whole world and the breath of God, women the rib and the crooked piece of man."[100] Browne also, it is said, "could never resist an anti-feminist joke."[101]

Most curious of Browne's attitudes regarding women was his expressed distaste for sexual intercourse. "I could be content," he wrote as a young man, before his marriage, "that we might procreate like trees, without conjunction, or that there were any way to perpetuate the world without this triviall and vulgar way of coition; It is the foolishest act a wise man commits in all his life."[102] The purpose served by distinguishing "a wise man" (himself?) in these lines from other men is unclear, except perhaps as a literary counterfoil to "foolishest." Browne later pointed out that the effect of opium on users was "not so much to invigorate themselves in coition, as to spin out the motions of carnality,"[103] and it is suggested that he himself used laudanum, perhaps for this purpose. During his marriage to Dorothy Mileham, who was sixteen years his junior, she produced twelve children in a period of eighteen years. Browne's coital reservations would lead Samuel Johnson to wonder "[w]hether the lady had yet been informed of these contemptuous positions" or "whether she was pleased with the conquest of so formidable a rebel . . . or whether, like most others, she married upon mingled motives, between convenience and inclination."[104]

Browne's odd view on sex is further reflected in the advice he offered his son Edward, also a doctor, regarding a lecture Edward was to deliver at Chirurgeon's Hall. "You may be asked," Sir Thomas wrote, "why nature did not make the penis double, as she did so many organs of the body." To this Edward should respond: "Oh, no, God forbid, one is too much."[105]

How much influence did Sir Thomas Browne's testimony have upon the verdict in the Bury St. Edmunds witchcraft trial? The matter has been addressed with considerable heat by a number of partisan writers. The deepest thrust has been to condemn Browne soundly for the part he played in the trial. The classic diatribe is that of Edmund Gosse, who calls Browne's testimony "the most culpable and most stupid act of his life." Of the accused women Gosse says: "[T]heir blood, poor creatures, was on the head of the author of *Religio Medici*," and he sees the trial record demonstrating that Hale was opposed to the prosecution, and that a word by Browne in favor of the accused, or silence, would have saved Amy Denny and Rose Cullender.[106] It also has been emphasized that since Browne's testimony was that of an "expert witness" it could not but have had a great effect on the jury.[107]

But Browne has not gone without defenders. The most common rehabilitative strategy has been to link him with an impressive array of contemporaries who shared similar views regarding the supernatural powers of the devil. Malcolm Letts, Browne's most impassioned defender, insisted that critical writers have relied on Hutchinson's jaundiced review of Browne's part in the trial rather than going to the original source. Letts stressed that Browne did not specify that Denny and Cullender were witches, but merely stated his opinion that the young accusers were somehow bewitched[108]—perhaps an attempt to attune his testimony to the objection voiced by Keeling. But Letts' point seems niggling, since the connection had been made between the accusers and the accused, and Browne could only break that linkage by openly and forcefully crediting the girls' condition to a natural cause. As it was, his testimony played into the strongest element of the witchcraft system, an element built upon a distinction between mechanistic matters and cause in a purposive sense.[109] In witchcraft cases, the controverted matter was not how a person died or languished—that could be explained quite sensibly, as Browne's testimony, read carefully, suggests. What is never explicable is *why* this person instead of another or this moment instead of a different time were involved in the tragedy.[110] Ernest Jones, a founding father of psychoanalysis, makes the following significant observation:

> The average man of today does not hesitate to reject the same evidence of witchcraft that was so convincing to the man of three centuries ago, though he usually knows no more about the true explanation than the latter did.[111]

Others, such as Joan Bennett, have concluded, reading the trial report, that Browne's testimony "was a small factor: it seems certain that they were doomed in any case."[112] This view is shared by William Dunn, who maintains that what Browne said was "noncommittal at best" and that "the fate of the women was almost sealed before the trial began."[113] Simon Wilkin takes the position that we ought to be slow to pronounce judgment on Browne for his part at Bury St. Edmunds, not only because he echoed the views of his time, but because "it must surely be admitted that he had nothing whatever to do with the justice or injustice of the law which made witchcraft a capital offense."[114] Dorothy Tyler, along the same lines, finds it "unquestionable" that the result of the trial would have been the same had Browne not testified, and she argues that "[o]ne cannot state too clearly that there is no evidence that Browne's opinion had any undue influence upon the jury, or that Hale depended upon him for any part of his view of the matter."[115]

Browne himself may have had second thoughts about his performance at Bury St. Edmunds. Some years after the trial he included in his *Commonplace Book* the following observation about witchcraft:

> Wee are no way doubtfull that there are wiches, butt have not been alwayes satisfied in the application of their wichcrafts or whether parties accused or suffering have been guiltie of that abomination, or persons under affliction suffered from such hands. In ancient time wee reade of many possessed & probably there are many still, butt the common crye & general opinion of wiches hath confounded that of possession, men salving such strange effections from veneficall [poisoning by sorcery] agents & out of partie suffering.[116]

The most notable word in this subsequent reflection by Browne has to be the hedge word "probably" in its second sentence. That the subject of witchcraft recurs in Browne's work might testify to some sense of guilt at his performance at the trial.

Are there lessons of contemporary relevance to be learned from Browne's testimony at Bury St. Edmunds? Several seem evident, highlighted by the fact that rarely are purely fictive fantasies spun by reputable medical practitioners so readily apparent as they are in the annals of witchcraft. A victim is created; falsehoods are sworn to that often promote self-serving ends—to assuage guilt, to posture, to maintain privilege, to eliminate an enemy or a pest, or to earn credits for here or hereafter.

Browne was a person who tuned out conflict. Joan Bennett, comparing him to John Milton, noted that Milton was eager to engage in controversy and to extend toleration so that all should have the right to argue their case. Browne, on the other hand, "delighted not in controversies,"[117] a quality much different than that of the quarrelsome Keeling. Browne had, Bennett points out, "little faith in the effectiveness of argument; therefore, sure of his own beliefs he evaded intellectual combat."[118] Robert Ketton-Cremer has observed: "No book could have been less in tune than *Religo Medici* with the angry times in which it first appeared. Although composed in the 1630s, it never touched on the political issues of those years—monarchy, prelacy, power."[119] "You might read every word of Sir Thomas Browne's writing and never discover that a sword had been unsheathed or a shot fired in England all the time he was living and working there," another writer points out.[120] Like Richard Baxter and Matthew Hale, Browne gloried in understanding and tolerance—to a point. *Religio Medici* abounds with sentiments expressing his respect for other religious points of view: "I bend my knee in glorious sympathy with continental worship," he would write of Catholic rites.[121] But his tolerance extended only to the boundary of a basic orthodox theodicy, and Browne often expressed his loathing for what he regarded as the fickle and irresponsible masses.

Browne was a pedant, and Julio Caro Baroja, a leading scholar in the field of witchcraft, has pointed out the peril of pedantry in a witchhunting age:

> [P]edants with power in their hands, supported by a whole arsenal of authorities and the opinions of other pedants like themselves, can be dangerous; more especially if there is a mass of people only too willing to give in to their ideas and pay tribute to their pedantry.[122]

In the end, it was Browne himself who pronounced the most memorable epitaph on his performance in the 1662 witch trial at Bury St. Edmunds, though placing it in a different context. "[T]is as dangerous," he once wrote, "to be sentenced by a Physician as a Judge."[123]

7

Of fear and drear

As judge at the trial, Sir Matthew Hale inevitably played a pivotal role—likely *the* pivotal role—in judicially elbowing the jury toward its verdict of guilty. We have noted the striking power that judges of the time possessed to indicate to jurors how they felt about the case being tried before them. We also have seen the words with which Hale charged the jury, his emphasis that witchcraft was unquestionably real: the Bible had so decreed and, besides, witchcraft was condemned by laws in all nations. We have also seen Hale's kindness to John Bunyan's widow and his more merciful approach, contrasted to Keeling's behavior, toward some miscreants. How are we to reconcile such sterling qualities of intellect and feeling with the part that Hale played at Bury St. Edmunds? A much closer look at the man and his beliefs is in order.

Hale departed Bury St. Edmunds for Cambridge the morning after he had pronounced the sentence of death upon Amy Denny and Rose Cullender. It was Hale's habit as "a devotionair and moralist"[1] to set out his religious views during the interval between the late afternoon sermon and supper time.[2] "When he had resolved on the subject," Hale's son-in-law observed, "the first thing he usually did, was with his pen upon some loose piece of paper, and sometimes upon a corner or the margin of the paper he wrote on, to draw a scheme of his whole discourse, or of so much of it as he designed at that time to consider." This done, Hale "tap'd his thoughts and let them run."[3] His purpose was not to recommend his ideas to others, but to concentrate his mind: the writing process, in the words of Alan Cromartie, who has studied the Hale manuscripts, involved "a curious mixture of relaxation and religious exercise."[4] The material, Cromartie notes, tends to be flaccid in style and repetitious in content, "while the abominable handwriting testifies to the hastiness of his thought." Hale often started pieces, then abandoned them, leaving gaps that were never filled. For

OF FEAR AND DREAR

those seeking to study the manner in which Hale's mind worked, however, these unpolished materials enable the reader, again in Cromartie's words, "to listen to Hale thinking aloud."[5]

At Cambridge the Sunday after he arrived there—three days after he had sentenced Amy Denny and Rose Cullender to death—Hale wrote about witchcraft. His reflections on the subject later would be incorporated into a book, published in 1693 and titled *A Collection of Modern Relations of Matter of Fact Concerning Witches & Witchcraft Upon the Persons of People. To Which is Prefixed a Meditation Concerning the Mercy of God, In Preserving Us from the Malice and Power of Evil Angels, Written by the Late Lord Chief Justice Hale, Upon Occasion of a Trial of Several Witches Before Him.* The book is said to be Part I of a series, but a second part never appeared. The editor is Socrates Christanus, the pseudonym of Edward Stephens, Hale's son-in-law. Stephens indicates in his preface that he "thought it very proper" to include such a meditation, though unfinished, of "that no less wise, profound, sagacious, and ingenuous, than just and good man," a man "so cautious, circumspect and tender in manner in matters of justice, and especially in matters of life and death."[6]

Hale's satisfaction with the jury verdict, Stephens argues, can be seen from the fact that he wrote the meditation so soon after the trial, and Stephens urges anyone inclined toward a disbelief in witchcraft to learn from Hale's thoughts. Perhaps Hale's observations, Stephens notes, will reverse

the impiety, the vanity, the self-conceitedness, or baseness of such witch-advocates, as either confidently maintain that there are no witches at all, making their shallow conceptions an adequate measure for the extent of the powers of nature, and of the wisdom and power of God.[7]

Stephens' preface castigates magistrates who, "contrary to their duty and their oaths, make light of the examination and trial of them [witches], when brought before them." Such officials, he scolds, "have cause to be ashamed of themselves, after notice of such a judgment [that is, Hale's thoughts], and others may hereby be admonished what to think of [such magistrates], if they persist in such assertions, or pretenses."[8]

Hale's essay takes only eight of the sixty-four pages of the volume, which otherwise is made up of a conglomerate collection of wild tales, such as that by Dr. John Portage about his encounter in 1649 with "wonderful apparitions, visions and unusual things."[9] The meditation echoes Hale's direction to the jury, rooting his belief in witchcraft in biblical sources. "That there are such as evil angels, it is without all question," Hale proclaims. Adam and Eve, Saul and the witch of Endor, Job, and the prophecy of the desolation of Babylon provide Old Testament verifications of diabolic action. The New Testament "more explicitly and abundantly" clarifies the matter, with the story of the demoniacal symptoms cured by Jesus, the vision of the fall of Satan from heaven like lightning, and similar demonstrations of the work of the devil. Besides, the matter is "confirmed to us by daily experience of the power and energy of these evil spirits in witches, and by them."

Such evil spirits, Hale insists, because they are not clogged or encumbered by matter, have extraordinary strength and energy. This is why possessed demoniacs in the Bible and those of contemporary times "could not be holden by the strength of man, when possessed with this powerful and malignant influence." Such feats of strength occur because the evil one possesses experience and subtlety, invisibility and swiftness, "whereby he can secretly and powerfully mingle himself with the subject he means to mischief." The devil is able to work the blood of his victims up into choler or lust, and "abuse the fancy with false representations or disturbances of trust" by taking advantage of his shrewd knowledge of how the human mind operates.

The wickedness of the evil spirits, Hale maintains, is "most lively seen in that display of the invisible administration and exercise of it toward Job," and the awful malice shown by the devil toward Job's children, his name, his body and the peace of his soul and mind. Job was a biblical figure with whom Hale was said to have shown particular affinity. Evan Griffith, minister of the Alderly church, in his funeral sermon, listed as the second of Hale's seven great virtues "[h]is patience under all his crosses and tryals, whereof he had no small portion, and his long continued affliction in this excellent virtue, that he was another mirror, after the holy Job."[10]

In his essay, Hale indicates that the devil, that Prince of Darkness, constantly tempted the Lord. Since the devil's malice is insatiable—"it is his business every day to go about seeking whom he may devour"— some forces must be able to thwart him; otherwise he would long since have prevailed. The most significant counterforce is the dominion the Lord retains over impure spirits: "though they hate to obey him, they dare not disobey him." The Lord always has the final word. God punishes the evil spirits with "certain torments . . . which they fear and drear as much as malefactors do the whip and the pillory." Nobody can be afflicted by the evil one "without leave and permission from God."

Besides this, good angels, "no whit inferior to [the evil angels] in power . . . are benevolent and loving to the children of men." Another major impediment to the devil's work, Hale indicates, lies in God's fortification of the will of man by the privilege of free choice, which evil angels "may sollicit, perswade and tempt" but which "all the devils in Hell cannot take from him." This free will is for Hale "an impregnable fort, that can only be taken by dedition [yielding], but never by storm of assault." If the devil is resisted, he will flee the battle site.

Hale's essay abruptly concludes at this point. In large type centered at the bottom of the page the editor notes: "Not Finished."

Another piece of evidence on Hale's views concerning witches surfaced recently among the voluminous Lambeth horde of his papers. He was writing in Dorchester sometime before September 1664 and mentions witches because he seeks to prove that accurate prophecy is a mark of divine inspiration. The key passage states: "Those evil spirits that must be the instructors of those witches either do merely abuse them with lies and falsities or if any of their presages be true they are such as lie in the power of those evil spirits by the permission of God to effect or such as they by their observation and understanding of antecedents they do prudentially conjecture."[11] For Hale, if witches possessed the gift of prophecy, then biblical foretellings cannot be used as evidence for the Christian faith. His reasoning, Cromartie observes, takes the following form:

1   if witches prophesize, they must have been fed the information by evil spirits;

2   if what they foretell happens to be correct, it is not because they can see the future, but because they either:

     (a)   are capable of producing the predicted state; or

     (b)   have enough information about the present to know, as a scientist might, the likely outcome of an existing situation.[12]

It is mildly surprising that Hale does not include any mention of the witchcraft trial at Bury St. Edmunds, though there was nothing specific that marked that case that would have buttressed his theme.

Hale's observations provide a strong endorsement of the reality of witchcraft and an elaboration of the theological rationale that dictated his actions at Bury St. Edmunds. They justify the theme that witches deserve to die because they have defied God and willingly have given hostage to the devil. Reading Hale's Cambridge essay centuries later Lord Campbell would note with disapproval its "extreme complacency,"[13] while an anonymous commentator would find that the writing "reflected with entire satisfaction on what he had done."[14]

Hale's extraordinarily deep religious commitment, unusual even in a period in which other-worldly concerns occupied so many people, seems basic in his condemnation of Amy Denny and Rose Cullender. Among others, the eminent legal historian William Holdsworth, an ardent admirer of Hale, notes that his charge to the jury at Bury St. Edmunds was ruled by "sincere religious beliefs": "a man of Hale's mind and temper could hardly be expected to doubt," Holdsworth notes, adding callously: "And these are, after all, small matters."[15] The hanging rope that strangled Amy Denny and Rose Cullender was set in place by Hale's inability to question witchcraft because he was so certain that it was supported by unchallengeable biblical doctrine. As Hale wrote:

> [W]hatever God saith, is most certainly true (as needs it must be, because truth is an essential attribute of God), and if we be persuaded surely, that these scriptures are the word of God, then of necessity we must believe whatsoever Almighty God in the scriptures reveals.[16]

Reading carefully through the 1,145 tightly printed pages of Hale's religious thought in the two volumes edited by Thomas Thirlwall is to experience the fearsome theological inflexibility of an otherwise curious mind. There is in Hale's writings a notable absence of the humanity of zealots who lay out their weaknesses, wring their hands about worldly matters that tempt them, and on occasion tell a touching tale of their fall from grace. Hale shows no such redeeming qualities; he is unrelenting in his emphasis on the self-abasing rules by which he orders his life and by which others, if they value their immortal souls, ought to arrange theirs.

The writing displays an obsession with death and a striking fear of the omnipresent possibility of sudden disabling disease. Earthly benefits, Hale stresses, are but snares for disappointment. The man with the most friends and largest family, unlike the man with fewer such resources, only runs the greater risk of being devastated by the death or disablement of those close to him. Personal beauty should not be treasured "[b]ecause a small matter quite spoils it; a fall, or a disease spoils the greatest strength; a humor in the face, a rheum in the eye, a palsy, or the smallpox ruins the great beauty; or if none of these happen, yet either old age or death, turn all into weakness, deformity, or rottenness."[17] "I have looked upon a spider framing his web with a great deal of curiosity and care," Hale tells his reader, "and after his industry of many days, the maid with the broom, at one brush, spoils all."[18] The evanescent, subject-to-sudden-spoilage nature of the good things of life pervades Hale's theological writing. The mood throughout, while not frantic, is edgy, as if Hale is busily writing away in order to persuade someone—God, or perhaps himself—of his impeccable qualifications for a heavenly berth.

Hale's thinking was overpowered by a burden of uncritical "religiosity," using that term in the same sense that the social psychologist Hadley Cantril employed it when he discussed the absence of criticality in persons taken in by an Orson Welles radio broadcast describing an invasion of the United States from Mars. Cantril found religiosity, defined as being "unusually zealous," to be inversely related to critical judgment. Critical persons reassured themselves by checking their newspapers to determine the program to which they were listening. Credulous persons looked out their windows, saw street lights, and interpreted these as Martian torches, or they switched their radio dial, heard the Mormon choir broadcasting from Salt Lake City, and concluded that throughout the United States people had flocked to the churches to pray for relief from the alien intrusion.[19]

Richard Baxter tells us that when a horse that Hale was riding from the west of England to London on the Sabbath was lamed, and then another horse of his died, this struck Hale "with such a sense of divine rebuke" that he never again profaned the holy day.[20] Hale himself testifies to the way that he sees God's hand at work: "I have seen and observed both in myself and others, our sins and offenses so suitable, and proportionately answered with punishments, that though they seem to be produced by strange and most casual conjectures, yet so exactly conformable to the nature, quality, and degree of the offense, that they carried in them the very effigies of the sins, and made it legible in the punishment, *sic ille manus, sic ora gerebat* [thus he exhibited himself in his form and countenance]." Having written this, Hale addresses God directly:

> And from these observations I found that those sins were displeasing to thee; that thou were most wise to discover, and most just and powerful to punish them; and did thereupon conclude, *Verily there is a reward for the righteous; verily he is a God that judgeth in the earth.*[21]

There is a striking contrast between Hale's observation on the concordance of piety and consequent events and a wry note by Edward Gibbon, that most rational of historians. Hale observed: "I am not apt to be superstitious, but this I have certainly and infallibly found to be true, that by my deportment in my duty towards God in the times devoted to his service, especially on the Lord's Day, I could make a certain conjecture of my success in my secular occasions the rest of the week after."[22] Gibbon's tone is one of bemusement when he puts forth an observation on the same point: "I shall not, I trust, be accused of superstition," he writes, "but I must remark that, even in this world, the natural order of events will sometimes afford the strong appearances of moral retribution."[23]

Orphaned before his fifth birthday, rather than attending grammar school as would have been more usual, Hale had been placed during his childhood and adolescence under the tutorship of Anthony Kingscot, a man holding strong Puritan views. At Oxford, he was enrolled in Magdalene Hall, famous as a training ground for Puritan ministers,[24] and "the only college where . . . strict puritans would have trusted their boy."[25] Though, like John Bunyan and, much later, Mahatma Gandhi, Hale may have indulged in a carefree lifestyle during his twenties, guilt and training soon yanked him back to strict orthodoxy. His youthful conceptions of faith never grew or broadened, Gerald Hurst maintains. He disliked all music. He hated intoning in religious services, and for thirty-six years he never missed going to church twice every Sunday, all matters leading Hurst to an acid judgment: "Thus, his endurance matched his piety."[26]

Kai Erikson, in his discussion of the Salem trials, has captured the essence of a belief system such as Hale's—one that would allow the results of the courtroom experiment at Bury St. Edmunds with the blindfolded girl to be thrust aside:

> The hard logic of their creed required the Puritans always to doubt the evidence of their own senses but never to doubt the fundamental precepts of their religion. . . . If a persuasive argument should jar a Puritan's certitude or a clever line of reasoning confuse him, he had every right to suspect that some devilish mischief was afoot.[27]

Similarly, Richard Hofstadter notes that "[a]s a chosen people, living under a special covenant with God, the Puritans did not believe that any of their fortunes were attributable to environmental circumstances or accidents." If they were subject to a plague of witches, it was because the devil had special reasons for trying to invade God's earthly bastion: these were signs of God's disfavor.[28] The Puritans believed that evil was a palpable presence in the world, and the universe a struggle between darkness and light. There was no horror that mortal man was incapable of committing.[29]

The necessity that theological doctrine dictate secular court proceedings, essential in the condemnation of Amy Denny and Rose Cullender, is well illustrated in the *Tayler* case, in which Hale served as judge. Tayler was an intrepid blasphemer who was charged with declaring, among other things, that "Christ is a whoremaster, and religion is a cheat . . . [and] I am Christ's younger brother . . . and Christ is a bastard." Hale's judgment that such words were cognizable offenses before the King's bench reflects his view that religion forms the basis of all government and its tenets must be protected by state law. He wrote:

> these words, though of ecclesiastical cognizance, yet that Religion is a cheat, tends to the dissolution of all government, and therefore punishable here, and so of contumelious reproaches of God or the religion established. . . . Christian religion is a part of the law itself, therefore injuries to God are as punishable as to the King, or any common person.[30]

It would be unfair to consider Hale's religiosity without specifying that it could produce admirable as well as reprehensible consequences. It was this ambiguity of outcome that caused Roger North to move back and forth between high praise and strong condemnation of Hale. In many situations, Hale's strict conformity to biblical dictate made him a powerful and appealing voice for reform. Commissioned to study the state of the poor in England, Hale was warmly sympathetic to their plight. He noted that "[a]t this day, it seems to me that the English nation is more deficient in their prudent provision for the poor than any other cultivated and Christian state; at least that have so many opportunities and advantages to supply them,"[31] and he argued that it was "better [to] relieve twenty drones than let one bee perish."[32] Hale insisted that the relief of poverty and the provision of a decent education for poor children "would do more good to this kingdom than all the gibbets, and cauterizations, and whipping posts, and jayls in this kingdom, and would render these kinds of discipline less necessary and less frequent."[33]

George Onslow, a speaker of the House of Commons a century following the Bury St. Edmunds trial, wrote of the death sentence imposed on Amy Denny and Rose Cullender that Hale was "afterwards much altered in his notions as to this matter, and had great concern upon him for what had befallen these persons."[34] Onslow's presumption, Wallace Notestein observes, is hardly a trustworthy story.[35] Onslow might well have been confusing Hale with Samuel Sewall, one of the judges at the Salem witchcraft trials. Five years after that trial, in a statement to his church's congregation, Sewall had acknowledged his shameful error in condemning the Salem defendants.[36]

Nonetheless, there are hints that Hale might have had second thoughts about what he had allowed to happen at Bury St. Edmunds. In his *Historia Placitorum Coronae*, probably written about 1675, a dozen or so years after the trial, Hale observed that homicide by witchcraft was "a secret thing," and not a felony at common law, and that it consisted of working upon the "fancy" of the victim.[37] He mentions enactment of the Jacobean statute outlawing witchcraft, but offers no comment or justification for the law, only associating it historically with popery and the ecclesiastical writ *De Heretico Comburendo*, regarding the burning of heretics.[38] Yet, Hale often provided illustrative material in *Historia Placitorum Coronae* from his own experience to flesh out discussion of a juridical point: remember, for instance, his reference to the man accused of rape who was physically incapable of the act. But no such exegetic exercise accompanies the consideration of witchcraft: Hale's brief discussion seems rather uncomfortable.

Alan Cromartie suspects that after the Bury trial Hale may have brought his ideas about witchcraft more into line with those of John Selden, "as he usually did, at least on every matter about which the latter expressed a view."[39] Hale, twenty-five years younger than Selden, had been one of the executors when Selden died in 1654, though, on the face of it, the two men represent an odd linkage. Selden was a notably secular personality known for his anti-clericalism, his bawdy wit, and his irregular relationship with the Countess of Kent and her complaisant husband.[40] Anthony Wood noted that Selden possessed a strong body and a vast memory, both of which he employed to make him "a prodigy in most parts of learning, especially in those which were not common." He was, Wood wrote, "a great philologist, antiquary, herald, linguist, statesman and what not."[41] This paean is supplemented by equally high praise from Lord Clarendon:

> He was of so stupendous learning in all kinds and in all languages . . . that a man might have thought he had been entirely conversant among books, and had never spent an

hour but in reading and writing; yet his humanity, courtesy, and affability was such that he would have been thought to have been bred in the best courts, but that his good-nature, charity, and delight in doing good, and in communicating all he knew, exceeded that breeding.[42]

It was Selden who, bored with a long and obtuse Parliamentary debate about the theological implications of Christ's descent into hell, proposed that a committee be appointed to visit the site and personally check out the matter.[43] Selden's observation on witchcraft has been much quoted over the centuries, undoubtedly more for its colorful content than for its good sense:

If one should profess that by turning his hat thrice and crying "Buz" he could take away a man's life, though in truth he could do no such thing, yet this were a just law made by the state, that whosoever should turn his hat thrice, and cry "Buz," with an intention to take a man's life, shall be put to death.[44]

As Reginald Scot had written much earlier, if the mere expression of ill-will were to be punished, then men would be driven to the slaughterhouse by the thousands.[45]

That neither Hale nor Sir Thomas Browne made any known mention of the Bury St. Edmunds witchcraft trial in their writings, commonplace books, or letters may testify that neither saw the matter as of much significance. But this conclusion comes up against the fact that what went on at that assize was dramatic, controversial, memorable, and relatively unusual. In the history of England probably no more than 500 persons were hanged as witches. Besides, the charges at Bury St. Edmunds had occupied several days of trial, and the marshal had thought it important enough to make a transcript of the proceedings. Hale and Browne might well have failed to offer any later mention of the trial because they wanted to forget it or because they hoped that it would remain buried.

Cromartie, noting this oddity of omission—the dog that did not bark—points out that Hale seemingly would have used witchcraft phenomena as part of his argument against Hobbesian materialism. The main focus of Hale's considerable though puerile scientific writing concerned matters such as gravity and magnetism, phenomena that could not be accounted for by mechanistic explanations; Hale interpreted them as verification of the existence of non-material forces.[46]

He also believed that atheism was the product of materialism and was rooted in the denial that man had an immortal and immaterial soul. Atheism could be disproved by showing the inadequacy of materialism as an accurate account of reality. Given these considerations, Cromartie finds it "very surprising that Hale's voluminous, repetitious and self-indulgent papers at Lambeth Palace, most of them composed between 1664 and 1676, make no reference to his personal experience of a witchcraft trial."[47]

Neither does Hale mention the Bury St. Edmunds or other witchcraft cases in his correspondence with Richard Baxter, who himself referred to numerous episodes of supposed witchcraft to support the existence of the "spirit."[48] In 1662, Hale had strong reasons—judicial, theological, and scientific—to welcome a demonstration of and a criminal conviction for alleged witchcraft. Subsequently, he had very strong reasons to publicize what had taken place at Bury St. Edmunds. That he failed to do so could suggest that there was an uneasiness in his mind about the part that he had played in that trial.

If North's portrait of the dynamics involved in presiding at a witchcraft case is correct, then we should consider most seriously his repeated allegations that Hale's fundamental character flaw lay in the necessity he felt to play into popular sentiments. Hale was a survivor. In this, he was far from alone in a world that at the time was ominously unstable. John Wilkins, a politically astute man who had "a firm and familiar relationship with Hale," observed that in the rapidly changing times in which they lived "it is not mere integrity without great prudence that can preserve a man in a constant and clear reputation,"[49] while Selden, Hale's mentor, had written that "[w]ise men say nothing in dangerous times," illustrating the theme with a fable:

> The lion . . . called the sheep to ask if his breath smelt: she said, Aye; he bit off her head for a fool: He called the wolf and asked him; he said no; he tore him in pieces for a flatterer. At last he called the fox and asked him; truly he had got a cold and could not smell.[50]

Hale flourished under the royalist regimes of Charles I and Charles II as well as during Cromwell's interregnum. Frederick Inderwick, indeed, found it a "degrading and saddening spectacle" to see Hale in 1660 involved in the deaths of accused regicides who earlier had been his professional colleagues and friends, and noted that in his time Hale had sworn "so many oaths that if they all had been written on one sheet of paper he would probably have been ashamed to look them in the face."[51]

What Inderwick particularly had in mind was Hale's endorsement during the interregnum of the Engagement. Promulgated early in 1651, it required that the person swear: "I do declare and promise that I will be true and faithful to the Commonwealth of England as it is now established without a King or a house of lords." At the Inner Temple, where Hale resided, every barrister who desired to appear in court had to come to the end of the bench table in the hall at dinner time and there publicly affix his name to a long role of parchment to signify his attachment to the Engagement.

Burnet in his biography denied that Hale had taken the Engagement, but the *State Trials* report a direct inquiry to Hale about the issue by the Lord President of the High Court when Hale appeared as a counsel, and his reply: "My Lord, I have done it."[52] Hale, who was appointed a justice of the court of common pleas by Cromwell, also subscribed to the Solemn League of Covenant, which would be burned by the hangman upon Charles II's return in 1661. Thomas Thirlwall, who thought very highly of Hale's religious writing, is contemptuous of his adherence to the Covenant, and wrote: "I feel at a loss for reasons to exculpate him in this instance from the charge of pusillanimity, selfishness, or versatility of principle. . . . "[53]

Hale's situation brings to mind that of Sancho Panza who declared that oaths were "very bad for the health and very harmful to the conscience,"[54] a matter which is said to have led Samuel Butler to compose a verse that could well characterize Hale:

> I've took so many oaths before
> That now without remorse
> I take all oaths the state can make
> As merely things of course.[55]

The only nonlegal piece of Latin that Hale chose to translate into English— Cornelius Nepos' biography of his friend, Titus Pomponius Atticus, a man who lived near the time of Christ—presents a portrait of a person much in Hale's image; indeed, Hale may well have modeled his career on that of the Roman consul. Hale notes that the book is about "the wise methods which that excellent man used to preserve his honor, innocence, and safety of his person from the dangers that might occur."[56] Atticus, Lord Bolingbroke observed, was noted "for keeping well with all sides, and venturing on none."[57] Another commentary on Atticus observes that "amidst the civil wars of his country, when he saw the designs of all parties equally tended to the subversion of liberty,

[he] constantly preserved the esteem and affection of both the competitors."[58]

There are other ways as well of looking at Hale's willingness to go along, within reason, with whatever forces managed to obtain power. One commentator on Hale's life had indicated the value of conciliation notably well:

> [I]t is obvious that the evils of a revolutionary or transition state of things would be incalculably increased, nay, that down-right anarchy might ensue—if all men of honor and principle were to decline acting in a magisterial capacity, under a government whose title was disputed; or if it were made a test of integrity and patriotism . . . to go heart and soul with one faction or another; in which case no compromise could ever be practicable, and no honest mediator could exist.[59]

The dilemma is classic: was Keeling a better man than Hale for having gone off to sulk in isolated indignation during the inter-regnum? Or was Hale's willingness to compromise a few of his principles in order to achieve what might be viewed as a greater good the better part of discretion? The dangers of each position are apparent: the person who abdicates leaves the field to those who remain. But the person who finds initial compromise palatable runs the risk of further corruption about less palatable matters once the first step has been taken. Each of us compromises daily in unending ways, but for Hale there was the blatant (but perhaps understandable) step of swearing contradictory oaths of fealty.

Note, in this regard, Hale's apparent concern with money. Burnet maintains that Hale left a piddling estate,[60] though Samuel Johnson thought that he passed on a considerable sum to his family.[61] The historian of Wotton-under-Edge, the major town near Hale's residence at Alderly, tells us that Sir Matthew seemed to have had an obsession about making sure of his legal rights to his land. He believed, we are told, that Lady Berkely, from whom he had bought the land, might be able to recover the estate by a claim of rights of dower, which would cut through the conveyance to him, so that he sold the property to his sons and employees, and later bought it back with the idea of producing a fog which no dower claim could penetrate.[62]

Nor does Hale's failure to publish his legal writings during his life-time appear to be a matter of modesty or self-effacement: rather it seems to accord with the sentiment of the antiquarian Elias Ashmole, who wrote: "I thought it not prudence to have my name then (as tymes stood) appeare in print."[63] In 1680, four years after Hale's death, his *Historium Placitorum Coronae* was ordered by the House of Commons to be published, though the treatise did not find its way into print until 1736. Hale, however, allowed the contemporaneous publication of innumerable homiletics that he had written.[64] By the most generous interpretation, these offerings must be regarded as decidedly banal. Even two of Hale's most ardent admirers found them trying. Sir William Holdsworth, who calls Hale "remarkable," "a literate lawyer," and "the greatest historian of English law before Maitland," concludes that his theological effusions are "tedious."[65] Lord Campbell, whose fulsome panegyric regarding Hale we have met with earlier, suggests that the use of Hale's tracts in the English schools for "domestic education" had led the younger generation to regard Hale as a "great bore."[66]

It was Roger North who seems to have captured best those traits of character that allowed Hale to act as he did at Bury St. Edmunds. North, born in 1653, was the youngest of four successful brothers. He was trained in law and spent most of the first part of his adult life in a sycophantic relationship with Francis, the eldest brother. As a neophyte lawyer, Francis had avidly and with some awe followed proceedings in Hale's courtroom; ultimately, Francis would rise first to the position of Lord Chief Justice and then to that of Lord Keeper.

Following the death of Francis and the political revolution of 1688, Roger North, refusing to take the oath of allegiance to the new regime, retired to the seclusion of his country home in Rougham in Norfolk and absorbed himself as a "life-writer," publishing an autobiography as well as biographies of his brothers. North obviously thought deeply about how to go about such work: he wanted to portray "the characters of persons [rather] than the nature of things, being desirous to know what they were rather than what they did." He desired to write "even and smooth, not too extended or cambd with parentheses, which makes us forget the nominative case before we come at the verb." But neither did he want sentences too short and "snatching," "moving in fitts and girds [sudden movements or jerks], as a hog pisses."[67]

There is some controversy regarding how objective North was when he dealt with those who did not share his intense royalist sympathies or his undiscriminating admiration for his eldest brother. Thomas Macaulay, his severest detractor, called North "a most intolerant Tory and a most affected writer," though granting that he was "a vigilant observer of all those minor circumstances which throw light on the disposition of men."[68] Others have looked more kindly on his abilities. Arthur Bryant believes that North was traduced by Macaulay, and notes that a collation of North's writings with contemporary documents fails to support any allegation of partisanship or inaccuracy.[69] The second Earl of Clarendon, commenting in his diary in 1689, labelled North one of only two honest lawyers he had ever met.[70] Paul Delany, surveying autobiographical writing, regards North as only a "little inferior" to Gibbon or Mill.[71] North was not pompous, filled with a sacred sense of himself. Note, for instance, his sophomoric jest that "[I]t was ordinary for pickpockets to travel the circuits; nay, I mean not lawyers, but literally such."[72] Perhaps the most balanced comment on North is that of Osmund Airy. Airy thought that North was only mildly overmodest when he described himself as "a plant of slow growth, and when mature but slight wood," but that his work was marked by "shrewd if somewhat garrulous chat."[73]

North's first task in his depiction of Hale was to relegate Burnet's fawning spiritual biography of the chief justice to its proper place, noting that Burnet "had pretended to write a life, but wanted both information and understanding for such a task."[74] For his part, North tiptoed between high praise and astringent criticism of Hale. Hale, North wrote, "became the cushion exceedingly well: His manner of hearing patient, his directions pertinent, and his discourses copious, and, although he hesitated often, fluent. His stop, for a word, by the produce, always paid for the delay; and, on some occasions, he would utter sentences heroic."[75] Hale, in North's eyes, was "sagacious," but he also was subject to "prejudices," "as most mortal men are."[76] A particular prejudice was that Hale was "habituated to not bearing contradiction, and had no value for any person whatever that did not subscribe to him." In addition, though an "upright judge," when Hale was partial to an issue "his inclination or prejudice, insensibly to himself, drew his judgment aside." "If one party was a courtier, and well dressed, and the other a sort of puritan, with a black cap and plain clothes, [Hale] insensibly thought the justice of the cause with the latter." Hale also, North insisted, was biased toward dissenters and against loyalists. This view is seconded by Cromartie, who notes in his recent study that Hale had "a tenderness for nonconformists,"[77] and displayed "a sympathy for the suffering of dissent."[78] It was a dissenter, Samuel Pacy, of course, who led the judicial attack on the alleged witches before Hale at Bury St. Edmunds.

Basically, as North saw the matter, Hale's problem as a judge was his "leaning toward the popular,"[79] shown by fear and pusillanimity. Hale was said to be afraid of the "impetuous fury of the rabble," a fear nourished by the rebellious times when the government was, at best, "but rout and riot." North thought Hale's conceit excessive, an "insuperable pride and vanity,"[80] and that it grew out of "self-conversation, being little abroad" and consequent "conversation with none but flatterers. . . . He was the most flatterable person ever was known."[81] Throughout his depiction of Hale, North continued to shift between praise and attack. Hale was, he declared, the most profound lawyer of his time, and "he knew it": "lawyers and laymen idolized him as if there had never been such a miracle of justice since Adam. His voice was oracular, and his person little less than adored." Hale's abilities "were extraordinary, being of an indefatigable industry, ready apprehension, and wonderful memory; and having bent all his force to the study of the law, English history and records, was arrived to the highest degree of learning that any age hath known in that profession."[82] But, moving now to the other side, North maintained that Hale's "overruling temper," while it did not manifest itself much in small matters, and those between common men, "for there his justice shined most," surfaced when he handled major cases; had he only dealt in great causes "he might have been accounted the worst judge that ever sat." Nor could North resist a sideswipe at Hale's nonlegal writings: "He published much in speculative devotion, part prose, part verse; and the latter hobbled so near the style of the other, as to be distinguished chiefly by being worse."[83]

Now, some decades after Hale's death, North wrote that he believed it necessary to show him in a truer light than when an age did not allow such freedom, "but accounted it a delerium, or malignancy at least, not to idolize him." North wants to put on record his judgment that Hale was not "a very touchstone of law, probity, justice, and publick spirit as, in his own time, he was accounted." "In short," North summarizes, "to give every one his due, there was in him the most of learning and wisdom, joined with ignorance and folly, that ever was known to coincide in the character of any one man in the world."[84] Later, in his autobiography, North would conclude another, largely repetitive examination of Hale's character with a notably kind comment: "So I leave the discourse of this great man, wishing I may be happy to live to see such another, with all his faults." This sentiment, however sporting, undoubtedly is not one that either Amy Denny or Rose Cullender, long since dead, likely would have endorsed. The best that they might have been able to do would have been to mock posthumously Hale's self-righteous boast that "I did faithfully execute justice according to that station I had; I rescued the oppressed from the cruelty, malice, and insolence of their oppressors; I cleared the innocent from unjust calumnies and reproaches."[85]

8

An age of so much knowledge and confidence

In English witchcraft cases, Keith Thomas has noted, "[t]he most common situation of all was that in which the victim . . . had been guilty of a breach of neighborliness, by turning away old women who had come to the door to beg or borrow some food or drink, or the loan of some household utensil."[1] A major element of the explanatory scheme for witchcraft accusations developed by Alan Macfarlane and by Thomas is that the failure to provide charity to their needy neighbors aroused hurtful and contradictory feelings in the minds of those who had turned their backs. These people were trapped between the emergent ethos of capitalist self-interest and the powerful religious impulse of concern for those less fortunate than themselves. On one hand, householders who now paid a regular poor rate did not expect to answer the beggar's knock at the door.[2] On the other hand, they were keenly aware of the injunction of Proverbs xxviii: 27: "He that giveth unto the poor shall not lack: but he that hideth his eyes shall have many a curse."[3] Beleaguered emotionally, they sought to cleanse their conscience by indicting the alms-seekers as unworthy and malevolent, as servants of the devil rather than as deserving children of God.

They were aided in this deed by medical testimony which often constituted a basic element of witchcraft prosecutions. As early as 1486, the *Malleus Maleficarum*, the manual for inquisitors, had pronounced that "if asked how it is possible to distinguish whether an illness is caused by witchcraft or by some natural physical defect, we answer that the first [way] is by means of the judgment of doctors."[4] More detailed guidelines were suggested a century later by the Italian scholar, Franceso Maria Guazzo. He maintained that witchcraft could be presumed "when the bewitched patient's illness is very hard to diagnose, so that doctors hesitate and are in doubt, and keep changing their minds, and fear to make any positive statement."[5]

In England, Richard Bernard, in his authoritative *Guide to Grand-*

Jury Men, specified physicians as particularly suitable witchcraft witnesses,[6] and Richard Boulton, writing in 1712, would declare that in cases of suspected witchcraft "men of judgment in physick . . . ought to be consulted." The testimony of doctors, Boulton presumed, would readily establish whether witchcraft was or was not at work, for "they must be mad themselves, or senseless, that cannot distinguish distracted persons from such as are possessed with Devils."[7]

George Beard, himself a doctor, has pointed out that "a skilled physician seemed to be in the ground-plan of nearly every witchcraft case in New England,"[8] though exception might be taken to his collegial use of the adjective "skilled." Some later writers, such as Leland Estes, have maintained that doctors, frustrated by their lack of adequate medical knowledge, were the fundamental progenitors of the witchcraft panics.[9] Ignorance and the concomitant desire to protect a privileged position, he believes, underlay their recourse to witchcraft diagnoses. There were orthodox views about what caused certain diseases, such as smallpox, but witchcraft filled the gap when no standard explanation was available.[10] The doctors of the time were "children in knowledge." Therefore, "to attribute a disease, the symptoms of which they could not comprehend, to a power outside their control . . . was a safe method of screening a reputation that otherwise might have suffered."[11] Thomas Ady, writing near the time of the Bury trial, described the process:

> Seldom goeth any man or woman to a physician for cure of any disease, but one question they ask the physician is . . . "Sir, do you not think the party is bewitched?", and to this many an ignorant physician will answer, "Yes, verily." The reason is *ignorantine pallium maleficium et icantio*—a cloak for a physician's ignorance. When he cannot find the nature of the disease, he saieth the party is bewitched.[12]

Others, such as Lucy Mair, focusing in particular on witchcraft in preliterate societies, while not necessarily disagreeing, find that diagnoses of witchcraft are functional, not only for the medical man, but also for the patient, given certain conditions. Mair notes that she "starts from the premise that in a world where there are few assured techniques for dealing with everyday crises, particularly sickness, a belief in witches, or the equivalent of one, is not only not foolish, it is indispensable." She finds that such beliefs flourish in societies where for the most part those who fall ill must simply let the illness run its course.[13] An alternate strategy is that the physician might say: "I don't know." Perhaps Montaigne best expressed this position: "After all," he wrote, "it is putting a very high price on one's conjectures to have a man roasted alive because of them."[14]

Sanford Fox, analyzing the roles played in witchcraft prosecutions by the professional elite—the doctors, ministers, and judges—concluded that it was in the self-interest of members of each group to allow those in the others to proceed unchallenged, however self-evidently sketchy and inadequate was the basis for their behavior.[15] In regard to the courts' passive acceptance of medical testimony Fox observes:

> The validity or basis of a physician's pronouncement that his patient was a victim of witchcraft is nowhere questioned. Such judgments were readily accepted and given weight. . . . There was no inquiry into the problems of why, in some uncurable and baffling physical illnesses, witchcraft appeared, and in others it did not. Why some physicians quickly reached the conclusion that a witch was involved in their patients' suffering, while other practitioners never ventured such an opinion, seemed to be a matter of no concern to anyone.[16]

For their part, ministers could readily broadcast witchcraft as a scourge visited upon those without sufficient faith. As such, it represented a compelling call—a threat—for firmer allegiance to the church and particularly to its representatives on earth who were in a position to protect the devout from the ubiquitous forces of diabolic evil.

In terms of witchcraft and the Bury St. Edmunds trial, both of which occupied his attention, Richard Baxter, a Puritan, the leading dissenting minister of the time, exemplifies this arrangement among members of those elite callings who had the power to reject or to align themselves with popular sentiments concerning witchcraft and its presence in any particular circumstance.

Baxter has been described as a man with sad, sincere eyes, a high Roman nose, lean cheeks, firm, thin lips, and an ample brow partly concealed by a skull cap from which the hair fell down in what was then called "lovelocks."[17] He and Sir Matthew Hale were neighbors during the years 1667–1669, when both lived in Acton in Middlesex.[18] Baxter was at Acton in order to comply with the Five Mile Act, which required that dissenting ministers remove themselves at least that distance from where they had been preaching. Hale, as Alan Cromartie notes, had chosen to reside "in this inconvenient place because of his somewhat ostentatiously modest tastes."[19] It is believed that Hale was influential in obtaining Baxter's release in 1669 for illegally holding conventicles at Acton.[20] "I scarce ever conversed so profitably with any other person in my life," Baxter would write of Hale.[21] When Baxter took up another residence, Hale bought the house that Baxter had been renting.

Hale left Baxter 40 shillings in his will, with which Baxter purchased the largest Cambridge Bible available, inscribed an encomium to Hale in it, and put the Bible on display in his house with a picture of Hale alongside it.[22] Hale also bequeathed to Baxter two manuscripts he had written about dissensions within the church and methods to alleviate them.[23] This was a gift, however, about which Baxter might have been less than enthusiastic, since he notes honestly, if not charitably, of Hale's religious writings: "The only fault I found with them was that great copiousness, the effect of his fullness and patience, which will be called tediousness by impatient readers."[24] Despite an express prohibition in Hale's will against doing so, Baxter published the treatises in 1684, saying that lawyers had convinced him to put the material before the public. The essays are particularly charitable to dissent, as long as it remains within the realm of protestantism, "the only true religion given to the world by Almighty God, through his son, Jesus Christ, wherein and whereby [believers] may expect everlasting salvation."[25] Hale inveighs against the spirit of revenge, an eye for an eye, as being "as much against the doctrine of Christ, as any thing in the world."[26]

Baxter was deeply involved in the fierce religious quarrels of the time, the acidulous tone of which often startles those accustomed to more restrained criticism. One of Baxter's treatises, for instance, drew from Thomas Long, the prebendary of Exeter, the comment that it was marked by "putrid, pestilent stinks and corruptions and so unlike the breathing of a mortified Christian, that the like never proceeded from any dying man, except such a one as hath been dying twenty years altogether."[27]

"If you want to know what a Puritan really was you cannot do better than to turn to the autobiographical sketch of Richard Baxter," one writer later noted,[28] while another would find him "the most representative Puritan in history."[29] On this basis, Baxter's greatest fame would come posthumously from the use by Max Weber and Richard Tawney of his writings to demonstrate the hospitality of seventeenth-century theological doctrine to the advent of capitalism.[30] Baxter was largely self-educated ("As for myself, my faults are no disgrace to any university," he would genially write, "for I was of none.")[31] He was a compulsive writer, producing, according to how you count them, 168,[32] 161,[33] 141,[34] or 116[35] books. Margaret

Charlton, the woman Baxter married when she was just over twenty years old and he was approaching fifty, would tell him, Baxter observes, that "I had done better to have written fewer books, and to have done those few better."[36] Samuel Johnson, however, thought otherwise: responding to Boswell's question about which books of Baxter to read, he had said: "Read any of them; they are all good."[37] Read today, however, Baxter's work seems mercilessly nitpicking about inconsequential matters. Even in his lifetime some thought this as well, for a critic in 1681 would crudely comment on Baxter's ability to "distinguish himself into a fart."[38] Among Baxter's more charming eccentricities was his unwillingness to correct most of the errors from the first edition of his *The Saint's Everlasting Rest*, on the ground that a perfect second edition text would be an affront to those who had bought the original version.[39]

In 1691 the last year of his life (his dotage, marked by "aged imbecility," Robert Calef would say[40]), Baxter published *The Certainty of the World of Spirits*. The book was assembled from materials he had been collecting for some time, and it offers, among other matters, the only near-contemporary commentary on the Bury St. Edmunds trial that we have found except for Hale's son-in-law's brief mention, noted earlier. The story that Baxter tells is a wild tale that makes us suspect his good sense, at least in regard to matters of witchcraft: or, perhaps, it testifies tellingly to Baxter's intense need to believe in supernatural forces. This is what Baxter reports about the Bury trial:

> Mr. Emlin a preacher in Dublin told me the story of the bewitching of two gentlewomen, sisters to Mr. Pacy, now a pious justice in Leostoft in Suffolk. He and his sisters, now married, are all yet living. They were used much like those in New-England, mentioned by Mr. Cotton Mather[,] being children then about nine and eleven years old. But I understand that the story is in print, and it is also in MS. from Judge Hale himself, who condemned the witches, (which no man was more backward to do without full evidence). A lady of my acquaintance, hath it under his hand. Therefore I forebear the particulars: Only one odd passage that Mr. Emlin told me I shall recite. A godly minister, yet living, sitting by to see one of the girls in her fits, suddenly felt a force pull one of the hooks from his breeches. And while he looked, with wonder what was become of it, the tormented girl, vomited it up out of her mouth: Any that doubteth of this story, may be satisfied of Mr. Pacy, and both his sisters, yet

living, and may know all the evidence and circumstances which I pass over.[41]

Mr. Emlin was Thomas Emlyn, a well-known dissenter, who is considered to have been England's first Unitarian minister.[42] One commentator, noting Emlyn's feeding to Baxter of "circumstantial narratives of a ghost-story and of a case of witchcraft," sensibly concluded that Emlyn's mind "was not of a rationalistic order."[43] Emlyn very likely had picked up the tale of the minister's bewitched breeches on site: he had preached in Lowestoft for a year and a half beginning in 1688,[44] and is said to have gotten along well with the Church of England minister.[45] Emlyn left Lowestoft for Dublin, where in 1703 he would be dismissed from his position when the grand jury, incited by other clerics in the city, indicted him for what they insisted was a blasphemous libel. A heavy fine was later remitted, but Emlyn had to serve a year in prison.[46] A generation later, Emlyn's son Sollom would meticulously edit Hale's posthumously published legal classic, *Pleas of the Crown*.

Who was the "godly minister" to whom Baxter refers? John Youell was the rector in Lowestoft at the time that the Pacy girls claimed to be bewitched, but he had died in 1676, twelve years before Emlyn came to town. Joseph Hudson was rector during Emlyn's short stay in Lowestoft, but it is unlikely that he had personal acquaintance with a trial that had occurred before he took up his post. A minister active in Lowestoft both during the trial and when Emlyn lived there was a dissenter, Samuel Manning, who was bequeathed £5 in Samuel Pacy's will. Manning was a firm believer in witchcraft; he insisted in 1665 that he and Thomas Spatchett had been the victims of the diabolic actions of Abre Grinset of Dunwich, a town fourteen miles south of Lowestoft. Manning is also believed to be the author of an undated letter which tells a standard tale of witchcraft:

> There was one Mr. Collett, a smith by trade, of Haveningham [Heveningham] in the county of Suffolk and formerly a servant in Sir John Duke's family . . . who, (as it was customary with him) assisted the dairy maid to churn or to make butter and not being able (as the phrase is) "to make butter come" he threw an hot iron into the churn under a notion that there was witchcraft in the case. At that time a man, who was employed as laborer and then at work carrying off dung in the yard, cryed out in a terrible manner "They have killed me" still keeping his hand upon his back inti-

mating where the pain was and died on the spot. The poor mans cloaths were taken off and the servants found to their surprise, the mark of the iron that was heated and thrown into the churn deeply imprinted upon his back. This account I heard from Mr. Collett's own mouth, who, being a man of unblemished character I verily believe to be a matter of fact.[47]

The attitude toward both witches and dissenters held by some officials is shown by the magistrate's comment on the accusation of Grinset by Manning and his colleague: "If she bewitched but Spatchett and Manning, and such as they are, she should never be hanged by me," he declared.[48] Manning likely played a very active role as provocateur in the Lowestoft witch trial.

Baxter's tale about the Bury witchcraft trial indicates that he was aware of the existence of a manuscript version of the proceedings, though apparently he had not read it. The handwritten copy of the report which we have referred to earlier is to be found among Baxter's papers in Dr. Williams' Library. On the last page of the manuscript, written at right angles to the remainder of the text, are the words:

Judges Hales his papers
Concerning witches 1676

These words presumably were written by the cataloguer, since all the documents of this volume of manuscripts of Baxter's are endorsed in the same handwriting. Librarians at Dr. Williams' Library believe that the date indicates when Baxter received the manuscript: 1676 is the year in which Hale died. Perhaps though it was the lady of his acquaintance who gave it to Baxter.

We have earlier noted discrepancies between the manuscript and the published version of the trial. In addition to the two that confined the objections to the proceedings to Keeling alone rather than to him and two others, there is a variation near the end of the report, where in the manuscript it is written: "The next morning, the 3 children with their parents all of them spake perfectly, and were as in good health as ever they were. . . . " A different hand has written in after "with their parents" that the group "came to my Lord's lodgings." The printed report substitutes "the Lord Chief Baron Hale's lodgings" for "my Lord's," an alteration that suggests the original editorial hand of Hale's marshal or, at least, that of some other subordinate.

In his own writings, Baxter continuously threatens the faithless and those wavering between orthodoxy and godlessness with a fate much worse than death. Witches are part of the arsenal he mounts to get potential sinners in line, with the line obviously forming at the doorstep of the church at which he or his colleagues preach. On witchcraft, he calls attention to the works of Increase and Cotton Mather, declaring that anyone who reads them would "see enough to silence any incredulity that pretendeth to be rational." In his preface to the second edition of Cotton Mather's *Late Memorable Providences Relating to Witchcrafts and Possessions*, Baxter wrote: "He must be an obdurate Sadducee that will not believe it."[49] Like so many clerics before and after him, Baxter obviously yearns, unrequited, for a modern-day miracle, unquestionably performed by God before masses of reputable people. Lacking such proof for his theology, he is forced to rely on past authority and argument. In the latter category, for instance, he responds rhetorically to the question of why the Devil had come to New England by noting: "Where will the Devil show most malice, but where he is hated most: Where will he cast his net, but where is the best prey."[50] Baxter turns querulous when he finds skeptics demanding to see the Devil "or a departed soul in a true apparation," people who truculently refuse to rely on the kinds of reports that he and Mather have gathered. In a clever bit of illogic, Baxter insists that because the mechanisms of witchcraft cannot be seen does not argue against their truth. For, he notes, "the sun [does not] shine on the infant in the womb," nor does that infant "see our building and tradings, and business in the world," though it is obvious to everybody that these phenomena most certainly are real. God permits humans to perceive only those things that are necessary to their existence.

With apparent forthcomingness, Baxter grants that there have been fraudulent accusations of witchcraft, and briefly discusses one of them, the 1620 case of William Perry, known as the Boy of Bilson. Perry, thirteen years old, but, as the author of the report of the case observes, "for subtilty far exceeding his age,"[51] had accused an old woman, Jane Clark, of bewitching him. Richard Baddeley, who reported the case, describes Perry's condition:

> In those fits hee appeared both deafe and blinde, writhing his mouth aside, continually groning and panting, and (although often pinched with mens fingers, pricked with needles, tickled also on his sides, and once whipped with a rod, besides other like extremities) yet could he not be discerned by either shrieking or shrinking, to bewray the least passion or feeling.[52]

Perry vomited up rags, thread, straw, and crooked pins. The black-
ness of his urine convinced physicians that "nature had left her usual
operations." But a servant, charged with watching Perry through a
hole in the wall after Perry had been told that the entire family had
gone to church, uncovered one part of the ruse: "Finding all quiet,
[Perry] lifts up himself, and stares, and listens, and at length gets out
of his bed, and in the straw or mat under it, takes out an inkpot and
makes water in the chamber-pot." Perry then added black ink to the
urine, and "for a reserve, if he should be forced to make water before
company," saturated a piece of cotton with the ink, and put it into his
prepuce, covering it with his foreskin.[53]

Another ruse also was employed to trap Perry. Thomas Morton, the
Bishop of Lichfield, finding that Perry went into fits on the reading of
the opening verse of the first chapter of St. John's Gospel, suggested to
him that the devil, as a scholar of some six thousand years' standing,
undoubtedly also knew Greek, and that it would be interesting to
determine his response to the verse when read in that language.
Morton, however, read a different section of the Bible. Perry, misled,
threw a fit, but he remained unmoved when the provocative Biblical
passage subsequently was recited to him in Greek.[54]

Baxter argues that the deception by the Boy of Bilson was the
product of training by "past priests (later turned Quaker)." This allows
him to damn in one indictment the two religious groups that fiercely
eluded his otherwise wide latitudinarian embrace. Besides papists and
Quakers, Baxter finds that the ranks of those who fake bewitchment
are filled by "lustful, rank girls and young widows, that plot for some
amorous, procacious [forward or saucy] design, or have imaginations
conquered by lust." When these women reach a state of hysteria, Satan
takes over. Thereafter, Baxter reasonably argues that though some
"cheats of pretended possession" have been discovered this provides
no reason for "weak, injudicious men to think that all are such."[55] As
did many others, including Sir Matthew Hale at the end of the Bury
St. Edmunds trial, Baxter maintains that because witchcraft accusations
are common and have persisted over a long period of time, they must
therefore be reasonable. "Sure it were strange," he insists, "if in an age
of so much knowledge and confidence, there should be so many score
of poor creatures put to death as witches, if it were not clearly manifest
that they were such. We have too many examples lately among us, to
leave any doubt of the truth of this."[56]

Baxter's work reflects the interdependence that he believed ought
to exist between the state and the church. A primary function of
government authorities, Baxter believed, was to encourage religious

affiliation and punish disbelief. He distrusted the masses—the profane multitude that he saw as hostile to religion[57]—and argued that magistrates should "restrain deceivers from preaching against the unquestionable truths of the Gospel, and give public countenance and encouragement to those master-truths."[58] He campaigned to bar anyone not a church member from taking part in an election for any state position.[59]

Baxter's core message is expressed in a pithy proclamation on the utility of virtue: "Time is short, souls are precious, hell is dreadful, heaven is joyful, devils and their wicked servants are busy."[60] Geoffrey Nuttall has summarized excellently the core tenets of the belief system which lay behind Baxter's ideas about witchcraft and those that characterized Matthew Hale's mindset at Bury St. Edmunds:

> The fact is that, while Baxter gives reason what he believes to be its due place, he never gives it primacy. Divine grace, inspiration, sanctification must also receive their due place. Alongside his strenuous defense of rationality is a quivering sensitiveness to the world of faith: an overpowering sense of God's presence; constantly renewed gratitude for God's mercies and responses to God's demand for serious holiness; and a controlling assurance of life beyond death and of things not seen but eternal.[61]

Ministers such as Baxter did not play as direct a role in the trial at Bury St. Edmunds as did representatives of the law and medicine, but their interests permeated the courtroom.

One thing that stands out in the trial of Amy Denny and Rose Cullender is the strong representation of dissenters and latitudinarians among those declaring for guilt. Opposing them were the rigid, intolerant Anglican John Keeling and other conformists among the landed gentry who, as justices of the peace or serjeants-at-law, shared Keeling's religious position if not his peppery personality.

Matthew Hale, raised in the Puritan tradition, though a practicing Anglican, was for his time an extraordinarily easygoing man in regard to neighboring faiths so long as their practitioners submitted to some divine sovereignty. Note this admirable theological embrace:

> A man whether he be an Episcopal, or a Presbyterian, or an Independent, or an Anabaptist; whether he wears a surplice, or wears none, whether he hears organs, or hears none;

whether he kneels at communion, or for conscience sake stands or sits, he hath the life of religion in him, and that life acts in him, and will conform his soul to the image of his Savior, and walk along with him to eternity, notwithstanding his practice or nonpractice of these indifferencies.[62]

Hale even was mildly indulgent toward Catholics, perhaps because of (or despite) the fact that his first wife was from a Roman Catholic family; she presumably had some influence in shaping Hale's argument that Catholics ought not be forced to take unpalatable oaths for fear of making them desperate.[63]

Sir Thomas Browne was similarly gracious and indulgent about forms of worship other than his own and unusually tolerant of Catholics ("We have reformed from them, not against them," Browne wrote[64]), though he too was unbending on the point that godliness was essential. Similarly, Richard Baxter persistently has been lauded as a man not given to harping on minor variations in diverse faiths and one who sought alliances among them all, though with the notable exception of Catholics and Quakers. Both Browne and Baxter are given individual chapters in Edward Augustus George's *Seventeenth Century Men of Latitude: Forerunners of the New Theology* (1908). Baxter, for his part, emphasized that Hale, when they were neighbors, was thoroughly understanding of Baxter's dissenting positions. Roger North, it may be remembered, had believed that Hale was altogether too partial to dissenters.

The Pacys were dissenters, as we noted earlier; they were adherents of the Congregational or, as it then was called, the Independent church. The Congregationalists in the mid-sixteenth century had formed part of the left wing of the Puritan movement, and of all the separatist surges theirs was considered to be the most politically dangerous. In 1593, fearing persecution, most of the Congregational leaders had fled to Holland, at the time a center of religious tolerance. Later, others went farther afield, many settling in New England.

The Congregationalists believed that a Christian baptism did not automatically qualify its recipient to be a church member; rather the church should consist only of persons who had consciously and openly dedicated themselves to Christ in the form of a covenant. They favored the autonomy of each gathered congregation, with members appointing a priest and establishing their own procedures. They opposed a set prayer book and the use of vestments and other religious trappings.[65]

Under the guidance of the exiled leaders in Holland, the Congregational movement gained particular strength in Norfolk, Suffolk, and Essex.[66] It flourished in the fifteen-year period of religious tolerance during the civil war and the interregnum, but found itself again under fire after the restoration in 1660 brought with it "holy violence" against the "fanatic vermin" whose conventicles were said to threaten the country's security.[67]

Samuel Pacy lived near the center of this religious ferment and played a considerable role in it. At Wrentham, nine miles south of Lowestoft, the rector, John Phillip, undoubtedly officiated at the 1638 marriage there of Samuel Pacy's brother, Nicholas, to Katherine Moore of Corton, a village three miles north of Lowestoft.[68] Presumably the couple chose to obtain a special license to wed elsewhere than where they resided because of the minister's persuasion.

Shortly after the Pacy wedding, Phillip, who had been excommunicated for his nonconformity two years earlier, left Wrentham because of his persecution by the church.[69] With a party of friends, including Nicholas Pacy and his wife, he sailed to New England and settled in Salem, Massachusetts.[70] Nicholas Pacy was granted ten acres of land in Salem on November 21, 1638,[71] and the following year he received another thirty acres.[72] His wife died at Salem in March 1640, probably shortly after the birth of a child.[73] The following year John Phillip returned to Wrentham, but Pacy apparently stayed on in Salem and he was admitted to the church there in 1650.[74] Living in Salem at this time was Phillip's sister-in-law, Joan Ames, the widow of the famous nonconformist divine, William Ames, who had been the Minister of the English Congregational Church at Rotterdam. Ames died there in 1633 and his widow emigrated to Massachusetts in 1637.[75] At Cambridge, William Ames had been a disciple of William Perkins, the prominent puritan theologian and demonologist.[76]

Evidence of Samuel Pacy's direct involvement in nonconformist activities and his ties to the Wrentham congregation can be read from an order by the justices of the peace sitting at the quarter sessions in Beccles on October 5, 1663, a year and a half after the witch trial:

> The court doth desire Henry Bacon Barronnett, one of his Majs. Justices of the Peace for this county, to send for John Smyth of Lowestoffe [a tanner by trade who had been elected constable] in this countie and cause him to be bound over by recognizance with conditions for his appearance at the next general quarter session of the peace here to be holden then and there to give in evidence against Samuell Pacy of Lowestoft, William Riseing of the same, Thomas Porter of the

same, and Edward Barker of Wrentham, upon a certain indictment performed against them and others and not to depart
this court without licence of said court.[77]

On January 1 of the following year, the justices supplemented this
order by noting that there were two indictments against Samuel Pacy
and others for meeting at illegal conventicles and that they should be
tried on the charges at or before the summer assize.[78]

Isaac Gillingwater, reporting that he had the information from his
mother's mother, who had been a servant to the Pacy family, said that
the Pacy's north parlor was a usual meeting place for the nonconformist communicants. Gillingwater observed that "from the
disorderly conduct of the said audience this practice was soon discon-
tinued." These meetings probably led to Pacy's indictment.
Unfortunately, there is no record of the outcome of the case.

Edward Barker is the most interesting to us of the three men
indicted with Pacy since he establishes a link between Pacy and
dissenting ministers with virulent views about the threat of witchcraft.
Barker, a graduate of Caius College, Cambridge, was ejected in 1662
from his living as rector of Eye in north Suffolk. He then went to live
at Wrentham, where he obviously had earlier connections since its
parish register lists the birth of a son to Barker and his wife on January
22, 1661, ten days before the ejection of nonconformists.[79] Barker
probably chose Wrentham because of its particular hospitality to
dissenters.[80] Francis Brewster, the lord of the manor, and a member of
Parliament, had been one of the first members of Phillip's church,[81]
and was related by marriage to the Ames family.

Samuel Petto, a nonconformist minister who had been ejected from
the parish of St. Cross, South Elmham, fifteen miles southwest of
Lowestoft, was a close friend of Barker and presumably a friend of Pacy.
Petto was also very active in the embryonic nonconformist movement
and often visited Great Yarmouth during the early years of the church.
During the period 1677–1684 he corresponded regularly with Increase
Mather in Massachusetts.[82] Petto, a staunch believer in witches, would
publish in 1693 the tract, mentioned earlier, that detailed the alleged
bewitchment in March 1662, the same month as the Denny–Cullender
trial, of Thomas Spatchett and Samuel Manning by an "old bastard
beggar woman."[83] Spatchett was also a nonconformist clergyman. In
1645, when he was the curate of Dunwich, he had been employed by
Matthew Hopkins as one of the "searchers" there. He examined two
alleged witches, both of whom were convicted.[84]

Very close relationships prevailed at the time between the many

Congregational churches in the area. Besides his connection with the Wrentham group, Pacy probably also had ties both to the Great Yarmouth congregation and to the emergent Lowestoft conventicle. Until 1689, when Thomas Emlyn took the position, Lowestoft did not employ a permanent nonconformist minister, though transient preachers often stayed briefly in the town. The Lowestoft dissenters customarily repaired for prayer to Great Yarmouth.[85] The dissenters of Great Yarmouth also had links with Salem. In 1649 a Great Yarmouth Puritan, William Towne, emigrated to Salem, taking with him his wife and two small daughters, Rebecca and Mary. Forty-three years later, as Rebecca Nurse and Mary Easty, these two Great Yarmouth emigrants were among the many "witches" executed at Salem. Their youngest sister, Sarah Cloyse, who had been born in Salem, also was arrested and accused of witchcraft, but she survived after spending a period in jail.

The communication between the towns was two-way, for the Church Book of the Yarmouth Congregational Church records: "Admitted [into the congregation] 19 March 1650, Elizabethe Edwarde by dismission from ye church of Xt [Christ] in Salem, New England."[86]

The Great Yarmouth nonconformist church had been established in 1643, splitting off amicably from the Norwich congregation.[87] Matthew Hopkins, invited to Great Yarmouth in 1645 by the corporation to search for witches, "discovered" sixteen of them, all of whom were said to have been convicted on their own confession.[88] Among those involved in the cases were John Brinsley, a Presbyterian, the parish minister who had been dismissed by the Archbishop of Canterbury in 1627, but remained in his living on the sufferance of the town authorities until 1632, when the Archbishop prevailed. In one of the tales of witchcraft published in *A Collection of Modern Relations*, Hale's son-in-law Edward Stephens identifies Brinsley as examining witches "discovered" by Matthew Hopkins at Great Yarmouth.[89]

After Brinsley left Great Yarmouth he became rector of nearby Somerleyton where many of his Yarmouth friends resorted to hear him.[90] Among those friends were Matthew Arnold and Samuel Pacy's sister, Margaret, the woman who played so important a role in the trial of Denny and Cullender. Although both residents of Lowestoft, Matthew and Margaret obtained a special license to be married by Brinsley at Somerleyton. Brinsley returned to Great Yarmouth in 1644 as one of the two town preachers, the other being his good friend and supporter, William Bridge, the Congregationalist. In 1662, with so many others, both men were ejected as dissenters.

Among documents discovered recently in the parish church at Lowestoft was one written and signed by Samuel Pacy in which he claimed expenses incurred in 1658 while trying to arrange a consolidation of the livings of Lowestoft and the small adjoining parish of Gunton. The attempt perhaps was to increase the income at Lowestoft so that a permanent dissenting Minister could be recruited for the town as had been suggested by Bridge at that time.[91]

Pacy's Puritan links with Great Yarmouth are reflected in his association with John Woodroffe, who handled the purchase Pacy and Thomas Mighells made in the 1650s of the derelict site of the old Greyfriars Priory. Woodroffe, later one of the executors of Pacy's will, and described in it as "my loveing friend,"[92] was one of Great Yarmouth's leading Presbyterian nonconformists. A government report in 1688 says that as the town's head bailiff Woodroffe had sought to have removed from his oath of office such phrases as "You shall keep secret the King's counsel" and "shall govern by law and reason."[93]

What might all this mean? Why should the stance of Keeling, a man so uniformly awful under so many other circumstances, be the decent one at Bury St. Edmunds? Why should the dissenters and such theologically tolerant men as Hale, Browne, and Baxter be on the side of intolerance in regard to witchcraft?

Part of the answer may lie in how the theological practices of the religious groups influenced the manner in which they viewed witchcraft, a matter that has been raised in studies of English witchcraft. In 1947, Reginald Trevor-Davies suggested that Puritan and anti-Royalist beliefs might lie at the core of an explanatory scheme for witchcraft prosecutions.[94] Royalist sympathies are not, however, significant correlates of the sides chosen at Bury St. Edmunds. Keeling's intense pro-Royalist position is notable, but those favoring conviction, particularly Sir Thomas Browne, certainly Matthew Hale, and very likely Samuel Pacy, also held pro-Royalist views.

Trevor-Davies' hypothesis received scant attention as later research on English witchcraft typically sought to discover processes rather than affiliations and belief-systems involved in witchcraft accusations, though in 1973 Leland Estes observed that "witch hunting had become a partisan religious issue, with insurgent Puritan interests using it to further highlight the shortcomings of the Anglican establishment."[95]

The basis of the ideological battle between Puritans and Anglicans lay in the different tactics available to the religious groups to respond to witchcraft. Witchcraft always had fitted comfortably with the Catholic church's repertoire of the miraculous. Catholic theology, indeed, might well have been instrumental in arousing beliefs in witchcraft, for, as Paul Carus notes, "as soon as a religion of magic becomes an established institution, it will develop the notion of witchcraft by a distinction between its own miracles and those of other people who are unbelievers," since "witchcraft is nothing but the performance of miracles without the license of the established church, which claims to have a monopoly on supernaturalism."[96] Another writer puts the same matter more flatly: "The theistic and satanistic hypotheses are, from the standpoint of logic and evidence, exactly on par."[97] Catholicism with its exorcism rites and its arsenal of rituals was thoroughly prepared to deal with witches. Following the Reformation, however, Anglicans no longer could make the sign of the cross, sprinkle holy water throughout their dwellings, hang medals of the saints, or use other tactics traditionally employed to ward off diabolic power.[98]

Anglican preachers, as Mary Douglas observes, "reaffirmed the power of evil, but left believers disarmed before the old enemy. The only way out in these circumstances was recourse to countermagic (and this had to be clandestine) or, better still, to the now approved method of legal prosecution. Hence the multiplication of witch trials during the following century." This theme in place, Douglas then deals with the anomaly that witchcraft accusations were common in continental jurisdictions that had not experienced the Reformation. In these areas, she maintains, "theologians seem to have lost faith in the curative power of religious systems long before the Reformation; and trials were accordingly initiated much earlier."[99]

In England, devout Puritans were an exception to the general rule of Protestant impotence in the face of visitations from the realm of the devil, and witchcraft became one of the killing grounds on which the orthodox church, and several theological systems which challenged it, battled. Puritans believed that prayer and fasting, accompanied by inner-searching and reform among those straying from orthodoxy, could overcome diabolic forces. Armed with such weapons, they discovered grounds for their deployment, since they had a sacred arsenal that they were convinced was superior to that of the Anglicans who dominated them in the secular world.

Dissenters, who made up only a small portion of the population, amounting to barely 5 per cent at the time of the Bury witchcraft trial,[100] also were likely to put more pressure on their children than establishment families. C. John Sommerville noted that for the dissenters, children were the necessary hope for their religious survival. He theorizes that the optimism that inspired the dissenting movement turned into a survivor mentality when it came to bringing up the next generation: "an overdeveloped inner life and imagination were no doubt necessary if they were to live as Dissenting strangers in a hostile world."[101]

Witch prosecutions in England were sharpest in Essex and Lancashire, two counties where Puritan evangelists were particularly energetic.[102] Matthew Hopkins, the self-appointed witch-finder who spurred a devastating witch-hunt in East Anglia, was a "Puritan run to seed"[103] and his cohort, John Stearne, a rigid Puritan.[104] The witch-hunt spurred by Hopkins in 1644–1645 represents the English parallel to the Salem Village outbreak almost five decades later.

Not all historians, however, have accepted interpretations that place an onus on the Puritans for witch-hunting. Wallace Notestein, a preeminent early scholar, believed that Francis Hutchinson, who tied Hopkins' Puritanism with his persecution of witches, was biased by his own Anglican standing. Besides, Hutchinson was confusing correlation with cause. There was, Notestein grants, a "coincidence in time between the great witch prosecution" of 1645 and the power of Puritanism which "makes it hard to escape the conclusion that these two unusual situations must in some way have been connected."[105] Notestein maintains that the witch frenzy during 1645 in East Anglia was the result of judicial anarchy in which local authorities, who often saw witches all about them, momentarily gained control. "The coming of Hopkins and Stearne gave them their chance, and there was no one to say stop."[106]

Alan Macfarlane, however, has pointed out that Notestein was not aware when he wrote in 1911 that the assize courts had convened in 1645, and that "judicial anarchy" had not prevailed then. For Macfarlane, the explanation for the 1645 witchcraft prosecutions lies not in the Puritanism of Hopkins, but in "a combination of particular factors, especially the disruption of local government and justice by the Civil War and, possibly, the economic, spiritual, and other tensions which the war created, with beliefs in witchcraft which, though usually kept just below the surface, were no less widespread and powerful than they had been in the sixteenth century."[107]

The view that Puritanism and dissent may have played a strong role in at least some English witchcraft trials was reinforced in a 1991 study by Michael MacDonald of the dynamics of the 1602 trial in which Dr. Edward Jorden testified as an expert witness on behalf of Elizabeth Jackson, who had been accused of witchcraft. Jorden, it may be remembered, told the court that the accuser, fourteen-year-old Mary Glover, a member of a prominent Puritan family, was suffering from hysteria, a view that was scornfully thrust aside by the judge. Jorden's later publication of *Suffocation of the Mother* (1603) always had been regarded as an attempt by a repudiated expert witness to find another forum in which to carry his point. But MacDonald insists that Jorden's book primarily was a work of religious propaganda rooted in a bitter and protracted struggle between the Anglican church hierarchy and its Puritan opponents about the reality of witchcraft.

The dénouement of the case of Elizabeth Jackson is the basis for MacDonald's position that inter-sect conflict underlay the proceedings. On her conviction, Jackson was sentenced to the maximum one year of imprisonment permitted under the existing statute. Meanwhile, Mary Glover continued to suffer from the fits that had led to her original charge. At the end of December in 1602 a group of Puritan divines and laymen "cured" her by holding a prayer and fasting session,[108] basing their action on the biblical text in which Jesus relieves a youth afflicted with a deaf and dumb spirit.[109] The cure of Mary Glover achieved considerable notoriety and is said to have "enraged the [Anglican] clergy and alarmed the government,"[110] particularly as Mary Glover tied her condition to the glory of the Puritan cause:

> At the moment of her deliverance, she used the same words that her grandfather, a victim of the Marian persecutions, had uttered as he died on the pyre. The equation of the famous martyr and the godly young demoniac . . . was seized upon by all of the Puritan writers who described her dispossession. To Puritan eyes . . . the girl had become the central figure in a struggle between religious truth and official persecution.[111]

MacDonald believes that Jorden's book on hysteria was reluctantly written and almost certainly was the product of prodding from Richard Bancroft, the Bishop of London. On its first page, for instance, Jorden declares: "I have not undertaken this businesse of mine owne accord."[112] Jorden's commission, it is said, was to provide scientific argument as part of an ongoing pamphlet war for disputing the validity of cases of possession, witchcraft, and exorcism "that both Catholics and Puritans were exploiting to win public approval and make converts."[113]

A Puritan, Stephan Bradwell, who had attended the trial, entered the fray after Jorden had published *Suffocation of the Mother*, insisting that during the Jackson trial a pair of physicians had effectively rebutted the testimony that hysteria underlay Mary Glover's accusations. Besides, the girl was young and innocent, incapable of sham: "[a] man would scarse looke for such subtletie, under so milde a counternance." Nor could Mary Glover have been suffering from hysteria because of menstrual suppression, since she had not yet begun to menstruate. Merely because other girls, such as Rachel Pinder "and too many such," had faked symptoms of bewitchment was no reason to question a legitimate case. Bradwell concluded that "all the booke cases and private observations, which Dr. Jorden bringeth, when they are compared with thus, are but idle and addle instaunces." Besides, since the basilisk can kill with a stare, Bradwell noted triumphantly, why should anyone take amiss the idea that witches can achieve the same thing?[114] The witch-believing Puritan had locked horns with the skeptical Anglican in a preview of the similar alignments that prevailed at Bury St. Edmunds.

Deeper inquiry into the religious beliefs that may have determined and permeated other cases of witchcraft in England is essential to determine if in London in 1602 and at Bury St. Edmunds sixty years later we have an unusual pattern, or whether there is substance in insights regarding the force of Puritan belief in sustaining the prosecution of witches in England and, by report, in New England. There can be no doubt that the same Puritan beliefs, originating from a small group of nonconformists in England, played no small role in both the activities of Matthew Hopkins in 1644–1645, the trial of Amy Denny and Rose Cullender and, in the long term, the trials at Salem in 1692. These beliefs, especially concerning witchcraft, largely were promulgated by William Perkins. As Brian Levack notes, "it is impossible to explain witch-hunting in New England without recognizing the importance of the Puritan ideas held by members of the ruling elite."[115] Among many others, Perry Miller explains the thought process in New England that fueled Puritan acceptance of witchcraft. Puritans, he writes, "could never banish from their minds the consciousness of something mysterious and terrible in life, of something that leaped when least expected, that upset all the regularities of technology and circumvented the laws of logic, that cut across the rules of justice, of something behind appearances that could not be tamed and brought to heel."[116]

Our examination of the proceedings against the two Lowestoft women offers support for the crisis interpretations that appear in many analyses of witchcraft. There were great social and economic pressures on the people of Lowestoft, particularly those prominent in prosecuting Amy Denny and Rose Cullender. These pressures were inherent in the intense conflict for economic survival that lay at the heart of the bitter contest between Lowestoft and Great Yarmouth over fishing rights. Although not obvious when reading the original trial report, our research has also shown that religion, to be more accurate a particular style of nonconformist belief, was probably the driving force behind the accusations against Amy Denny and Rose Cullender. It is likely that without these underlying beliefs the accusations would not have been made and there would have been no trial. We also have seen how spatial and social proximity between the accused and their accusers played so prominent a role in the case. The pretrial contact between Samuel Pacy and the leading Lowestoft townsmen and Hale and other legal luminaries seems likely to have triggered the formal charges, a possibility heightened by Hale's foreknowledge of the proceedings before he went on his assize journey.

The witch trial at Bury St. Edmunds, the hanging of two women guilty of nothing more sinister than being a nuisance, offers a tragic lesson in the consequences of a failure in logic and decency. It will not do to whitewash the episode as merely a reflection of the ideas of the time in which the major participants played out roles that reflected the best judgment then prevailing. At Bury St. Edmunds, there were cross-currents of opinion regarding the reality of witchcraft. Those who participated in the trial had a real choice, between death for the accused or their acquittal. They undoubtedly were convinced that what they were doing was correct. We can understand, perhaps appreciate this, but understanding does not relieve us from judging the behavior of those who sent Amy Denny and Rose Cullender to their deaths.

In putting together the historical record of this case we often have revisited the gravesites of the Pacys at St. Margaret's. When the old Pacy house on High Street was recently refurbished, we discovered behind some seventeenth-century paneling, in a first floor bedroom, nails of the kind that the Pacy girls claimed the Devil had inserted into their mouths. It reminded us of the haunting words of historian G.M. Trevelyan:

> The poetry of history lies in the quasi-miraculous fact that once, on this earth, on this familiar spot of ground, walked other men and women, as actual as we are today, thinking their own thoughts, swayed by their own passions, but now all gone, one generation vanishing into another, gone as utterly

as we ourselves shall shortly be gone, like ghosts at cock-crow.[117]

For a brief moment, then, we have tried to restore to their place two women who deserved better, and we have attempted to locate some explanations for why they were sacrificed. In the end, we repeat our earliest point: there are lessons of contemporary importance to be learned from this report of a bygone prosecution for witchcraft. They include lessons about human arrogance, lessons about the flaws of judicial process, and, perhaps most important, lessons about the extraordinary ability of people to rely uncritically on tainted information to do awful things.

Part III

Post mortem

9

A matter of adipocere

The remains of Sir Matthew Hale now lie in the churchyard at Alderly in Gloucestershire, entombed in a sarcophagus-like rectangular stone box five feet wide, nine feet long, and four feet high. Hale's final home dominates the fifteen other tombs and tombstones surrounding his. The churchyard site reportedly was preferred by Hale to the more prestigious church interior because he believed that churches were for the living, churchyards for the dead.[1] Straggly weeds grow about half a foot high from cracks in the slab above Hale's last resting place, while daffodils appear on the other gravesites.

Hale died on Christmas Day in 1676. Richard Baxter observed that "when he found his belly swell, his breath and strength much abate, and his face and flesh decay, he cheerfully received his sentence of death."[2] Hale was so renowned that it was difficult for some ordinary mortals to believe that he had come to his end in a manner no different from that of other humans. "Here are 2 or 3 stories," Sir Ralph Verney wrote to his eldest son, "about Judge Hales foretelling the time of his death; in the maine, I beeleeve them true, but the circumstances are too long for a letter." The son was similarly convinced: "I am persuaded," he replied, "that such an excellent vertuous man as Honest Judge Hales might have the spirit of prophecie given him, to prophecie anything according to the analogie of faith."[3]

Edmund Verney thought Hale, "that incomparably learned and upright man and just," would be "more missed than any man in England except his Majesty."[4] At the funeral, Hale was eulogized by Evan Griffith, pastor of the Alderly Church, for "his temperance and sobriety, in the midst of a sottish and swinish generation," and for his "humility, meekness, gentleness, and self-denial," graces which were claimed to make Hale "another Moses." Hale also was praised by Griffith for his patience, piety, charity, and mercifulness, as well as for a strong sense of justice. "To hinder him from administering of justice impartially to high, low, rich, poor, without fear or favor," said Griffith, "was to stop the sun in the firmament, and to divert its course."[5] Griffith's stylized praise, abundantly flattering, nonetheless fails to approach the heights of Baxter's tribute to Hale:

> [He has] gone off the stage with more universal love and honor for his skill, wisdom, piety, and resolved justice than ever I heard or read that any Englishman ever did before him or any magistrate of the world of his rank since the days of the Kings of Israel.[6]

In his will, Hale had left precise instructions for his interment: "I desire [my body] may be buried in the churchyard at Alderly," he had prescribed, "on the south side of the tomb of my former wife," the wife he had regarded as distressingly extravagant and self-indulgent. It may have been free association when he added thereafter in the will that the burial arrangement ought to be made only "if it may be done without much inconvenience and expense." Otherwise, Hale indicates, he will settle for burial at the town of Acton, where at that time the body and the tomb of his first wife lay. When all was settled, the wife's tomb was relocated at Alderly, while her remains stayed in the ground at Acton.[7] It was a compromise that Hale undoubtedly would have endorsed: adequately symbolic, less troublesome, and cheaper.

The Latin inscription on Hale's tombstone, its phrasing of his choosing,[8] reads in translation as follows:

Here is buried
Matthew Hale, the Only Son
Of Robert Hale and
Joann his Wife
Born in this
Parish of Alderly
First Day of November in the Year
of Our Lord 1609
And Deceased in Truth in the Same Place
the Twenty Fifth Day
in December The Year of Our Lord
1676
His Age 67[9]

The vista today at Hale's burial site is tranquil and bucolic, though the church is locked and the glass in several of its windows is gone, the spaces covered with cardboard.

Alderly Grange, the house in which Matthew Hale was born, still stands. A brick tablet placed in the upper reaches of an outside wall tells when the building was constructed. ANNODO, it reads on one line, and 1608 on the next. The house was spanking new when Hale entered life there in 1609. The present owner cannot resist taking a pair of visitors upstairs to the room in which Hale had been born, even though he and his wife were about to leave when the two arrived unannounced. The owner now uses the cramped space as a dressing room; he keeps a miniature portrait of Hale on an end table. A full-length Van Dyck portrait of Henry Holland, who died on the scaffold in 1649 for his loyalty to the King, is visible in one of the drawing rooms in the house.[10] The painting belongs to his wife, the man says. He himself is a descendant of Hale; while she, he notes with pride, traces her ancestry to James I.

The owner of Alderly Grange, however, is not named Hale. The male line had died out only a few generations after Sir Matthew, though it was revived near the end of the eighteenth century. In 1779, John Blagden married Anne Hale, heiress to the Hale family estates. On the death in 1784 of the last descendant bearing the Hale family name, the Blagdens came into possession of sizable property holdings. Presumably in gratitude, John Blagden took Hale as his last name.[11] Descendants of his family can still be found in Gloucestershire. In this way at least, Hale's name escaped the fate of Samuel Pacy's: we were unable to locate any patronymic descendants of Samuel and Elizabeth Pacy.

A further memento of Hale can be found in the Old Library in the Guildhall in London in the form of a life-size portrait that hangs over the fireplace in the main room. The painting is one of a series of twenty-two done by Michael Wright, an Englishman trained in Scotland and Italy,[12] to commemorate the judges who performed the formidable job of settling disputes growing out of the Great Fire of London in 1666.[13] Critics have it that the paintings are of nondescript quality: Walpole insists that they would have been better if the commission had gone to Peter Lely. But Lely had refused to attend the judges in their chambers, as they desired, instead demanding that they come to his studio.[14]

The portraits, completed in 1671, were done on bed ticking and primed on both sides for strength.[15] In his, Hale is shown wearing his scarlet robe and fur mantle. He is standing on a step with a balustrade behind him, his face turned three-quarters to the left with his eyes fixed ahead. He wears a close-fitting black skull cap, and carries his square-topped hat with a roll of paper in his right hand. The thumb of his left hand is placed within the narrow black girdle which encircles his waist, a pose said to be typical.[16] He wears a rather poorly painted gold chain over his shoulders. The collar, which fits close to his cheek, is plain, flat, and square cut. By the time of the picture, the ruff, previously worn by all judges of Hale's stature, had been abandoned. A black and gold embroidered glove is tucked within Hale's girdle on his right side.[17]

Hale looks portly in the Guildhall painting. "I think it's partly the robes," the lady showing the portrait suggests, "though his face is chubby, hands rounded, fleshy." A later examination of Hale's judicial robes, with their ermine collars and sleeves, taken out of storage for us at the Gloucester Folk Museum where they are being held prior to being sent to the Tate Gallery in London for cleaning, indicates clearly that their owner was a bulky man. The robes, cut without a hem, are of fine scarlet cloth, richly dyed in grain; their quality, as J.H. Baker points out, is testified to by the fact that three centuries later they show no fraying.[18]

The Guildhall portrait of Hale bears marks from water and it bulges slightly from the soaking it suffered during a firebomb raid on December 12, 1940, even though it had been placed underground for safekeeping. Today, of the original twenty-two portraits of the Fire Judges, only those of Hale and Sir Hugh Wyndham remain at the Guildhall. Some of the others—including that of John Keeling—were distributed here and there, usually to heirs, though the majority no longer exist.[19] This seems appropriate. As we observed earlier, Hale was a survivor.

The remains of Sir Thomas Browne are interred in a vault in St. Peter Mancroft, a church which had been constructed in Norwich between 1430 and 1455.[20] Browne's corpse was to be involved in a wild, implausible saga, one particularly ironic given their mortal possessor's preoccupation with the undisturbed rest of the deceased. Browne had written movingly in *Urne-Burial* about the discovery in nearby Walsingham of between forty and fifty cinerary pots containing human bones and ashes.[21] He had mistakenly identified the remains as those of Roman soldiers; they were later found to be Saxon. But such an error of fact did not deter Browne from using his discovery as the basis for soaring observations on the conditions of human existence. *Urne-Burial* has been judged to contain "reflections of life, death, immortality in some of the loveliest and most solemn passages in the

English language."[22] Another commentator regards it as "probably the greatest literary expression of all antiquarianism."[23] Among Browne's strongest observations are those of horror at the disturbance of the remains. "To be gnaw'd out of our graves, to have our sculs made drinking-bowls, and our bones turned into pipes, to delight and sport our enemies"—such "tragicall abominations," he observed, could be escaped only "in burning burials."[24]

There is but one comfort gainsaid to mortals, Browne wrote: anything and anyone can deprive us of life, but nothing can take death away from us. Browne himself died in 1682—twenty years after he had participated in the witchcraft prosecution. Death came to him on October 19, the same day as his birth.[25] What makes the matter singular is that Browne had been fascinated with the idea of people dying on their birthdays. In *A Letter to a Friend, Upon Occasion of the Death of his Intimate Friend*, a touching attempt by Browne at consolation, he had mused about the fact:

> that the first day should make the last, that the tail of the snake should return into its mouth precisely at that time, and they should wind up on the day of their nativity, is indeed a remarkable coincidence.[26]

Browne might have gotten the idea that people are more apt to die on their birthdays than at other times from the fact that William Herbert, the third Earl of Pembroke, one of Shakespeare's patrons (and a leading candidate for the role of the "Lord of my love" and the "onlie begetter" of the sonnets[27]), had died on his birthday. The Oxford college that Browne attended had been named for Herbert while Browne was in residence there.[28] Common belief also had it that Plato had passed away on his birthday, a matter which Browne declared placed his death "somewhat above humanity."[29] Other instances are reported by John Gibbon, a notably eccentric seventeenth-century antiquarian (and an older brother of Robert Gibbon, Hale's factotum and one of his executors), who wrote an essay called "Day-Fatalities." They include Alexander the Great, Pompey, and Henry VII's wife, in addition to Gibbon's own maternal uncle.[30]

Following his death on his birthday, Browne's body was placed into a vault on the south side of the chancel at St. Peter Mancroft. The vault already contained the bodies of one of Browne's daughters and two of his grandsons. Browne's wife would be interred there two years later. The epitaph on her tomb, as Sir Geoffrey Keynes has poignantly observed, "is the only tangible relic of her life that remains, except for the illiterate postscripts which she was in the habit of adding to Sir Thomas' letters to his children."[31] In 1723—more than half a century later—officials placed the remains of Dr. John Jeffery, the man who had edited Browne's *Christian Morals*, into the Browne vault. It then was sealed and filled with earth.

The burial site remained undisturbed for the next seventeen years, until workmen digging a grave for Mary Bowman, the recently deceased wife of St. Peter Mancroft's rector, accidentally pick-axed their way into the Browne vault. It was at first reported that they had discovered large deposits of adipocere, the waxy substance into which muscles and the albuminoid portions of the body are sometimes transformed after death: the discovery of adipocere is regarded as Browne's sole scientific contribution.[32] But this report was scotched by a statement that only skeletons remained in the vault, plus a mop of auburn hair. This was taken to signify the lasting quality of Sir Thomas' vividly-brown hair,[33] until an authority on such matters pointed out that the hair of all corpses is turned reddish by materials absorbed from the earth.

Browne's skull was removed from the tomb under mysterious circumstances. Several casts of it later came to light, but it would be seven years before the original was donated to the Norfolk and Norwich Hospital Museum by a doctor who did not want to divulge how he had obtained possession of it. Only a fringe of hair remained; a lock of hair, said to be from the original find, was later to come into the possession of Sir William Osler, a preeminent Canadian physician (later a Regius professor at Oxford), and a worshipful admirer of Browne.[34] That lock is on display today at McGill University.

In 1893, officials at St. Peter Mancroft threatened to sue the Museum to have the skull returned, but lawyers advised that a man's bones do not constitute legal property and that consequently the surrender of the skull could not be accomplished by means of judicial process.[35] When the skull was recovered by the Museum, Osler donated a silver casket in 1901 to house it in a more dignified manner.[36] Among the inscriptions on the plates around its pedestal were two of Browne's more trenchant opinions on the nature of death and its consequences:

> At my death, I mean to take a total adieu of the world, not caring for a monument, history or epitaph, not so much as the bare memory of my name to be found anywhere but in the universal register of God.[37]

And:

> I believe that our estranged and divided ashes shall unite again;
> that our separated dust, after so many pilgrimages and transfor-
> mations into the parts of minerals, plants, animals, elements,
> shall at the voice of God return into their primitive shapes and
> join again to make up their primary predestinate forms.[38]

It was decided in 1922 to reunite Browne's skull with what remained
of his body. Before that was done, however, the skull was dispatched by
messenger to the Royal College of Surgeons in London. There an elaborate attempt was made to determine which of a considerable number
of portraits said to be of Browne accurately represented him.

As Figure 7 shows, the skull was arranged precisely to test the
authenticity of the so-called Buccleuch miniature portrait, one of the
only two renderings which passed the test. Another aim of the investigation was to answer the question: "Can the body really tell us
anything about the mind of a man and, if so, how much?"—though
not much hope was held out for an affirmative answer. Sir Arthur
Keith, who supervised the inquiry, noted that Browne had a low-
browed skull with a receding forehead, "features which are not
universally associated with a high intellect." But, at the same time,
Browne was said to possess a brain considerably larger than that of the
average Englishman.[39] In the end it appeared that little more than a
vague sort of scientific excuse had prompted the exhaustive examination of Sir Thomas Browne's skull. The writer of the report on the
matter said about as much:

> We feel we do not know a man unless we know what he looks
> like, and our curiosity is very strong in the case of men dead
> and gone whom we have learnt to know in part through their
> works.[40]

The analysis completed, the skull was put back with the body under
the sanctuary at the east end of St. Peter Mancroft on July 4, 1922.
"But who knows the fate of his bones, or how often he is to be
buried," Browne had written, with stunning prescience in regard to his
own remains.[41] A Monumental Inscription to Browne can be found
today on the south pillar above the altar rail. On it, Browne is
described as "per orbem Notissimus Vir Prudentissimus, Integerrimus,
Doctissimus"—known throughout the world as a man outstanding in
prudence, judgment, and learning.

Figure 7 Sir Thomas Browne's skull

Source: Photo from Miriam L. Tildesley, "Sir Thomas Browne: His Skull, Portraits and Ancestry," in *Biometrika*, Vol. xv (August 1923). CEFAS Library, Lowestoft, is gratefully acknowledged for permission to reproduce it here.

While Browne's skull was still in its peripatetic status, its original owner's reputation—the epitaph notwithstanding—was being brought into question. In preparation in 1904 for the tercentenary of Browne's birth, the British Medical Association sought subscriptions to underwrite the cost of a statue to Browne, to be placed in a central location in Norwich.[42] Dr. Conolly Norman, an eminent Irish physician, objected strenuously, harking back to the witchcraft trial. Browne's record, Norman insisted, was "stained with innocent blood, the blood of poor and defenseless people shed with his connivance almost, one might say, at his instigation." Norman suggested to the Medical Association that the least it could do would be to erect a memorial to Amy Denny and Rose Cullender. Their figures, he said, could be used as background in the Browne statue, there to provide "interesting evidences of Sir Thomas's repute."[43]

The suggestion was ignored, and a larger-than-life statue of Sir Thomas can be found in the Haymarket in Norwich, his gaze directed to a broken urn in his outstretched palm; if the statue were to raise its head, it would be looking directly at the house in which Browne lived.[44] Shoppers rest beside it, and teenagers use it as a convenient meeting place. The large plinth on which the statue stands bears the marks of contemporary times. On one side is scribbled in crayon: "Norwich punks are a sad pathetic sight." On another is a fascist symbol in red paint, while Ruth, Karen, Sal, and Dave commemorate themselves on other portions of the statue. Nearby, a group of elderly men and women hand out pamphlets that Browne might well have appreciated. They proclaim that "because of Immorality and Covetousness the Wrath of God is Coming."

Sir Edmund Bacon, the magistrate who set the judicial wheels in motion, lies buried in the Bacon family vault in St. Botolph's, the isolated and ancient parish church of Redgrave. He is commemorated on a small slab, set in the wall above the vault in the corner of the church. The inscription reads:

> In the vault under this marble
> Lyeth the body of Sir Edmond Bacon of
> Redgrave Baronet who marryed
> Elizabeth daughter of Sir Robert Crane
> of Chilton Hall in Suff: Knt and Bartt
> and lived with her in marriage 35 years
> had issue by her 6 sons and 10 daughters
> He lived in the Love and Honorable
> Esteeme of his country
> Loyal to his King constant
> To the Government in God and State
> A Generous Colonel
> a Good Magistrate
> A Just Man
> A learned and most Accomplished Gentleman
> and Dyed

a Pious Christian
on the 12 Day of September 1685
in the yeare of his age 52

The church is dominated by the lavish white marble memorial to Sir John Holt who, as a judge in the early eighteenth century, was instrumental in bringing the witch trial craze to an end. Holt had purchased the Redgrave Hall estate from the Bacon family in 1710.

Samuel Pacy would live almost two decades after the witchcraft trial. On his death in 1680, his body was interred in St. Margaret's Church, Lowestoft. Burial inside churches was a new fashion, having come into usage during the Civil War and the Interregnum. Such a burial "always argued unusual standing in the community";[45] the consent of the churchwarden had to be obtained. Those offended by the new custom labeled the areas where bodies were placed as the "charnel-chapel"[46] or "charnel-house."[47] To counteract unpleasant odors arising from the shallow graves, juniper and frankincense were burned on special occasions, such as the great festivals and the visits of important dignitaries.[48]

In St. Margaret's, the black marble slabs commemorating Samuel Pacy and several members of his family are embedded in the floor in a prominent position in the chancel, almost directly in front of the altar. The presence of the Pacy tombstone in so conspicuous a spot might seem to belie his reputation as "an eminent dissenter";[49] instead it merely demonstrates the complexities of religious affiliation in seventeenth-century England. Despite doctrinal disputes with the Church of England, dissenters often lived on amiable terms with the established church at a parochial level. In his will, for instance, Pacy bequeathed forty shillings to Joseph Hudson, Lowestoft's vicar.

Some dissenters attended both public or private nonconformist services as well as those of the Church of England, where they sometimes took communion.[50] Many of the others who shunned their local church for worship continued to view it as a house of God, a hallowed site in which to be baptized, married, and eventually buried. Like Samuel Pacy, William Bridge, the radical nonconformist preacher in Great Yarmouth, was also interred in his parish church. Pacy's family, being wealthy, readily could have purchased a place inside St. Margaret's in which to inter his body, knowing perfectly well that in doing so they would not be violating his religious beliefs.

The slab inside St. Margaret's marking the grave of Samuel Pacy's wife is the most conspicuous of those of the family. It is slightly more than seven feet long and three-and-three-quarter feet in width. On the upper portion it reads:

> HERE LAYETH THE BODY OF
> ELIZABETH THE WIFE OF
> SAMUEL PACY MERCHANT OF
> THIS TOWNE WHO DEPARTED
> THIS LIFE THE 4th OF AVGVST
> ANNO DOMINI 1682 AGED 58
> YEARS

The gray slab commemorating Samuel is a foot-and-a-half shorter and to the left of Elizabeth's, facing from the altar rail. It reads:

> HERE VNDER RESTETH THE
> BODY OF SAMUELL PACY THE
> BROTHER OF NICHOLAS PACY
> WHO DEPARTED THIS LIFE THE
> 17th OF SEPTEMBER ANNO
> DOMINI 1680 AGED 56 YEARES

Despite the grammar, it is the death date of Samuel, not that of his older brother, that the slab notes. The reference to Nicholas, rather than Samuel's wife, may be testimony to the fact that he had paid for the entombment or, perhaps, it demonstrates the unimportance of wives in such public memorials. That Samuel and Elizabeth were about the same age represents a slight variation on the convention of the time for men to marry women about three years younger than they were.[51] Samuel, the parish register indicates, was buried in linen, a mark of status. A payment of £5 had been mandated in 1667 for every corpse so clothed, a measure that was intended to reduce the importation of French and Dutch linens and to advance the price of domestic wool.[52] A clever ruse was sometimes employed to reduce the fine. When paid, it was divided into two parts. Half went to the person who had informed against the violators and the other half to the parish poor. By arranging that the informer should be a member of his family, or a servant, the violator could insure that half the sum was returned to him.[53]

The slab immediately to the right of Samuel Pacy's can no longer be read with the naked eye. It lies on a direct path from the chancel door to the interior of the church and countless footsteps have eroded its inscription. Nineteenth-century records indicate that it memorializes

Nicholas Pacy, who, aged 66, died November 5, 1680, less than two months after his youngest brother, Samuel. This is the same Nicholas Pacy who had for a time lived in Salem; the date of his return to Lowestoft is unknown. More than fifty years later—in September 1736—the body of Samuel Church, Samuel Pacy's grandson, was interred under the floor at St. Margaret's and his name was appended onto the memorial slab to Nicholas Pacy, his great-uncle.[54]

Two of the Pacy children are buried to the right of their mother and father. Immediately adjacent to that of her mother's is a stone commemorating Susan, the family's eldest daughter, the one girl of the three sisters who, as far as we know, played no significant part in the 1662 witchcraft prosecution. The inscription indicates that Susan had been the wife of Richard Church and that she had died March 22, 1708, at the age of sixty. Susan Pacy, therefore, was just short of her fourteenth birthday when Amy Denny and Rose Cullender were tried for witchcraft.

Susan's marriage to Richard Church, a Lowestoft merchant, had been her second alliance. She previously was wed to Edward Brown, a tanner, who died in 1669 at age 25, less than two years after the marriage. She bore him one child, a son named Edward, who died the same year as his father. Susan married Richard Church four months later and he died eight years after that. Susan herself likely elected to be laid to rest with the Pacys and to have her husband's remains interred elsewhere. In his will, Church had committed his body "to the earth from whence it was taken" and asked only that his executrix—Susan— have the body "buried in such desent Christian Mannor" as she "thought moote and convenient."[55] His wife remained a widow for the 31 years until her death. By 1680, when Samuel Pacy died, Susan was living with her three children in a house owned by him.[56]

The church floor was prised up again almost a century after Susan was interred to receive the body of Matilda Church, Samuel Pacy's great-great-granddaughter. Both Susan and her sister, Deborah, were great-grandmothers of Matilda Church because of the intermarriage of Richard Church, Susan's son, with Elizabeth Pake, Deborah's daughter. Matilda Church was a spinster, "a notable eccentric,"[57] who had lived most of her life in Great Yarmouth. In her will, she had requested that she be buried in linen in the same church grave as her ancestors and that she be carried there by six men who were to have a guinea apiece.[58]

John Barker Church of Lowestoft, Matilda's brother, may well have been a man cut from the same mold as Samuel Pacy. Church amassed a large fortune while serving as *commissaire* for the Count de Rochambeau, General-in-Chief of the French contingent during the American Revolution. Rochambeau was present at Yorktown for the surrender of the British general, Lord Cornwallis,[59] a direct descendant of the justice of the peace who had been in attendance at the trial of Amy Denny and Rose Cullender.

In 1778, John Barker Church had eloped with Angelica, the eldest daughter of General Philip Schuyler, a member of one of the wealthiest New York families. The General was much put out by the elopement: he was, he wrote a friend, "un-acquainted with [Church's] family connections and his situation in life," so that he found the matter "exceedingly disagreeable."[60] Alexander Hamilton was married to Angelica's younger sister, Elizabeth, and some writers maintain that Angelica, "charming" and "witty,"[61] was Hamilton's mistress.[62]

John Barker Church fought a pistol duel with Aaron Burr on September 2, 1799, based on Church's allegation that Burr had accepted a bribe from the Holland Land Company.[63] No one was hurt in the first round of shots; then Church ended the affair by apologizing, saying that he had been indiscreet, and was sorry for it.[64] When Hamilton was killed in a duel with Burr at Weehawken on July 11, 1804, it was Church's pistols that Hamilton used for the encounter.[65]

Church later returned to England, and was elected to Parliament for six years from 1790 for Wendover, a rotten borough of 180 inhabitants that he had purchased from the Earl of Varney. He was an intimate of the Prince of Wales as well as a friend of Lafayette and Talleyrand. Church died in Paris in 1818, on the eve of a planned visit to Lowestoft.

The Church family history includes a passing incident whose larger irony very likely was unbeknown to the participants. In 1835, Elizabeth Church—her first name an echo of the Bury trial—had attended a fancy masquerade ball in New York with two male friends, the three dressed as the witches in *Macbeth*, "looking as horrible as possible, with serpents entwined around their hats and waists. At the ball they danced around the devil who appeared with a long tail."[66]

The remains of Deborah Pacy, one of Susan's younger sisters, and a key figure in the witch trial, are interred immediately to the right of Susan's and Matilda Church's. The inscription on Deborah Pacy's commemorative slab reads:

HERE LIETH THE BODY OF
DEBORAH THE WIFE OF IO:
SEPH PAKE AND THE DAUGHTER OF
SAMUEL AND ELIZABETH PACY
DECEASED WHO DIED JAN 23
1695/6 AGED 42 YEARS

The 1695/6 refers, of course, to the practice, slowly fading at that time, of adherence to the Julian calendar, which dated a new year from March 25 rather than from the beginning of January, a practice only officially abandoned in 1752. According to the Lowestoft Parish Register, Deborah was baptized on April 12, 1654—presumably fairly soon after her birth—at the font of the church in which she would be buried. That would have made her just short of eight years old when the witch trial took place, rather than nine, which is what the trial record maintains. The parish register entry also disputes the age at death recorded on the slab: it indicates that Deborah would not have been forty-two for another two-and-a-half months. It appears likely, given these contradictions, that Deborah was not baptized soon after her birth, as was the usual but far from universal custom, but instead when she was at least several months old. The most reasonable explanation for such a delay would be the child's fragility.[67]

Added to Deborah's tomb, in a different lettering style, is notice of the interment in the same space of Deborah Plumstead, "Eldest daughter of Doctor JOSEPH PAKE and DEBORAH his wife." The daughter had died on September 6, 1723, at the age of forty-one years. Deborah's husband was to outlive his wife by seventeen years. Eighteen months after Deborah's death, he married Mary Knight, née Mighells, the widowed daughter of a family close to the Pacys. She died in 1710 and was buried in St. Margaret's near other members of the Knight family. Pake himself died three years later; in his will he designated 40 shillings to be given to the poor of Lowestoft, adding as a caveat: "But if any of the poor shall molest or disturb my funerall or trouble the house, such of them shall have no share or part of said money."[68] His gravestone, also in St. Margaret's, testifies to his "34 years successful practice of pharmacy and surgery, in which his approved fidelity and clear judgement rendered him the happy instrument of affording great relief to those who were in sickness; for which Death sent him to receive his reward from God, in the 58th year of his age."[69]

Samuel Pacy thus lies buried amidst his wife and two of his daughters, both of whom, though married, were not put to rest with their husbands. The remains of Elizabeth Pacy, the middle sister, the other key protagonist in the witchcraft proceedings, also rest at St. Margaret's, but no memorial was erected to her and the exact site of her interment is not known. She had married Henry Ward, a Lowestoft mariner and distant relative of the Pacys, in 1677, and the couple had settled in Stepney, then a hamlet outside London. The marriage was short. Henry Ward died in 1680; eight months before his death he had written his will, noting that he was "now in health of body . . . but going to sea and not knowing how soon it may please God to take me out of this fraile and transitory life." Elizabeth, together with an infant daughter, returned to Lowestoft,[70] where she died in December 1684.[71] At the time of her death she was one month short of her thirty-fifth birthday.

Neither the remains of Mary, a daughter who died shortly after birth,[72] nor those of any of the four sons of Samuel and Elizabeth Pacy are memorialized in St. Margaret's Church. The first son was William, who was born in 1655 and died in infancy. Then came Samuel who was born about 1659 or 1660. Samuel, who later became a Justice of the Peace, was also a dissenter and a trustee of the first Congregational Chapel which opened in Lowestoft in 1696.[73] In addition, he was named one of the country's fifty unpaid Receiver-Generals, political nominees who were appointed in each county of the realm, and often made use of the money they gathered for their own purposes in the interval before it was handed in. The positions were regarded as juicy prizes for rewarding or creating local electoral influence.[74] The junior Samuel Pacy died suddenly in 1708 while taking the baths at Epsom, owing the government £18,628.13s.8d. (18,628 pounds, 13 shillings and 8 pence) that he had collected in taxes, and leaving his affairs, a Parliamentary declaration observed, "in great confusion."[75] Despite strenuous efforts, the money never was found. Another William was born late in 1662 or in early 1663, and the youngest boy, John, in 1664. The second William, also a dissenter,[76] later became mayor of Great Yarmouth, and saw his daughter married to the Reverend Roger Donne, a descendant of the poet.[77]

The Pacy burial vaults presumably remained undisturbed after Matilda Church was interred amidst her ancestors in 1805. Then, in the spring of 1983, some members of the Fabric Committee at St. Margaret's, responsible for the upkeep of the building, looked longingly at the space taken up by the burial vaults as a possible direction for underground expansion. To explore the possibilities, a builder was employed who drilled a porthole-sized opening in what proved to be a four-foot-thick wall between the crypt (now used as the vestry) and the burial vault. The work was done with a minimum of publicity since it might have been deemed blasphemous—disturbing the repose of the dead lying in consecrated ground—and could have led to community censure. After several days of effort, when the workers finally broke through the wall, they placed a light bulb at the end of a wire attached to a cane and thrust it into the opening at almost exactly the spot where Elizabeth Pacy's bones should be. Two wooden coffins, both resting on trestles, could be made out lying side by side in a brick-lined vault some twelve feet square. The left-hand coffin was perfectly intact. Made from plain wood, it was devoid of any ornamentation save an unreadable inscription on the top. The other coffin, seemingly much older, had collapsed in on itself.

Committee members, who had hoped that the vault somehow would be empty, now decided that there was no likelihood that the rector would care to undertake the elaborate process necessary to obtain permission to move the Pacy remains elsewhere. So they sealed up the hole. One man who had participated in the venture sought words to express his feelings about the intrusion into the final resting place of the Pacys. "There was no smell," he said finally, a note of considerable surprise in his voice. "No smell at all."

That today there remain prominent vestiges of the major personages in the 1662 witchcraft case—Samuel Pacy, Matthew Hale, Edmund Bacon and Thomas Browne—testifies to their impression on their own times and, at least in regard to Hale and Browne, to the extension of their significance into our time. It probably would go without saying that we have been unable to discover any certain indication of the final resting place of either Amy Denny or Rose Cullender.

A

TRYAL

OF

WITCHES,

AT THE

ASSIZES

HELD AT

Bury St. Edmonds for the County of *SUFFOLK*; on the Tenth day of *March*, 1664.

BEFORE

Sir MATTHEW HALE Kt.

THEN

Lord Chief Baron of His Majefties Court of EXCHEQUER.

Taken by a Perfon then Attending the Court

LONDON,

Printed for *William Shrewsbery* at the Bible in *Duck-Lane*. 1682.

Figure 8 The front cover of the trial report, 1682
Source: Authors' collection.

Appendix

A tryal of witches

TO THE READER

This trial of witches hath lain a long time in a private gentleman's
hands in the country, it being given to him by the person that took it at
the court for his own satisfaction; but it came lately to my hands, and
having perused it, I found it a very remarkable thing, and fit to be
published; especially in these times, wherein things of this nature are
much controverted, and that by persons of much learning on both sides.
I thought that so exact a relation of this trial would probably give
more satisfaction to a great many persons, by reason that it is pure
matter of fact, and that evidently demonstrated; than the arguments
and Reasons of other very Learned Men, that probably may not be so
Intelligble to all Readers; especially this being held before a Judge,
whom for his Integrity, Learning, and Law, hardly any Age, either
before or since could parallel; who not only took a great deal of paines,
and spent much time in this Tryal himself: but had the Assistance and
Opinion of several other very Eminent and Learned Persons: So that
this being the most perfect Narrative of any thing of this Nature hith-
erto Extant, made me unwillingly to deprive the World of the Benefit
of it: which is the sole Motive that induced me to Publish it.

Farewel.

A TRYAL OF WITCHES

At the Assizes and General Gaol delivery, held at Bury St. Edmonds *for*
the County of Suffolk, *the Tenth day of* March, *in the Sixteenth Year of*
the Reign of our Sovereign Lord King Charles II: *before* Matthew Hale,
Knight, Lord Chief Baron of His Majesties Court of Exchequer: Rose
Cullender *and* Amy Duny, *Widows, both of* Leystoff *in the County afore-*

said, were severally indicted for Bewitching Elizabeth *and* Ann Durent, Jane Bocking, Susan Chandler, William Durent, Elizabeth *and* Deborah Pacey: *And the said* Cullender *and* Duny, *being arraigned upon the said Indictments, pleaded* Not Guilty: *And afterwards, upon a long Evidence, were found* Guilty, *and thereupon had Judgment to dye for the same.*

The Evidence whereupon these Persons were convicted of Witchcraft, *stands upon divers particular Circumstances.*

I. Three of the Parties above-named, viz. *Anne Durent, Susan Chandler,* and *Elizabeth Pacy* were brought to *Bury* to the Assizes and were in reasonable good condition: But that Morning they came into the Hall to give Instructions for the drawing of their Bills of Indictments, the Three Persons fell into strange and violent fits, screeking out in a most sad manner, so that they could not in any wise give any Instructions in the Court who were the Cause of their Distemper. And although they did after some certain space recover out of their fits, yet they were every one of them struck Dumb, so that none of them could speak neither at that time, nor during the Assizes until the Conviction of the supposed Witches.

As concerning *William Durent*, being an Infant, his Mother *Dorothy Durent* sworn and examined deposed in open Court, That about the Tenth of *March, Nono Caroli Secundi*, she having a special occasion to go from home, and having none in her House to take care of her said Child (it then sucking) desired *Amy Duny* her Neighbour, to look to her child during her absence, for which she promised her to give her a Penny: but the said *Dorothy Durent* desired the said *Amy* not to Suckle her Child, and laid a great charge upon her not to do it. Upon which it was asked by the Court, why she did give that direction, she being an old Woman and not capable of giving Suck? It was answered by the said *Dorothy Durent*, that she very well knew that she did not give suck, but that for some years before, she had gone under the Reputation of a *Witch*, which was one cause made her give the caution: Another was, That it was customary with old Women, that if they did look after a sucking Child, and nothing would please it but the Breast, they did use to please the Child, to give it the breast, and it did please the Child, but it sucked nothing but Wind, which did the Child hurt. Nevertheless after the departure of this deponent, the said *Amy* did Suckle the Child: And after the return of the said *Dorothy*, the said *Amy* did acquaint her, *That she had given Suck to the Child* contrary to her command. Whereupon the Deponent was very angry with the said

Amy for the same; at which the said *Amy* was much discontented, and used many high Expressions and Threatening Speeches towards her: telling her; *That she had as good to have done otherwise than to have found fault with her, and so departed out of her House*: And that very Night her Son fell into strange fits of swounding, and was held in such terrible manner, that she was much affrighted therewith, and so continued for divers weeks. And the said Examinant farther said, that she being exceedingly troubled at her Childs Distemper, did go to a certain Person named Doctor *Jacob*, who lived at *Yarmouth*, who had the reputation in the Country, to help children that were Bewitch'd: who advis'd her to hang up the Childs Blanket in the Chimney-corner all day, and at night when she put the Child to Bed, to put it into the said blanket, and if she found any thing in it, she should not be afraid, but to throw it into the Fire. And this Deponent did according to his direction; and at night when she took down the Blanket with an intent to put her Child therein, there fell out of the same a great Toad, which ran up and down the hearth, and she having a young youth only with her in the House, desired him to catch the Toad, and throw it into the Fire, which the youth did accordingly, and held it there with the Tongs; and as soon as it was in the Fire it made a great and horrible Noise, and after a space there was a flashing in the Fire like Gun-powder, making the noise like the discharge of a Pistol, and thereupon the Toad was no more seen nor heard. It was asked by the Court, if that after the noise and flashing, there was not the Substance of the Toad to be seen to consume in the fire? And it was answered by the said *Dorothy Durent*, that after the flashing and noise, there was no more seen than if there had been none there. The next day there came a young Woman a Kinswoman of the said *Amy*, and a neighbour of this Deponent, and told this Deponent, that her Aunt (meaning the said *Amy*) was in a most lamentable condition having her face all scorched with fire, and that she was sitting alone in her House, in her smock without any fire. And thereupon this Deponent went into the House of the said *Amy Duny* to see her, and found her in the same condition as was related to her; for her Face, her Leggs, and Thighs, which this Deponent saw, seemed very much scorched and burnt with Fire, at which this Deponent seemed much to wonder. And asked the said *Amy* how she came into that sad condition? and the said *Amy* replied, she might thank her for it, for that she this Deponent was the cause thereof, but that she should live to see some of her Children dead, and she upon Crutches. And this Deponent farther saith, that after the burning of the said Toad, her child recover'd, and was well again, and was living at the time of the Assizes. And this Deponent farther saith,

That about the *6th. of March, 11° Car. 2.* her Daughter *Elizabeth Durent*, being about the Age of Ten Years, was taken in a like manner as her first Child was, and in her fits complained much of *Amy Duny*, and said, That she did appear to her, and Afflict her in such manner as the former. And she this Deponent going to the Apothecaries for some thing for her said Child, when she did return to her own House, she found the said *Amy Duny* there, and asked her what she did do there? and her answer was, *That she came to see her Child, and to give it some water.* But she this Deponent was very angry with her, and thrust her forth of her doors, and when she was out of doors, she said, *You need not be so angry, for your Child will not live long:* and this was on a *Saturday*, and the Child dyed on the *Monday* following. The cause of whose Death this Deponent verily believeth was occasion'd by the Witchcraft of the said *Amy Duny:* for that the said *Amy* hath been long reputed to be a *Witch*, and a person of very evil behaviour, whose Kindred and Relations have been many of them accused for *Witchcraft*, and some of them have been Condemned.

The said Deponent further saith, that not long after the death of her Daughter *Elizabeth Durent*, she this Deponent was taken with a Lameness in both her Leggs, from the knees downward, that she was fain to go upon Cruches, and that she had no other use of them but only to bear a little upon them till she did remove her Crutches, and so continued till the time of the Assizes, that the *Witch* came to be Tryed, and was there upon her Crutches, the Court asked her, *That at the time she was taken with this Lameness, if it were with her according to the Custom of Women?* Her Answer was, that it was so, and that she never had any stoppages of those things, but when she was with Child.

This is the Substance of her Evidence to this Indictment.

There was one thing very remarkable, that after she had gone upon Crutches for upwards of Three Years, and went upon them at the time of the Assizes in the Court when she gave her Evidence, and upon the Juries bringing in their Verdict, by which the said *Amy Duny* was found Guilty, to the great admiration of all Persons, the said *Dorothy Durent* was restored to the use of her Limbs, and went home without making use of her Crutches.

II. As concerning *Elizabeth* and *Deborah Pacy*, the first of the Age of Eleven Years, the other of the age of Nine Years or thereabouts: as to the Elder, she was brought into the Court at the time of the Instructions given to draw up the Indictments, and afterwards at the time of Tryal of the said Prisoners, but could not speak one Word all the time, and for the most part she remained as one wholly senseless as one in a deep Sleep, and could move no part of her body, and all the Motion of Life that appeared in her was, that as she lay upon Cushions in the Court upon her back, her stomack and belly by the drawing of her breath, would arise to a great height: and after the said *Elizabeth* had lain a long time on the Table in the Court, she came a little to her self and sate up, but could neither see nor speak, but was sensible of what was said to her, and after a while she laid her Head on the Bar of the Court with a Cushion under it, and her hand and her Apron upon that, and there she lay a good space of time: and by the direction of the Judg, *Amy Duny* was privately brought to *Elizabeth Pacy*, and she touched her hand; whereupon the Child without so much as seeing her, for her Eyes were closed all the while, suddenly leaped up, and catched *Amy Duny* by the hand, and afterwards by the face; and with her nails scratched her till Blood came, and would by no means leave her till she was taken from her, and afterwards the Child would still be pressing towards her, and making signs of Anger conceived against her.

Deborah the younger Daughter was held in such extream manner, that her Parents wholly despaired of her life, and therefore could not bring her to the Assizes.

The Evidence which was given concerning these Two Children was to this Effect.

Samuel Pacy a Merchant of *Leystoff* aforesaid, (a man who carried himself with much soberness during the Tryal, from whom proceeded no words either of Passion or Malice, though his Children were so greatly Afflicted), Sworn and Examined, Deposeth, That his younger Daughter *Deborah*, upon *Thursday* the Tenth of *October* last, was suddenly taken with a Lameness in her Leggs, so that she could not stand, neither had she any strength in her Limbs to support her, and so she continued until the Seventeenth day of the same Month, which day being fair and Sunshiny, the Child desired to be carried on the *East* part of the House, to be set upon the Bank which looketh upon the Sea; and whil'st she was sitting there, *Amy Duny* came to this Deponents House to buy some Herrings, but being denyed she went away discontented, and presently returned again, and was denyed, and likwise the third time and was denyed as at first; and at her last going away, she went away grumbling; but what she said was not perfectly understood. But at the very same instant of time, the said Child was taken with most violent fits, feeling most extream pain in her Stomach, like the pricking of Pins, and Shreeking out in a most dreadful manner like unto a Whelp, and not like unto a sensible Creature. And in this extremity the Child continued to the great grief of the Parents until the Thirtieth of the Same Month. During this time this Deponent sent for one Dr. *Feavor*, a Doctor of Physick, to take his advice concerning his Childs Distemper: the Doctor being come, he saw the Child in those fits, but could not conjecture (as he then told this Deponent, and afterwards affirmed in open Court, at this Tryal) what might be the cause of the Childs Affliction. And this Deponent farther saith, That by reason of the circumstances aforesaid, and in regard *Amy Duny* is a Woman of an ill Fame, & commonly reported to be a *Witch & Sorceress*, and for that the said Child in her fits would cry out of *Amy Duny* as the cause of her Malady, and that she did affright her with Apparitions of her Person (as the Child in the intervals of her fits related) he this Deponent did suspect the said *Amy Duny* for a *Witch*, and charged her with the injury and wrong to his child, and caused her to be set in the Stocks on the Twenty eighth of the same *October*: and during the time of her continuance there, one *Alice Letteridge* and *Jane Buxton* demanding of her (as they also affirmed in Court upon their Oathes) what should be the reason of Mr. *Pacy's* Childs Distemper? telling her, That she was suspected to be the cause thereof; she replyed, Mr. Pacy *keeps a great stir about his Child, but let him stay until he hath done as much by his Children, as I have done by mine.* And being further examined, what she had done to her Children? She answered, *That she had been fain to open her Child's Mouth with a Tap to give it Victuals.*

And the said Deponent further desposeth, That within two days after speaking of the said words being the Thirtieth of *October*, the eldest Daughter *Elizabeth*, fell into extream fits, insomuch, that they could not open her Mouth to give her breath, to preserve her Life without the help of a Tap which they were enforced to use; and the younger Child was in the like manner Afflicted, so that they used the same also for her Relief.

And further the said Children being grievously afflicted would severally complain in their extremity, and also in the intervals, That *Amy Duny* (together with one other Woman whose person and Cloathes they described) did thus Afflict them, their Apparitions appearing before them, to their great terrour and affrightment: And sometimes they would cry out, saying, *There stands* Amy Duny, *and there* Rose Cullender; the other Person troubling them.

Their fits were various, sometimes they would be lame on one side of their Bodies, sometimes on the other: sometimes a soreness over their whole Bodies, so as they could endure none to touch them: at other times they would be restored to the perfect use of their Limbs, and deprived of their Hearing; at other times of their Sight, at other times of their Speech; sometimes by the space of one day, sometimes for two; and once they were wholly deprived of their Speech for Eight days together, and then restored to their Speech again. At other times they would fall into Swounings, and upon the recovery to their Speech they would Cough extreamly, and bring up much Flegme, and with the same crooked Pins, and one time a Two-penny Nail with a very broad head, which Pins (amounting to Forty or more) together with the Two-penny Nail were produced in Court, with the affirmation of the said Deponent, that he was present when the said Nail was Vomited up, and also most of the Pins. Commonly at the end of every fit they would cast up a Pin, and sometimes they would have four or five fits in one day.

In this manner the said Children continued with this Deponent for the space of two Months, during which time in their Intervals this Deponent would cause them to Read some Chapters in the *New Testament*. Whereupon this Deponent several times observed, that they would read till they came to the Name of Lord, or Jesus, or Christ; and then before they could pronounce either of the said Words they would suddenly fall into their fits. But when they came to the Name of Satan, or Devil, they would clap their Fingers upon the Book, crying out, *This bites, but makes me speak right well.*

At such time as they be recovered out of their fits (occasion'd as this Deponent conceives upon their naming of Lord, or Jesus, or Christ,) this Deponent hath demanded of them, what is the cause they cannot pronounce those words, They reply and say, *That* Amy Duny *saith, I must not use that name.*

And farther, the said Children after their fits were past, would tell, how that *Amy Duny*, and *Rose Cullender* would appear before them, holding their Fists at them, threatning, *That if they related either what they saw or heard, that they would Torment them Ten times more than ever they did before.*

In their fits they would cry out, *There stands* Amy Duny, *or* Rose Cullender; and sometimes in one place and sometimes in another, running with great violence to the place where they fancied them to stand, striking at them as if they were present; they would appear to them sometimes spinning, and sometimes reeling, or in other postures, deriding or threatning them.

And this Deponent farther saith, That his Children being thus Tormented by all the space aforesaid, and finding no hopes of amendment, he sent them to his Sisters House, one *Margaret Arnold*, who lived at *Yarmouth*, to make tryal, whether the change of the Air might do them any good. And how, and in what manner they were afterwards held, he this Deponent refers himself to the Testimony of his said Sister.

Margaret Arnold, Sworn and Examined, saith, That the said *Elizabeth* and *Deborah Pacy* came to her House about the Thirtieth of *November* last, her Brother acquainted her, that he thought they were Bewitch'd, for that they vomited Pins; and farther Informed her of the several passages which occurred at his own House. This Deponent said, that she gave no credit to that which was related to her, conceiving possibly the Children might use some deceit in putting Pins in their mouths themselves. Wherefore this Deponent unpinned all their Cloathes, and left not so much as one Pin upon them, but sewed all the Clothes they wore, instead of pinning of them. But this Deponent saith, that notwithstanding all this care and circumspection of hers, the Children afterwards raised at several times at least Thirty Pins in her presence, and had most fierce and violent Fitts upon them.

The Children would in their Fitts cry out against *Rose Cullender* and *Amy Duny*, affirming that they saw them; and they threatned to Torment them Ten times more, if they complained of them. At some times the Children (only) would see things run up and down the House in the appearance of Mice; and one of them suddainly snapt one with the Tongs, and threw it into the fire, and it screeched out like a Rat.

At another time, the younger Child being out of her Fitts went out of Doors to take a little fresh Air, and presently a little thing like a Bee flew upon her Face, and would have gone into her Mouth, whereupon the Child ran in all haste to the door to get into the House again, screeking out in a most terrible manner; whereupon, this Deponent made haste to come to her, but before she could get to her, the Child fell into her swooning Fitt, and at last with much pain straining herself, she vomited up a Two-penny Nail with a broad Head; and after that the Child had raised up the Nail she came to her understanding; and being demanded by this Deponent, how she came by this Nail? she Answered, *That the Bee brought this Nail and forced it into her Mouth.*

And at other times, the Elder Child declared unto this Deponent, that during the time of her Fitts, she saw Flies come unto her, and bring with them in their Mouthes crooked Pins; and after the Child had thus declared the same, she fell again into violent Fits, and afterwards raised several Pins.

At another time, the said Elder Child declared unto this Deponent, and sitting by the Fire suddainly started up and said, *she saw a Mouse*, and she crept under the Table looking after it, and at length, she put something in her Apron, saying, *she had caught it*; and immediately she ran to the Fire and threw it in, and there did appear upon it to this Deponent, like the flashing of Gunpowder, though she confessed she saw nothing in the Childs Hand.

At another time the said Child being speechless, but otherwise of perfect understanding, ran round about the House holding her Apron, crying, *hush, hush*, as if there had been some Poultrey in the House; but this Deponent could perceive nothing: but at last she saw the Child stoop as if she had catch't at something, and put it into her Apron, and afterwards made as if she had thrown it into the Fire: but this Deponent could not discover anything: but the Child afterwards being restored to her speech, she this Deponent demanded of her what she saw at the time she used such a posture? who answered, *That she saw a Duck*.

At another time, the Younger daughter being recovered out of her Fitts, declared, *That* Amy Duny *had been with her, and that she tempted her to Drown her self, and to cut her Throat, or otherwise to Destroy her self.*

At another time in their Fitts they both of them cryed out upon *Rose Cullender* and *Amy Duny*, complaining against them; *Why do not you come your selves, but send your Imps to Torment us?*

These several passages as most remarkable, the said Deponent did particularly set down as they daily happen'd, and for the reasons aforesaid, she doth verily believe in her conscience, that the Children were bewitched, and by the said *Amy Duny*, and *Rose Cullender*; though at first she could hardly be induced to believe it.

As concerning *Ann Durent*, one other of the Parties, supposed to be bewitched, present in Court.

Edmund Durent her Father Sworn and Examined: said, That he also lived in the said, Town of *Leystoff*, and that the said *Rose Cullender*, about the latter end of *November* last, came into this Deponents House to buy some Herrings of his Wife, but being denyed by her, the said *Rose* returned in a discontented manner; and upon the first of *December* after, his Daughter *Ann Durent* was very sorely Afflicted in her Stomach, and felt great pain, like the pricking of Pins, and then fell into swooning fitts, and after the Recovery from her Fitts, she declared, *That she had seen the Apparition of the said* Rose, *who threatned to Torment her*. In this manner she continued from the first of *December*, until this present time of Tryal; having likewise vomited up divers Pins (produced here in Court). This Maid was present in Court, but could not speak to declare her knowledge, but fell into most violent fits when she was brought before *Rose Cullender*.

Ann Baldwin Sworn and Examined, Deposeth the same thing as touching the Bewitching of the said *Ann Durent*.

As concerning *Jane Bocking* who was so weak, she could not be brought to the Assizes.

Diana Bocking Sworn and Examined, Deposed, That she lived in the same Town of *Leystoff*, and that her said Daughter having been formerly Afflicted with swooning fitts recovered well of them, and so continued for a certain time; and upon the First of *February* last, she was taken also with great pain in her Stomach, like pricking with Pins; and afterwards fell into swooning fitts and so continued till the Deponents coming to the Assizes, having during the same time taken little or no food, but daily vomited crooked Pins; and upon Sunday last raised Seven Pins. And whilst her fits were upon her she would spread forth her Arms with her hands open, and use postures as if she catched at something, and would instantly close her hands again; which being immediately forced open, they found several Pins diversly crooked, but could neither see nor perceive how or in what manner they were conveyed thither. At another time, the same *Jane* being in another of her fitts, talked as if she were discoursing with some persons in the Room, (though she would give no answer nor seem to take notice of any person then present) and would in like manner cast abroad her Arms, saying, *I will not have it, I will not have it*; and at last she said, *Then I will have it*, and so waving her Arm with her hand open, she would presently close the same, which instantly forced open, they found in it a Lath-Nail. In her fitts she would frequently complain of *Rose Cullender* and *Amy Duny*, saying, That *now she saw* Rose Cullender *standing at the Beds feet, and another time at the Beds-head, and so in other places*. At last she was stricken Dumb and could not speak one Word, though her fitts were not upon her, and so she continued for some days, and at last her speech came to her again, and she desired her Mother to get her some Meat; and being demanded the reason why she could not speak in so long time? She answered, *That* Amy Duny *would not suffer her to speak*. This Lath-Nail, and divers of the Pins were produced in Court.

As concerning *Susan Chandler*, one other of the Parties supposed to be Bewitched and present in Court.

Mary Chandler Mother of the said *Susan*, Sworn and Examined, Deposed and said, That about the beginning of *February* last past, the said *Rose Cullender* and *Amy Duny* were Charged by *Mr. Samuel Pacy* for Bewitching of his Daughters. And a Warrant being granted at the request of the said Mr. *Pacy*, by Sir *Edmund Bacon* Baronet, one of the Justices of the Peace for the County of *Suffolk* to bring them before him, and they being brought before him were Examined, and Confessed nothing. He gave order that they should be searched; whereupon this Deponent with five others were appointed to do the same: and coming to the House of *Rose Cullender*, they did acquaint her with what they were come about, and asked whether she was contented that they should search her? she did not oppose it, whereupon they began at her Head, and so stript her naked, and in the lower part of her Belly they found a thing like a Teat of an Inch long, they questioned her about it, and she said, *That she had got a strain by carrying of water which caused that Excrescence.* But upon narrower search, they found in her Privy Parts three more Excrescencies or Teats, but smaller than the former: This Deponent farther saith, That in the long Teat at the end thereof there was a little hole, and it appeared unto them as if it had been lately sucked, and upon the straining of it there issued out white milkie Matter.

And this Deponent farther saith, That her said Daughter (being of the Age of Eighteen Years) was then in Service in the said Town of *Leystoff*, and rising up early the next Morning to Wash, this *Rose Cullender* appeared to her, and took her by the hand, whereat she was much affrighted, and went forthwith to her Mother, (being in the same town) and acquainted her with what she had seen; but being extreamly terrified, she fell extream sick, much grieved at her Stomach; and that Night after being in Bed with another young Woman, she suddenly scrieked out, and fell into such extream fits as if she were distracted, crying against *Rose Cullender*; saying, *she would come to bed to her.* She continued in this manner beating and wearing her self, insomuch, that this Deponent was glad to get help to attend her. In her Intervals she would declare, *That some time she saw* Rose Cullender, *at another time with a great Dog with her.* She also vomited up divers crooked Pins; and sometimes she was stricken with blindness, and at another time she was Dumb, and so she appeared to be in Court when the Tryal of the Prisoners was; for she was not able to speak her knowledge; but being brought into the Court at the Tryal, she suddenly fell into her fits, and being carryed out of the Court again, within the space of half an hour she came to her self and recovered her speech, and thereupon was immediately brought into the Court, and asked by the Court, whether she was in condition to take an Oath, and to give Evidence, she said she could. But when she was Sworn, and asked what she could say against either of the Prisoners? before she could make any answer, she fell into her fits, screeking out in a miserable manner, crying *Burn her, burn her,* which were all the Words she could speak.

Robert Chandler father of the said *Susan* gave in the same Evidence, that his Wife Mary Chandler had given, only as to the searching of *Rose Cullender* as aforesaid.

This was the sum and Substance of the Evidence which was given against the Prisoners concerning the Bewitching of the Children before mentioned. At the hearing this Evidence there were divers known persons, as Mr. Serjeant *Keeling*, Mr. Serjeant *Earl*, and Mr. Serjeant *Barnard*, present. Mr Serjeant *Keeling* seemed much unsatisfied with it, and thought it not sufficient to Convict the Prisoners: for admitting that the children were in Truth Bewitched, yet said he, it can never be applyed to the Prisoners, upon the Imagination only of the Parties Afflicted; For if that might be allowed, no person whatsoever can be in safety, for perhaps they might fancy another person, who might altogether be innocent in such matters.

There was also Dr. *Brown* of *Norwich*, a Person of great knowledge; who after this Evidence given, and upon view of the three persons in Court, was desired to give his Opinion, what he did conceive of them: and he was clearly of Opinion, that the persons were Bewitched; and said, That in *Denmark* there had been lately a great Discovery of Witches, who used the very same way of Afflicting Persons, by conveying Pins into them, and crooked as these Pins were, with Needles and Nails. And his Opinion was, That the Devil in such cases did work upon the Bodies of Men and Women, upon a Natural Foundation, (that is) to stir up, and excite such humours superabounding in their Bodies to a great excess, whereby he did in an extraordinary manner Afflict them with such Distempers as their Bodies were most subject to, as particularly appeared in these Children; for he conceived, that these swouning Fits were Natural, and nothing else but that they call the Mother, but only heightned to a great excess by the subtilty of the Devil, co-operating with the Malice of these which we term Witches, at whose Instance he doth these Villanies.

Besides the particulars above-mention'd touching the said persons Bewitched, there were many other things Objected against them for a further proof and manifestation that the said Children were Bewitched.

As *First*, during the time of the Tryal, there were some experiments made with the Persons Afflicted, by bringing the Persons to touch them; and it was observed, that when they were in the midst of their Fitts, to all Mens apprehension wholly deprived of all sense and understanding, closing their Fists in such manner, as that the strongest Man in the Court could not force them open; yet by the least touch of one of these supposed Witches, *Rose Cullender* by Name, they would suddenly shriek out opening their hands, which accident would not happen by the touch of any other person.

And least they might privately see when they were touched, by the said *Rose Cullender*, they were blinded with their own Aprons, and the touching took the same Effect as before.

There was an ingenious person that objected, there might be a great fallacy in this experiment, and there ought not to be any stress put upon this to Convict the Parties, for the Children might counterfeit this their Distemper, and perceiving what was done to them, they might in such manner suddenly alter the motion and gesture of their Bodies, on purpose to induce persons to believe that they were not natural, but wrought strangely by the touch of the Prisoners.

Wherefore to avoid this scruple it was privately desired by the Judge, that the Lord *Cornwallis*, Sir *Edmund Bacon*, and Mr. Serjeant *Keeling*, and some other Gentlemen there in Court, would attend one of the Distempered persons in the farther part of the Hall, whilst she was in her fits, and then to send for one of the Witches, to try what would then happen, which they did accordingly: and *Amy Duny* was conveyed from the Bar and brought to the Maid: they put an Apron before her Eyes, and then one other person touched her hand, which produced the same effect as the touch of the Witch did in the Court. Whereupon the Gentlemen returned, openly protesting, that they did believe the whole transaction of this business was a meer Imposture.

This put the Court and all persons into a stand. But at length Mr. *Pacy* did declare, That possibly the Maid might be deceived by a suspition that the Witch touched her when she did not. For he had observed divers times, that although they could not speak, but were deprived of the use of their Tongues and Limbs, that their understandings were perfect, for that they have related divers things which have been when they were in their fits, after they were recovered out of them. This saying of Mr. *Pacy* was found to be true afterwards, when his Daughter was fully recovered (as she afterwards was) as shall in due time be related: For she was asked, whither she did hear and understand any thing that was done and acted in the Court, during the time that she lay as one deprived of her understanding? and she said, *she did*: and by the Opinions of some, this experiment, (which others would have a Fallacy) was rather a confirmation that the Parties were really Bewitched, than otherwise: for say they, it is not possible that any should counterfeit such Distempers, being accompanied with such various Circumstances, much less Children; and for so long time, and yet undiscovered by their Parents and Relations: For no man can suppose that they should all

Conspire together, (being out of several families, and, as they Affirm, no way related one to the other, and scarce of familiar acquaintance) to do an Act of this nature whereby no benefit or advantage could redound to any of the Parties, but a guilty Conscience for Perjuring themselves in taking the Lives of two poor simple Women away, and there appears no Malice in the Case. For the Prisoners themselves did scarce so much as Object it. Wherefore, say they, it is very evident that the Parties were Bewitched, and that when they apprehend or understand by any means, that the persons who have done them this wrong are near, or touch them; then their spirits being more than ordinarily moved with rage and anger at them being present, they do use more violent gestures of their Bodies, and extend forth their hands, as desirous to lay hold upon them; which at other times not having the same occasion, the instance there falls not out the same.

2ly. One *John Soam* of *Leystoff* aforesaid, Yeoman, a sufficient Person, Deposeth, That not long since, in harvest time he had three Carts which brought home his Harvest, and as they were going into the field to load, one of the Carts wrenched the Window of *Rose Cullenders* House, whereupon she came out in a great rage and threatned this Deponent for doing that wrong, and so they passed along into the Fields and loaded all the Three Carts, the other two Carts returned safe home, and back again, twice loaded that day afterwards; but as to this Cart which touched *Rose Cullenders* House, after it was loaded it was overturned twice or thrice that day; and after that they had loaded it again the second or third time, as they brought it through the Gate which leadeth out of the Field into the Town, the Cart stuck so fast in the Gates-head, that they could not possibly get it through, but were inforced to cut down the Post of the Gate to make the Cart pass through, although they could not perceive that the Cart did of either side touch the Gate-posts. And this Deponent further saith, That after they had got it through the Gate-way, they did with much difficulty get it home into the Yard; but for all that they could do, they could not get the Cart near unto the place where they should unload the Corn, but were fain to unload it at a great distance from the place, and when they began to unload they found much difficulty therein, it being so hard a labour that they were tired that first came; and when others came to assist them, their Noses burst forth a bleeding: so they were fain to desist and leave it until the next Morning; and then they unloaded it without any difficulty at all.

Robert Sherringham also Deposeth against *Rose Cullender*, That about Two Years since, passing along the Street with his Cart and Horses, the Axletree of his Cart touched her House, and broke down some part of it, at which, she was very much displeased, threatning him, that his Horses should suffer for it; and so it happen'd, for all those Horses, being Four in Number, died within a short time after: since that time he hath had great Losses by the suddain dying of his other Cattle; so soon as his Sows pigged, the Pigs would leap and caper, and immediately fall down and dye. Also, not long after, he was taken with a Lameness in his Limbs that he could neither go nor stand for some days. After all this, he was very much vexed with great Number of Lice of an extraordinary bigness, and although he many times shifted himself, yet he was not anything the better, but would swarm again with them; so that in the Conclusion he was forc'd to burn all his Clothes, being two suits of Apparel, and then was clean from them.

As concerning *Amy Duny,* one *Richard Spencer* Deposeth, That about the first of *September* last, he heard her say at his House, *That the Devil would not let her rest until she were Revenged on one* Cornelius Sandeswell's *Wife.*

Ann Sandeswel Wife unto the above-said *Cornelius,* Deposed, That about Seven or Eight Years since, she having bought a certain number of Geese, meeting with *Amy Duny,* she told her, *If she did not fetch her Geese home they would all be Destroyed*: which in a few days after came to pass.

Afterwards the said *Amy* became Tenant to this Deponents Husband for a House, who told her, *That if she looked not well to such a Chimney in her House, that the same would fall*: Whereupon this Deponent replyed, That it was a new one; but not minding much her Words, at that time they parted. But in a short time the Chimney fell down according as the said *Amy* had said.

Also this Deponent farther saith, That her Brother being a Fisherman, and using to go into the *Northern Seas,* she desired him to send her a Firkin of Fish, which he did accordingly; and she having notice that the said Firkin was brought into *Leystoff-Road,* she desired a Boatman to bring it ashore with the other Goods they were to bring; and she going down to meet the Boat-man to receive her Fish, desired the said *Amy* to go along with her to help her home with it; *Amy* Replyed, *She would go when she had it.* And thereupon this Deponent went to the Shoar without her, and demanded of the Boat-man the Firkin, they told her, That they could not keep it in the Boat from falling into the Sea, and they thought it was gone to the Divel, for they never saw the like before. And being demanded by this Deponent, whether any other Goods in the Boat were likewise lost as well as hers? They answered, *Not any.*

This was the substance of the whole Evidence given against the Prisoners at the Bar; who being demanded, what they had to say for themselves? They replyed, *Nothing material to any thing that was proved against them.* Whereupon, the Judge in giving his direction to the Jury, told them, That he would not repeat the Evidence unto them, least by so doing he should wrong the Evidence on the one side or on the other. Only this acquainted them, That they had Two things to enquire after. *First*, Whether or no these Children were Bewitched? *Secondly*, Whether the Prisoners at the Bar were Guilty of it?

That there were such Creatures as *Witches* he made no doubt at all; For *First*, the Scriptures had affirmed so much. *Secondly*, The wisdom of all Nations had provided Laws against such Persons, which is an Argument of their confidence of such a Crime. And such hath been the judgment of this Kingdom, as appears by that Act of Parliament which hath provided Punishments proportionable to the quality of the Offence. And desired them, strictly to observe their Evidence; and desired the great God of Heaven to direct their Hearts in this weighty thing they had in hand: *For to Condemn the Innocent, and to let the Guilty go free, were both an Abomination to the Lord.*

With this short Direction the Jury departed from the Bar, and within the space of half an hour returned, and brought them in both *Guilty* upon the several Indictments, which were Thirteen in Number, whereupon they stood Indicted.

This was upon *Thursday* in the Afternoon, *March* 13. 1662.

The next Morning, the Three Children with their Parents came to the Lord Chief Baron *Hale's* Lodging, who all of them spake perfectly, and were as in good Health as ever they were; only *Susan Chandler*, by reason of her very much Affliction, did look very thin and wan. And their friends were asked, At what time they were restored thus to their Speech and Health? And Mr. *Pacy* did Affirm, That within less than half an hour after the *Witches* were Convicted, they were all of them Restored, and slept well that Night, feeling no pain; only *Susan Chandler* felt a pain like pricking of Pins in her Stomach.

After, they were all of them brought down to the Court, but *Ann Durent* was so fearful to behold them, that she desired she might not see them. The other Two continued in the Court, and they Affirmed in the face of the Country, and before the *Witches* themselves, what before hath been Deposed by their Friends and Relations; the Prisoners not much contradicting them. In Conclusion, the Judge and all the Court were fully satisfied with the Verdict, and thereupon gave Judgment against the *Witches* that they should be Hanged.

They were much urged to confess, but would not.

That Morning we departed for *Cambridge*, but no Reprieve was granted: And they were Executed on *Monday*, the Seventeenth of *March* following, but they confessed nothing.

FINIS.

Notes

PREFACE

1 Salo W. Baron, *The Contemporary Relevance of History: A Study in Approaches and Methods*, New York: Columbia University Press, 1986, p. 52.

2 Robert Jay Lifton, *The Nazi Doctors: Medical Killing and the Psychology of Genocide*, New York: Basic Books, 1986, p. xiii.

3 David Cannadine, *G.M. Trevelyan: A Life in History*, New York: Norton, 1993, p. 226.

4 Cannadine, *Trevelyan*, p. 226.

5 Bertrand Russell, *Unpopular Essays*, New York: Simon & Schuster, 1950, p. 162.

6 Wallace Notestein, *A History of Witchcraft in England from 1558 to 1718*, Washington DC, American Historical Association; C. L'Estrange Ewen, *Witch Hunting and Witch Trials: The Indictments for Witchcraft from the Records of 1372 Assizes Held for the Home Circuit, 1559–1736 AD* (1929), London: F. Muller, 1971 reprint; George L. Kittredge, *Witchcraft in Old and New England*, Cambridge: Harvard University Press, 1929; Keith Thomas, *Religion and the Decline of Magic*, New York: Scribner, 1971; James Sharpe, *Instruments of Darkness: Witchcraft in England 1550–1750*, London: Hamish Hamilton, 1996.

7 Alan Macfarlane, *Witchcraft in Tudor and Stuart England: A Regional and Comparative Study*, London: Routledge & Kegan Paul, 1970.

8 Joyce Gibson, *Hanged for Witchcraft: Elizabeth Lowys and Her Successors*, Canberra: Tudor Press, 1988.

9 Michael MacDonald (ed.), *Witchcraft and Hysteria in Elizabethan England: Edward Jorden and the Mary Glover Case*, London: Tavistock/Routledge, 1991.

10 Edgar Peel and Pat Southern, *The Trials of the Lancashire Witches: A Study of Seventeenth-Century Witchcraft*, New York: Taplinger, 1969; Annabel Gregory, "Witchcraft, Politics and 'Good Neighbourhood' in Early Seventeenth Century Rye," in *Past & Present*, 133 (1991), pp. 31–66; Anne Reiber DeWitt, "Witchcraft and Conflicting Visions of the Ideal Village Community," *Journal of British Studies*, 34 (1994), pp. 427–464

11 Paul S. Boyer and Stephen Nissenbaum, *Salem Possessed: The Social Origins of Witchcraft*, Cambridge: Cambridge University Press, 1974;

Bernard Rosenthal, *Salem Story: Reading the Witch Trials of 1692*, Cambridge: Cambridge University Press, 1993; Frances Hill, *A Delusion of Satan: The Full Story of the Salem Witch Trials*, New York: Doubleday, 1995; Gustav Henningsen, *The Witches Advocate: Basque Witchcraft and the Spanish Inquisition (1609–1614)*, Reno: University of Nevada Press, 1980; Michael Kunze, *Highroad to the Stake: A Tale of Witchcraft*, William E. Yuile (trans.), Chicago: University of Chicago Press, 1987.

12 Carlo Ginzburg, *The Night Battles: Witchcraft and Agrarian Cults in the Sixteenth and Seventeenth Centuries*, John and Anne Tedeschi (trans.), Baltimore: Johns Hopkins University Press, 1983.

13 *The Salem Witchcraft Papers: Verbatim Transcripts of the Legal Documents on the Salem Witchcraft Outbreak of 1692*. Compiled and transcribed in 1938 by the Works Progress Administration, New York: Da Capo Press, 1977.

14 Russell Baker, "The Historian Glut," *New York Times*, April 9, 1994, p. 15.

15 Bernard Rosenthal, *Salem Story: Reading the Witch Trials of 1692*, Cambridge: Cambridge University Press, 1993, pp. 7–8.

16 Anthony M. Orum, Joe R. Feagin, and Gideon Sjoberg, "Introduction: The Nature of the Case Study," in Feagin, Orum, and Sjoberg (eds.), *A Case for the Case Study*, Chapel Hill: University of North Carolina Press, 1991, p. 2.

17 William Godwin, *Lives of the Necromancers*, London: Frederick J. Mason, 1834, p. 443.

18 Rosenthal, *Salem Story*, p. 186.

19 Rosenthal, *Salem Story*, p. 189.

20 J.A. Sharpe, *Witchcraft in Seventeenth-Century Yorkshire: Accusations and Counter Measures*, York: Borthwick Institute of Historical Research, 1992, pp. 5, 23.

21 Kai T. Erikson, *Wayward Puritans: A Study in the Sociology of Deviance*, New York: Wiley, 1966.

22 Louise Creighton, *Life and Letters of Mandell Creighton*, London: Longmans, Green, 1904, Vol. I, p. 372.

23 Creighton, *Mandell Creighton*, Vol. II, p. 338.

24 George Lincoln Burr, "New England's Place in the History of Witchcraft," *Proceedings of the American Antiquarian Society*, 21 (1911), p. 217.

25 G.R. Elton, *The Practice of History*, London: Sydney University Press, 1967, p. 17.

1 WITCHCRAFTS HERE RESEMBLE WITCHCRAFTS THERE

1 *A Tryal of Witches Held at Bury St. Edmunds*, London: William Shrewsbery, 1682.

2 William Paley, *The Works of William Paley*, London: Longman, 1838, Vol. II, p. 388. The same note is sounded in fictional form in Herman Melville's *Billy Budd, Foretopman*, London: J. Lehmann, 1924. Billy is sentenced to hang by the ship's captain who understands that Billy had

killed the master-at-arms inadvertently, not deliberately. The captain desires to quell incipient mutiny by demonstrating his toughness.

3 John Bunyan, *A Relation of the Imprisonment of Mr. John Bunyan, Minister of the Gospel at Bedford*, London: James Buckland, 1745.

4 Frederic W.N. Bayley, *The Wife of Bunyan Interceding with Chief Justice Hale for the Release of Her Husband from Prison and an Evening Scene in John Bunyan's Prison Life*, Bedford: The Times Office, 1851, p. 11.

5 Thomas Thirlwall, *The Works, Moral and Religious, of Sir Matthew Hale*, London: H.D. Symonds, 1805, p. xxii.

6 Thirlwall, *Works of Hale*, pp. 147–8. Foss, among many others, repeats this theme. He notes that the witch trial forms a "blot that cavillers have discovered in Hale's reputation." Edward Foss, *The Judges of England*, London: John Murray, 1964, Vol. VII, p. 114.

7 John Aikin, Thomas Morgan, and William Johnston, *General Biography; Or Lives, Critical and Historical, of the Most Eminent Persons of All Ages, Countries, Conditions, and Professions*, London: G.G.J. & J. Robinson, 1804, Vol. V, p. 11.

8 John Lord Campbell, *The Lives of the Chief Justices*, London: John Murray, 1849, Vol. I, p. 512.

9 Campbell, *Chief Justices*, Vol. I, p. 562.

10 John T. Rutt (ed.), *Diary of Thomas Burton, Esq*, London: Henry Colburn, 1828, Vol. I, p. 26.

11 See Brock P. McAllister, "Lord Hale and Business Affected with a Public Interest," *Harvard Law Review*, 43 (1930), pp. 759–91; and Walton H. Hamilton, "Affectation with a Public Interest," *Yale Law Journal*, 39 (1930), pp. 1089–1112.

12 Peckham J., in *Budd v. New York*, 117 N.Y. Reports 1, 47, 1889. The leading American precedent was *Munn v. Illinois*, 94 US 113, 1877. See also Max Lerner (ed.), *The Mind and Faith of Justice Holmes*, Boston: Little, Brown, 1943, p. 144; Louis B. Boudin, *Government by Judiciary*, New York: Godwin, 1932, pp. 420–4.

13 See generally Dennis G. Donovan, Magaretha G. Hartley Herman, and Ann E. Imbrie (eds.), *Sir Thomas Browne and Richard Burton: A Reference Guide*, Boston: G.K. Hall, 1981, pp. 1–326.

14 James N. Wise, *Sir Thomas Browne's Religio Medici and Two Seventeenth Century Critics*, Columbia: University of Missouri Press, 1973, p. 51.

15 William Osler, *Religio Medici*, London: Chiswick Press, 1906, p. 30.

16 Wallace Notestein, *A History of Witchcraft in England from 1558 to 1718*, Washington: American Historical Association, 1911, p. 260.

17 Alan Macfarlane, *Witchcraft in Tudor and Stuart England: A Regional and Comparative Study*, London: Routledge & Kegan Paul, 1970, p. 60.

18 Joyce Gibson, *Hanged for Witchcraft: Elizabeth Lowys and Her Successors*, Canberra: Tudor Press, 1988, p. 237.

19 Geoffrey R. Quaife, *Wanton Wenches and Wayward Wives: Peasants and Illicit Sex in Early Seventeenth Century England*, New Brunswick, NJ: Rutgers University Press, 1979, p. 31.

20 Anne Llewellyn Barstow, *Witchcraft: A New History of the European Witch Hunts*, New York: Pandora, 1994, p. 72.

21 Dorothy Tyler, "A Review of the Interpretation of Sir Thomas Browne's Part in the Witch Trial of 1664," *Anglia*, 54 (1930), p. 181.
22 George Lincoln Burr, *Narratives of the Witchcraft Cases*, New York: Charles Scribner's, 1914, p. 215.
23 Cotton Mather, "A Modern Instance of Witches Discovered and Condemned, in a Tryal, before that Celebrated Judge, Sir Matthew Hale," in *Wonders of the Invisible World*, Boston: Benjamin Harris, 1693, p. 83. See further M. Wynn Thomas, "Cotton Mather's *Wonders of the Invisible World:* Some Metamorphoses of Salem Witchcraft," in Sydney Anglo (ed.), *The Damned Art: Essays in the Literature of Witchcraft*, London: Routledge & Kegan Paul, 1977, pp. 202–26.
24 Perry Miller, *The New England Mind: From Colony to Province*, Cambridge: Harvard University Press, 1953, p. 207.
25 John Hale, *A Modest Enquiry into the Nature of Witchcraft*, Boston: Benjamin Eliot, 1702, pp. 27–8. See also Samuel G. Drake, *Annals of Witchcraft in New England, and Elsewhere in the United States*, Boston: W.E. Woodward, 1869, p. xl.
26 Thomas Hutchinson, *The History of the Colony and Province of Massachusetts-Bay* [1764], Edited by Lawrence S. Mayo, Cambridge: Harvard University Press, 1936, Vol. II, pp. 17–18. See further Charles W. Upham, *Lectures on Witchcraft Comprising a History of the Delusion in Salem in 1692*, Boston: Carter, Hendee & Babcock, 1831, p. 180. John Greenleaf Whittier indicated the connection between Bury and Salem in a poem regarding Samuel Sewall:

> When he sat on the bench of the witchcraft courts
> With the laws of Moses and Hale's Reports
> And spake in the name of both, the word
> That gave the witch's neck to the cord.

John Greenleaf Whittier, "The Prophecy of Samuel Sewall" [1859], in *Narrative and Legendary Poems*, Boston: Houghton Mifflin, 1892, p. 211. See also William Nelson Gemmill, *The Salem Witch Trials: A Chapter of New England History*, Chicago: A.C. McClure, 1924, p. 218.
27 Richard Weisman, *Witchcraft, Magic, and Religion in 17th Century Massachusetts*, Amherst: University of Massachusetts Press, 1984, pp. 209–16.
28 Rosenthal, *Salem Story*, p. 109.
29 Montesquieu, *De l'esprit des lois* [1748], in *The Spirit of Laws*, edited by David W. Carrithers, Berkeley: University of California Press, 1977, Book XII, Chapter V, p. 221. For a sociological statement on the same matter see Jack Katz, "Deviance, Charisma, and Rule-Defined Behavior," *Social Problems*, 20 (1972), pp. 186–202.
30 Julio Caro Baroja, *The World of Witches*, O.N.V. Glendinning (trans.), Chicago: University of Chicago Press, 1964, p. 212.
31 Alan C. Kors and Edward Peters, *Witchcraft in Europe: A Documentary History*, Philadelphia: University of Pennsylvania Press, 1972, pp. 32–4.
32 Henry Charles Lea, *Materials Toward a History of Witchcraft*, Edited by Arthur C. Howland, New York: Thomas Yoseloff, 1957, Vol. II, p. 904.

33 David Butcher, *The Development of Pre-Industrial Lowestoft, 1560–1730*, M.Phil. thesis. Norwich: University of East Anglia, 1991, p. 298.

34 John T. Appleby, *Suffolk Summer*, Ipswich: East Anglian Magazine, 1948, p. 12.

35 Edmund Gillingwater, *An Historical Account of the Ancient Town of Lowestoft*, London: G.G.J. & J. Robinson, 1790, pp. 49–50.

36 Butcher, *Pre-Industrial Lowestoft*, p. 94.

37 R.L. Whitehead, "Foreword," to Hugh H.W. Lees, *The Chronicles of a Suffolk Parish Church: Lowestoft St. Margaret*, Lowestoft: Flood & Sons, 1949, p. v.

38 Eilert Ekwall, *The Concise Oxford Dictionary of English Place-names*, 4th edition, Oxford: Clarendon Press, 1960, p. 305.

39 Francis D. Longe, *Lowestoft in Olden Times*, 2nd edition, Lowestoft: McGregor & Fraser, 1905, p. 63.

40 James T. Jenkins, *The Herring and the Herring Fisheries*, Westminster: P.S. King & Son, 1927, p. 46.

41 *Love's Labour's Lost*, IV, i, 145; Frances A. Yates, *A Study of Love's Labour's Lost*, Cambridge: Cambridge University Press, 1936, p. 5.

42 Machell Stace, *Cromwelliana: A Chronological Detail of Events in Which Oliver Cromwell was Engaged; From the Year 1642 to His Death 1658*, London: G. Smeeton, 1810, pp. 2–3; Alfred Kingston, *East Anglia and the Great Civil War*, London: Elliot Stock, 1897, pp. 93–4.

43 Beth Britten, *My Brother Benjamin*, Abbotsbrook, Bucks.: Kensal Press, 1986.

44 Walter de la Mare, "I Saw Three Witches," in *Songs of Childhood*, London: Longmans, Green, 1902, pp. 31–2; also *The Complete Poems of Walter de la Mare*, New York: Knopf, 1970, p. 8.

45 Donald Mitchell and Philip Reed (eds.), *Letters from a Life: The Selected Letters and Diaries of Benjamin Britten, 1913–1976*, Berkeley: University of California Press, 1991, Vol. I, pp. 120, 149.

46 Vera Brittain, *Testament of Youth: An Autobiographical Story of the Years 1900–1925*, London: Victor Gollancz, 1983, p. 183.

47 Brittain, *Testament of Youth*, p. 183.

48 The term "last" had originally meant a load, but then became a variable measure depending on the commodity and the locality (Nesta Evans, *The East Anglian Linen Industry: Rural Industry and Local Economy, 1500–1800*, Aldershot, Hants.: Gower, 1985, p. 52). In the East Anglian herring trade, there were two lasts: a "fisherman's last" and a "merchant's last." A fisherman's last was made up of 1,200 fresh fish (ten barrels each containing "a long hundred of fish"—120 herring). After curing the fish, the merchants repacked them into barrels of 100: ten such barrels or 1,000 fish constituted a merchant's last. In this way, for every five lasts of fresh fish purchased, the merchant could retail six lasts of cured fish.

49 Edmund Gillingwater, *Town of Lowestoft*, pp. 153–6.

50 Edmund Gillingwater, *Town of Lowestoft*, p. 6.

51 Tobias Gentleman, *England's Way to Win Wealth, and to Employ Ships and Marriners*, London: Nathaniel Butter, 1614, p. 31.

52 Statute of Herring, 31 Edw. III, c. 1 & 23 (1357), which decreed that no fish were to be sold within seven leucae of Great Yarmouth. The statute

was confirmed by 45 Edw. III, c. 3 (1373) which also placed Kirkley Road, a stretch of coastal water near Lowestoft, under Yarmouth's jurisdiction.

53 2 Rich. II, c. 7 (1379). The full chronology of the dispute is found in Isaac S. Leadam and James F. Baldwin (1918), *Select Cases Before the King's Council, 1243–1482*, London: Selden Society. See also A. Saul, "Local Politics and the Good Parliament," in Tony Pollard (ed.) (1984), *Property and Politics: Essays in Later Medieval English History*, Gloucester: Alan Sutton, pp. 156–71; Geoffrey R. Elton (1986), "Piscatorial Politics in the Early Parliaments of Elizabeth I," in Neil McKendrick and R.B. Outhwaite (eds.), *Business Life and Public Policy: Essays in Honour of D.C. Coleman*, Cambridge: Cambridge University Press, pp. 1–20.

54 Robert E. Zupko, *British Weights & Measures: A History from Antiquity to the Seventeenth Century*, Madison: University of Wisconsin Press, 1977, pp. 6–7.

55 Edmund Gillingwater, *Town of Lowestoft*, p. 155; Charles J. Palmer (1872–1875), *Perlustration of Great Yarmouth, with Charleston and Southtown*, Great Yarmouth: G. Nall, Vol. II, pp. 236–7.

56 John Bellamy, *Criminal Law and Society in Late Medieval and Tudor England*, Gloucester: Alan Sutton, 1984, pp. 40–1.

57 *Dictionary of National Biography*, Vol. 18, p. 1058; see also Philip Bliss (ed.), *Reliquiae Hearnianae: The Remains of Thomas Hearne, M.A., of Edmund Hall*, London: John Russell Smith, 1838, Vol. I, p. 63, Vol. III, pp. 36, 37.

58 *A Collection of Modern Relations of Matters of Fact Concerning Witches & Witchcraft Upon the Persons of People*, Socrates Christanus (ed.), London: John Harris, 1693, pp. A6–A7.

59 *A Collection*, pp. A4–A7.

60 C. L'Estrange Ewen, *Witch Hunting and Witch Trials: The Indictments for Witchcraft from the Records of 1373 Assizes Held for the Home Circuit, 1559–1736 AD*, London: F. Muller, 1971, pp. 250–1.

61 Evelyn Curtis, *Crime in Bedfordshire, 1660–1688*, Bedford: Elstow Moot Hall, 1957, p. 8.

62 8 Rich. II, c. 2 (1384).

63 J.S. Cockburn, *A History of English Assizes, 1558–1714*, Cambridge: Cambridge University Press, 1972, p. 49.

64 Edmund Gillingwater, *Town of Lowestoft*, p. 222.

65 Edmund Gillingwater, *Town of Lowestoft*, p. 224.

66 Edmund Gillingwater, *Town of Lowestoft*, p. 226.

67 Edmund Gillingwater, *Town of Lowestoft*, p. 244.

68 Edmund Gillingwater, *Town of Lowestoft*, p. 237.

69 Edmund Gillingwater, *Town of Lowestoft*, p. 239.

70 Some of the legal aspects of the case are briefly discussed by Matthew Hale, *The Prerogatives of the King*, D.E.C. Yale (ed.), London: Selden Society, 1976, p. 295.

71 John R. Elder, *The Royal Fisheries Companies of the Seventeenth Century*, Aberdeen: University Press, 1912, pp. 91–2.

72 House of Lords Record Office, Main Papers, House of Lords, June 27, 1661 (Brief to Examine Witnesses, etc.).

73 Robert Hawkins, *The Perjur'd Phanatick*, 3rd edn, London: J. Wilford, 1728, pp. vii–viii.
74 A.C. Sturgess (ed.), *Register of Admissions to the Honourable Society of the Middle Temple From the Fifteenth Century to the Year 1944*, London: Butterworth, 1949, p. 89.
75 Edmund Heward, *Matthew Hale*, London: Robert Hale, 1972, p. 331.

2 THE TOAD IN THE BLANKET

1 Edmund Gillingwater, *An Historical Account of the Ancient Town of Lowestoft*, London: G.G.J. & J. Robinson, 1790, pp. 221–39.
2 Frank L. Huntley, *Sir Thomas Browne: A Biographical and Critical Note*, Ann Arbor: University of Michigan Press, 1968, pp. 184–203.
3 Thomas Browne, *Hydriotaphia, Urne-Buriall*, together with *The Garden of Cyrus*, London: Hen. Brome, 1658, p. A7b.
4 John H. Gleason, *The Justices of the Peace in England, 1588 to 1640*, Oxford: Clarendon Press, 1969, p. 68.
5 Larry M. Boyer, "The Justice of the Peace in England and America from 1506 to 1776: A Bibliographic History," *Quarterly Journal of the Library of Congress*, 34 (1977), pp. 315–26.
6 Richard Baxter, *Directions to Justices of Peace, Especially in Corporations, for the Discharge of their Duty to God*, London: Robert White, 1657 (single folio sheet).
7 Gleason, *Justices of the Peace*, p. 53.
8 Redgrave and Botesdale Parish Registers, Suffolk Record Office, Ipswich, FB132/D1/1.
9 Thomas G. Barnes, "Examination Before a Justice in the Seventeenth Century," *Notes and Queries for Somerset and Dorset*, 27 (1955), pp. 40–1.
10 1 and 2 Philip and Mary, c. 13 (1554–1555) and 2 and 3 Philip and Mary, c. 10 (1555).
11 John H. Langbein, *Prosecuting Crime in the Renaissance: England, Germany, France*, Cambridge: Harvard University Press, 1974, p. 18.
12 Langbein, *Prosecuting Crime*, p. 31.
13 J.S. Cockburn, "Early-Modern Assize Records as Historical Evidence," *Journal of the Society of Archivists*, 5 (1975), p. 216.
14 Jane Crawford, "Evidences for Witchcraft in Anglo-Saxon England," *Medium Aevum*, 32 (1963), pp. 107–8.
15 33 Henry VIII, c. 8 (1542).
16 1 Edw. VI, c. 12 (1547).
17 An Act Against Conjurations, Enchantments and Witchcrafts, 5 Eliz. I, c. 16 (1563). The Act is reproduced in Rossell H. Robbins, *Encyclopedia of Witchcraft and Demonology*, New York: Crown, 1959, pp. 158–9.
18 Selma R. Williams and Pamela J. Williams, *Riding the Nightmare: Women & Witchcraft*, New York: Atheneum, 1978, p. 110.
19 On the use of love philters, see Angus McLaren, *Reproductive Rituals: The Perception of Fertility in England from the Sixteenth to the Nineteenth Century*, London: Methuen, 1984, p. 39.

20 Robert Filmer, *An Advertisement to Jury-men of England Touching Witches*, London: R. Royston, 1653, p. 18.
21 1 Jac. I, c. 12 (1604); repealed by 9 Geo. II, c. 5 (1736). A particularly useful tabular comparison of the 1563 and 1604 statutes is found in Alan Macfarlane, *Witchcraft in Tudor and Stuart England: A Regional and Comparative Study*, London: Routledge & Kegan Paul, 1971, p. 15.
22 Langbein, *Prosecuting Crime*, p. 7; John M. Beattie, *Crime and the Courts in England, 1660–1800*, Princeton: Princeton University Press, 1986, p. 271.
23 Anthony Fletcher, *Reform in the Provinces: The Government of Stuart England*, New Haven: Yale University Press, 1986, p. 117.
24 Cyrus H. Karraker, *The Seventeenth-Century Sheriff*, Chapel Hill: University of North Carolina Press, 1930, p. 7.
25 Charles G. Harper, *The Newmarket, Bury, Thetford, and Cromer Road*, London: Chapman & Hall, 1904, p. 285.
26 Diarmard MacCulloch (ed.), *The Chorography of Suffolk*, Ipswich: Boydell Press, 1976, p. 19. The original manuscript was compiled by an unknown hand. Fragments still exist in the Suffolk Record Office at Ipswich and in the Bodleian Library (Bodley MS Tanner 135, ff. 1–28).
27 Roger Latham and William Matthews, *The Diary of Samuel Pepys*, London: G. Bell, 1970, Vol. III, p. 10 (January 15, 1662).
28 Isaac Gillingwater, *Trial of the Lowestoft Witches*, unpublished manuscript, p. 2, Suffolk Record Office, Lowestoft, AR992/1.
29 George Fox, the Quaker leader, apparently was imprisoned in the Bury jail (see *The Grounds and Causes of Our Sufferings Related in Short: Who Suffer by the Cruelty of Oppressors in Edmonds-Bury Gaol in Suffolk*, London: Thomas Simonds, 1656), though there is no reference to this episode in Fox's journal which mentions numerous imprisonments throughout England: John L. Nicholls (ed.), *The Journal of George Fox*, rev. edition, Cambridge: Cambridge University Press, 1952. We know that George Whitehead and other Quakers were in the Bury jail in 1655: Samuel Tuke, *Memoirs of George Whitehead: A Minister of the Gospel in the Society of Friends*, Philadelphia: Nathan Kite, 1832, Vol. I, pp. 83–9; Norman Penney (ed.), *The Journal of George Fox*, Cambridge: Cambridge University Press, Vol. I, 1911, p. 442.
30 Joan Parkes, *Travel in England in the Seventeenth Century*, Oxford: Clarendon Press, 1925, pp. 243–4.
31 Augustus Jessop (ed.), *The Autobiography of the Hon. Roger North*, London: David Nutt, 1887, p. 136.
32 Cockburn, *English Assizes*, p. 65.
33 John Patten, "Population Distribution in Norfolk and Suffolk During the Sixteenth and Seventeenth Centuries," *Transactions of the Institute of British Geographers*, 65 (1975), p. 49. Peter Clark and Paul Slack put the figure at 6,200 persons in 1671: *English Towns in Transition, 1500–1700*, London: Oxford University Press, 1976, p. 83, while Hervey sets it at 4,500 persons in 1674: S.H.A. Hervey, *Bury St. Edmunds: St. James Parish Registers—Marriages 1562–1800*, Suffolk Green Books, Vol. XVII, Woodbridge: George Booth, 1916, p. viii.

34 Henry E. Marsh (ed.), *Bury St. Edmunds*, Norwich: Jarrold & Sons, 1970, p. 9.

35 Robert S. Gottfried, *Bury St. Edmunds and the Urban Crisis, 1290–1539*, Princeton: Princeton University Press, 1982, p. 193.

36 Daniel Defoe, *Tour Through the Eastern Counties* [1724], Ipswich: East Anglian Magazine Ltd, 1949, p. 68.

37 Penelope Corfield, "Urban Development in England and Wales in the Sixteenth and Seventeenth Century," in Jonathan Barry (ed.), *The Tudor and Stuart Town: A Reader in English History, 1530–1688*, London: Longman, 1990, p. 47.

38 Samuel Tymms, *A Handbook of Bury St. Edmunds in the County of Suffolk*, 2nd edition, Bury St. Edmunds: F. Lankester, 1859, p. 46.

39 Historical Manuscript Commission, *The Manuscripts of Rye and Hereford Corporations, Capt. Loder-Symonds, Mr. E.R. Wodehouse, MP and Others*, 13th Report, 1892, Part 4, p. 64.

40 Suffolk Record Office, BB c/11.

41 Lowestoft Parish Register, p. 109. The Lowestoft Parish Registers are in three volumes: (1) R.E. Steel and F.D. Longe (trans.), *The Parish Registers of Lowestoft*, Lowestoft: Flood & Sons, 1892. This volume lists baptisms and burials 1561–1720 and marriages 1561–1650; (2) *The Parish Registers of Lowestoft*, compiled and privately printed by Frederick Arthur Crisp, Lowestoft: 1901. This volume contains baptisms and burials 1724–1750 and marriages 1650–1750; and (3) *The Parish Registers of Lowestoft*, compiled and privately printed by Frederick Arthur Crisp, Lowestoft: 1904. This volume contains baptisms, burials, and marriages 1751–1812. Unless otherwise indicated, parish register citations are to the first volume.

42 David Butcher, *The Development of Pre-Industrial Lowestoft, 1560–1730*, M.Phil. thesis. Norwich: University of East Anglia, 1991, p. 64.

43 Hugh H.W. Lees, *The Chronicles of a Suffolk Parish Church: Lowestoft St. Margaret*, Lowestoft: Flood & Sons, 1949, p. 241.

44 Lowestoft Manor Court Book, 194/A10/7, Suffolk Record Office, Lowestoft.

45 David Butcher, *The Development of Pre-Industrial Lowestoft, 1560–1730*, M.Phil. thesis. Norwich: University of East Anglia, 1991, p. 69.

46 Edward A. Wrigley, "Mortality in Pre-Industrial England: The Example of Colyton, Devon, Over Three Centuries," *Daedalus*, 97 (1968), pp. 546–80.

47 Steven R. Smith, "Growing Old in Early Stuart England," *Albion*, 8 (1976), pp. 125–41.

48 Henry Cuffe, *The Differences of the Ages of Mans Life; Together with the Original Causes, Purpose, and End Thereof*, London: B. Alsop, 1633, p. 24.

49 Percy H. Reaney, *A Dictionary of British Surnames*, London: Routledge & Kegan Paul, 1958, p. 93.

50 Beccles Parish Registers, Suffolk Record Office, Lowestoft, FC3/D2/11.

51 The seventeenth-century antiquarian William Camden says of Emma (he spells it Emme): "some will have to be the same with Amie, in Latine

Amata." *Remains Concerning Britain* [1605], London: John Russell Smith, 1870, p. 102.

52 C. L'Estrange Ewen, *Witch Hunting and Witch Trials: The Indictments for Witchcraft from the Records of 1373 Assizes Held for the Home Circuit, 1559–1736 AD*, London: F. Muller, 1971, p. 311.

53 Samuel Wilton Rix (1837), *Brief Records of the Independent Church at Beccles*, London: Jackson & Walford, pp. 36–43.

54 Lowestoft Parish Register, p. 113.

55 Lowestoft Manor Court, 194/A10/8 & 9.

56 SRO, 194/A1/1 & 2.

57 Lowestoft Parish Register, p. 119.

58 PRO File ASSI/16/4/1. We are grateful to Gordon Glanville for retrieving this material for us.

59 PRO ASSI/16/4/1.

60 PRO ASSI/16/4/1.

61 John S. Morrill, *The Cheshire Grand Jury, 1625–1659: A Social and Administrative Study*, Leicester: Leicester University Press, 1976.

62 Beattie, *Crime and the Courts*, p. 271.

63 Matthew Hale, *The History of the Pleas of the Crown* [1736], Philadelphia: Robert H. Small, 1847, Vol. I, p. 219.

64 Edward Waterhouse, *Forescutus Illustratus*, London: T. Raycroft, 1663, p. 342; see further James C. Oldham, "The Origins of the Special Jury," *University of Chicago Law Review*, 50 (1983), pp. 137–221.

65 Alan Macfarlane and Sarah Harrison, *The Justice and the Mare's Ale: Law and Disorder in Seventeenth-Century England*, New York: Cambridge University Press, 1981, pp. 100–1.

66 *A Tryal of Witches at the Assizes Held at Bury St. Edmunds*, London: William Shrewsbery, 1682, pp. 1–2. Subsequent quotations from the trial report, including the testimony of Dorothy Durrant, will not be given individually: all appear in the first twelve pages of the report.

67 Matthew Hale, *Pleas of the Crown*, Vol. I, p. 169.

68 Donald Veall, *The Popular Movement for Law Reform*, Oxford: Clarendon Press, 1970, p. 18.

69 PRO, ASSI/16/4/1. We want to express our gratitude to Elisabeth Leetham-Green of the Cambridge University Library for reading of the indictment.

70 Ewen, *Witch Hunting*, pp. 90–6.

71 Lowestoft Parish Register, p. 117.

72 Lowestoft Parish Register, Vol. II, p. 1.

73 It has been said that "a quarter, or a third, of all the families in the country contained servants in Stuart times." Peter Laslett, *The World We Have Lost: Further Explored*, 3rd edition, London: Methuen, 1984, p. 13. There is a teasing possibility of a Durrant connection with the 1645 crusade in East Anglia against witches directed by Matthew Hopkins, since the child of a woman named Annabelle Durrant was an alleged victim of Mary Johnson, one of the so-called Manningtree witches. E. Lyon Linton, *Witch Stories*, London: Chapman & Hall, 1861, pp. 315, 324. The case is reported in the tract, *A True and Exact Relation of the Severall Informations, Examinations, and Confessions of the*

Late Witches Arraigned and Executed in the County of Essex, London: Henry Overton and Benj. Allen, 1645, pp. 18–20.

74 Lowestoft Parish Register, p. 116.

75 Valerie Fildes, "The Age of Weaning in Britain, 1500–1800," *Journal of Biosocial Science*, 14 (1982), p. 233.

76 François Mauriceau, in the most highly regarded book of the time on childhood diseases, specifically mentions the swallowing of air as a cause of colic: *Diseases of Women with Child, and in Child-Bed*, Hugh Chamberlen (trans.), London: Andrew Hall, 1710, pp. 331–2.

77 Robert Burton, *The Anatomy of Melancholy*, Oxford: Henry Cripps, 1621, Part I, Sect. 4, p. 433.

78 Nicholas Culpeper, *Culpeper's Discovery for Midwives, or, A Guide for Women: The Second Part*, London: Peter Cole, 1663, p. 68.

79 Patricia Crawford, "Attitudes to Menstruation in Seventeenth-Century England," *Past & Present*, 9 (1981), p. 49.

80 Dorothy McLaren, "Fertility, Infant Mortality, and Breast Feeding in the Seventeenth Century," *Medical History*, 22 (1978), p. 381.

81 Jeffrey M.N. Boss, "The Seventeenth-Century Transformation of the Hysteric Affection, and Sydenham's Baconian Medicine," *Psychological Medicine*, 9 (1979), p. 222.

82 Lazare Riviere, *The Practice of Physick*, Nicholas Culpeper, A. Cole, and W. Rowland (trans.), London: Peter Cole, 1655, p. 420.

83 Crawford, "Menstruation," p. 54.

84 Crawford, "Menstruation," p. 54.

85 For an excellent summary of the history in medicine of the concept of hysteria see Mark S. Micale, *Approaching Hysteria: Disease and its Interpretation*, Princeton, NJ: Princeton University Press, 1995. See also Sander L. Gilman, Helen King, Roy Porter, G.S. Rousseau, and Elaine Showalter, *Hysteria Beyond Freud*, Berkeley: University of California Press, 1993.

86 Eliot Slater, "Diagnosis of 'Hysteria'," *British Medical Journal*, 1 (1965), p. 1399.

87 Francis A. Whitlock, "The Aetiology of Hysteria," *Acta Psychiatrica Scandinavica*, 43 (1967), p. 144.

88 Paul Chodoff and Henry Lyons, "Hysteria, the Hysterical Personality and 'Hysterical' Conversion," *American Journal of Psychiatry*, 114 (1958), p. 734.

89 Josef Breur and Sigmund Freud, *Studies in Hysteria*, New York: Nervous and Mental Disease Publications, 1936, p. 61.

90 Frederick J. Ziegler, John B. Imboden, and Eugene Meyer, "Contemporary Conversion Reactions: A Clinical Study," *American Journal of Psychiatry*, 116 (1960), pp. 901–20.

91 Benjamin Brodie, *Local Nervous Afflictions from Lectures Illustrative of Certain Nervous Afflictions*, London: Longman, Rees, Orme, Browne, Green & Longman, 1838, pp. 59–60.

92 Brodie, *Nervous Afflictions*, p. 37. See further Timothy Holmes, *Sir Benjamin Collins Brodie*, London: T. Fisher, 1898.

93 Wallace Notestein, *A History of Witchcraft in England from 1558 to 1718*, Washington, DC: American Historical Association, 1911, p. 343.

94 Francis Hutchinson, *An Historical Essay Concerning Witchcraft*, London: Knaplock, 1718, p. v.
95 For further details on the case see C. L'Estrange Ewen, *Witchcraft in the Star Chamber*. Privately printed, 1938, pp. 44–54.
96 John H. Rivett-Carnac, "Witchcraft: the Rev. John Lowes," in *Notes and Queries*, 8th series, 9 (March 21, 1896), pp. 223–4.
97 Hutchinson, *Concerning Witchcraft*, p. 109.
98 Hutchinson, *Concerning Witchcraft*, p. 110.
99 Hutchinson, *Concerning Witchcraft*, pp. 110–11.
100 Hutchinson, *Concerning Witchcraft*, p.101. Church proscriptions against recourse to counter-magic find their most authoritative expression in St. Thomas Aquinas' *Commentary on the Four Books of Sentences*: "It is never proper that that which is accomplished by witchcraft should be destroyed by yet other witchcraft, as if witchcraft were to testify to its own authenticity." Quoted in Alan C. Kors and Edward Peters, *Witchcraft in Europe: A Documentary History*, Philadelphia: University of Pennsylvania Press, 1972, p. 74.
101 Hutchinson, *Concerning Witchcraft*, p. 112.
102 Richard Boulton, *A Compleat History of Magic, Sorcery, and Witchcraft*, London: E. Curll, 1715.
103 Richard Boulton, *The Possibility and Reality of Magick, Sorcery, and Witchcraft Demonstrated*, London: J. Roberts, 1922, pp. 102–3.
104 Charles G. Chambers, *A Corner of Suffolk: Notes Concerning Lowestoft and the Hundred of Mutford and Lothingland*, Lowestoft: Flood & Son, 1926, p. 13.
105 Chambers, *Suffolk*, pp. 1–16.
106 Isaac Gillingwater, *Lowestoft Witches*, p. 5.
107 Isaac Gillingwater, *Lowestoft Witches*, p. 5.
108 Alice O.D. Claxton, *The Suffolk Dialect of the 20th Century*, Ipswich: Norman Adlard, 1954, p. 46.
109 Malcolm Smith, *The British Amphibians and Reptiles*, London: Collins, 1964, pp. 168–220.
110 Ted Ellis, letter to Ivan Bunn, February 10, 1983.
111 William Godwin, *Lives of the Necromancers*, London: Frederick J. Mason, 1834, pp. 310–11; Montague Summers, *The History of Witchcraft and Demonology*, London: Kegan Paul, Trench, Trubner, 1926, pp. 158–60.
112 William Shakespeare, *The Tragedy of Macbeth*, IV, i, 6–7.
113 Katharine M. Briggs, *Pale Hecate's Team*, New York: Humanities Press, 1952, p. 80.
114 Pennethorne Hughes, *Witchcraft*, London: Longmans, Green, 1952, p. 141.
115 Robert Muchembled, "The Witches of the Cambresis: The Acculturation of the Rural World in the Sixteenth and Seventeenth Centuries," in James Obelkevich (ed.), *Religion and the People, 800–1700*, Chapel Hill: University of North Carolina Press, 1979, pp. 232–41.
116 *A Detection of Damnable Driftes, Practized by Three Witches Arraigned at Chelmsford in Essex . . . April 1579*, London: Edward White, 1579, p. 12.
117 George Lyman Kittredge, *Witchcraft in Old and New England*, Cambridge: Harvard University Press, 1929, p. 182.

118 Alexander Roberts, *A Treatise of Witchcraft ... with a True Narration of the Witchcrafts which Mary Smith, Wife of Henry Smith, Glover, Did Practice*, London: N.O., 1616, p. 18.
119 Rossell H. Robbins, *Encyclopedia*, p. 325.
120 Christina Hole, *A Mirror of Witchcraft*, London: Chatto & Windus, 1957, p. 58; F. Bartham Zinckle, *Some Materials for the History of Wherstead*, London: Simpkin, Marshall, 1887.
121 Rossell H. Robbins, *Encyclopedia*, p. 344.
122 Rossell H. Robbins, *Encyclopedia*, p. 344.
123 William Perkins, *A Discourse on the Damned Art of Witchcraft*, Cambridge: Thomas Pickering, 1608; Rossell H. Robbins, *Encyclopedia*, p. 174.
124 Rossell H. Robbins, *Encyclopedia*, p. 174. The remaining three items were (5) if a fellow witch or magician testified against them, this was ground for further inquiry; (6) if a devil's mark were found upon the suspect; (7) if the suspect's answers were unconstant or if he were "contrary to himself in his answers." Perkins was cautious on this final matter, however, noting that the innocent could be cowed and confused in the presence of the greatness of the crown courts.
125 Barry Reay, "Popular Culture in Early Modern England," in Reay (ed.), *Popular Culture in Seventeenth-Century England*, London: Croom Helm, 1985, pp. 6–7.
126 Roger Thompson, "Salem Revisited," *Journal of American Studies*, 6 (1972), p. 381.
127 Preserved Smith, *A History of Modern Culture*, New York: Henry Holt, 1930, Vol. I, p. 436. See also Jeffrey Russell, *A History of Witchcraft, Sorcerers, Heretics, and Pagans*, London: Thames & Hudson, 1980, p. 92.
128 Brian P. Levack, *The Witch-Hunt in Early Modern Europe*, 2nd edition, London: Longman, 1995, p. 200.
129 John Bellamy, *The Tudor Law of Treason: An Introduction*, London: Routledge & Kegan Paul, 1979, p. 111.
130 H.C. Erik Midelfort, *Witch Hunting in Southwestern Germany*, Stanford: Stanford University Press, 1972; Midelfort, "Witch Hunting and the Domino Theory," in James Obelkevich (ed.), *Religion and the People*, pp. 277–88.
131 John H. Langbein, *Torture and the Law of Proof: Europe and England in the Ancien Régime*, Chicago: University of Chicago Press, 1976, p. 7.
132 Langbein, *Torture*, p. 67.
133 Frederick Pollock and Frederic W. Maitland, *The History of English Law*, 2nd edition, Cambridge: Cambridge University Press, 1898, Vol. II, p. 660.
134 H.C. Erik Midelfort, "Were There Really Witches?," in Robert M. Kingdon (ed.), *Transition and Revolution: Problems and Issues of European Renaissance and Reformation History*, Minneapolis: Burgess, 1974, p. 192.
135 Beatrice White, "Introduction," to George Gifford, *A Dialogue Concerning Witches and Witchcraftes* [1593], Oxford: Oxford University Press, 1931, p. v.

136 See, for instance, Alan Anderson and Raymond Gordon, "The Uniqueness of English Witchcraft: A Matter of Numbers?" *British Journal of Sociology*, 30 (1979), pp. 359–61; Ronald Holmes, *Witchcraft in British History*, London: Tandem, 1976, p. 12.

137 Christina Larner, "Witch Beliefs and Accusations in England and Scotland," in Larner, *Witchcraft and Religion: The Politics of Popular Belief*, Oxford: Basil Blackwell, 1984, pp. 70–1.

138 Christina Larner, "James VI and James I and Witchcraft," in Alan G.R. Smith (ed.) *The Reign of James VI and I*, London: Macmillan, 1973, p. 89.

3 THE SWOUNING SISTERS

1 *A Tryal of Witches at the Assizes Held at Bury St. Edmunds*, London: William Shrewsbery, 1682, pp. 12–13. Subsequent quotations from the trial report appear on pages 12 through 40.

2 For a similar kind of in-court confrontation in Italian criminal trials see Wayland Young, *The Montesi Scandal*, New York: Doubleday, 1958, p. 214.

3 See, e.g., George Giffard [Gifford], *A Dialogue Concerning Witches and Witchcraft*, London: John Winstead, 1593, p. E4; Gillian Tindall, *A Handbook of Witches*, New York: Atheneum, 1966, p. 118.

4 "The Case of Mary Smith for Witchcraft," in T.B. Howell (ed.), *Cobbett's Complete Collection of State Trials and Proceedings for High Treason and Other Crimes From the Earliest Period*, London: Longman, Hurst, Rees, Orme, and Brown, 1816, Vol. II, p. 1058.

5 William Perkins, *A Discourse on the Damned Art of Witchcraft*, Cambridge: Thomas Pickering, 1608, pp. 206–7.

6 Howell, *State Trials*, Vol. II, p. 1058.

7 Matthew Hale, *The History of the Pleas of the Crown* [1736], Philadelphia: Robert H. Small, 1847, Vol. I, pp. 279–80.

8 Matthew Hale, *Pleas of the Crown*, p. 302. In 1895, the US Supreme Court would rule that a child of five-and-a-half was competent to appear as a witness in a murder trial. The court, enunciating common law, declared that his "capacity and intelligence, . . . his appreciation of the difference between truth and falsehood, as well as his duty to tell the former" were what counted. *Wheeler v. United States*, 159 U.S. 523, 524 (1895).

9 Anne Llewellyn Barstow, *Witchcraft: A New History of the European Witch Hunts*, New York: Pandora, 1994, p. 85.

10 Wallace Notestein, *A History of Witchcraft in England from 1558 to 1718*, Washington: American Historical Association, 1911, pp. 44–5.

11 Thomas Potts, *The Wonderfull Discoverie of Witches in the County of Lancaster*, London: John Barnes, 1613.

12 Similarly, in Brouamount in Lorraine, a 9-year-old accused every member of her family of witchcraft—father, mother, grandparents, uncles, and aunts. Her father confirmed her accusations, and her relatives were burned at the stake. E. William Monter, *European Witchcraft*, New York: Wiley, 1969, p. 105.

13 Lynn Thorndike, *A History of Magic and Experimental Science: The Seventeenth Century*, New York: Columbia University Press, 1958, Vol. VII, p. 303. There is a record of a marriage between a Pierre Passé and Elisabeth Udric in London in 1573. The couple is said to have migrated from Holland. Bernard Cottret, *The Huguenots in England: Immigration and Settlement, 1550–1799*, Peregrine and Adriana Stevenson (trans.), Cambridge: Cambridge University Press, 1991, pp. 258–9.

14 Lowestoft Parish Register, p. 27.

15 Lowestoft Manor Court Books, Suffolk Record Office, Lowestoft, 194/A10/5.

16 Probate records of the Archdeaconry of Suffolk, Suffolk Record Office, Ipswich, IC/A2/36/37.

17 Archdeaconry of Suffolk, IC/AA1/56/128.

18 *A Calendar of Marriage Licenses Issued by the Consistory Court, Norfolk*, Norfolk Record Office, Norwich, Vol. 1589–1648, p. 263.

19 Edmund Gillingwater, *An Historical Account of the Ancient Town of Lowestoft*, London: G.G.J. & J. Robinson, 1790, p. 263.

20 Lowestoft Parish Register, p. 80.

21 Extract from the Court Roll of Topcroft with Denton, May 13, 1652, Norfolk Record Office, Norwich, MS 14674,36 D 3.

22 Lowestoft Manor Court, 194/A10/8.

23 PRO, Perogative Court of Canterbury Wills, PROB II/227.

24 Edmund Gillingwater, *Town of Lowestoft*, p. 242.

25 David Ogg, *England in the Reign of Charles II* (1934), Oxford: Clarendon Press, 1955, Vol. I, p. 220.

26 Mary Anne Everett Green (ed.), *Calendar of State Papers—Domestic Series*, Nedeln/Lichtenstein: Kraus Reprints, 1968, Vol. 68, p. 39.

27 PRO, SP29/68PT1.

28 PRO, SP29/84.

29 Indenture of Mortgage, March 20, 1679, Lucas and Wyllys Collection, Norfolk Record Office, Norwich, Y/D22/338; Ibid., February 20, 1689, Y/D22/339.

30 "Suffolk in 1674, Hearth Tax Returns," *Suffolk Green Books*, Woodbridge, 1905, Vol. 13, p. 29.

31 Lowestoft Manor Court, 194 A/10/12.

32 Lowestoft Manor Court, 194 A/10/12.

33 Lowestoft Town Book , Norfolk Record Office, Norwich, PD589/112.

34 *Topcroft Cum Denton Manor Court Book*, NRO, Gervais Steele 27/3/72, R176Bff.

35 PRO, Perogative Court of Canterbury Wills, PROB II/364.

36 David Butcher, *The Development of Pre-Industrial Lowestoft, 1560–1730*, M.Phil. thesis. Norwich: University of East Anglia, 1991.

37 Lowestoft Town Book.

38 Hugh H.W. Lees, *The Chronicles of a Suffolk Parish Church: Lowestoft St. Margaret*, Lowestoft: Flood & Sons, 1949, pp. 212–13.

39 Lowestoft Manor Court, 194 A/10/7–12.

40 Quarter Sessions Order Books, Suffolk Record Office, Ipswich, B105/2/1,5,7,10, pp. 130, 135.

41 Ronald Hutton, *The Restoration: A Political and Religious History of England and Wales, 1658–1667*, Oxford: Clarendon Press, 1985, pp. 208–9.

42 Alan Macfarlane, *Witchcraft in Tudor and Stuart England: A Regional and Comparative Study*, London: Routledge & Kegan Paul, 1971, p. 105.

43 Isaac Gillingwater, *Lowestoft Witches*, p. 11.

44 Lowestoft Parish Register, p. 137.

45 Edmund Gillingwater, *Town of Lowestoft*, p. 298.

46 Lowestoft Parish Register, p. 143.

47 Hilda Smith, "Gynecology and Ideology in Seventeenth Century England," in *Liberating Women's History: Theoretical and Ideological Essays*, Urbana: University of Illinois Press, 1976, p.108.

48 Wallace Notestein, *The English People on the Eve of Colonization*, New York: Harper, 1954, p. 101.

49 Quoted in Carl Bridenbaugh, *Vexed and Troubled Englishmen, 1590–1646*, New York: Oxford University Press, 1968, p. 108.

50 Edward Coke, *The Second Part of the Institutes of the Laws of England* (1642), London: E. & R. Brooke, 1797, pp. 70–1. See also Walter J. King, "Early Stuart Courts Leet Still Needful and Useful," *Social History*, 23 (1990), p. 290.

51 Walter J. King, "Early Stuart Court Leets"; see also King, "Untapped Resources for Social History: Court Leet Records," *Journal of Social History*, 15 (1982), pp. 699–705.

52 David R. Hainsworth, *Stewards, Lords and People: The Estate Steward and His World in Late Stuart England*, London: Cambridge University Press, 1992.

53 William Andrews, *Bygone Punishments*, 2nd edition, London: Philip Allan, 1931, p. 175.

54 Leonard A. Parry, *The History of Torture in England*, London: Sampson, Low, Marston, 1934, pp. 162–3.

55 Alice Morse Earle, *Curious Punishments of Bygone Days*, Chicago: Herbert S. Stone, 1896, pp. 36–7.

56 James Heath, *Torture and English Law: An Administrative and Legal History from the Plantagenets to the Stuarts*, Westport, CT: Greenwood, 1982, p. 265.

57 Frederick J. Powicke, *A Life of the Reverend Richard Baxter, 1615–1691*, London: Cape, 1924, p. 109.

58 Lowestoft Parish Register, Vol. II, p. 2.

59 Francis Hutchinson, *An Historical Essay Concerning Witchcraft*, London: Knaplock, 1718, p. 149. A tap was inserted on the advice of John Locke, the renowned philosopher and physician to the first Earl of Shaftesbury, into the Earl's stomach to drain fluid from a hydatid cyst. Kenneth H.D. Haley, *The First Earl of Shaftesbury*, Oxford: Clarendon Press, 1968, pp. 27, 205. Its use supplied the basis for mockery by Shaftesbury's political opponents: "His belly carries still a tap/Through which black treason, all its drege doth strain/At once both excrements of guts and brain." Tim Harris, *London Crowds in the Reign of Charles II: Propaganda and Politics from the Restoration Until the Exclusion Crisis*, Cambridge: Cambridge

University Press, 1987, p. 147. Wits of the day called a vessel with a turn-stock, constructed for holding wine, a "Shaftesbury," and the Earl's common nickname was "Tapski." William Osler, "John Locke as a Physician," in *An Alabama Student and Other Biographical Essays*, London: Oxford University Press, 1926, p. 95.

60 M. Wynn Thomas, "Cotton Mather's *Wonders of the Invisible World: Some Metamorphoses of Salem Witchcraft*," in Sydney Anglo (ed.), *The Damned Art: Essays in the Literature of Witchcraft*, London: Routledge & Kegan Paul, 1977, p. 26.

61 Gifford, *Dialogue*, p. A3.

62 Charles Upham, *Salem Witchcraft*, Boston: Wiggin & Lunt, 1867, Vol. II, p. 107.

63 Charles Upham, *Salem Witchcraft*, Vol. II, p. 147.

64 Quoted in Andrew Amos, *Ruins of Time Exemplified in Matthew Hale's History of the Pleas of the Crown*, London: W. and R. Stevens, and G.S. Norton, 1856, p. 239.

65 *Ipswich Probate Court Marriage Licenses*, Suffolk Record Office, Ipswich, Book 18, folio 7.

66 Stuart Browne (ed.), *Baptisms and Deaths Recorded in the Church Book of Great Yarmouth Independent Church, 1643–1705*, Norfolk Record Society (1951), Vol. 22, pp. 14, 16.

67 A.L. Rowse, *Matthew Arnold: Poet and Prophet*, London: Thames & Hudson, 1976, p. 9.

68 John P. Jump, *Matthew Arnold*, London: Longmans, Green, 1955, p. 176.

69 Matthew Arnold, "A Psychological Parallel," in *Complete Prose Works*, Edited by Robert H. Super, Ann Arbor: University of Michigan Press, 1977, pp. 111–47. See further: Gilbert Geis and Ivan Bunn, "Matthew Arnold and the Lowestoft Witches," *Nineteenth Century Prose*, 20 (1993), 1–17.

70 Sidney Coulling, *Matthew Arnold and His Critics: A Study of Arnold's Controversies*, Athens: Ohio University Press, 1974, p. 20; Basil Wiley, "Arnold and Religion," in Kenneth Allott (ed.), *Matthew Arnold*, Athens: Ohio University Press, 1975, p. 239; Jump, *Matthew Arnold*, p. 157.

71 Peter Laslett, *The World We Have Lost Further Explored*, London: Routledge & Kegan Paul, 3rd edition, 1983, p. 84.

72 Lowestoft Parish Register, p. 89.

73 Lowestoft Parish Register, p. 137.

74 Lowestoft Parish Register, p. 143.

75 Lowestoft Parish Register, p. 110.

76 Archdeaconry of Suffolk, IC/AAI/105/150.

77 Lowestoft Parish Register, p. 111.

78 Archdeaconry of Suffolk, IC/AAI/105/150.

79 Lowestoft Parish Register, Vol. 2, p. 5.

80 Lowestoft Parish Register, Vol. 2, p. 5.

81 J. Duncan, *Copy of the Original Record of the Yarmouth Congregational Church, 1642–1855*, Typescript. London: Dr. Williams' Library, 1960, p. 39.

82 Brian Levack, *The Witch-Hunt in Early Modern Europe*, New York: Longman, 1987, p. 46.

83 E. William Monter, *Witchcraft in France and Switzerland: The Borderlands During the Reformation*, Ithaca: Cornell University Press, 1976, p. 158.

84 Henri Boguet, *An Examinen of Witches*, E. Allen Ashwin (ed.), Montague Summers (trans.), London: J. Rodker, 1929, p. 128.

85 Hutchinson, *Concerning Witchcraft*, p. 57.

86 Thomas Ady, *A Candle in the Dark, or a Treatise Concerning the Natures of Witches & Witchcraft*, London: T. Newberry, 1656, p. 7.

87 Keith Thomas, *Religion and the Decline of Magic: Studies in Popular Beliefs in Sixteenth and Seventeenth Century England*, London: Weidenfeld & Nicolson, 1971, p. 445.

88 Gifford, *Dialogue*, p. G3.

89 Ronald Seth, *Children Against Witches*, London: Robert Hale, 1969, p. 16.

90 C. L'Estrange Ewen, *Witchcraft and Demonianism*, London: Heath Cranton, 1933, pp. 142–3.

91 Ewen, *Witchcraft and Demonianism*, p. 283.

92 Richard Bernard, *A Guide to Grand-Jury Men*, London: Edward Blackmore, 1627, p. 218 *et seq.*

93 Eric Maple, *The Dark World of Witches*, New York: A.S. Barnes, 1946, p. 79.

4 LICE OF EXTRAORDINARY BIGNESS

1 *A Tryal of Witches at the Assizes Held at Bury St. Edmunds*, London: William Shrewsbery, 1682, pp. 45–59.

2 Eric Stockdale, "Sir John Kelyng, Chief Justice of the King's Bench," *Publications of the Bedfordshire Historical Record Society*, 59 (1980), p. 47.

3 Quoted in Alexander Pulling, *The Order of the Coif*, London: William Clowes, 1897, p. 3.

4 J.H. Baker, *The Order of Serjeants at Law: A Chronicle of Creations, with Related Texts and a Historical Introduction*, London: Selden Society, 1984, pp. 28, 62, 64, 73, 98.

5 Baker, *Serjeants at Law*, p. 97.

6 Anthony Trollope, *Lady Anna* [1874], Stephen Orgel (ed.), New York: Oxford University Press, 1974, p. 322.

7 J.S. Cockburn, letter, September 18, 1981. Although both Hale and Keeling rode the Norfolk circuit on several later occasions, they never again were present there together.

8 Francis Blomefield, *An Essay Towards a Topographical History of the County of Norfolk*, London: William Miller, 1808, Vol. IV, p.246.

9 Baker, *Serjeants at Law*, p. 59.

10 Baker, *Serjeants at Law*, p. 192.

11 *Dictionary of National Biography*, Vol. XV, p. 247.

12 Baker, *Serjeants at Law*, p. 441.

13 Baker, *Serjeants at Law*, p. 529.

14 Lawrence Stone, "The Size and Composition of the Oxford Student Body, 1580–1909," in Stone (ed.), *The University in Society: Oxford and Cambridge from the 14th to the 19th Century,* Princeton: Princeton University Press, 1974, p. 94.

15 Their paths had crossed very indirectly, when William Dugdale, seeking access to the papers of John Selden, for whom Hale was one of the executors, wrote to Browne on November 17, 1658 asking for his intervention with another of the executors, mentioning that Hale had already granted permission. Simon Wilkin (ed.), *Sir Thomas Browne's Works Including His Life and Correspondence,* London: William Pickering, 1836, Vol. I, p. 189.

16 Thomas Browne, *"Religio Medici,"* in Charles Sayle (ed.), *The Works of Sir Thomas Browne,* Edinburgh: John Grant, 1912, Part I, sect. 5, p. 11.

17 Stephan Bradwell, "Mary Glover's Late Woeful Case, Together with Its Joyfull Deliverance" [1603], in Michael MacDonald (ed.), *Witchcraft and Hysteria in Elizabethan England: Edward Jorden and the Mary Glover Case,* London: Tavistock/Routledge, 1991, p. 28. We have relied heavily on MacDonald's excellent introduction for our review of the Mary Glover trial.

18 Rhodes Dunlap, "King James and Some Witches: The Date and Text of *Daemonologie," Philological Quarterly,* 54 (1975), pp. 40–6.

19 Christina Larner, "James VI and James I and Witchcraft," in Alan G.R. Smith (ed.), *The Reign of James VI and I,* London: Macmillan, 1973, pp. 74–90; Christina Larner (1975), "Anne of Denmark: Queen of Scotland: A Demonological Dowry?" *Glasgow University Gazette,* 78 (June), pp. 1–2.

20 See, e.g., Dorothy Tyler, "A Review of the Interpretation of Sir Thomas Browne's Part in the Witch Trial of 1664," *Anglia,* 54 (1930), p. 187. Tyler mistakenly places the Krøge trial in the late 1650s and says that only four women were burned.

21 Wilkin, *Sir Thomas Browne's Works,* Vol. I, p. 184.

22 Letter from Johansen, October 10, 1991. See also Jens Christian Johansen, *Da Djavelen Var Ude: Trolldom i det 17. Arhundredes Danmark* [The Missing Devil: Witchcraft in 17th Century Denmark], Odense: Odense Universitetsforlag, 1991.

23 Knud Bogh, "Thomas Browne og Gabriel Ackeleye: Den Først Oversaettelse of Vulgar Errors," *Fund og Forskning i Det Kongelige Biblioteks Samlinger,* 18 (1971), p. 19.

24 Thomas Bartholin, *Epistolarum Medicinalium . . . Centuria,* Copenhagen: Petri Haubold (1663), Vol. III, pp. 242ff.

25 James Crossley (ed.), Editorial note in *Diary and Correspondence of Dr. John Worthington,* Manchester: Charles Simms, 1848, Vol. II, pp. 84–5.

26 Johan Brunsmand, *Krøges Huskors,* Edited by Anders Baeksted, Copenhagen: Ejnar Munksgaard, 1953, pp. 159–61, 288.

27 W.H. Davenport Adams, *Witch, Warlock, and Magician: Historical Sketches of Magic and Witchcraft in England and Scotland,* London: Chatto & Windus, 1889, p. 286.

28 Cotton Mather, "A Modern Instance of Witches," in *Wonders of the Invisible World* [1692], New York: Bell, 1974, Sect. 10, p. 97.

29 Matthew Hale, *The Primitive Origination of Mankind, Considered and Examined According to the Light of Science*, London: William Shrewsbery, 1677, p. 120.
30 Lowestoft Parish Register, p. 110.
31 Lowestoft Parish Register, p. 100.
32 Lowestoft Parish Register, p. 103.
33 Vincent B. Redstone (ed.), *The Ship Money Returns for the County of Suffolk, 1639/40*, Ipswich: Suffolk Institute of Archaeology and Natural History, 1904. See also Mildred Campbell, *The English Yeoman Under Elizabeth and the Early Stuarts*, New Haven: Yale University Press, 1942.
34 Lowestoft Overseers Accounts, 1656–1691, Suffolk Record Office, Lowestoft, 01/13/1/1.
35 Hugh H.W. Lees, *The Chronicles of a Suffolk Parish Church: Lowestoft St. Margaret*, Lowestoft: Flood & Sons, 1949, p. 212.
36 Lowestoft Manor Court, 194/A10/8.
37 Lowestoft Parish Register, p. 118.
38 Francis Hutchinson, *An Historical Essay Concerning Witchcraft*, London: Knaplock, 1718, p. 41.
39 Isaac Gillingwater, *Lowestoft Witches*, p. 22.
40 Ewen, *Witchcraft and Demonianism*, pp. 159–60.
41 Rossell H. Robbins, *Encyclopedia of Witchcraft and Demonology*, New York: Crown, 1959, p. 52.
42 Arthur Campling (ed.), *East Anglian Pedigrees*, Norwich: Norfolk Record Society, 1940, pp. 200–2.
43 Beccles Parish Registers, Suffolk Record Office, Lowestoft, PR 109/D2/11.
44 Lowestoft Parish Register, pp. 88–91.
45 Lowestoft Parish Register, p. 137.
46 Lowestoft Manor Court, 194/A10/8.
47 Julian Franklyn, *Death by Enchantment: An Examination of Ancient and Modern Witchcraft*, London: Hamish Hamilton, 1971, p. 33.
48 Lowestoft Parish Register, pp. 83 and 90.
49 Lowestoft Manor Court, 194/A10/8 & 11.
50 Lowestoft Parish Register, p. 111.
51 Lowestoft Parish Register, p. 76.
52 Lowestoft Parish Register, p. 96.
53 Lowestoft Parish Register, p. 96.
54 C. L'Estrange Ewen, *The Ewens of East Anglia*, London: Privately published, 1928.
55 Lowestoft Parish Register, p. 73.
56 Suffolk Probate Records, IC/AA1/78/581.
57 Lowestoft Manor Court, 194/A10/8.
58 SRO, IC/AA1/19/161.
59 Eric Maple, *The Dark World of Witches*, New York: A.S. Barnes, 1946, p. 88.
60 Enid Porter, *The Folklore of East Anglia*, London: Batsford, 1974, p. 34.
61 John Bellamy, *The Tudor Law of Treason: An Introduction*, London: Routledge & Kegan Paul, 1979, p. 164.

62 James Fitzjames Stephen, *A History of the Criminal Law of England*, London: Macmillan, 1883, Vol. I, p. 383.

63 Matthew Hale, *History of the Common Law of England* [1713], Charles M. Gray (ed.), Chicago: University of Chicago Press, 1971, p. 133.

64 Matthew Hale, *Common Law*, p. 165.

65 T.S. Hughes (ed.), *The Works of Dr. Isaac Barrow*, London: A.J. Valpy, 1830, Vol. 1, p. 277.

66 John M. Beattie, "Crime and the Courts in Surrey, 1736–1753," in J.S. Cockburn (ed.), *Crime in England, 1550–1800*, Princeton: Princeton University Press, 1977, pp. 167–8. See also J.S. Cockburn, *A History of English Assizes, 1558–1714*, Cambridge: Cambridge University Press, 1972, p. 122.

67 John Hawles, *The English-man's Right: A Dialogue Between a Barrister at Law and a Jury-man*, London: R. Janeway, 1680, pp. 14, 58.

68 Gilbert Burnet, *The Life and Death of Sir Matthew Hale, Kt. Sometime Lord Chief Justice of His Majesties Court of Kings Bench*, London: William Shrewsbery, 1682, p. 92.

69 Thomas Thirlwall, *The Works, Moral and Religious, of Sir Matthew Hale*, London: H.D. Symonds, 1805, Vol. II, pp. 283–4.

70 Robert Hawkins, *The Perjur'd Phanatick*, 3rd edition, London: J. Wilford, 1728, p. 59.

71 Hawkins, *Perjur'd Phanatick*, p. 69.

72 Stephen, *Criminal Law*, Vol. I, p. 380.

73 J.M. Kaye, Book review, *Law Quarterly Review*, 94 (1978), p. 464.

74 Quoted in Jack Adamson and H.F. Folland, *Sir Harry Vane: His Life and Times (1613–1662)*, Boston: Gambit, 1973, p. 199.

75 The admonition of William Perkins (stated in 1608), though of the same nature, seems more even-handed: "I would therefore wish and advise all jurors who give their verdict upon life and death in course of assizes, to take good heed that as they be diligent in zeal of God's glory and take good of his church in detecting of witches by all sufficient and lawful means, so likewise they would be careful what they do and not to condemn any party suspected upon bare presumptions without sound and sufficient proofs, that they be not guilty through their own rashness of shedding innocent blood." William Perkins, *A Discourse on the Damned Art of Witchcraft* [1608], in Ian Breward (ed.), *The Works of William Perkins*, Abingdon, Berks.: Sutton Courtenay Press, 1970, p. 606.

76 James I, *Daemonologie, in the Form of a Dialogue*, Edinburgh: Robert Walde-Grave, 1597, Bk III.

77 Quoted in George Birbeck Hill and Lawrence F. Powell (eds.), *Boswell's Life of Samuel Johnson*, 2nd edition, London: Clarendon Press, 1964, Vol. I, p. 31.

78 Increase Mather, "Cases of Conscience Concerning Evil Spirits," in Cotton Mather, *Wonders of the Invisible World*, London: John Russell Smith, 1862, p. 282.

79 David Lanham, "Hale, Misogyny, and Rape," *Criminal Law Journal*, 7 (1983), p. 153.

80 Adams, *Witch, Warlock*, p. 287. Others who believe that the charge tilted against the defendants include Anthony Harris, *Night's Black Agents:*

Witchcraft and Magic in Seventeenth-Century English Drama, Manchester: Manchester University Press, 1980, p. 174; F.A. Inderwick, *Side Lights on the Stuarts*, 2nd edition, London: Sampson, Low, Marston, Searle & Rivington, 1891, p. 167; Reginald Trevor-Davies, *Four Centuries of Witch-beliefs*, London: Methuen, 1947, p. 177.

81 Barbara J. Shapiro, *Probability and Certainty in Seventeenth-Century England: A Study of the Relationships Between Natural Science, Religion, History, Law, and Literature*, Princeton: Princeton University Press, 1983, p. 208.

82 Keith Thomas, *Religion and the Decline of Magic: Studies in Popular Beliefs in Sixteenth and Seventeenth Century England*, London: Weidenfeld & Nicolson, 1971, p. 657.

83 Ewen, *Witchcraft and Demonianism*, p. 125.

84 Roger North, *The Life of the Right Honourable Francis North, Baron of Guilford*, London: John Whiston, 1742, p. 129.

85 North, *Francis North*, p. 129.

86 T.W., *The Clerk of the Assize, Judges, Marshall and Cryer*, London: Timothy Twyford, 1660, pp. 48–9.

87 Bellamy, *Treason*, p. 168.

88 T.W., *Clerk*, pp. 48–9; Beattie, "Crime and the Courts," p. 395.

89 T.W., *Clerk*, p. 16.

90 T.W., *Clerk*, p. 16.

91 Quoted in Richard Boulton, *The Possibility and Reality of Magick, Sorcery, and Witchcraft Demonstrated*, London: J. Roberts, 1922, p. 109.

92 Boulton, *Witchcraft Demonstrated*, p. 109.

93 Cynthia B. Herrup, *The Common Peace: Participation and the Criminal Law in Seventeenth-Century England*, Cambridge: Cambridge University Press, 1987, p. 192.

94 Matthew Hale, *The History of the Pleas of the Crown* [1736], Philadelphia: Robert H. Small, 1847, Vol. II, p. 412.

95 John Murray, *Handbook for Essex, Suffolk, Norfolk, and Cambridgeshire*, 2nd edition, London: John Murray, 1875, p. 134.

96 Bellamy, *Treason*, p. 191.

97 Edmond Bower, *Doctor Lamb Revived* [1653]; cited in Keith Thomas, *Religion and the Decline of Magic: Studies in Popular Beliefs in Sixteenth and Seventeenth Century England*, London: Weidenfeld & Nicolson, 1971, pp. 34–6.

98 Margaret A. Murray, *The Witch-cult in Western Europe*, Oxford: Clarendon Press, 1962, p. 17; Edgar Peel and Pat Southern, *The Trials of the Lancashire Witches: A Study of Seventeenth-Century Witchcraft*, New York: Taplinger, 1969, p. 158.

5 WRINKLED FACE, FURROWED BROW, AND GOBBER TOOTH

1 Kirsten Hastrup, "Iceland's Sorcerers and Paganism," in Bengt Ankarloo and Gustav Henningsen (eds.), *Early Modern European Witchcraft: Centres and Perspectives*, Oxford: Clarendon Press, 1990, p. 386; E.

William Monter, "Scandinavian Witchcraft in Anglo-American Perspective," in ibid., p. 426.

2 Alan C. Kors, Book Review, *Journal of Interdisciplinary History*, 9 (1979), pp. 544–5.

3 Brian Levack, *The Witch-Hunt in Early Modern Europe*, 2nd edition, London: Longman, 1995, pp. 2–3.

4 Christina Larner, "English and Scotch Witches," *New Edinburgh Review*, February 1971, p. 26.

5 Geoffrey Scarre, *Witchcraft and Magic in 16th and 17th Century Europe*, Atlantic Highlands, NJ: Humanities Press International, 1987, p. 38.

6 Julio Caro Baroja, *The World of Witches*, O.N.V. Glendinning (trans.), Chicago: University of Chicago Press, 1964, p. 81.

7 Stuart Clark, "Protestant Demonology: Sin, Superstition, and Sorcery (c.1520–c.1630)," in Ankarloo and Henningsen, *European Witchcraft*, p. 60.

8 Thomas Thirlwall, *The Works, Moral and Religious, of Sir Matthew Hale*, London: H.D. Symonds, 1805, Vol. II, p. 346.

9 Richard Bernard, *A Guide to Grand-Jury Men*, London: Edward Blackmore, 1627, p. 104.

10 Lucy Mair, *Witchcraft*, New York: McGraw-Hill, 1969, pp. 7–9.

11 Alan Macfarlane, "A Tudor Anthropologist: George Gifford's *Discourse* and *Dialogue*," in Sydney Anglo (ed.), *The Damned Art: Essays in the Literature of Witchcraft*, London: Routledge & Kegan Paul, 1977, pp. 151–2.

12 Lynn Sandra Kahn, "The Dynamics of Scapegoating: The Expulsion of Evil," *Psychotherapy: Theory, Research, and Practice*, 17 (1980), pp. 79–84. See also Tom Douglas, *Scapegoats: Transferring Blame*, London: Routledge, 1995.

13 Ann Kibbey, "Mutations of the Supernatural: Witchcraft, Remarkable Providences, and the Power of Puritan Men," *American Quarterly*, 34 (1982), pp. 141–2.

14 Jeremy Kingston, *Witches and Witchcraft*, Garden City, NY: Doubleday, 1976, pp. 137–9.

15 Lawrence Stone, "The Disenchantment of the World," *New York Review of Books*, 17 (December 2, 1971), p. 20.

16 Mair, *Witchcraft*, p. 152.

17 A person in New England who was accused of witchcraft was involved in more than one hundred lawsuits—"he seems to have gone out of his way to make enemies, which could be dangerous in a society on the lookout for witches." Edgar J. McManus, *Law and Liberty in Early New England: Criminal Justice and Due Process, 1620–1692*, Amherst: University of Massachusetts Press, 1993, p. 142.

18 Keith Thomas, *Religion and the Decline of Magic: Studies in Popular Beliefs in Sixteenth and Seventeenth Century England*, London: Weidenfeld & Nicolson, 1971, pp. 552–3.

19 R.B. Lee, "Work Effort, Group Structure, and Land-Use in Contemporary Hunter-Gatherers," in Peter J. Ucko, Ruth Tringham, and Geoffrey W. Dimbleby (eds.), *Man, Settlement and Urbanism*, London: Duckworth, 1972, p. 182.

20 James L. Brain, "Witchcraft and Development," *African Affairs*, 81 (1982), p. 381.
21 Philip Mayer, "Witches," in Max Marwick (ed.), *Witchcraft and Sorcery*, Harmondsworth: Penguin, 1970, p. 55.
22 Gustav Henningsen, "Witchcraft in Denmark," *Folklore*, 93 (1982), p. 132.
23 David Butcher, *The Development of Pre-Industrial Lowestoft, 1560–1730*, M. Phil. Thesis, Norwich: University of East Anglia, 1991, pp. 74/76 and 572
24 James I, *Daemonologie, in the Form of a Dialogue*, Edinburgh: Robert Walde-Grave, 1597, p. 43. Stuart Clark, "King James' *Daemonologie: Witchcraft and Kingship*," in Anglo, *Damned Art*, p. 164; Larner, "James VI and I," p. 89.
25 Monter, *France and Switzerland*, p. 120; Muchembled, "Cambresis," pp. 227–8; Hans Sebald, "Nazi Ideology Redefining Deviants: Himmler's Witch-Trial Survey and the Case of the Bishop of Bamberg," *Deviant Behavior*, 10 (1989), p. 260; H.C. Erik Midelfort, "Witchcraft, Magic, and the Occult," in Steven Ozmen (ed.), *Reformation Europe: A Guide to Research*, St. Louis: Center for Reformation Research, 1982, p. 191.
26 John Gaule, *Select Cases of Conscience Touching Witches and Witchcraft* [1646], quoted in E. Lynn Linton (ed.), *Witch Stories*, London: Chatto & Windus, 1883, p. 177.
27 C. L'Estrange Ewen, *Witch Hunting and Witch Trials: The Indictments for Witchcraft from the Records of 1373 Assizes Held for the Home Circuit, 1559–1736 AD*, London: F. Muller, 1971, pp. 102–8.
28 Alexander Rysman, "How the 'Gossip' Became a Woman," *Journal of Communications*, 27 (1977), p. 176.
29 Alan Macfarlane, *Witchcraft in Tudor and Stuart England: A Regional and Comparative Study*, London: Routledge & Kegan Paul, 1971, pp. 161–2.
30 Marianne Hester, *Lewd Women and Wicked Witches: A Study of the Dynamics of Male Domination*, London: Routledge, 1992, pp. 107–97.
31 William Gouge, *Of Domesticall Duties: Eight Treatises*, 3rd edition, London: George Miller, 1634, p. 21.
32 Barbara Rosen (ed.), *Witchcraft*, New York: Taplinger, 1969, p. 12.
33 Pennethorne Hughes, *Witchcraft*, London: Longmans, Green, 1952, p. 167.
34 Heinrich Kramer and James Sprenger, *Malleus Maleficarum* [1487], Montague Summers (trans.), London: John Rodker, 1928, p. 71.
35 Bernard, *Grand-jury Men*, pp. 88–90.
36 Karen Horney, "The Dread of Women," *International Journal of Psycho-analysis*, 13 (1932), p. 349.
37 Keith Thomas, *Religion*, p. 679. See further George Rosen, "Psychopathology in the Social Process: A Study of the Persecution of Witches in Europe as a Contribution to the Understanding of Mass Behaviors and Psychic Epidemics," *Journal of Health and Human Behaviors* (1960), pp. 200–11.
38 Hughes, *Witchcraft*, p. 134.

39 Reginald Scot, *The Discoverie of Witchcraft*, London: W. Broome, 1584, p. 134.

40 Macfarlane, *Tudor and Stuart*, p. 17.

41 Macfarlane, *Tudor and Stuart*, p. 17.

42 Alice Clark, *Working Life of Women in the Seventeenth Century*, London: George Routledge, 1919, p. 302.

43 Christina Larner, *Enemies of God: The Witch-Hunt in Scotland*, London: Chatto & Windus, 1981, pp. 101–2.

44 Christina Larner, "Was Witch-Hunting Woman Hunting?" *New Society*, October 1, 1981, p. 11.

45 Alan Cromartie, *Sir Matthew Hale, 1609–1676: Law, Religion and Natural Philosophy*, Cambridge: Cambridge University Press, 1995, pp. 5, 43.

46 Matthew Hale (1816), *Letters of Advice to His Grandchildren*, London: Taylor & Hessey, 1816, p. 19.

47 *Lord Leigh's Case*, 84 English Reports 807 (1676). *R. v. Lister* [93 English Reports 645, 646 (1721)] agrees that where a wife was either "squandering away her husband's estate, or going into lewd company" it was "lawful for the husband, in order to preserve his honor and estate, to lay such a wife under restraint." But see further *R. v. Jackson* [1 Queen's Bench Division 671, 679 (1891)], with Lord Halsbury's observations on this "quaint and absurd dicta."

48 Matthew Hale, *Letters of Advice*, pp. 116–17. Hale's depiction of his first wife parallels the stereotype of women of the time:

> Their emotions ran riot; they had no sense of discipline; they squandered money on dress, on strange china, on entertainments, on cards, on every form of dissipation. After the fire of youth had departed, every vice which want of education permits to flourish grew rank and luxuriant. The spirit of enquiry degenerated into a vulgar and impertinent curiosity. Usual capacity for the communication of ideas became empty and frivolous gossip. Thwarted energy was distorted into a peevish and querulous discontent. Generous emotions which, fixed upon big things, might have doubled the strength of the forces of improvement, were concentrated upon petty things, and dwindled into trifling and irresponsible whims and humors.
>
> (Walter Lyon Blaise, *The Emancipation of Women*, London: Constable, 1910, pp. 30–1)

49 John B. Williams, *Memoirs of the Life, Character, and Writings of Sir Matthew Hale*, London: Jackson & Walford, 1835, p. 162.

50 Richard Baxter, *Additional Notes on the Life and Death of Sir Matthew Hale*, London: Richard Janeway, 1682, p. A4.

51 Roger North, *The Life of the Right Honourable Francis North, Baron of Guilford*, London: John Whiston, 1742, p. 63.

52 Williams, *Memoirs*, pp. 341–56. See also Wilfrid Prest, "Hale as a Husband," *Legal History*, 14 (1933), pp. 142–4.

53 Susan D. Amussen, *An Ordered Society: Gender and Crime in Early Modern England*, Oxford: Blackwell, 1988, p. 81.

54 Erasmus Middleton, *Biographia Evangelina; Or, An Historical Account of the Lives and Deaths of the Most Eminent and Evangelical Authors or Preachers, Both British and Foreign*, London: J.W. Parham, 1779, Vol. III, p. 424.
55 Matthew Hale, *The History of the Pleas of the Crown* [1736], Sollom Emlyn (ed.), Philadelphia: Robert H. Small, 1847, Vol. I, p. 290.
56 Matthew Hale, *Pleas of the Crown*, Vol. I, p. 635.
57 Matthew Hale, *Pleas of the Crown*, Vol. I, p. 636.
58 Statute of Westminster, 13 Edw. I, c. 30 (1285).
59 J.M. Kaye, "The Making of English Criminal Law: (1) The Beginnings— a General Survey of Criminal Law and Justice Down to 1500," *Criminal Law Review*, January 1977, p. 9.
60 Henry de Bracton, "Pleas of the Crown," in *On the Laws and Customs of England*, Edited by Samuel E. Thorne, 1968, Cambridge: Harvard University Press, 1968, Vol. II, pp. 414–15, 418.
61 Kaye, "English Criminal Law," p. 8.
62 Joel Samaha, *Crime in Elizabethan England*, Ph.D. dissertation, Northwestern University, 1972, p. 52.
63 *State v. Floyd*, 177 S.E. 375, 385 (So. Car. 1934).
64 *US v. Wiley*, 492 F.2d 547, 554 (DC Dist. 1973).
65 "300 Years On," *Economist*, August 16, 1975, p. 51.
66 *People v. Benson*, 6 Calif. 221, 223 (1856).
67 The Hale jury charge was jettisoned in California by *People v. Rincon-Pineda*, 538 P.2d 247, 254, 1975, in a decision followed by other jurisdictions [*State v. Settle*, 531 P.2d 151 (Ariz.) 1975]; [*State v. Feddersen*, 230 N.W. 2d 510 (Iowa 1975)]. A Wyoming judge summed up the development: "Rincon-Pineda," he noted, "has literally taken the bull by the horns and exploded Hale's myth." *Lopez v. State*, 544 P.2d 855, 868 (Wyo. 1976).
68 Matthew Hale, *Pleas of the Crown*, Vol. I, p. 636.
69 Thomas, *Religion*, p. 689.
70 Samuel Harsnett, *A Discovery of the Fraudulent Practises of John Darnell* [1599], quoted in Charles Upham, *Salem Witchcraft*, Boston: Wiggin & Lunt, 1867, Vol. I, p. 370.
71 Jeffrey Russell, *A History of Witchcraft, Sorcerers, Heretics, and Pagans*, London: Thames & Hudson, 1980, p. 110.
72 Prudencio de Sandoval, *Historia del Emprador Carlos V, Rey de Ispana*, Madrid: La Illustracion, 1847, Vol. V, pp. 53–7.
73 Paul Boyer and Stephen Nissenbaum, *Salem Possessed: The Social Origins of Witchcraft*, Cambridge: Harvard University Press, 1974, p. 2.
74 Russell Zguta, "Witchcraft Trials in Seventeenth-Century Russia," *American Historical Review*, 82 (1977), p. 1196.
75 For a sophisticated examination of this point see James Sharpe, *Instruments of Darkness: Witchcraft in England, 1550–1750*, London: Hamish Hamilton, 1996.
76 Francis Hill, *A Delusion of Satan: The Full Story of the Salem Witch Trials*, New York: Doubleday, 1995, pp. 32–3.
77 Holmes, "Women: Witnesses and Witches," *Past and Present*, 140 (1993), p. 49.

78 See generally Lydal Roper, "Witchcraft and Fantasy in Early Modern Germany," *History Workshop: A Journal of Socialist and Feminist Historians*, 32 (1991), pp. 19–43.

79 Deborah Willis, *Malevolent Nurture: Witch-Hunting and Maternal Power in Early Modern England*, Ithaca, NY: Cornell University Press, 1995, pp. 13–14.

80 Nicholas P. Spanos, "Witchcraft in Histories of Psychiatry: A Critical Analysis and an Alternative Conceptualization," *Psychological Bulletin*, 85 (1978), p. 423.

81 Monica Hunter Wilson, "Witch Beliefs and Social Structure," *American Journal of Sociology*, 41 (1951), p. 308.

82 Daniel P. Walker, *Unclean Spirits: Possession and Exorcism in France and England in the Late Sixteenth and Early Seventeenth Centuries*, Philadelphia: University of Pennsylvania Press, 1981, p. 15.

83 Samuel B. Guze, Letter, June 10, 1985.

84 Gabriel Garcia Marquez, *The General in His Labyrinth*, Edith Grossman (trans.), New York: Knopf, 1990, p. 216.

85 See Alan A. Kane, Benjamin Ginn, and Bernardo A. Mora, "Multiple Foreign Bodies in the Stomach," *Journal of the American Medical Association*, 174 (1969–70), pp. 2073–4.

86 *The Disclosing of a Later Counterfeyted Possession by the Devyl in Two Maydens within the Citie of London* (1574), in Rosen, *Witchcraft*, pp. 231–9.

87 Stephen H. Cassan, *Lives and Memoirs of the Bishops of Sherborne and Salisbury*, Salisbury: Brodie & Downing, 1824, Part II, p. 83.

88 C. L'Estrange Ewen, *Witchcraft in the Star Chamber*. Privately printed, 1938, pp. 28–36.

89 Thomas Guidott, Preface to Edward Jorden, *A Discourse of Natural Bathes and Mineral Waters*, 3rd edition [1673], quoted in George Lyman Kittredge, *Witchcraft in Old and New England*, Cambridge: Harvard University Press, 1929, p. 321–2.

90 Christina Hole, *Witchcraft in England*, London: B.T. Batsford, 1947, pp. 192–4.

91 W.H. Davenport Adams, *Witch, Warlock, and Magician: Historical Sketches of Magic and Witchcraft in England and Scotland*, London: Chatto & Windus, 1889, p. 296.

92 Maple, *Dark World*, p. 107.

93 Edward T. Withington, "Dr. John Weyer and the Witch Mania," in Charles J. Singer (ed.), *Studies in the History and Method of Science*, Oxford: Clarendon Press, 1917–1921, Vol. I, pp. 216–17.

94 Henry Charles Lea, *Materials Toward a History of Witchcraft*, Edited by Arthur C. Howland, New York: Thomas Yoseloff, 1957, Vol. II, p. 591.

95 Lea, *Materials*, Vol. II, p. 989.

96 Sascha Talmor, *Glanville: The Use and Abuses of Skepticism*, Oxford: Pergamon Press, 1981; Moody E. Prior, "Joseph Glanvill, Witchcraft, and Seventeenth Century Science," *Modern Philology*, 30 (1932), pp. 167–93.

97 Joseph Glanvill, *Saducismus Triumphatus: Or, Full and Plain Evidence Concerning Witches and Apparitions* [1681], in *Collected Works*, New York: George Olms Verlag, 1978, Vol. II, p. 28.

98 Glanvill, *Saducismus*, Vol. IX, pp. 116–17.

99 Roger Latham and William Matthews, *The Diary of Samuel Pepys*, London: G. Bell, 1970, Vol. VII, p. 382 (November 24, 1666).

100 Gregory Zilboorg, *The Medical Man and the Witch During the Renaissance*, Baltimore: Johns Hopkins University Press, 1935, p. 73.

101 Jessie O'Dwyer and Pat Carlen, "Josie: Surviving Holloway . . . and Other Women's Prisons," in Carlen (ed.), *Criminal Women: Autobiographical Accounts*, Cambridge: Polity Press, 1984, p. 170.

102 John Putnam Demos, *Entertaining Satan: Witchcraft and the Culture of Early New England*, New York: Oxford University Press, 1982, p. 441.

103 David C. Taylor, "Hysteria, Play-Acting and Courage," *British Journal of Psychiatry*, 149 (1986), p. 37.

104 Mark S. Micale, "Hysteria and Its Historiography: The Future Perspective," *History of Psychiatry*, 1 (1980), p. 38.

105 Mark S. Micale, "Hysteria and Its Historiography: A Review of Past and Present Writings (I)," *History of Science*, 27 (1989), p. 225.

106 Taylor, "Hysteria," p. 38.

107 Helen King, "Once Upon a Text: Hysteria from Hippocrates," in Sander L. Gilman, Helen King, Roy Porter, G.S. Rousseau, and Elaine Showalter, *Hysteria Beyond Freud*, Berkeley: University of California Press, 1993, pp. 3–90.

108 Ilza Veith, *Hysteria: The History of a Disease*, Chicago: University of Chicago Press, 1965.

109 Vern L. Bullough, *The Subordinate Sex: A History of Attitudes Toward Women*, Urbana: University of Illinois Press, 1973, pp. 60–1.

110 Mary R. Lefkowitz, *Heroines and Hysterics*, London: Duckworth, 1981, p. 15.

111 Thomas S. Szasz, *The Manufacture of Madness: A Comparative Study of the Inquisition and the Mental Health Movement*, New York: Harper & Row, 1970, p. 149.

112 Josef Breur and Sigmund Freud, "On the Psychical Mechanism of Hysterical Phenomena: Preliminary Communication," in *Standard Edition of the Complete Psychological Works of Sigmund Freud*, James Strachey (trans.), London: Hogarth Press, 1955, Vol. II, pp. 3–17. See also William J. McGrath, *Freud's Discovery of Psychoanalysis: The Politics of Hysteria*, Ithaca: Cornell University Press, 1986; Alan Krohn, *Hysteria: The Elusive Neurosis*, New York: International Universities Press, 1978.

113 Georges Guillain, *G.J.M. Charcot: His Life, His Work*, Pearce Bailey (trans.), New York: Hoeber, 1959, p. 73.

114 Aubrey Lewis, "The Survival of Hysteria," *Psychological Medicine*, 5 (1975), p. 9.

115 Lewis, "Survival of Hysteria," p. 12.

116 Pierre Janet, *The Mental State of Hystericals*, Caroline R. Corson (trans.), New York: Putnam's, 1901, p. 527.

117 Jonathan Pincus, "Hysteria Presenting to the Neurologist," in Alec Roy (ed.), *Hysteria*, Chichester: Wiley, 1982, p. 135.

118 George L. Engel, *Fainting*, 2nd edition, Springfield, IL: Thomas, 1962, p. 152.

119 Renato D. Alarcon, "Hysteria and the Hysterical Personality: How Come One Without the Other?" *Psychiatric Quarterly*, 41 (1973), pp. 265, 267.

120 Paul Chodoff, "Hysteria and Women," *American Journal of Psychiatry*, 139 (1982), p. 545.

121 R. Philip Snaith, "Family and Marital Hysteria," *British Journal of Psychiatry*, 114 (1968), pp. 644–5.

122 Chodoff and Lyons, "Hysteria," p. 739. See also Pauline B. Bart, "Social Structure and Vocabularies of Discontent: What Happened to Female Hysteria?" *Journal of Health and Social Behavior*, 9 (1968), pp. 188–93.

123 Quoted in Micale, "Hysteria and Its Historiography (I)," p. 322.

124 Robert E. Kendell, "A New Look at Hysteria," in Roy, *Hysteria*, p. 33.

125 Kendell, "Hysteria," p. 33.

126 Upham, *Salem Witchcraft*, Vol. II, pp. 4–5.

127 Rossell H. Robbins, *Encyclopedia of Witchcraft and Demonology*, New York: Crown, 1959, p. 435.

128 Marion L. Starkey, *The Devil in Massachusetts: A Modern Enquiry into the Salem Witch Trials*, Garden City, NY: Anchor Books, 1969, p. 47.

129 Francis Hutchinson, *An Historical Essay Concerning Witchcraft*, London: Knaplock, 1718, p. 6.

130 Walter Scott, *Letters on Demonology and Witchcraft*, London: George Routledge & Sons, 1884, p. 176.

131 C. L'Estrange Ewen, *Witchcraft and Demonianism*, London: Heath Cranton, 1933, p. 111.

132 Cotton Mather, *The Wonders of the Invisible World: Being an Account of the Tryals of Several Witches Lately Executed in New England*, London: John Dunton, 1693, p. 117.

133 Chadwick Hansen, *Witchcraft at Salem*, New York: George Braziller, 1969, p. x.

134 Ernest Caulfield, "Pediatric Aspects of the Salem Witchcraft Tragedy: A Lesson in Mental Health," *American Journal of Diseases of Children*, 65 (1943), p. 802.

135 C. David Marsden, "Hysteria—A Neurologist's View," *Psychological Medicine*, 16 (1986), p. 283.

136 David P. Allison and Mark Roberts, "On Constructing the Disorder of Hysteria," *Journal of Medicine and Philosophy*, 19 (1994), p. 239.

137 Slater, "Hysteria," p. 1396. See also Roberta Satow, "Where Has All the Hysteria Gone?" *Psychoanalytic Review*, 66 (1979), pp. 463–77.

138 Gustav Henningsen, "The Greatest Witch-Trial of All: Navarre, 1609–14," *History Today* (November 1980), pp. 38–9. See further Henningsen, *The Witches' Advocate: Basque Witchcraft and the Spanish Inquisition (1609–1614)*, Reno: University of Nevada Press, 1980.

139 Thomas Szasz, "Hysteria," in David L. Sills (ed.), *International Encyclopedia of the Social Sciences*, New York: Macmillian, 1968, Vol. VI, p. 51.

140 Hutchinson, *Concerning Witchcraft*, p. 39.

141 Silvio Benham, John Horder, and Jennifer Anderson, "Hysterical Epidemic in a Classroom," *Psychological Medicine*, 3 (1973), p. 369.

NOTES

6 A MAN OF BILIOUS COMPLEXION AND A PEDANT WITH POWER

1 John Lord Campbell, *The Lives of the Chief Justices*, London: John Murray, 1849, Vol. I, p. 512.
2 Campbell, *Chief Justices*, Vol. I, p. 510.
3 We have relied heavily on Eric Stockdale, "Sir John Kelyng, Chief Justice of the King's Bench," *Publications of the Bedfordshire Historical Record Society*, 59 (1980), for biographical information.
4 Stockdale, "Sir John Kelyng," p. 43.
5 Edward Foss, *The Judges of England*, London: John Murray, 1964, Vol. VII, p. 13. Ross Lee, *Law and Local Society in the Time of Charles I: Bedfordshire and the Civil War*, Bedford, Bedfordshire Record Society, 1986, p. 152. Keeling also was remorseless when it came to strict interpretation of the law against infanticide. See Leon Radzinowicz, *A History of English Criminal Law and Its Administration from 1750*, London: Macmillan, 1948, Vol.1 p. 431
6 Stockdale, "Sir John Kelyng," p. 43. See also *Another Cry of the Innocent & Oppressed for Justice*, London: no publisher indicated, 1664, which describes various trials in London before Keeling and his colleagues. An interchange typical of Keeling is this:

K: We care not what you did there, we have proved that you did meet.
Prisoner: I understand that God is a spirit, and I meet to worship the eternal God in spirit, and he perswade my heart and consciences, and must I be condemned to banishment for that?
K: Yes, yes, for the law is against it.

(*Another Cry*, p. 9)

7 Frank W. Jessup, *Sir Roger Twysden, 1597–1672*, New York: Barnes & Noble, 1967, p. 168.
8 Frederick Birkenhead, *Fourteen English Judges*, London: Cassell, 1926, p. 63.
9 Robert Hawkins, *The Perjur'd Phanatick*, 3rd edition, London: J. Wilford, 1728, p. 38.
10 John Kelyng, *A Report of Cases in the Pleas of the Crown, Adjudged and Determined in the Reign of Charles II*, London: Isaac Cleave, 1708, p. 51.
11 Alan Cromartie, *Sir Matthew Hale, 1609–1676: Law, Religion and Natural Philosophy*, Cambridge: Cambridge University Press, 1995, p. 71. Keeling, of course, did not seek to rationalize the practice, which at least offered a semblance of mercy, but only to see that it was enforced in a literal manner.
12 Stockdale, "Sir John Kelyng," p. 52.
13 Gwilym O. Griffith, *John Bunyan*, London: Hodder & Stoughton, 1927, p. 136.
14 Joseph Gurney, "John Bunyan," *Notes and Queries*, 7th series, 10 (1890), p. 345.

15 Roger Sharrock (ed.), "Introduction" to John Bunyan, *Grace Abounding to the Chief of Sinners*, Oxford: Clarendon Press, 1962, p. 2.

16 Jack Lindsay, *John Bunyan: The Maker of Myths*, London: Methuen, 1937, pp. 125–6.

17 Monica Furlong, "Bunyan in Prison," *History Today*, 25 (1975), p. 534.

18 John Brown, *John Bunyan (1628–1688): His Life, Times, and Work*, Frank M. Harrison (ed.), London: Hulbert, 1928, p. 144.

19 James Anthony Froude, *Bunyan*, London: Macmillan, 1888, p. 72.

20 W.T. Whitley, "Bunyan's Imprisonment: A Legal Study," *Transactions of the Baptist Historical Society*, 6 (1918–1919), pp. 1–24.

21 John Bunyan, *The Pilgrim's Progress*, London: Nath. Ponder, 1678, p. 128.

22 John Brown, *John Bunyan*, pp. 140–50.

23 Bunyan, *Grace Abounding*, pp. 126–9; Christopher Hill, *A Tinker and a Poor Man: John Bunyan and His Church, 1628–1688*, New York: Knopf, 1989, pp. 229–30.

24 Bunyan, *Grace Abounding*, pp. 125–31.

25 Griffith, *John Bunyan*, p. 137.

26 Griffith, *John Bunyan*, p. 190.

27 Monica Furlong (ed.), *The Trial of John Bunyan & the Persecution of the Puritans*, London: Folio Society, 1978, p. 20. See also Roger Sharrock, *John Bunyan*, Westport, CT: Greenwood Press, 1984, p. 40.

28 Hill, *Tinker*, p. 106; see also Richard L. Greaves, *Deliver Us from Evil: The Radical Underground in Britain, 1660–1663*, Oxford: Oxford University Press, 1986.

29 T.B. Howell (ed.), *Cobbett's Complete Collection of State Trials and Proceedings for High Treason and Other Crimes From the Earliest Period*, London: Longman, Hurst, Rees, Orme, and Brown, 1816, Vol. V, pp. 947–1363.

30 *The Victoria History of the County of Bedford*, Westminster: A. Constable, Vol. III, p. 258.

31 Violet A. Rowe, *Sir Henry Vane the Younger: A Study in Political and Administrative History*, London: Athlone Press, 1970, p. 224.

32 Jack Adamson and H.F. Folland, *Sir Harry Vane: His Life and Times (1613–1662)*, Boston: Gambit, 1973, p. 332.

33 Howell, *State Trials*, Vol. VI, p. 171.

34 Greaves, *Deliver Us from Evil*, p. 89.

35 34 Edward III, c. 1 (1361).

36 John G. Bellamy, *Criminal Law and Society in Late Medieval and Tudor England*, Gloucester: Alan Sutton, 1984, p. 54.

37 Frederick Pollock and Frederic Maitland, *The History of English Law Before the Time of Edward I*, Cambridge: Cambridge University Press, 1895, Vol. II, p. 503.

38 Walter G. Bell, *The Great Fire of London in 1666*, London: Bodley Head, 1951, p. 90.

39 Kelyng, *Report*, pp. 70–9.

40 David Ogg, *England in the Reign of Charles II* (1934), Oxford: Clarendon Press, 1955, Vol. I, pp. 513–14; Ilana K. Ben-Amos,

Adolescence and Youth in Early Modern England, New Haven: Yale University Press, 1994, pp. 183–4.

41 Harris, *London Crowds*; Tim Harris, "The Bawdy House Riots of 1668," *Historical Journal*, 29 (1986), pp. 537–56. Note also Max Beloff, *Public Order and Popular Disturbances, 1660–1714*, London: Oxford University Press, 1938, pp. 34–5.

42 Howell, *State Trials*, Vol. VI, p. 884; Alexander Luders, *Considerations on the Law of High Treason, In the Article of Levying War*, Bath: Richard Cruttwell, 1808, p. 46.

43 Howell, *State Trials*, Vol. VI, p. 884.

44 Kelyng, *Report*, p. 71.

45 Howell, *State Trials*, Vol. VI, p. 884.

46 Howell, *State Trials*, Vol. VI, p. 884

47 Matthew Hale, *Pleas of the Crown*, Vol. I, p. 134; see also Vol. I, pp. 141, 152.

48 Alfred E. Havighurst, "The Judiciary and Politics in the Reign of Charles II: Part I, 1660–1676," *Law Quarterly Review*, 66 (1950), p. 69; Erasmus Earle had been involved as head of a special judicial commission in judgment on a similar "riot." He had sentenced to death—on Christmas Day 1648, a time deliberately chosen "in accordance with a disagreeable Puritan foible"—eight ringleaders of a group of royalists who had protested against Parliament's suspension of the Mayor. Robert W. Ketton-Cremer, *Norfolk in Civil War: A Portrait of a Society in Conflict*, Hamden, CT: Archon Books, 1970, pp. 331–49.

49 William N. Welsby, *Lives of Eminent English Judges of the Seventeenth and Eighteenth Century*, London: S. Sweet, 1846, pp. 19–20.

50 Donald Veall, *The Popular Movement for Law Reform*, Oxford: Clarendon Press, 1970, p. 22.

51 Timothy A. Green, *Verdict According to Conscience: Perspectives on the English Criminal Jury Trial, 1200–1800*, Chicago: University of Chicago Press, 1984, pp. 141–2.

52 Matthew Hale, *Pleas of the Crown*, Vol. I, p. 159.

53 *Journal of the House of Commons* (n.d.), pp. 4, 20, 35–7.

54 Stockdale, "Sir John Kelyng," p. 50.

55 Anthony Fletcher, *Reform in the Provinces: The Government of Stuart England*, New Haven: Yale University Press, 1986, p. 51.

56 Caroline Robbins (ed.), *The Diary of John Milward, Esq*, Cambridge: Cambridge University Press, 1938.

57 *Dictionary of National Biography*, Vol. 30, pp. 361–2.

58 Barry Coward, *The Stuart Age: A History of England, 1603–1714*, London: Longmans, 1980, p. 288; J.S. Cockburn, *A History of English Assizes, 1558–1714*, Cambridge: Cambridge University Press, 1972, p. 109; John R. Western, *Monarchy and Revolution: The English State in the 1680s*, London: Blandford, 1972, p. 40.

59 Adamson and Folland, *Sir Harry Vane*, p. 372. "Whether or not Oliver did refer to 'Magna Farta,' the attribution is *ben trovato*," Christopher Hill notes. "Such remarks would go down well with the troops." *A Nation of Novelty and Change: Radical Politics, Religion, and Literature in Seventeenth-Century England*, London: Routledge, 1990, pp. 51–2.

60 Caroline Robbins, *John Milward*, p. 167.
61 Roger Latham and William Matthews, *The Diary of Samuel Pepys*, London: G. Bell, 1970, Vol. VIII, p. 578 (December 13, 1667).
62 Latham and Matthews, *Pepys*, Vol. VIII, p. 321 (July 4, 1667).
63 Caroline Robbins, *John Milward*, p. 168.
64 Caroline Robbins, *John Milward*, p. 169.
65 Caroline Robbins, *John Milward*, p. 170. The Commons' proceedings are set forth in Howell, *State Trials*, Vol. VI, pp. 992–5.
66 *Rex v. Bushell*, 124 English Reports 1006 (King's Bench, 1670).
67 Timothy A. Green, *Verdict*, pp. 200–11.
68 Campbell, *Chief Justices*, Vol. I, p. 510; *Historical Manuscripts Commission, Manuscripts of Lord Kenyon*, 14th Report, Appendix, Part IV, 1894, p. 81.
69 Caroline Robbins, *John Milward*, p. 166.
70 Campbell, *Chief Justices*, Vol. I, p. 512.
71 Laurence Echard, *The History of England*, London: Jacob Tonson, 1718, Vol. III, p. 288.
72 Thomas Raymond, *The Report of Divers Special Cases*, London: R. & E. Atkins, 1696, p. 209.
73 Christopher Hill, *Intellectual Origins of the English Revolution*, Oxford: Clarendon Press, 1980, p. 278; John H. Randall, *The School of Padua and the Emergence of Modern Science*, Padua: Editrice Antenore, 1961.
74 Phyllis Allen, "Medical Education in 17th Century England," *Journal of the History of Medicine and Allied Sciences*, 1 (1946), pp. 115–43.
75 John Whitefoot, "Some Minutes for the Life of Sir Thomas Browne," in Thomas Browne, *Posthumous Works*, London: E. Curll, 1712, p. xxvii–xxviii.
76 George Yost, "Sir Thomas Browne and Aristotle," in Robert Ralston Cawley and George Yost (eds.), *Studies in Sir Thomas Browne*, Eugene: University of Oregon Press, 1965, p. 102.
77 Latham and Matthews, *Pepys*, Vol. V, p. 27 (January 27, 1664). The other two books were Francis Osborne's *Advice to a Son: or Directions for Your Better Conduct Through the Various and Most Important Encounters of this Life*, Oxford: Thomas Robinson, 1658, and Samuel Butler's *Hudibras*, London: R. Parker, 1659.
78 William B. Bean, "The Doctor's Religion," *Archives of Internal Medicine*, 113 (1964), p. 6; Molly Lefebure, *Samuel Taylor Coleridge: A Bondage of Opium*, London: Victor Gollancz, 1974, p. 404.
79 William Hazlitt, "Of Persons One Would Wish to Have Seen," in *Literary Remains of the Late William Hazlitt*, London: Saunders & Ottley, 1836, Vol. II, p. 334. The other person was Sir Fulke Greville (1564–1628), a minor English writer and a statesman.
80 Charles Bodemer, "Embryological Thought in Seventeenth Century England," in Bodemer and Lester S. King, *Medical Investigation in Seventeenth Century England*, Los Angeles: William Andrews Clark Memorial Library, University of California, 1968, p. 18.
81 Peter Green, *Sir Thomas Browne*, London: Longman, Green, 1959, p. 7.
82 Samuel Johnson, "Dr. Johnson's Life of Sir Thomas Browne," in Wilkin, *Sir Thomas Browne's Works*, Vol. I, p. xxii.

83 Edmund Gosse, *Sir Thomas Browne*, London: Macmillan & Co., 1905, p. 193.

84 Jonathan F.S. Post, *Sir Thomas Browne*, Boston: Twayne, 1987, p. 58.

85 Thomas Browne, *Pseudodoxia Epidemica*, Robin Robbins (ed.), Oxford: Clarendon Press, 1981, Vol. I, pp. 28, 32; see generally Steven Shapin, *A Social History of Truth: Civility and Science in Seventeenth-Century England*, Chicago: University of Chicago Press, 1994.

86 Thomas Browne, *Pseudodoxia*, Vol. I, p. 643.

87 Thomas Browne, *Pseudodoxia*, Vol. I, p. 114.

88 Fred Braven, "Arthanasius Kircher (1602–1680)," *Journal of the History of Ideas*, 43 (1982), pp. 129–34. Similarly, it has been written that Kircher's works "in number, bulk, and uselessness are not surpassed in the whole field of learning." Thomas Browne, *Pseudodoxia*, Vol. II, p. 693.

89 Lynn Thorndike, *A History of Magic and Experimental Science: The Seventeenth Century*, New York: Columbia University Press, 1958, Vol. VII, pp. 569–70.

90 William P. Dunn, *Sir Thomas Browne*, 2nd edition, Minneapolis: University of Minnesota Press, 1950, p. 7.

91 Post, *Sir Thomas Browne*, p. 114.

92 Jean-Jacques Denomian, *Sir Thomas Browne's* Religio Medici: *A New Edition with Biographical and Critical Notes*, Cambridge: Cambridge University Press, 1955, p. xiv.

93 Stanley Fish, *Self-Consuming Artifacts: The Experience of Seventeenth-Century Literature*, Berkeley: University of California Press, 1972, p. 368.

94 Egon S. Merton, *Science and Imagination in Sir Thomas Browne*, New York: King's Crown Press, 1949, pp. 88–9.

95 Thomas Browne, *Pseudodoxia*, Vol. I, pp. 586–7.

96 William Murison, "Introduction," to Thomas Browne, *Hydriotaphia*, Cambridge: Cambridge University Press, 1937, p. x.

97 Joan Webber, *The Eloquent "I": Style and Self in Seventeenth-Century Prose*, Madison: University of Wisconsin Press, 1968, p. 182.

98 Geoffrey Keynes (ed.), *The Works of Sir Thomas Browne*, Chicago: University of Chicago Press, 1964, Vol. III, p. 293.

99 Kenelm Digby, "Observation on *Religio Medici*," in Wilkin (ed.), *Sir Thomas Browne's Works*, Vol. II, p. 129.

100 Simon Wilkin (ed.), *Sir Thomas Browne's Works*, London: William Pickering, 1835, Vol. II, pp. 105–6.

101 Joan Bennett, *Sir Thomas Browne*, Cambridge: Cambridge University Press, 1962, p. 176.

102 Browne, *Works*, Keynes (ed.), Vol. I, p. 83. Satirists scolded that Browne was "a reproach to his parents, who shuns the entertainment of Hymen, the blissful amours of the fair, without which he himself had not gained so much as the post of a cypher, in the numeration of mankind." Benjamin Bridgewater, *Religio Bibliopolae, in Imitation of Dr. Browns Religio Medicie, with a Supplement To It*, London: P. Smart, 1691, p. 77.

103 Browne, *Works*, Keynes (ed.), Vol. VI, p. 281.

104 Johnson, "Life of Browne," Vol. I, p. xxvi.

105 Thomas Browne to Edward Browne, June 14, 1676, in Browne, *Works*, Keynes (ed.), Vol. IV, pp. 61–2. See further Peter Green, *Sir Thomas Browne*, London: Longmans, Green, 1959; Jeremiah S. Finch, *Sir Thomas Browne: A Doctor's Life of Science and Faith*, New York: Henry Schuman, 1950, p. 239.
106 Edmund Gosse, *Browne*, p. 105.
107 John B. Thayer, *Legal Essays*, Boston: Boston Book Company, 1908, p. 332. See also Walter Scott, *Letters on Demonology and Witchcraft*, London: George Routledge & Sons, 1884, pp. 213–14; C. L'Estrange Ewen, *Witchcraft and Demonianism*, London: Heath Cranton, 1933, p. 350; Reginald Trevor-Davies, *Four Centuries of Witch-beliefs*, London: Methuen, 1947, p. 109.
108 Malcolm Letts, "Sir Thomas Browne and Witchcraft," *Notes and Queries*, 11th series, 5 (March 23, 1912), pp. 221–3.
109 Alan J. Macfarlane, "Witchcraft in Tudor and Stuart Essex," in J.S. Cockburn (ed.), *Crime in England, 1550–1800*, Princeton: Princeton University Press, 1977, p. 83.
110 See, for instance, Onesmus K. Mutungi, *The Legal Aspects of Witchcraft in East Africa with Particular Reference to Kenya*, Nairobi: East African Literature Bureau, 1977, pp. 18–19.
111 Ernest Jones, *On the Nightmare*, New York: Liveright, 1951, p. 229.
112 Bennett, *Sir Thomas Browne*, p. 13.
113 Dunn, *Sir Thomas Browne*, p. 27.
114 Wilkin (ed.), *Sir Thomas Browne's Works*, Vol. I, p. 43.
115 Tyler, "Sir Thomas Browne," p. 184, 188.
116 Geoffrey Keynes (ed.), *The Works of Sir Thomas Browne*, Chicago: University of Chicago Press, 1964, Vol. V, p. 252.
117 Whitefoot, "Minutes," p. 97.
118 Bennett, *Sir Thomas Browne*, p. 97.
119 Ketton-Cremer, *Norfolk*, p. 271.
120 Alexander Whyte, *Sir Thomas Browne: An Appreciation*, London: O. Anderson & Ferrter, 1898, p. 18.
121 Browne, *Works*, Keynes (ed.), Vol. I, p. 89.
122 Baroja, *World of Witches*, p. 250.
123 Keynes, *The Works of Sir Thomas Browne*, Chicago: University of Chicago Press, 1964, p. 102.

7 OF FEAR AND DREAD

1 Roger North, *The Life of the Right Honourable Francis North, Baron of Guilford*, London: John Whiston, 1742, p. 292.
2 [Edward Stephens], "Preface," to Matthew Hale, *A Discourse of the Knowledge of God, and of Our Selves*, London: William Shrewsbery, 1688, p. A4.
3 Stephens, "Preface," to Matthew Hale, *Discourse*, pp. A4, A5.
4 Alan Cromartie, Sir Matthew Hale (1609–1676). Ph.D. dissertation (history), Cambridge University, 1991, p. 170.
5 Cromartie, Hale, p. 170.

6 Edward Stephens, "Preface," to Matthew Hale, *A Collection of Modern Relations of Matter of Fact Concerning Witches & Witchcraft Upon the Persons of People*, London: John Harris, 1693, p. A7.
7 Stephens, "Preface," to Matthew Hale, *Collection*, p. A7.
8 Edward Stephens, "Preface," to Matthew Hale, *Collection*, p. A7.
9 In the printed version, the date of composition is given as March 26, 1661. The year probably is wrong because in England 1662 had begun only the day before. The manuscript source shows that the day also is wrongly given, the essay having been written on March 16th.
10 Evan Griffith, *A Sermon Preached in Alderly in the County of Gloucester January 4, 1676: At the Funeral of Sir Matthew Hale Kt*, London: William Shrewsbery, 1677, p. 28.
11 Lambeth MSS 3492, fo.157. The Lambeth Papers were bought by the Lambeth Palace Library about 1988 from James Fairhurst. Fairhurst had acquired the papers, which had been left to rot in a stable, from the Hale family in the 1940s. None of the papers, except for the essay discussed here, shows demonological interest (Alan Cromartie, Letter of October 15, 1991).
12 Alan Cromartie, Letter, May 23, 1992. See also Alan Cromartie, *Sir Matthew Hale, 1609–1676*, Cambridge: Cambridge University Press, 1995, p. 239.
13 John Lord Campbell, *The Lives of the Chief Justices*, London: John Murray, 1849, Vol. I, p. 566.
14 Book Review, *Edinburgh Review*, 84 (1846), p. 387.
15 William S. Holdsworth, "Sir Matthew Hale," *Law Quarterly Review*, 39 (1923), p. 407.
16 Thomas Thirlwall, *The Works, Moral and Religious, of Sir Matthew Hale*, London: H.D. Symonds, 1805, Vol. II, p. 323.
17 Thirlwall, *Works of Hale*, Vol. II, p. 288. There was, of course, a long tradition of such views; thus Thomas à Kempis wrote: "Do not be vain about your beauty or strength of body, which a little sickness can mar and disfigure." Thomas à Kempis, *Imitation of Christ* [1441], Edgar Daplyn (trans.), London: Marshall, Morgan & Scott, 1979, p. 34.
18 Thirlwall, *Works of Hale*, Vol. II, p. 288.
19 Hadley Cantril, *The Invasion from Mars: A Study in the Social Psychology of Panic*, Princeton: Princeton University Press, 1940. See also Barbara Leaming, *Orson Welles*, London: Weidenfeld & Nicolson, 1985, pp. 158–62; John Houseman, "The Man from Mars," in Don Corigdon (ed.), *The Thirties: A Time to Remember*, New York: Simon & Schuster, 1962, pp. 583–97.
20 Richard Baxter, *Additional Notes on the Life and Death of Sir Matthew Hale*, London: Richard Janeway, 1682, p. 24; see also Baxter, "Preface," Thomas Gouge, *The Surest and Safest Way of Thriving*, London: N. Simmons, 1676, p. A8v. The Reverend Henry Newcome reports in his diary similar misadventures on horseback, and also takes them as divine messages. The diary editor sarcastically observes that Newcome's "self-delusion" prompted him to "read in all [such] events a hint for himself, and generally, sanctioning the course most to his own liking." This process, the editor notes, had been described by Francis Bacon as "taking

nOCES

an aim at Divine matter by human, which cannot but breed mixture of imaginations." Thomas Heywood (ed.), *The Diary of the Rev. Henry Newcome from September 30, 1661 to September 29, 1663*, Manchester: Chatham Society, 1849, pp. xi–xii.

21 Thirlwall, *Works of Hale*, Vol. II, p. 267.
22 Thirlwall, *Works of Hale*, Vol. II, p. 244.
23 Edward Gibbon, *Decline and Fall of the Roman Empire* [1845], Edited J.B. Bury, New York: Heritage Press, 1946, Vol. VI, p. 479.
24 Lawrence Stone, "The Size and Composition of the Oxford Student Body, 1580–1909," in Stone (ed.), *The University in Society: Oxford and Cambridge from the 14th to the Early 19th Century*, Princeton: Princeton University Press, 1974, Vol. I, p. 341.
25 Elizabeth Godfrey, *Home Life Under the Stuarts, 1603–1649*, London: Grant Richards, 1903, p. 89.
26 Gerald Hurst, "Sir Matthew Hale," *Law Quarterly Review*, 70 (1954), p. 343.
27 Kai T. Erikson, *Wayward Puritans: A Study in the Sociology of Deviance*, New York: Wiley, 1966, p. 51.
28 Richard Hofstadter, "The Age of the College," in Hofstadter and Walter B. Metzger, *The Development of Academic Freedom in the United States*, New York: Columbia University Press, 1955, p. 92.
29 David H. Fischer, *Albion's Seed: Four British Folkways in America*, New York: Oxford University Press, 1989, p. 23.
30 84 English Reports 906; I Ventris 293 (1676).
31 Matthew Hale, "Preface," in *A Discourse Touching Provision for the Poor*, London: William Shrewsbery, 1683, p. A2V.
32 Quoted in an unsigned book review, "On the Means of Improving the People," *Quarterly Review*, 19 (1918), p. 112.
33 Hale, "Preface," in *Provision for the Poor*, p. A3V.
34 [Great Britain]. Historical Manuscripts Commission, "A Manuscript Belonging to the Earl of Onslow," 14th Report, Appendix, Part IX. London: Her Majesty's Stationery Office, 1895, p. 480.
35 Wallace Notestein, *A History of Witchcraft in England from 1558 to 1718*, Washington: American Historical Association, 1911, p. 268.
36 Ola Elizabeth Winslow, *Samuel Sewall of Boston*, New York: Macmillan, 1964, p. 135.
37 Matthew Hale, *Pleas of the Crown*, Vol. I, p. 429.
38 Matthew Hale, *Pleas of the Crown*, Vol. I, p. 442.
39 Cromartie, Letter, September 5, 1991.
40 Cromartie, *Hale*, p. 171.
41 Anthony A. Wood, *Athenae Oxonienses* [1813], 3rd edition, Amsterdam: Georg Olms Verlag, 1969, Vol. I, p. 98.
42 Edward Clarendon, *The Life of Edward Earl of Clarendon, Lord High Chancellor of England*, Oxford: Oxford University Press, 1857, Vol. I, pp. 28–9.
43 Jack Adamson and H.F. Folland, *Sir Harry Vane: His Life and Times (1613–1662)*, Boston: Gambit, 1973, pp. 220–1.
44 John Milward (ed.), *The Table Talk of John Selden, Esq. (1689)*, London: William Pickering, 1847, p. 225.

45 Reginald Scot, *The Discoverie of Witchcraft*, London: W. Broome, 1584, p. Alllj.

46 Matthew Hale, *Difficiles Nugae, or, Observations Touching the Torricellian Experiment and the Various Solutions of the Same*, London; W. Godbid, 1674; Matthew Hale, *An Essay Touching the Gravitation and Non-Gravitation of Fluid Bodies, and the Reasons Thereof*, 2nd edition, London: W. Godbid, 1675; Matthew Hale, *Observations Touching the Principles of Natural Motions, and Especially Touching Rarefaction and Condensation* . . . , London: W. Godbid, 1677.

47 Cromartie, Letter, September 5, 1991.

48 Cromartie, Letter, September 5, 1991.

49 Barbara J. Shapiro, *John Wilkins, 1614–1672: An Intellectual Biography*, Berkeley: University of California Press, 1969, pp. 70, 175–6.

50 Milward, *Table-Talk*, p. 277.

51 Frederick Inderwick, *The Interregnum (1648–1660)*, London: Sampson, Low, Marston, Searle & W. Rivington, 1891, pp. 217–18.

52 Howell, *State Trials*, Vol. V, p. 211; Andrew Amos, *Ruins of Time Exemplified in Sir Matthew Hale's History of the Pleas of the Crown*, London: V. and R. Stevens and G.S. Norton, 1856, p. 66.

53 Thirlwall, *Works of Hale*, Vol I, p. 138.

54 Miguel de Cervantes, *Don Quixote* [1605], Samuel Putnam (trans.), Harmondsworth: Penguin Books, 1992, p. 82.

55 Samuel Butler, *The Posthumous Works of Mr. Samuel Butler*, London: R. Baldwin, 1754, p. 139, though Hill doubts the authenticity of attribution to Butler. Christopher Hill, *Society and Puritans in Pre-Revolutionary England*, London: Secker & Warburg, 1964, p. 42. On the same subject, Selden had written: "New oaths are so frequent, they should be taken like pills, swallowed whole; if you chew them you will find them bitter; if you think what you swear 'twill hardly go down." Milward, *Table-Talk*, p. 138.

56 Thirlwall, *Works of Hale*, Vol. I, p. 419.

57 Edward Berwick, *Lives of Marcus Valerius Messala, Corvinus, and Titus Pomponius Atticus*, Edinburgh: James Ballantyne, 1813, p. 113.

58 Berwick, *Atticus*, p. 117.

59 Anonymous, Book Review, *Edinburgh Review*, 84 (October 1846), pp. 382–3.

60 Gilbert Burnet, *The Life and Death of Sir Matthew Hale, Kt, Sometime Lord Chief Justice of His Majesties Court of Kings Bench*, London: William Shrewsbery, 1682, p. 154.

61 George Birbeck Hill and Lawrence F. Powell (eds.), *Boswell's Life of Samuel Johnson*, 2nd edition, London: Clarendon Press, 1964, Vol. II, p. 34.

62 Edward S. Lindley, *Wotton Under Edge*, London: Museum Press, 1962, pp. 259–60.

63 C.H. Josten, *Elias Ashmole (1617–1692)*, Oxford: Clarendon Press, 1966, Vol. I, p. 63.

64 See, e.g., Thirlwall, *Works of Hale*.

65 Holdsworth, "Sir Matthew Hale," pp. 402–3.

66 Campbell, *Chief Justices*, Vol. I, p. 584.

67 Franciscus J.D. Korsten, *Roger North (1651–1734): Virtuoso and Essayist*, Amsterdam: Holland University Press, 1981, p. 96.
68 Thomas B. Macaulay, *The History of England from the Accession of James II*, New York: Hurd & Houghton, 1872, Vol. I, p. 102.
69 Arthur Bryant, *Samuel Pepys: The Savior of the Navy*, New York: Macmillan, 1939, p. 107.
70 Edward Clarendon diary, Jan. 16, 1689.
71 Paul Delany, *British Autobiography in the Seventeenth Century*, London: Routledge & Kegan Paul, 1969, p. 172.
72 Roger North, *The Autobiography of Francis North*, Augustus Jessop (ed.), London: David Nutt, 1887, p. 136.
73 Osmund Airy, Book Review, *English Historical Review*, 3 (1888), p. 174.
74 North, *Francis North*, p. 95.
75 North, *Francis North*, p. 62.
76 North, *Francis North*, pp. 60–1.
77 Cromartie, *Sir Matthew Hale*, p. 135.
78 Cromartie, *Sir Matthew Hale*, pp. 122–3.
79 North, *Francis North*, pp. 61–2.
80 North, *Autobiography*, p. 103.
81 North, *Francis North*, p. 64.
82 North, *Autobiography*, p. 102.
83 North, *Francis North*, p. 63.
84 North, *Francis North*, p. 64.
85 Thirlwall, *Works of Hale*, Vol. II, p. 295.

8 AN AGE OF SO MUCH KNOWLEDGE AND CONFIDENCE

1 Keith Thomas, *Religion and the Decline of Magic: Studies in Popular Beliefs in Sixteenth and Seventeenth Century England*, London: Weidenfeld & Nicolson, 1971, p. 661.
2 Anthony Fletcher, *Reform in the Provinces: The Government of Stuart England*, New Haven: Yale University Press, 1986, p. 228.
3 As George Lyman Kittredge notes, the legend of the Beggar's Curse—the fearful malediction upon those who refused alms—enjoyed continuous currency from the Dark Ages through the nineteenth century. George Lyman Kittredge, *Witchcraft in Old and New England*, Cambridge: Harvard University Press, 1929, p. 132.
4 Henricus Institoris and James Sprenger, *Malleus Maleficarum* [1487], Montague Summers (trans.), London: J. Rodker, 1928, p. 51.
5 Franceso Guazzo, *Compendium Maleficarum* [1608], quoted in Roger Hart, *Witchcraft*, London: Wayland, 1971, p. 51.
6 Richard Bernard, *A Guide to Grand-Jury Men*, London: Edward Blackmore, 1627, pp. 228–38.
7 Richard Boulton, *The Possibility and Reality of Magick, Sorcery, and Witchcraft Demonstrated*, London: J. Roberts, 1922, p. 10.
8 George M. Beard, *The Psychology of the Salem Witchcraft Excitement of 1692 and Its Practical Application to Our Own Time*, New York: G.P. Putnam's, 1882, p. 17.

9 Leland L. Estes, "The Medical Origins of the European Witch Craze: A Hypothesis," *Journal of Social History*, 17 (1983), pp. 271–84.

10 Christina Larner, *Enemies of God: The Witch-Hunt in Scotland*, London: Chatto & Windus, 1981, p. 82.

11 Thomas A. Spalding, *Elizabethan Demonology*, London: Chatto & Windus, 1880, p. 63.

12 Thomas Ady, *A Candle in the Dark, or a Treatise Concerning the Natures of Witches & Witchcraft*, London: T. Newberry, 1656, p. 115.

13 Lucy Mair, *Witchcraft*, New York: McGraw-Hill, 1969, pp. 8–9.

14 *The Complete Works of Montaigne*, Donald M. Frame (trans.), Stanford: Stanford University Press, 1957, p. 790.

15 Sanford J. Fox, *Science and Justice: The Massachusetts Witchcraft Trials*, Baltimore: Johns Hopkins University Press, 1968.

16 Fox, *Science and Justice*, p. 111.

17 Frederick J. Powicke, *A Life of the Reverend Richard Baxter, 1615–1691*, Boston: Houghton Mifflin, 1924, p. 11.

18 A local street in Acton, Hale Gardens, commemorates the justice, but a land development about 1905 that was to include a Baxter Street fizzled. Letter from R.N.G. Roland, October 23, 1978.

19 Alan Cromartie, *Sir Matthew Hale, 1609–1676: Law, Religion and Natural Philosophy*, Cambridge: Cambridge University Press, 1995, p. 206.

20 William M. Lamont, *Richard Baxter and the Millennium*, London: Croom Helm, 1979, p. 17.

21 Matthew Sylvester (ed.), *Reliquiae Baxterianae*, London: T. Parkhurst, J. Lawrence, & J. Dunton, 1696, Vol. III, p. 47.

22 Sylvester, *Baxterianae*, Vol. III, pp. 43–5.

23 Richard Baxter, *Additional Notes on the Life and Death of Sir Matthew Hale*, London: Richard Janeway, 1682, p. A4.

24 Baxter, *Additional Notes*, p. 28.

25 Matthew Hale, *On the Nature of Religion*, London: B. Simmons, 1684, p. 36.

26 Matthew Hale, *Religion*, p. 36.

27 Thomas Long, *A Review of Mr. Baxter's Life*, London: E. Whitlock, 1697, p. 132.

28 Charles Bigg, *Wayside Sketches in Ecclesiastical History*, London: Longmans, Green, 1906, p. 37.

29 John S. Flynn, *The Influence of Puritanism on the Political and Religious Thought of the English*, London: J. Murray (1920), p. 138.

30 Max Weber, *The Protestant Ethic and the Spirit of Capitalism*, Talcott Parsons (trans.), London: G. Allen & Unwin, 1930; Richard H. Tawney, *Religion and the Rise of Capitalism*, New York: Harcourt, Brace, 1926. See also Winthrop S. Hudson, "Puritanism and the Spirit of Capitalism," *Church History*, 18 (March 1949), pp. 3–17.

31 John H. Davies, *The Life of Richard Baxter of Kidderminster*, London: W. Kent, 1889, p. 10.

32 William Orme, *The Practical Works of the Rev. Richard Baxter*, London: J. Duncan, 1830, p. 73.

33 A.B. Grossard, "Appendix" to Richard Baxter, *Grand Question Resolved*, London: Tho. Parkhurst, 1868.

34 Arnold G. Matthews, *The Works of Richard Baxter. An Annotated List*, London: Wyman & Sons, 1932.

35 George Birbeck Hill and Lawrence F. Powell (eds.), *Boswell's Life of Samuel Johnson*, 2nd edition, London: Clarendon Press, 1964, Vol. III, p. 521. This count is of the number of Baxter volumes on the shelf in Dr. Williams' Library, which houses his papers.

36 Quoted in Geoffrey F. Nuttall, *Richard Baxter*, London: Nelson, 1965, p. 115.

37 Hill and Powell, *Johnson*, Vol. IV, p. 226.

38 John Browne, *Kidarminster-Stuff, A New Piece of Print*, London: Rondal Taylor, 1681, p. 16.

39 Joan Webber, *The Eloquent "I": Style and Self in Seventeenth-Century Prose*, Madison: University of Wisconsin Press, 1968, p. 133.

40 Samuel G. Drake, *The Witchcraft Delusion in England*, Roxbury, MA: Elliott Woodward, 1866, Vol. II, p. xviii.

41 Richard Baxter, *The Certainty of the World of Spirits*, London: T. Parkhurst, 1691, pp. 80–81.

42 *Dictionary of National Biography*, Vol. VI, pp. 774–8.

43 *Dictionary of National Biography*, Vol. VI, p. 775.

44 John Browne, *History of Congregationalism and Memorials of the Church in Norfolk and Suffolk*, London: Jarrold & Sons, 1877, p. 214.

45 Sollom Emlyn, "Memoirs of the Life and Writings of Mr. Thomas Emlyn," in Thomas Emlyn, *Works*, 4th edition, London: John Noon, 1646, Vol. I, p. xiii.

46 Emlyn, "Memoirs," in Emlyn, *Works*, Vol. I, p. x.

47 E.R. Cooper, *Mardles from Suffolk* [1932], Woodbridge: Barbara Hopkins Books, 1984, pp. 139–40. Cooper relates that he found the letter in manuscript form in a copy of a nineteenth-century book.

48 Samuel Petto, *A Faithful Narrative of the Wonderful and Extraordinary Fits Which Mr. Tho. Spatchet (Late of Dunwich & Cookly) Was Under by Witchcraft*, London: John Harris, 1693.

49 Richard Baxter, "Preface," to Cotton Mather, *Late Memorable Providences Relating to Witchcrafts and Possessions*, 2nd edition, London: T. Parkhurst, 1691, p. 3.

50 Baxter, "Preface," to Mather, *Providences*, p. 6.

51 Richard Baddeley, *The Second Part of the Boy of Bilson*, London: E. Whitlock, 1698, p. 60.

52 Baddeley, *Boy of Bilson*, pp. 63–4.

53 Baddeley, *Boy of Bilson*, p. 69.

54 Baddeley, *Boy of Bilson*, p. 73.

55 Baxter, *Certainty*, p. 2.

56 Richard Baxter, *The Saint's Everlasting Rest: Concerning the Proofes of the Truth and Certain Futurity of Our Rest . . .* , London: Thomas Underhill & Francis Tyton, 1649, pp. 261–2.

57 Richard A. Baxter, *A Holy Commonwealth*, London: Thomas Underhill & Francis Tyton, 1659, pp. 92–4, 226–9; see also Christopher Hill, *The*

World Turned Upside Down: Radical Ideas During the English Revolution, Harmondsworth: Penguin Books, 1976, p. 103.

58 Davies, *Richard Baxter*, p. 160.

59 Richard Schlatter, *Richard Baxter and Puritan Politics*, New Brunswick, NJ: Rutgers University Press, 1957, p. 645; Christopher Hill, *Society and Puritans in Pre-Revolutionary England*, London: Secker & Warburg, 1964, p. 242.

60 Baxter, *Certainty*, p. 14.

61 Nuttall, *Richard Baxter*, p. 124.

62 Thirlwall, *Works of Hale*, Vol. I, pp. 316–17.

63 Basil Duke Henning, *The House of Commons, 1660–1690*, London: Secker & Warburg, 1983, Vol. II, p. 462.

64 Browne, *Works*, Keynes (ed.), Vol. I, p. 48.

65 Robert W. Dale and Alfred W. W. Dale, *History of English Congregationalism*, 2nd edition, London: Hodder & Stoughton, 1907.

66 John D. Gay, *The Geography of Religion in England*, London: Duckworth, 1971, p. 135.

67 Ole Peter Grell, Jonathan I. Israel, and Nicholas Tyacke (eds.), *From Persecution to Toleration*, Oxford: Clarendon Press, 1991, p. 331.

68 *Marriage Licenses at the Ipswich Probate Court, 1613–1674*, Ipswich: F.A. Crisp, 1903, Bk. 15, f. 32.

69 A.G. Mathews, *Calamy Revised (Being a Revision of Edmund Calamy's Account of the Ministers and Others Ejected and Silenced) 1660–1662*, Oxford, 1934, p. 389.

70 Charles Edward Banks, *Topographical Dictionary of 2885 English Emigrants to New England 1620–1650*, Philadelphia: Genealogical Publishing Company, 1937.

71 *Historical Collection of the Essex Institute*, Salem: Essex Institute Press, 1869, Vol. IX, p. 78.

72 *Historical Collection*, 1863, Vol. V, p.169.

73 *The Records of the First Church in Salem Massachusetts, 1629–1736*, Robert E. Moody (ed.), Salem: Essex Institute, 1974, p. 11.

74 James Savage, *A Genealogical Dictionary of the First Settlers of New England*, Baltimore: Genealogical Publishing Co., 1896, Vol. III, p. 327.

75 John Browne, *Congregationalism*, p. 429.

76 Ian Breward (ed.), *The Works of William Perkins*, Abingdon, Berks.: Sutton Courtenay Press, 1970, p. 9.

77 *Quarter Sessions*, B105/2/1,5,7,10, p. 130.

78 *Quarter Sessions*, p. 135.

79 Wrentham Parish Registers. Suffolk Record Office, Lowestoft, 168/D2/1.

80 John Browne, *Congregationalism*, p. 431.

81 Daniel Neal, *The History of Puritans; or Protestant Nonconformists*, London: William Baynes, 1822, Vol. IV, p. 173.

82 Mathews, *Calamy Revised*, p. 343.

83 Samuel Petto, *Faithful Narrative*.

84 C. L'Estrange Ewen, *Witchcraft and Demonianism*, London: Heath Cranton, 1933, pp. 298–9. Peter Elmer, "State-Building and Witch-Burning in Early Modern Europe," in Jonathan Barry, Marianne Hester,

and Gareth Roberts (eds.), *Witchcraft in Early Modern Europe: Studies in Culture and Belief*, Cambridge: Cambridge University Press, 1996, p. 175.

85 Edmund Gillingwater, *An Historical Account of the Ancient Town of Lowestoft*, London: G.G.J. & J. Robinson, 1790, p. 356.

86 J. Duncan, *Copy of the Original Record of the Yarmouth Congregational Church, 1642–1855*, Typescript, London: Dr. Williams' Library, 1980.

87 John Browne, *Congregationalism*, pp. 214–66.

88 Richard Deacon, *Matthew Hopkins: Witch Finder General*, London: Frederick Muller, 1976, pp. 153–6.

89 *A Collection of Modern Relations of Matter of Fact Concerning Witches & Witchcraft Upon the Persons of People*, London: John Harris, 1693, pp. 46–8.

90 John Browne, *Congregationalism*, pp. 214–66.

91 J.E. Clowes, *Chronicles of the Old Congregational Church at Great Yarmouth*, Great Yarmouth: 1642–1658. Privately published, 1906, p. 29.

92 PRO B11/364, Public Record Office, London.

93 Calendar of State Papers (Domestic), 14 Dec. 1668; George E. Evans, "Early Nonconformity in Yarmouth," *Transactions of the Congregational Historical Society*, 2 (1905–1906), pp. 402–9.

94 Reginald Trevor-Davies, *Four Centuries of Witch-beliefs*, London: Methuen, 1947.

95 Estes, "Witch Craze," p. 274.

96 Paul Carus, *The History of the Devil, and the Idea of Evil, from the Earliest Times to the Present Day*, Chicago: Open Court, 1900, pp. 274, 278.

97 Curt J. Ducasse, *A Philosophical Scrutiny of Religion*, New York: Ronald Press, 1953, p. 205.

98 Brian Levack, *The Witch-Hunt in Early Modern Europe*, New York: Longman, 1987, p. 102.

99 Mary Douglas, "Introduction: Thirty Years After *Witchcraft, Oracles, and Magic*," in Douglas (ed.), *Witchcraft Confessions & Accusations*, London: Tavistock, 1970, p. 58.

100 C. John Sommerville, *The Discovery of Childhood in Puritan England*, Athens: University of Georgia Press, 1992, p. 13.

101 Sommerville, *Childhood*, pp. 10–11.

102 Hugh R. Trevor-Roper, "The European Witch-Craze," in Max Marwick (ed.), *Witchcraft and Sorcery*, Harmondsworth: Penguin Books, 1970, p. 132.

103 Ewen, *Witchcraft and Demonianism*, p. 261.

104 Rosemary Ellen Guilley, *Encyclopedia of Witches and Witchcraft*, New York: Facts on File, 1989, p. 45.

105 Notestein, *History of Witchcraft*, p. 196.

106 Notestein, *History of Witchcraft*, p. 201.

107 Alan Macfarlane, *Witchcraft in Tudor and Stuart England: A Regional and Comparative Study*, London: Routledge & Kegan Paul, 1971, p. 142.

108 See Patrick Collinson, *The Religion of Protestants: The Church in English Society, 1559–1625*, Oxford: Oxford University Press, 1982, pp. 260–3.

NOTES

109 Mark ix: 14–18.
110 Michael MacDonald, "Introduction," in MacDonald (ed.), *Witchcraft and Hysteria in Elizabethan London: Edward Jorden and the Mary Glover Case*, London: Tavistock/Routledge, 1991, p. xix.
111 MacDonald, "Introduction," p. xix.
112 Edward Jorden, *A Brief Discourse of a Disease Called the Suffocation of the Mother*, London: John Windet, 1603, p. 1.
113 MacDonald, *Witchcraft and Hysteria*, pp. viii–ix.
114 Stephen Bradwell, "Mary Glover's Late Woeful Case," in MacDonald, *Witchcraft and Hysteria*, pp. 33, 68, 106.
115 Brian Levack, "Introduction," to Levack (ed.), *Witchcraft in Colonial America*, New York: Garland, 1992, p. ix.
116 Perry Miller, *The New England Mind: From Colony to Province*, Cambridge: Harvard University Press, 1953, p. 487.
117 David Cannadine, *G.M. Trevelyan: A Life in History*, New York: W. Norton, 1993, p. 190.

9 A MATTER OF ADIPOCERE

1 John Southerden Burn, *History of Parish Registers in England*, London: Edward Suter, 1829, p. 89; Edmund Heward, *Matthew Hale*, London: Robert Hale, 1972, p. 123.
2 Richard Baxter, *Additional Notes on the Life and Death of Sir Matthew Hale*, London: Richard Janeway, 1682, p. 8.
3 Margaret M. Verney, *Memoirs of the Verney Family from the Restoration to the Revolution, 1660 to 1696*, London: Longmans, Green, 1899, Vol. IV, pp. 232–3.
4 Verney, *Memoirs*, p. 233.
5 Evan Griffith, *A Sermon Preached in Alderly in the County of Gloucester January 4, 1676: At the Funeral of Sir Matthew Hale Kt*, London: William Shrewsbery, 1677.
6 Matthew Sylvester (ed.), *Reliquiae Baxterianae*, London: T. Parkhurst, J. Lawrence, & J. Dunton, 1696, Vol. III, p. 176.
7 John B. Williams, *Memoirs of the Life, Character, and Writings of Sir Matthew Hale*, London: Jackson & Walford, 1835, pp. 327, 406.
8 Williams, *Memoirs*, p. 159.
9 The translation from the Latin was done by Richard Frank, University of California, Irvine, who pointed out that *denati*, the term for "deceased" on Hale's tombstone, is a made-up word, and might have been employed to contrast with *nati* ("born"). Perhaps though the inscription speaks to the scorn that Roger North visited upon Hale for what North claimed was the poor quality of his translation from the Latin of Cornelius Nepos' life of Pomponius Atticus. Roger North, *The Life of the Right Honourable Francis North, Baron of Guilford*, London: John Whiston, 1742, p. 63. In agreement with North on Hale's inadequacy as a translator is Edward Berwick, *Lives of Marcus Valerius Messala, Corvinus, and Titus Pomponius Atticus*, Edinburgh: James Ballantyne, 1813, pp. 146–7.
10 Regarding the painting see Christopher Brown, *Van Dyck*, New York: Phaidon, 1982, pp. 203, 206.

11 Edward S. Lindley, *Wotton Under Edge*, London: Museum Press, 1962, p. 312.

12 Sara Stevenson and Duncan Thompson, *John Michael Wright: The King's Painter*, Edinburgh: Scottish National Gallery, 1982; C.H. Collins Baker, *Lely and the Stuart Painters: A Study of English Portraiture Before and After Van Dyck*, London: Philip Warner, 1912, Vol. I, pp. 182–95; John Evelyn noted in his diary: "I went . . . to see the pictures of all the judges and eminent men of the long robe newly painted by Mr. Write, & set up in Guild-hall . . . most of them very like the persons they are made to represent, though I never took Write to be any considerable artist." Esmond S. de Beer (ed.), *The Diary of John Evelyn*, Oxford: Clarendon Press, 1955, Vol. IV, p. 17.

13 Walter G. Bell, *The Great Fire of London in 1666* [1920], London: Bodley Head, 1951, pp. 356–7; Thomas F. Reddaway, *London 1666: Fire and Rebuilding*, London: Bedford College, University of London, 1966, p. 11.

14 Horace Walpole, *Anecdotes of Painting in England with Some Account of the Principal Artists*, George Vertue (ed.), 4th edition, London: J. Dodsley, 1786, Vol. III, p. 91. Pepys felt the same about the relative merits of Wright and Lely. On June 18, 1662, he wrote in his diary: "I walked to Lilly's the painter; where we saw . . . rare things. . . . Thence to Wrights the painter: but Lord, the difference that is between their two works." Roger Latham and William Matthews, *The Diary of Samuel Pepys*, London: G. Bell, 1970, Vol. III, pp. 112–13.

15 Philip E. Jones, *The Fire Court*, London: William Clowes & Sons, 1966, Vol. I, p. xi.

16 North, *Francis North*, p. 61.

17 George Scharf, "Portraits of Judges in the Guildhall," *Archaeological Journal*, 50 (1983), pp. 264–73.

18 J.H. Baker, *The Order of Serjeants at Law: A Chronicle of Creations, with Related Texts and a Historical Introduction*, London: Selden Society, 1984, p. 68.

19 James L. Howgego, "The Guildhall Fire Judges," *Guildhall Miscellany*, 1 (February 1953), pp. 20–30.

20 A.D. Bayne, *A Comprehensive History of Norwich*, London: Jarrold & Sons, 1869, pp. 66–7.

21 Thomas Browne, *Hydriotaphia, or Urne-Burial or, A Brief Discourse of the Sepulchrall Urnes Lately Found in Norfolk* [1658], in Geoffrey Keynes (ed.), *The Works of Sir Thomas Browne*, Chicago: University of Chicago Press, 1964.

22 Jeremiah S. Finch, *Sir Thomas Browne: A Doctor's Life of Science and Faith*, New York: Henry Schuman, 1950, p. 522.

23 Egon S. Merton, *Science and Imagination in Sir Thomas Browne*, New York: King's Crown Press, 1949, p. 6.

24 Thomas Browne, *Urne-Burial*, p. 155.

25 Johnstone Parr, "Sir Thomas Browne's Birthday," *English Language Notes*, 11 (1973), pp. 44–6.

26 Thomas Browne, *A Letter to a Friend, Upon Occasion of the Death of His Intimate Friend* [1690], in Keynes, *The Works of Sir Thomas Browne*, Vol. I, p. 105.
27 John Dover Wilson, *An Introduction to the Sonnets of Shakespeare for the Use of Historians and Others*, New York: Cambridge University Press, 1964, pp. 72–91.
28 Douglas Macleane, *Pembroke College*, London: F.E. Robinson, 1900, p. 73.
29 Thomas Browne, *Pseudodoxia Epidemica*, Robin Robbins (ed.), Oxford: Clarendon Press, 1981, Vol. I, p. 345.
30 John Gibbon, "Day-Fatality: Or Some Observations on Days Lucky and Unlucky," in John Aubrey, *Three Prose Works*, edited by John B. Brown, Carbondale: Southern Illinois University Press, 1972, pp. 7–20.
31 Geoffrey Keynes, *The Commonplace Book of Elizabeth Littleton, Daughter of Sir Thomas Browne*, Cambridge: Cambridge University Press, 1919, p. 22.
32 William H. Barnes, "Browne's 'Hydrotaphia,' with a Reference to Adipocere," *Isis*, 20 (1934), pp. 337–43. Browne's observations were only casual. The true discoverer of adipocere was Antoine François de Fourcroy, who examined more than 1,000 corpses removed from the Cimetière des Innocents when it was closed in 1786: William A. Smeaton, *Fourcroy: Chemist and Revolutionary, 1755–1809*, Cambridge: W. Heffer & Sons, 1962. For a good summary of Fourcroy on adipocere see Andrew Ure, *A Dictionary of Chemistry*, 3rd edition, London: Thomas Tegg and others, 1828, pp. 103–8.
33 Andrew Clark, *The Colleges of Oxford*, London: Methuen, 1891, pp. 415–16.
34 See Peter Martens, "The Faith of Two Doctors: Thomas Browne and William Osler," *Perspectives in Biology and Medicine*, 36 (1992), pp. 120–30.
35 Arthur J. Cleveland, *A History of Norfolk and Norwich Hospital, From 1900 to the End of 1946*, Norwich: Jarrold, 1948, p. 139.
36 Harvey Cushing, *The Life of Sir William Osler*, London: Oxford University Press, 1940, pp. 530–l; F.J. Myrick, "Sir Thomas Browne: The Story of His Skull, His Wig, and His Coffin Plate," *British Medical Journal*, 1 (May 6, 1922), pp. 725–6.
37 Browne, *Works*, Keynes (ed.), Vol. I, p. 57.
38 Browne, *Works*, Keynes (ed.), Vol. I, Sect. xlviii, p. 63.
39 Arthur Keith, *An Autobiography*, London: Watts, 1950, p. 454; see also Keith, *Phrenological Studies of the Skull and Brain Cast of Sir Thomas Browne of Norwich*, Edinburgh: University of Edinburgh, 1924.
40 Miriam L. Tildesley, "Sir Thomas Browne and His Skull, Portraits and Ancestry," *Biometrika: A Journal for the Statistical Study of Biological Problems*, 15 (1923), pp. 1–76.
41 Thomas Browne, *Urne-Burial*, p. 131.
42 John Knott, "Medicine and Witchcraft in the Days of Sir Thomas Browne," *British Medical Journal*, 2A (October 14, 1905), p. 957.
43 Conolly Norman, "Sir Thomas Browne: Adui Alteram Partem," *British Medical Journal*, 2 (August 27, 1904), p. 474.

44 Anthony Batty Shaw, *Sir Thomas Browne of Norwich*, Norwich: Jarrold & Sons, 1987, p. 8.

45 Margaret Spufford, *Contrasting Communities: English Villages in the Sixteenth and Seventeenth Centuries*, Cambridge: Cambridge University Press, 1974, p. 109.

46 Edmund Gillingwater, *An Historical Account of the Ancient Town of Lowestoft*, London: G.G.J. & J. Robinson, 1790, p. 369.

47 John Bowle, *John Evelyn and His World: A Biography*, London: Routledge & Kegan Paul, 1981, p. 181.

48 Christina Hole, *English Home Life, 1500 to 1800*, London: B.T. Batsford, 1947, p. 76.

49 Edmund Gillingwater, *Town of Lowestoft*, p. 369.

50 Douglas R. Lacey, *Dissent and Parliamentary Politics in England, 1661–1689: A Study in the Perpetuation and Tempering of Parliamentarianism*, New Brunswick, NJ: Rutgers University Press, 1969, p. 27.

51 Lawrence Stone, "Social Mobility in England, 1500–1700," in W. R. Owens (ed.), *Seventeenth Century England: A Changing Culture*, London: Ward Lock Educational, 1980, Vol. II, p. 12.

52 Touching Burying in Woolen, 18 Car. 2, cap. 4; see Caroline Robbins, *John Milward*, pp. 58–9.

53 Christina Hole, *The English Housewife in the Seventeenth Century*, London: Chatto & Windus, 1953, p. 226.

54 St. Margaret's Church, Lowestoft—Inscriptions. This unpublished manuscript in the Suffolk Record Office, Lowestoft, is unsigned, but is attributed to J. L. Clemence.

55 *Norfolk Consistory Court Wills*, Norwich: Norfolk Record Office, OW 85.

56 Prerogative Court of Canterbury Wills, Prob II/227. 230 Dawson.

57 Charles J. Palmer, *The Perlustration of Great Yarmouth*, Great Yarmouth: George Nall, 1938, Vol. II, p. 321.

58 Palmer, *Perlustration*, Addenda.

59 Arnold Whitbridge, *Rochambeau*, New York: Macmillan, 1965, pp. 225–9.

60 Nathan Schachner, *Alexander Hamilton*, New York: Thomas Yoseloff, 1946, p. 229.

61 Schachner, *Hamilton*, p. 104.

62 Philip Young, *Revolutionary Ladies*, New York: Knopf, 1977, p. 174; James T. Flexner, *The Young Hamilton: A Biography*, Boston: Little, Brown, 1978, pp. 329, 445. In one letter, Angelica wrote to her sister of Hamilton: "I love him very much, and if you were so generous as the old Romans, you would lend him to me for a little while." Schachner, *Hamilton*, p. 344.

63 Allan McLane Hamilton, *The Intimate Life of Alexander Hamilton*, New York: Scribner's, 1911, p. 408.

64 Samuel H. Wandell and Meade Minnigerode, *Aaron Burr*, New York: G.P. Putnam's, 1925, Vol. I, pp. 180–1; Mary-Jo Kline and Joanne Wood Ryan (eds.), *Political Correspondence and Public Papers of Aaron Burr*, Princeton: Princeton University Press, 1983, p. 410.

65 Willard M. Wallace, "Introduction," in Harold C. Syrett and Jean G. Cook (eds.), *Interview in Weehawken: The Burr–Hamilton Duel as Told in the Original Documents*, Middletown, CN: Wesleyan University Press, 1960; Matthew L. Davis, *Memoirs of Aaron Burr with Miscellaneous Selections from His Correspondence*, New York: Harper, 1837, Vol. II, p. 424.

66 Helen Putnam, *The Man Who Owned the Pistols: John Barker Church and His Family*, Interlaken, NY: Heart of the Lakes Publishing, 1981, p. 185.

67 B. Midi Berry and R.S. Schoefield, "Age at Baptism in Pre-Industrial England," *Population Studies*, 25 (November 1971), pp. 453–63. The authors note that "it would be dangerous to assume that the interval between birth and baptism in any parish at any point in time, is either early or late" (p. 463); that is, either two days or two weeks.

68 *Norfolk Wills*, 230 Dawson.

69 Hugh H.W. Lees, *The Chronicles of a Suffolk Parish Church: Lowestoft St. Margaret*, Lowestoft: Flood & Sons, 1949, p. 126.

70 *Norfolk Wills*, 143 Bishop.

71 Lowestoft Parish Register, p. 146.

72 According to Steel and Longe's transcription of the Lowestoft Parish Register (p. 135), Mary Pacy was baptized on August 24, 1657. For October 14 of the same year, they list the burial of "Elizabeth," a daughter of Samuel and Elizabeth Pacy. Their copying, however, is in error: the original Parish Registers at the church indicate the burial of Mary Pacy on this date.

73 John Browne, *Congregationalism*, p. 528.

74 Henry Roseveare, *The Treasury: The Evolution of a British Institution*, New York: Columbia University Press, 1969, p. 95.

75 *[An Act] to Empower the Lord High Treasurer to Compound with the Sureties of Samuel Pacy Deceased Late Receiver General for the County of Suffolk*, 7 Anne (1708).

76 S. Wilton Rex (ed.), *The Diary and Autobiography of Edmund Bohun, Esq*, Beccles: Reed Crisp, 1853, p. 85. Bohun so identifies William in his June 6, 1869 entry, indicating that both he and Pacy had been named justices of the peace for Suffolk.

77 Palmer, *Perlustration*, Vol. I, p. 286.

Index

Note: The letter 'n' following a page number indicates a reference in the notes.